Encyclopaedic History of Indian Freedom Movement Series

MUTINY AND ITS AFTERMATH

Edited by
OM PRAKASH

ANMOL PUBLICATIONS PVT. LTD.
NEW DELHI - 110 002 (INDIA)

ANMOL PUBLICATIONS PVT. LTD.
4374/4B, Ansari Road, Daryaganj
New Delhi - 110 002
Ph.: 23261597, 23278000
Visit us at: www.anmolpublications.com

Mutiny and Its Aftermath

First Edition, 2004

ISBN 81-261-1518-1

[Responsibility for the facts stated, opinions expressed, conclusions reached and plagiarism, if any, in this book is entirely that of the Editor. The Publisher bears no responsibility for them, whatsoever.]

PRINTED IN INDIA

Published by J.L. Kumar for Anmol Publications Pvt. Ltd., New Delhi - 110 002 and Printed at Mehra Offset Press, Delhi.

Contents

Preface

'Golden bird' as India was known in yore days, rich in natural resources and well-developed cottage industries it was considered an affluent country. Indian spices, fabrics and other handicrafts were in great demand the world over. In the lure of having these goods and riches, many European powers made adventurous voyages to locate India.

The story of European expansions in Asia forms one of the great epics of modern times. India was the cornerstone of European imperialism in Asia. It was the lure of the lucrative 'Indian trade' which incited European adventurers to seek a new route to India, thus inaugurating a new era of contact between these two distant lands. Among the European empires in Asia, the British empire was the most enduring and prosperous one. And India was the finest jewel of the British dominion. It is worthwhile to remember that European exploration and adventure in the east were encouraged by the great demand in Europe for the products from Malabar like spices and calicoe cloth. Symbolically, the European age in Indian and indeed Asian history began with the landing of Vasco-de-Gama at Calicut on the 27th of May 1498. During this period, there was a continuous struggle between European traders and their native rivals and among the Europeans themselves. By the end of the eighteenth century this struggle for supremacy had been resolved in favour of the English.

The European traders were originally in the position of supplicants before the native rulers in India. For example, when William Hawkins arrived at the court of Jehangir with a letter from King James I asking for trade facilities, he had brought with him, a gift of 25,000 Gold pieces. As Lane Poole observes,

"There was nothing to suggest the most distant dream that in two centuries and a half the slight introduction Hawkins was then effecting between England and India would culminate in the sovereignty of a British Queen over the whole empire."

But unlike their European rivals like the Portuguese and the Dutch, the English made their bid for power in India only when the powerful Mughal empire had begun to decline. In any case the Portuguese and the Dutch had only small coastal settlements in India even at the height of their power and influence in this country.

By the end of the seventh Century, the Portuguese had been displaced by their Dutch rivals in Malabar and in the islands, of the East Indies. As for the Dutch, they were compelled by force of circumstances to regard the factories "which they established on the main land merely as marketing points for the products of an Empire which had its capital at Batavia in the East Indies."

Moreover, the Dutch power in India was largely jeopardised on European battle fields.

The wars with England and France drained the resources of this nation. Thus, it was left to the French to provide real opposition to the English in India.

The same pattern can be detected in the story of European activity in Malabar. Here the intensity of their rivalry was greater because of three main reasons. Malabar with its many fine harbours and backwaters was more accessible from the sea, increasing the scope for European interference.

Thus, European powers who came to India with the intention of trade snatched the political power and sovereignty from the local states, principalities and feudal lords. And established complete control over India. After over hundred years colonial rule, the feeling of national integration and freedom from the clutches of foreign power developed among the Indians. Thus, began the saga of freedom movement.

This encyclopaedic study is phased into two most significant and historic diversions having deep bearing on varied kinds of events which moulded the destiny of millions of people of Indian sub-continent. These events having complete political overtones, became a glaring phenomenon with the downfall of the Mughal Empire almost with the commencement of the 18th century. The ambitious piercing eyes of four European powers — the British, the French, the Portuguese and the Dutch—did cast upon several gainful economic successes in India.

Of these powers, the East India Company's government, with well organised force, bureaucracy and diplomats achieved phenomenal successes against their adversaries. The first phase,—therefore has been marked from Plassey to the Mutiny of 1857 (The First War of Independence) when the Company's role came to an end.

The second phase, naturally, came very much in the hands of the British Government functioning under the Whitehall and ended with the dawn of Swaraj on 15 August 1947.

This multi-volumes study would take up several themes, viz. political, socio-economic, religious, constitutional, educational, press, revolutionaries, local pioneers, legislation, revenues and judicial policy, on-going process of reaction — violent and non-violent, moderates and extremists, local and all India movements, reaction of the British Raj, efforts for conciliation, significant Acts passed by the Central Legislature, the impact of two global wars, 1914-1919 and 1939-1945; Congress, Muslim League, Hindu Mahasabha and the British Policy, a significant change in Britain soon after 1945, the Labour Government of Clement Attlee and Partition of India in August 1947.

In the first lot eleven volumes have appeared while in the present second lot ten volumes are being brought out namely the Marathas and their administration; Lord William Bentinck and Metcalf era of reforms; Raja Rammohun Roy: the reformer; Mutiny and its aftermath; History of Anglo-Sikh wars;

Emergence of Maharaja Ranjit Singh; Lord Hastings and his administrative measures; Ranjit Singh administration and British policy; British policy of intervention and expansion; and Lord Wellesley and policy of expansion.

This prestigious project is arranged, managed and looked after by a team of most dedicated and long experienced scholars of modern Indian history.

In gathering the authentic information, we have taken liberty to draw the material from the learned works of many great scholars in the field. We are deeply beholden to all those whose works are partially cited or substantially made use of in the project. I am indebted to Mr. J.L. Kumar, Managing Director, Anmol Publications Pvt. Ltd., New Delhi for his constant inspiration and moral support and finally to bring out this work. Last but not the least I am thankful to all those who have assisted me one way or other while preparing the manuscript.

—Om Prakash

1

Dalhousie's Administration and Annexations

Dalhousie entered on an outmoded system, which in fact broke down under his vigorous administration. The East India Company Proprietors entitled to vote numbered now 1800, each possessed of at least £1000 stock. Lord Derby summed up their duties and privileges thus: 'They receive the dividends upon their stock, and elect the members of the Court of Directors'. They also attended ceremonial dinners.

The Directors theoretically still possessed unlimited power, except that the Board of Control might overrule them. This exception, so important, was reinforced by the Board of Control's power of 'secret' communications with the Indian Government. The President of the Board was in the Cabinet, a precursor of the Secretary of State of Post Mutiny times. 'Thus the Court of Directors was tied hand and foot by the Board, which signified the President, while he in turn signified the Government or Crown'.[1] The system lasted a few years longer (till alarm and indignation over the Mutiny made the Company's end inevitable), only because Dalhousie, unlike Wellesley, always treated his nominal chiefs with courtesy. Even when matters were strained, he kept his dignity.[2]

He has first to become master in his own household. History does *not* repeat itself; yet British-Indian history seems to possess a static quality. We see, with deep variations yet with striking repetition of mood and action, resemblances in Wellesley, Dalhousie, Curzon; similarly we see crises and oppositions recur. The quarrel of Dalhousie and Napier appears a parallel to that of Curzon and Kitchener. If Wellesley also did not quarrel with his own military power, that was because it was largely represented by his brother.

Dalhousie's Commander-in-Chief, Sir Charles Napier, from old scars that had changed his physiognomy or warped his physical efficiency, had gone far to wards realising Tod's famous description of the Mewar chief who was' 'a fragment of a warrior'. But his energy, fire, and egoism flared as destructively and grandly as ever:

> 'He is wonderfully well preserved for a man of sixty-seven, still more so when it is recollected what a life of hardships he has led, what climates he had braved, how riddled and chopped to pieces with balls and bayonets and sabre wounds he is. His hair is now quite gray; and allowing it to grow as it will, he combs it back straight off his forehead to the back of his head. Under bushy eyebrows gleam a pair of piercing and a brilliant eyes...his nose, highly aquiline by nature, was made still more so by a bullet at Busaco, which went in at his right cheek, through his nose, shattering it as it passed....Sir Charles's manner is peculiarly young and gay. He is full of anecdote, such as his varied life was likely to supply; full of fun and full of cleverness. I never had a more agreeable inmate in my house' (Lord Dalhousie).

Since Cornwallis's time we have heard the constant grumbling of civilian and military that one service got all the jobs and honours. This ever-present squabble was renewed with particular fierceness, John Lawrence and his friends 'grousing' that only 'a red coat' was considered, Napier furious at the all-encroaching civilians. He said he would rather by far have been Governor of the Punjab, the province whose frontier fortresses peered towards those Central Arian plains where England and India (it was held) must grapple one day in the world's mightiest struggle, the rehearsal of Ragnarok and Armageddon. The dominant school of thought was divided as to whether it were better to await Russia behind strong natural walls, already British, or to annex Afghanistan, press boldly on, and bring the Muscovite to bay in his own deserts. Napier preferred the latter course; there were no limits to the regions into which he would march devastatingly. He found the new Governor-General utterly unawake to his chances and duties:

> 'I like this young man, for he is seemingly a good fellow, but he has no head for governing this empire and drawing forth all its wondrous resources! What the Koh-i-noor is among diamonds, India is among nations. Were I emperor of India for twelve years, she should be traversed by railroads, and have her rivers bridged; her seat of government at Delhi, or Meerut, or Simla, or Allahabad. No Indian prince should exist. The Nizam should be no more heard of, Nepal would be ours, and an ague fit should become the courtly imperial sickness at Constantinople, while the Emperor of Russia and he of China should never get their pulses below 100 !'
>
> 'Would that I were king of India! I would make Muscowa and Pekin shake .... The five rivers and the Punjab, the Indus and Scinde, the Red Sea and Malta! What a chain of lands and waters to attach England to India! Were I king of England I would, from the palace of Delhi, thrust forth a clenched first in the teeth of Russia and France. England's fleet should be all in all in the West, and the Indian army all in all in the East. Indian should not belong

another day to the "ignominious tyrants", nor should it depend upon opium sales, but on an immense population well employed in peacefull pursuits. She should suck English manufactures up her great rivers, and pour down those rivers her own varied products'.

He raved at the civilian government of the Punjab, and those incompetent Lawrences. He found Dalhousie 'as weak as water and as vain as a pretty woman or an ugly man'.

Napier inhabited a cinema world of his own creation. Everywhere, he roared, revolt and war were preparing. Gulab Singh was gathering for an invasion of British India, the Sikhs were casting cannon daily in the jungles and hinding them in holes. Mutiny, mutiny—it was being concerted on all sides, and anyone but these fools who were ruining India could have heard its mutterings. As for his own strategy, it was superbly simple. He thought in fifties, apparently; he would, if given his way, have placed 50,000 men on the Narmada, 50,000 on the Brahmaputra, 50,000 beyond the Satlej. Then, when ready, he would overrun Afghanistan and Southern China, and parcel them out among his legions. A war of acrimonious papers was waged between him and the Governor-General, with the Lawrences writing to the latter, sometimes with contempt, sometimes in wrath. John wrote sceptically of the wounderful Sind methods which were always being flung at his head:

> 'What a system for such a man as Sir Charles to advocate! Judicial—you flogged and fined up to 500 rupees without record or power of appeal. I fear some of your men must have done much harm. There was a Mr.—under me in the Jullandur who had been in Scinde, and I saw some terrible cases of oppression by him in this way, to which I speedily put a stop....'

'To suppose that a man ignorant of the manners, customs, habits, and language of a people, with untrained men under him, could really have governed a country as he thinks he did Scinde, seems to me an impossibility. He has always had one great advantage, namely, that he tells his own story. A man may make a good many mistakes, and still be a better ruler than an Ameer of Scinde'.

The last sentence hits the nail squarely. Napier's despotism had been experienced by a people used to caprice and certain of one thing only, that man was born to oppression as the sparks fly upward.

As for Napier's suspicion of mutiny all around, in 1850 alarm was caused by rumour that a Sikh regiment had refused *batta* for its share in putting down a trivial rebellion. The Governor-General enquired, and learnt that what happened was that they had refused to take 'bloodmoney' for fighting against their own countrymen. 'They said they had done their duty and were content with that they had received.[3] Marvelling, he dismissed the incident as 'highly creditable'. The final storm came over this *batta* business, which from first to last has raised so many tumults in India. Early in 1850 Napier, with the excuse that Dalhousie was then at sea, on his own authority cancelled a regulation disallowing certain special grants for dearness of provisions. When corrected he stuck to his guns, asserted a right to have so acted and his intention to repeat the action if he saw necessity. The Governor-General wrote to Sir John Hobhouse, President of the Board of Control: 'I have been exceedingly vexed, and with reason'. The war continued. Napier put in memorandums, one of which his opponent characterised privately as 'the most discreditable paper that ever was traced by the pen of a public man'. Napier proceeded to accuse the Governor-General of 'most extraordinary and most disingenuous' reasoning. He resigned, and left his command in December, 1850, going home to die, but to achieve in posthumous publications an explosion hardly less than those which had accompanied him through life. Especially was it believed that he had foreseen the Mutiny; and his countrymen, who naturally admired the old hero, set him on the same plane of exalted esteem as Nelson, Wellington, and Lord Roberts.

Napier asserted that all princes regarded us with 'venomous hatred'; and in this , as in this assertions of mutiny everywhere, there was enough of truth. There were disquieting incidents in a number of native regiments. But it is certain that his random and abounding accusations of disaffection everywhere and in everyone had behind them no genuine prescience. He threw such a cloud of missiles that some hit some mark. A far more striking example of prophecy was Henry Lawrence's playful forcecast[4] written in 1842, which even to details, as in its prediction of events at Delhi and at 'Meerut itself, at all times unquiet', reads like a forgery composed after 1857. John also, in his parting shot[5] at his adversary, showed that the gift of prophecy was in the family:

> 'I think poor Charlie Napier will probably make an ass of himself in his posthumous work. Like Falstaff's which bore so large a proportion in his daily expenditure compared with bread, there will be in Napiers work very much about himself, and little about India. He was so eaten up with passion and prejudice that his really good qualities had not fair play'.

In 1842, when the title of Nawab of Surat was abolished, Lord Auckland declared his intention.

> 'to persevere in the one clear and direct course of abandoning no just and honourable accession of territory or revenue, while all existing claims of right are at the same time scrupulously maintained',

words which Lord Dalhousie echoed early:

> 'I take this opportunity of recording my strong and deliberate opinion, that in the exercise of a wise and

sound policy the British Government is bound not to put aside or neglect such rightful opportunities of acquiring territory or revenue as may from time to time present themselves'.

He changed the map, with a speed and thoroughness no campaign had equalled.

He was, however, not quite the sweeping annexationist he is usually made out. He made attempts to distinguish between States possessed of independent or quasi-independent power before the Company's rise to paramountcy, and those which were its creation. The right of adoption was disallowed to the latter class;[6] if their rulers died without male heirs of the body, they were held to have 'lapsed' to the company. Under this ruling, a number of important States were gathered in, one after another, till Indian opinion thought the foreigner looked on sovereignty as a tree whose fruits must all ultimately fall to his basket.

The story of Satara's annexation has been told too fully for effectiveness in a wordy, cantankerous book,[7] hard to read. Major Basu's version is, however, amply in accord with contemporary British testimony, and, despite his silly trick of digging at the word 'Christian' on every page, almost in every paragraph, is adequate polemic and a case hard to dispose of.

Elphinstone and others had used the Satara Raja, at the time of the last war with the Peshwas, as a means to localise and lessen the campaign and our enemies. There had been previous communication between the Raja and the British; and there is some reason to believe that the Raja understood that he had been promised complete restoration to the power once his ancestor Sivaji's. On the other hand, the British regarded him as a helpless tool, almost a prisoner, of the Peshwa. But they found him a valuable tool, and consciousness of this fact rankled afterwards. The course pursued may be indicated by a quotation from Thomas Munro's letter to Elphinstone, March 29, 1818:[8] 'The limits of his principality may be left undefined for the present. He should be required to summon Bajee Rao and his principal chiefs to his presence, and in case of their not obeying to proclaim Bajee Rao and all who adhered to him rebels'. This the Raja, whose person was wrested from the peshwa at the battle of Ashti, did, and it helped to huddle the war to a finish.

He was disappointed in the extent of the principality awarded him, though the British—who soon forgot his very real service in denouncing the Peshwa as an unfaithful servant who had forfeited all right to obedience himself, and underrated his assistance as much as he overrated it—considered their action generous , the giving of something to one whose own power to obtain it was nil. He was left also with a genuine grievance in the matter of certain *Jagirs* where he was promised feudal suzerainty, a promise which lapsed by some of the accidents due to changing personnel and policies in an administration that was manned from far overseas. Over his disappointment, and especially this definite loss, he brooded.

Pratap Singh was a ruler of exceptional ability and probity. The main complaint his English overlords had against him was one inherent in geographical conditions, and one which in times less unscrupulously realist and imperialist would have been ignored. It was exposed in a minute (January 30, 1837) by Sir Robert Grant,[9] Governor of Bombay, after the trouble had started:

> 'An opinion is now very commonly entertained that the erection of Sattara into a separate principality was a mistaken proceeding. It is at least clear that this principality includes the finest part of the Deccan, and by its position most awkwardly breaks the continuity of the British territory. There are those, therefore, who will hail the present crisis as affording an excellent opportunity of repairing the error alluded to, by pulling down the inconvenient pageant we have erected'.

Of particular annoyance to the British authorities was the habit of Hindus who had widows they wished to burn, of taking them into Satara territory, where the anti-suttee regulation did not hold, much as an interrupted prize-fight in old times would move across a county boundary.

Grant's minute contained another passage which deeply interested the surviving princes when Parliament incautiously ordered the Satara papers to be published:

> 'I am aware that it is the probable course, or, if I may so speak, the natural history of such an Empire as our in India, that it gradually absorbs all the petty and dependent state attached to it, nor is there any reason to suppose that Satara will not at length share the common fate'.

He noted at the same time that the Portuguese possessions were

> 'absolutely valueless, except as the shattered and fading memorials of past glory; to us they are most inconvenient neighbours, by breaking the continuity of our dominions, and by furnishing in very supposable cases rallying points for the discontent and disaffection of our own subjects....certainly it is our obvious policy to seize the earliest opportunity of barring up this most inconvenient and possibly mischievous inlet'.

In December, 1835, the East India Company took the exceptional step of sending Pratap Singh a jewelled sword worth £3000 for his 'exemplary fulfilment of the duties' of 'his elevated situation', which had filled their minds with 'feelings of unqualified satisfaction and pleasure'. He did not receive the sword, however, for early in 1836 his Resident reported that he believed the Raja was trying to seduce British sepoys stationed in Satara from their allegiance. The Bombay authorities prosecuted the enquiry 'with an eagerness that embarrassed the Government both at Calcutta and at home'.[10] After close examination of the evidence, Lord Auckland's Government decided (1837) that there was 'little or nothing in the evidence recorded.... to inculpate the Raja'. He should, however, be warned that suspicions had arisen, and advised to conduct himself warily to prevent such episodes, painful for both sides. Then the business might be dropped. Grant was not willing to drop it, and did not drop it. But he died, 1838, and others had to continue his researches. Further accusations of anti-Company intrigue with neighbouring Rajas, notably of Jodhpur, and with the Portuguese, were brought against the Satara ruler. The evidence did not seem considerable to many contemporary British officers who deserve respect. The Raja used titles which indicated that he considered himself the head of the Maratha people, and in general rather more important than the paramount Power considered him. But in India (where titles had always been cheap, and the company had never scrupled to go on giving them to Nawabs and Rajas who had been stripped of every shred of Power and territory) this one proven offence (if offence it was) did not justify annexation. In 1839 the Bombay Government

> 'took the singularly infelicitous step of inviting the accused prince to acknowledge the truth of the accusation, and renew in more stringent terms the treaty alleged to be broken. Intimation was given that, on his failing to criminate himself, he would be dethroned. The terms were indignantly rejected, and the dethroned prince went into exile'.[11]

That is, he preferred to be dismissed, rather than accept pardon for actions that had not been proved or even examined in fair court. He resided at Benares, until his death in 1847, conducting a campaign of protest both in India and England, with many British sympathisers, both soldier and civilian, and regarded as a martyr by Indian opinion. He quite possibly was guilty—he and the Portuguese may even have come to know Sir Robert Grant's statesmanlike plans for them, and have taken counsel together, as threatened men sometimes do; and it is very probable that he was not an enthusiastic subject of the Company, or sure of his own future under their expansive mood. But there is no justification for the way our historians assume a doubtful case as proved, as when the *Oxford History of India* compresses his story into,

> 'the Raja of Satara....engaged in a long-continued series of foolish treasonable intrigues with the Portuguese and other people. The Bombay government made every effort to convince the Raja of his folly, and gave him opportunities for repentance; but he refused to listen, and was necessarily deposed, his brother taking his place'.[12]

That brogher, Apa Sahib, a worthless debauchee, had been adequately described by Grant Duff in 1819: 'an obstinate, ill-disposed lad, with very low vicious habits, which all the admonition of the Raja cannot get the better of'. He was, however, amenable, and he introduced some needed measures, such as the abolition of suttee. He died in 1848, on his death-bed adopting a son and successor. The Company were now in thc full tide of their annexation-on-any-pretext fever, and Sir John Hobhouse, President of the Board of Control, had already sent Dalhousie, newly arrived and with his mind still fluid on the Satara business, 'this obvious incitement to annexation':[13]

> '.. The death of the ex-Raja of Satara certainly comes at a very opportune moment. The reigning Raja is, I hear, in very bad health, and it is not at all impossible we may soon have to decide upon the fate of his territory. I have a very strong opinion that on the death of the present prince without a son, no adoption should be permitted, and this petty principality should be merged in the British Empire'.

Satara was annexed, and the adoption swep aside, a blow to such reputation for straightforwardness as the Company still possessed:[14]

> 'I do not remember ever to have seen Mr. Elphinstone so shocked as he was at this proceeding. The treatment of the Sattara sovereignty as a jageer,

> over which we had claims of feudal superiority, he regarded as a monstrous one: but any opinion of the injustice done to this family was subordinate to the alarm which he felt at the dangerous principles which were advanced, affecting every sovereign state in India'.

The Satara family was the family of Sivaji, with peculiar claims to Maratha and Hindu reverence. The testimony of Sir John Low, a member of Dalhousie's Council, may serve to show how deeply such Indian opinion as existed was wounded:

> 'The confidence of our Native Allies was a good deal shaken by the annexation of Satara....When I went to Malwa, in 1850 where I met many old acquaintances, whom I had known when a very young man and over whom I held no authority. I found these old acquintances speak out much more distinctly as to their opinion of the Satara case: so much so, that I was, on several occasions, obliged to check them. It is remarkable that every native who ever spoke to me respecting the annexation of Satara, asked precisely the same question: "What crime did the late Rajah commit that his country should be seized by the Company?"[15]

It was held, soundly enough, that the merits or demerits of Apa Sahib or the boy he adopted were not relevant. The only question was, Had he been the Company's faithful vassal? He notoriously had—he lacked his predecessor's self-respect as conspicuously as he lacked his other qualities. The matter continued to exacerbate both British and Indian minds, and must be considered one of many incidents that forced on the Mutiny. When that event came, this affair had been ceaselessly agitated for twenty years, with much ensuing resentment. Native India thought the annexation high-handed in the extreme, and despaired of seeing *any* ancient rights or engagements respected.

The last chapter was written in the Mutiny. The agent who had spent fourteen years of exile in London trying to get justice for the family, fled from Satara with a price on his head. There was disaffection and a tiny rising, which cost the lives of four native policemen. Then a group of over twenty—which included a son and another relative of the lawyer who had caused so much trouble, both through the House of Commons and in India—were blown from guns.

Sambalpur, a gain of only 4693 square miles and a £7000 revenue, lapsed in 1849. Since 'a pestilential climate, with no roads or comforts', it was left to Indian subordinates, who raised extra money by a 25 per cent increase of the land tax, an increase doubled in 1854. Complaints went unheeded. In 1857, mutineers wrested from a British prison the nearest heir to the lapsed sovereignty, who had been serving a life sentence since 1840. His people welcomed him back, back he led a desperate hunted life, with one interval of renewed imprisonment, until caugt finally in 1864.

Karauli, a Rajput State, escaped annexation (1852), largely because Henry Lawrence, then Agent for Rajputana, pleaded on its behalf; partly, too in deference to Indian reverence for the Rajput clan and name. Dalhousie wrote:[16]

> 'It is not worth creating any alarm about; and perhaps after all it may be politic to let alone these Rajput states, even though we have strict right on our side....
>
> ..... I have received a letter from Colonel Low, in which he urges the *policy* or recognising the adoption with reference to Rajputs' feelings, so earnestly that I think it right to send you an extract from his letter. He is a temperate and safe man, and his views will probably incline you still more to the liberal view which I have anticipated that the Court would take. On the question of *right*, I would not have deferred to him; on the question of *policy* as regards

Rajputana I do not wish to insist upon my opinion against his'.

The Court of Directors demurred, but in the end Karauli was spared. It remained steadfastly loyal in the storm, so helpful that its Chief's salute was rasied to 17 guns, and his State's debt of £11,000 remitted. Rajput States stood fast in the Mutiny. The Rajputs had come under British protection in the main voluntarily, to escape from Maratha subjugation; to this day a steady regard has 'persisted towards them from us, in which Tod's enthusiastic book had helped. The Marathas, those stiff opponents have been less fortunate, and it is only now that esteem is belatedly growing up.

Two Maratha States, Jhansi and Nagpur, lapsed in 1854. The sequel of Jhansi's annexation, is beautiful young Rani's 'inveteracy' during the Mutiny, is known to everyone. Against the annexation of Nagpur, historically one of the leading four maratha States, Low wrote two desperately earnest minutes of protest. But Dalhousie 'had no difficulty (with the Directors and himself) 'in proving' that Nagpur was a dependent State created after its ruler's share in the last Maratha War. Facts, too, were against Nagpur; it consisted of no less than 80,000 square miles, whose annexation,

> 'would not only give the Company a revenue of forty lakhs of rupees, but it would consolidate their scattered dominions, and enclose Hyderabad in a ring fence. The road between Calcutta and Bombay would lie almost entirely in British territory, and, in short, "the possession of Nagpur would combine our military strength, would enlarge our commercial resources, and would materially tend to consolidate our power".[17]

The settlement, as commonly happened, was marred by unfortunate incidents.[18]

The Nizam, who passed into 'a ring fence', had a somewhat narrow escape from elimination. His dominions had never been much more happily governed than Oudh.

But there was nothing between him and the paramount Power except money differences and debts, and the Governor-General was a man just and scrupulous, far inferior to Wellesley in ability to work himself up into passionate acceptance of his own case; he could see other points of view:

> "The monthly subsidy for which the Resident maintains a perpetual wrestle with the Diwan, and which transforms the representative of the British Government, by turns, into an importunate creditor, and a bailiff in execution, is the pay of the contingent. Where that source of demand and dispute once adjusted, there is no Native State in India whose relations with the British Government would, as far as we know, be more friendly and unruffled. The Nizam has been our ally for much more than half a century. This Government disclaims not only the intention but the wish of doing any act by which the independence of the Nizam can be in any way impaired'.[19]

The districts known as the Berars were put under British control, their revenues to be taken in settlement of claims and for payment of the subsidiary force, all surplus to be paid to the Nizam's treasury.[20] The Nizam remained nominally their sovereign. In this manner, Dalhousie saved the Company's ancient ally, and re-established him as what he is to-day the only genuinely independent prince in India.

Dalhousie's reign was a crowded season of removing anomalies and of unifying and consolidating India. Nationalist opinion to-day is not sore about his actions, for the princess seem a survival adverse to the modernist dreams of a United Independent India. It would rejoice, had he gone further, and absorbed every State. But we are concerned only with the effect in that vanished semi-feudal age, an age of European princedoms such as we have forgotten entirely, and of public opinion everywhere which thought the people largely negligible, and only aristocratic 'rights' important. Some outbreak was certain, unless all Indians were willing to be relegated to inferiority for ever.

Yet with a State that was not Maratha and had unquestioned title-deeds of internal independence, Dalhousie could be forbearing, as we have seen. In 1852 a Muslim State, Bhawalpur, was allowed to have a disputed succession, which next year passed into civil war, resulting in the rebel's victory and enthronement. The Governor-General rejected John Lawrence's strong plea for interference, and was a wise Gallio; the troubles did not concern British India, unless fighting slopped over the border. This incident[21] shows how much rope was left native States within their limits; it is only by degrees that their rulers long afterwards, have been told that they must not torture to death, or even inflict capital punishment too readily and capriciously. For example, the next Nawab of Bhawalpur, after Dalhousie's time, was allowed to execute three uncles, who might have cherished kingly ambitions.

Dalhousie's quick humanity made him protest beyond strict political rights, against suttee, which persisted on a shocking scale in some of the Rajput State. But the most ancient and inveterately traditional of them all, Udaipur persisted in these sacrifices at its rulers' funerals (in 1861 the last *legal* widow-burning in India outside Nepal disgraced it).[22] Though the Governor-General could not coerce Udaipur, when suttee occurred in Dungapur, a Rajput State temporarily under British regency, he treated it as a crime, and punished it far more heavily than it is punished to-day.

We come to the last chapter but one of Oudh's misrule and misery. We have seen its Nawabs taken from nominal dependence on the Mogul to dependence on the Company: tossed a province and new subjectss by Hastings, in the subjugation of the Rohillas: robbed by authority and without authority: made 'kingss' by Lord Hastings: forced by Auckland to accept a treaty whose annulment was concealed from them: subjected by successive rulers to that iniquity which revolts us to-day 'unilateral' denunciation distortion and revision of solemn treaties:

> 'Most assuredly Warren Hastings, Lord Teignmouth, Lord Wellesley, Lord Hastings and Lord Auckland, would never have acted in private life as they did in the capacity of governor-general towards prostrate oude'.[23]

Under the aegis of British protection, Lucknow was infested for close on a century with pimps and panders, musicians, robbers and Europeans. Contemporary accounts show a populace armed and swaggering, and crowded streets where 'elephants and camels are the common labourers',[24] blocking traffic. The buffalo-hide shield, studded with brass knobs, is flung up on the left shoulder: fiercely-moustached Rajputs and Pathans, black-bearded Mussulmans, 'self-sufficient citizens', flaunt matchlock and tulwar. Midway ran the silvery streak of the river, between sprawling glittering palaces and those parks which still make Lucknow uniquely beautiful.

> 'Elephants in scores, tigers, rhinoceroses, antelopes, cheetahs or hunting-leopards, lynxes, Persian cats, Chinese dogs, might all be seen sunning themselves in this park, either in their cages, or stretched listlessly on the grass, as commonly as sheep and cows in an English meadow'.

The visitor was 'transported suddenly into some of the scenes....read in childish history and novels'. Such lunacy, even in the East, would have been swept away by revolution long before, but for the terrible puissance outside Oudh's borders, protecting its rulers.

Oudh, nevertheless, remained important. It had been loyal, slavishly so, to its engagements, and the paramount Power had no legal excuse for annexation. It remained, a vast and awkward gap in the Company's dominions.

Larger than Switzerland Saxony and Wurtemberg together, 'stripped as it has been of its rupees and its most valuable provinces by successive governors-general, Oude is still more populous than any of the German states....except Prussia and Austria'.[25] But at last something had to be done, within or without the cover of treaty rights. In 1847 Lord Hardinge warned the King that he must mend his atrocious government, or the British Government would take steps to see it mended. In 1848 Sleeman was sent to Lucknow by Dalhousie as Resident, to undertake 'the reconstruction of a great, rich and oppressed country.... a noble as well as an arduous task....[26] in 1849 he was instructed to make a tour and report on conditions. He found them fantastic in iniquity. His least trouble was with infanticide, the common practice of the Rajputs in the kingdom, practised with the indecency that so easily goes with ruthlessness. Yes, his colloquists told him, of course they killed their female children' they buried them alive, a after smothering them with the first faeces passed from the bowels, and on the thirteenth or fourteenth day afterwards the priest came and ate a meal in the room which had been both birthplace and tomb, thereby becoming a 'sineater'.[27] Lucknow, that 'overgrown city', was a' perpetual turmoil of processions, illuminations, and festivities'.[28] The King had settled down to a continuous Eisteddfod, his sole companions fiddlers and buffoons, his ambition 'limited to the reputation of being the best drum-beater, dancer, and poet of the day',[29] aspirations admirable in private individual but out of place in a ruler, and in any case not likely to appeal to an Indian official. Most of his fellow-artists were Doms, outcastes of the most scavenging and despised kind. Sleeman's sombre narrative is lit up with humorous interuldes, all verging on grimness. There were, for example, the activities of 'the King of the Fairies' (djinns), an enterprising Muslim who precipitated by means of a false ceiling messages from elfland, enjoining gifts to that region through himself, its representative.

The King's pastimes needed money, to procure which royal forces scoured the land. The peasantry grew swift-footed and long-sighted. They sometimes hit back, Oudh being full of sepoys, 'the great nursery of soldiers for the Company's army. The forces of the Bengal presidency come almost exclusively from Oudh'. But these armed groups were an added element to the universal lawlessness. Sleeman was often assured that annexation would be welcomed, if there were any way of evading our dreaded courts. In this desire he sympathised deeply, but, like others, unavailingly; when Oudh was ultimately annexed, little notice was paid to his witness that out legal methods. wrought more harm than all other evil agencies together.[30]

> 'The quality of testimony, no doubt, like that of every other commodity, deteriorates under a system, which renders the good of no more value in *exchanges* then the bad. The formality of our Courts here, as everywhere else, tends to impair, more or less, the quality of what they receive. The simplicity of Courts, composed of little village communities and elders, tends, on the contrary, to improve the quality of the testimony they get; and in India, it is found to be best in the isolated hamlets of hills and forests, where men may be made to do almost anything rather than *tell a lie*. A Marhatta pandit, in the valley of the Nerbudda, once told me, that it was almost impossible to teach a wild Gond of the hills and jungles the *occasional* value of a lie! It is the same with the Tharoos and Booksas, who are, almost exclusively, the cultivators of the Oude Tarae forest, and with the peasantry of the Himmalaya chain of mountains, before they have come much in contact with people of the plains, and become subject to the jurisdiction of our Courts. These Courts are, everywhere, our, *weak point* in the estimation of our subjects; and they should be, everywhere, simplified, to meet the wants and wishes of so simple a people'.

To sum up:

> 'A want of sympathy or fellow-feeling between the governing and governed is common in all parts of India, but in no part that I have seen is it so marked as in Oude. The officers of the Government delight in plundering the peasantry, and upon every local Governor who kills a landholder of any mark, rewards and honours are instantly bestowed, without the slightest inquiry as to the cause or mode. They know that no inquiry will be made, and therefore kill when they can; no matter how, or for what cause'.[31]

Yet the region tormented with this madness was nobly endowed:

> 'I have seen no soil finer; the whole plain of which it is composed is capable of tillage; it is everywhere intersected by rivers, flowing from the snowy chain of the Himmalaya, which keep the moisture near the surface at all times, without cutting up any of the land on their borders into deep ravines; it is studded with finest groves and single trees, as much as the lover of the picturesque could wish; it has the boldest and most industrious peasantry in India, and a landed aristocracy too strong for the weak and wretched Government; it is, for the most part, well cultivated; yet with all this, one feels, in travelling over it as if he was moving among a people suffering under incurable physical diseases, from the atrocious crimes every day perpetrated with impunity, and the numbers of suffering and innocent people who approach him in the hope of redress, and are sent away with despair'.[32]

Sleeman was strongly against annexation, and warned Lord Dalhousie in writing 'that the annexation of Oude would cost the British power more than the value of ten such kingdoms, and would inevitably lead to a mutiny of the Sepoys', a prediction he died just too soon to see fulfilled. He held, as others of his way of thinking did, that the native States were 'breakwaters, and when they are all swept away, we shall be left to the mercy of our native army, which may not always be sufficiently under our control'. Also, that they had an educational value; Indians, looking first on the quiet and security pervading the Company's dominions and then on the lunatic caprice and misery of such States as Oudh, would feel how lucky those in the former were. He knew, too, how valuable as a safety-valve native India was: the ambitious and energetic, who could serve only as subordinates on a pittance and without self-respect in British India, here could rise to places of responsibility or, at any rate, power and esteem. Those whose habits unfitted them' to occupy niches of humility and lowly service could here swagger with tulwar and matchlock.

But his report was too convincing, and was borne out by the Governor-General's own experience. In December, 1851, Dalhousie Journeyed on Oudh's borders, in the North-West Provinces, then under Thomason's beneficent rule, and noted:

> 'The district profits considerably by its proximity to Oudh, since the disturbances in that unfortunate land very frequently produce an emigration of good cultivators from some village that can stand squeezing no more. The other day the whole of the cultivators of one village, two hundred in number, fled into the Shahjehanpur district, and were all eagerly hired by the zamindars at once'.[33]

> 'All day I heard a heavy cannonading going on, and marvelled to think that we should be able to hear the artillery practice all the way from Cawnpore. Before the evening I discovered it was our neighbours in Oudh collecting their revenue! Nothing more common, the people say, all along this border'.[34]

Yet with amazing patience Dalhousie procrastinated. It is an example of the queer illogicality with which British Indian history is written that the annexation of Oudh has been so often reprobated, when actions flatly unethical are glossed over. This is because the Mutiny followed. There is not much open to criticism in the Oudh annexation, details apart; and as to details, 'it is impossible but that offences should come', and it is the historian's business not to stress the unavoidable that is also trivial.

In 1854 Outram was sent to Lucknow as Resident. He reported that there had been no improvement. His account, 'excellent, clear, concise, temperate in its tone, and decisive in its conclusion', reached Dalhousie at Coonoor in the Nilgiris, March 15, 1855; Oudh's administration was an orgy of massacre and corruption set to music.

Even yet Dalhousie pondered and hesitated: Wellesley's treaty of 1810, a gross injustice at the time and in its attendant bullying now stood the erring kingdom in good stead: it enjoined that reforms must be carried out by the Nawab's own officers, and Dalhousie believed in promises being kept. On January 2, 1856, a Court of Directors', decision reached him; he was to offer the King a kind of 'Vatican, Sovereignty, the title of King, adequate funds, and full jurisdiction short of death over the Lucknow palace, parks (and menageries). Outram, who had been recalled to Calcutta for conference, was sent back to Lucknow, reaching it January 30, with a British brigade close behind. He went to the palace, to find its guns dismounted in mourning, and a disarmed guard of honour saluting with empty hands signifying helplessness. The King placed his turban between his hands, and broke down when reading the treaty he was to sign. Glven a few days' grace he refused to accept the new position (February 7), was deposed, and went to Calcutta, where he resided, agitating and protesting, one more centre of pity and resentment.

Dalhousie's pledge of generous grants to those brought low was ignored, and in Canning's brief pre-Mutiny rule they were 'reduced to great pecuniary straits, with all the humiliations attendant upon such a state'.[35] Those who had sung and revelled starved; and with them starved royalty and nobility. An unsympathetic Chief Commissioner succeeded Outram the Resident, and chose to occupy a palace 'expressly set aside for the King's family'. Oudh was flooded with disbanded troops, under a new regime in which robbery was liable to heavy penalities. Not less than 40,000 Company's sepoys had their homes in the province, and they and their families, a large fraction of the total population, were troubled in their minds.

Dalhousie's words in his Diary[36] are movingly sincere:

> 'I believe the work to be just, practicable, and right. With that feeling on my mind, and in humble reliance on the blessing on the Almighty, I approach the execution of the duty gravely; and not without solicitude, but calmly and altogether without doubt'.

It seems hard, after careful weighing of three-quarters of a century of criticism that has followed the event, to see how he could have acted other than he did. But the mischief arose from the fact that now Indians, except within a restricted and threatened area, were debarred from hope of any post, civil of military, of any importance. Tolerant of much misrule and misery (explained by religious philosophy, as these were), the people of India until recently never attached as much weight to actual material improvement as we have imagined. They could see only that a very rich province, long pillarged and longer coveted, had been swallowed up, and an ancient family exiled, 'who, whatever may have been their offences towards their own subjects, have not been unfaithful to the British Government'.[37] This claim, which to the Directors appeared a mainly formal one, to them was essential: if the British both annexed when there had been the test of strength in war, as with the Punjab, and when there had been nothing but decades of slavish submission, where did anyone stand? As for the suffering under native rule, there were two sides to this question:[38]

> 'General Lowe, whom I have always known as a most indulgent judge of native governments and an enemy to annexation...used, in the particular case of Oude, to maintain that the people preferred their present misrule to our strict and meddling system, and the insolence and extortion of chuprassies and other petty officials; yet, after having been ten years and more Resident at Lucknow, he is now one of the most decided as to the impossibility of maintaining the present Government. Sleeman (the most vehement advocate of annexation)[39] is said to be in general a still greater friend to native governments'.

However, Oudh was annexed, and its teeming disorders dispersed rather than grappled with. As for the few surviving States, they drew into themselves, watchful, frightened, thinking such thoughts as even Englishmen have occasionally known:

> Another year! another deadly blow!
> Another mighty empire overthrown!
> And We are left, or shall be left, alone'.

Dalhousie ended other long-standing anomalies, as well as petty kingdoms that had outlived their real independence. In 1852 he secured the Delhi heir-apparent's promise to leave his palace (which was wanted for British military uses) when he succeeded his father; and 'regretted that the silly sentimentality of the Court[40] interposed any impediment to taking the crown as well as the palace'. We may doubt the wisdom of this yet further attenuation of a faded majesty venerated even in its relics; and again, may ponder, with the coming shadow of 1857 falling on our narrative. The same shadow falls with another name, the Peshwa's. He died, 1851, and the pension granted him by Malcolm was not renewed to his adopted son, the notorious Nana Sahib. Dalhousie argued:

> 'In thirty-three years the Peshwa received the enormous sum of more than two and a half million sterling. He had no charges to maintain, no sons of his own, and has bequeathed twenty-eight lacs to his family. Those who remain have no claim whatever on the consideration of the British Government. They have no claim on its charity, because the income left to them is amply sufficient for them'.

We may envy the people of India, and wish that the same reasoning might be used of British pensions granted for events in the far past and continued age after age. There seems no cause to cavil at it. In 1855, the Nawab of the Carnatic died, and the title was discontinued, his uncle, who succeeded, being now styled merely Prince of Arcot and becoming a nobleman. The same year, the 'rajas' of Tanjore died out, as their power had deed long ago. In this, as in the Nawabs case, Dalhousie intended a generous financial settlement. It was not his fault that the usual thing happened to the Ranis' personal property. One by one, princedoms whose ghosts had long haunted the Indian scene were exorcised and vanished.

A major campaign outside India was the second Burmese War, 1852. Frontier incidents had been accumulating since the first war; and in November, 1851, the foreign merchants of Rangoon made a detailed complaint of grievances. Dalhousie sent Commodore. Lambert to express his 'confidence' that the Court of Ava would right these, and would disclaim breaches of treaty. A party of naval officers (January 6) went to the Rangoon Governor's house; told to wait outside they pressed on to the foot of the steps, where they were informed that His Excellency was sleeping and could not be disturbed. A long stand in hot sun tried their tempers, as did the discovery that His Excellency was amusedly watching through a lattice. Lambert in reprisal seized a vessel belonging to the Burmese King and blockaded the rivers. Dalhousie remained patient, and sent a second letter. The Commodore's ship, bearing it, was fired on, but easily silenced its assailants. John Lawrence meanwhile had asked, 'Why did you send a Commodore to Burma if you wanted peace'?,; and Dalhousie himself remorsefully admitted (January 23, 1852) that 'these Commodores are too combustible for negotiations'.

At length a thrasonical answer arrived from the Rangoon Governor,

> 'commanding the forces, and appointed to go and rule a large territory and brave army after due prostration at the royal feet, and after taking counsel with Meng Tarahgyee Phooyah, who is all-powerful Lord of the Universe, Master of the Tshattang elephant, and all white Elephants, and Lord of Life, he who is like unto the Lotus-flower'.

The British officers were reproved for having invaded his privacy while he was sleeping, and for having been drunk when they did it.

Dalhousie's next communication went to the point. By April 1,

> 'if, untaught by former experience, forgetful of the irresistible power of the British arms...the King of Ava shall unwisely refuse the just and lenient conditions which are now set before him, the British Government will have no alternative but immediate war'.

War followed; it had minor setbacks, but no repetition of the mistakes of the former war. At first the British suffered more from pineapples, which were one hundred for a shilling, than from Burmese missiles. The Shwe-Dagon pagoda, in Rangoon, was stormed, April 14, 1852; other pagodas and strong points were stormed, till in

October the Burmese generalissimo, son of the Bandula who had fought so well in the first war, was ordered to appear before the Golden Foot in woman's dress,[41] for having been defeated. He preferred surrender to the British.

The war ended without treaty, the British annexing Pegu and the Burmese King, who explained that he was not at liberty to sign away territory, formally notifying the invaders (June, 1853) that he would allow them to remain in his country, and forbid his generals to molest them. His people, cut off from the sea, were almost starving; he asked that the Irawadi blockade might be lifted, and free trade established between his nation and the British.

The war had been marred by one sinister incident. The 38th Native Infantry, afraid of losing caste, had 'respectfully but firmly' refused to go to Burma by sea, though willing to march anywhere by land. It was technically within its rights, and the Governor-General acted with characteristic humanity:

> 'I could not fail to remember the melancholy incident in the same station of Barrackpore on the same occasion of the march of troops for a Burmese war, when from some misunderstanding and want of judicious and temperate handing the Native troops were at length massacred as mutineers. Bearing that sad scene in mind, I felt that while I should never advise the Government to permit open disobedience of its orders, to truckle to its Sepoys, or in any the slightest degree to compromise its own authority; yet if it were practicable to modify existing orders, so as to avert an occasion which stupidity or error might make use of for a manifestation of discontent, or even of open mutiny, it would be a wise act for the Government to avoid such occasion for misapprehension, and so to preserve the men from the certain consequences of their own folly.

The battalion had declared its willingness to march; and 'we thought it right that they should march'. They marched, therefore, though the hot weather had come, to Dacca, and relieved a less scrupulous unit there, which sailed for Burma.

Ever since the close of the second Sikh War, in which Dost Muhammad had attempted to wreak belated vengeance for his former suffering at out hands, the question of an understanding with Afghanistan had been pondered. John Lawrence, who wrote, 'The best attitude perhaps the only safe one, with Orientals, is that of complete superiority', and

> 'I look upon a Sikh chief as in every respect a more honourable and trustworthy man than an Afghan. Falsehood and villainy are the natural characteristics of an Afghan, and their rulers are probably much worse than the majority of their people'.
>
> 'All thinking men would say that it must, indeeed, be a terrible crisis—Russia must be a frightful foe—when the lords of the East—the English—backed by France and Turkey, hold out in this fashion the right hand of fellowship to Kabul!'[42]

represented one attitude, that of standing on dignity for the Dost's impertinence in interfering in the Sikh campaign. The Dost answered this by suspicion; 'I know that the English will never forgive me'.

Herbert Edwardes, the chief warden of the marches,[43] was the first who made negotiation possible. Of a frank and adventurous nature, he was ready to see unofficial emissaries. When a treaty was finally made, March, 1855, though Dalhousie preferred that John Lawrence should actually carry it through and sign it, the main credit was Edwardes's. It was perhaps fortunate that negotiations were not hustled through, but protracted until almost the eve of the Mutiny. Dost Muhammad in that immense upheaval kept to his side of the fence.

Next year (May 14, 1854) the Khan of Khelat was brought within the Indian system, and became a subsidised prince. The western frontier was now closed, except for the border tribes who kept it in a condition of constant petty warfare.

Inside India the Santal rebellion, 1855, at the time was taken as a portent, and aroused much of the alarm and savagery of repression which were to blaze out less than two years later. This was partly because it came so close to the capital. The Santals (Sonthals), aborigines who in a state of nature live by the chase, a people of extreme simplicity and lovableness, were suffering (as they continue to suffer) from Hindu infiltration. This meant change of habits and a whole train of perplexities. Their lands became alienated, they were entangled in debts to people far cleverer than themselves. They were under foolish local officials, who would not help them: 'The facile reply that the Santals should appeal to the civil courts, or prove their charges of oppression before the criminal courts, was the answer of the father who should offer his son a stone when he asked for bread'.[44] No one dreamed of insurrection by 'a race so gentle and harmless, with courts of justice ever open to them'; moreover, courts of British justice—which 'are open to everyone (like the Savoy Hotel)'. Planters, who were having trouble with the Bengali peasant , praised these 'laborious and patient' people'; railway contractors delighted in them. Then, without warning, a Santal inundation swept over the outlying regions of Bengal, reaching to within a hundred miles of Calcutta, cleaving open skulls of European and Indian alike, pouring out poisoned arrows, burning huts and bungalows. All ended, however, as it was bound to end, in massacre and executions. The blood of the martyrs—if we may for a minute forget their wrong-doing and remember only that except by such an outbreak no redress could ever have come to them for mere grumbling and representation has never brought humanity anything—proved the seed of better conditions. Their land was made into a non-regulation' district, and they shared with the Punjab the privilege of exemption from the blessings of justice as dispensed in the law-courts, experiencing in their stead straightforward protection.

Dalhousie, like the rest of Calcutta, was deeply impressed by this sudden fire out of the heart of aboriginal darkness:

> "This Santal outbreak has taught us a new and cogent lesson; and I trust very much that Her majesty's ministers and those who talk of drawing troops from India so glibly and confidently...will lay that lesson to heart'.

As these words show, a vague uneasiness was troubling men's minds; there was growing through many years an underground irritation of the sort that so often contributes to exceeding passion of anger, when at last its dimly suspected justifications seem to leap up in open menace. The irritation was felt by both sides. Its centres were in Oudh swarming with pillaged landowners and unemployed soldiery; in the, marathas, who felt that Sivaji's family had been wronged, and their rightful Peshwa (by adoption of his predecessor) deprived of the pension which kept a memory of ancient grandeur alive; in Delhi, where an ancient family knew that their tenure of the palace which was itself a city, within whose walls they could fool themselves that they were still regalities, was running out, and that a foreign soldiery would take their place there; and where ever (which was everywhere in North India—it is easy to see why South India was untouched by the Mutiny, which was as much outside its interests and passions as an outbreak in Poland or China, almost) European society had been exacerbated by the intense angers of the civilian-military quarrel which Napier had brought to a head.

In January, 1856, Lord Dalhousie went; but his going was followed by three events 'in rapid succession'[45] all part of the swiftly rising rapids that were sweeping tranquil India to the catastrophe. An order was issued, July 25, 1856, which made all units liable for general service, beyond the seas as in India; henceforward, refusal for caste prejudices was mutiny pure and simple. War was declared against Persia, November 1, 1856; India was deprived of a large part of its shrunken forces, not long after public opinion had been disquieted by the Crimean War, in which the clash which Government had anticipated for decades, with increasing apprehension and gravity, had come at last, and (rumour said) with not any great success to England. The Persian expedition, which was commanded by Outram and Havelock, won battles easily enough. But men remembered another war, that with Afghanistan, which was arose from the same obsessing dread of Russia; that one also had begun with victories, over which a pack of fuss was made at the time, but had passed into overwhelming disaster. Many agreed with John Lawrence when he scoffed (January 30, 1857) at this eternal Russian bugbear: 'I believe there is no man now alive who will ever see a Russian army in India, and no Asiatic army could stand for a day before our troops in the open field'. Again Indian troops were being sent far beyond their borders, to similar destruction! Moreover, India was left very low in British troops.

Lastly, on January 23, 1857, General Hearsey[46] (surely the most suggestive name that even a novelist could invent!) reported that there was 'an unpleasant feeeling' about cartridges which the men believed were smeared with cow and pig lard. What followed is known to the world.

It is natural that we should look back on Dalhousie's reign as a time of territorial expansion. But it was also one of intense and beneficent activity. James Thomason, perhaps the greatest of Indian Provincial governors after Munro, ruled the North-West Provinces, 1843-53. Wise, patient, pacific, he gathered no laurels of war; but he won a personal regard from wilder spirits such as only Henry Lawrence won. His administration was looked on as mine whence the Punjab could 'dig' first rate men for its own more exciting service. Even to that promotion they went, however eagerly, yet with sorrow at parting from such a master; Thomason's farewell letter to Sir Richard Temple on going to the Lawrences, Temple wrote in his retirement, 'still shines like the evening star in my recollection'.[47]

Thomason moved continually about his province, always with a mind at leisure to listen and be interested,

> 'till at length there was hardly a place or a road in an area of 70,000 square miles, scarcely a clan or tribe in a population of 30 millions, with which he was not acquainted'.[48]

He was the bureaucrat at his best and noblest; a machine of ungrudging effort. He would,

> 'set himself laboriously to learn how each kind of complex business should be performed from beginning to end, from the lowest to the highest step; having done that, he would reduce all his knowledge to lucid statement, so that what had perhaps been hard to him might be made easy to others. When he had thus instructed his officers of all degrees, he was extraordinarily patient and watchful in seeing that they acted up to his instructions'.[48]

In such a subordinate Dalhousie found a man who even foreran him in enthusiasm for the people's advancement. So much was done. In the North-West provinces, in the Punjab, throughout India generally that we can understand the vexation which accompanied deeper feelings when the Mutiny came. The mere record of the Lawrences' achievement in one year, which called out from John by Napier's criticisms, is staggering. Theirs was a system which did not admit of leave. The need was too enormous, the work too exciting; men must persist until they broke down. When Dalhousie had mentioned that his near relation, Lord William Hay, wanted leave, John had answered:

'If Lord W. Hay is left to our mercies, we must, in duty bound, refuse him leave. We have agreed not to recommend any leave unless when men are sick. There is still much to do, and will be so for the next two years. Every day is of value, and the best officer cannot work too hard or too long for the public interest'.

A tyranny of duty drove on the best men, as fiercely as any taskmaster's whip. After thirty years in which men's lives had gone in such work as extirpating thuggee and suttee, infanticide and slavery, we need not wonder that respect for Indian civilisation was low. The slavish superstition which made men refuse to cross the sea, lest defilement came, pressed on Dalhousie,

'the necessity for commencing the movement intended to uproot the absurd and unmeaning system, under which the whole Bengal army is practically no better than a collection of local corps, and to substitute for it a system of enlistment for general service of every man who may hereafter be recruited for any arm within its ranks'. (August 2, 1854.)

Dalhousie sanctioned Thomason's plans for an engineering college at Rurki and kept up at his own cost the girl's college founded in Calcutta by J. E. Drink water Bethune, a member of his Council, who died, 1851. He pressed on the Directors educational expenditure. He established for Bengal, hitherto a charge of the Governor-General, and too apt to be neglected for general responsibilities, a separate Lieutenant-governorship. He established a Central Legislative Council. He a even dreamed of a time when Indians might rise to authority themselves. He laid practically all the foundations of modern India and it is only when we look at the promise of this period and remember the prolonged setback which followed the Mutiny—an experience like the American

'Reconstruction' are after the Civil War—that we realise the tragedy of that episode, which substituted harsh judgment and bitterness for understanding and eagerness. He greatly increased the expenditure on public works, so much so that we may look on the gain of four and a half millions sterling to the revenue from his annextions as one for the good of India as a whole. The Grand Trunk Road was begun; canals were vastly extended, and the mighty Ganges Canal was finished in 1854, after eight years of work and the spending of £14,00,000 of which sum all but £170,000 was provided during his period of office. Its 525 miles (at this date) exceeded 'all the irrigation lines of Lombardy and Egypt together'; and Thomason, not a man to boast, claimed that it was unequalled among the efforts of civilised nations'. Dalhousie insisted, against strong opposition, that such benefactors as outstanding public engineers, though neither in red coats nor among the 'heaven-born' civilians, should be knighted. Prisoners were put under inspectors, first by Thomason in his territory, then by degrees in every other province; even criminals were acknowledged to have rights of protection. The final extirpation of the *Meriah* abominations was in Dalhousie's time. He introduced railways, the first line being opened in 1853, and a more important one between Calcutta and the Raniganj coal-area, in 1854. India saw (1853),

> 'the splendid sight of fifty Parsee ladies riding in a special train upon the rail from Bombay to Tanah'.[49]

He introduced the electric telegraph, and supported the man responsible, against every sort of official nonsense and red tape, having him directly under himself, and not under the Military Board. The Punjab was given a network of military roads, immensely valuable to its people. The inefficient postal arrangements were abolished, and the cheap half-anna rate of pre-War days established. The forests were conserved and tea-planting encouraged.

Macaulay's 'filtration theory' in education had worn very thin before the Mutiny, and a new policy was laid down in the Directors' despatch of 1854, which is usually ascribed to Sir Charles Wood, the President of the Board of Control.[50] The Bombay Government had already acknowledged the relative importance of elementary education, and by 1852 had 233 vernacular schools with over 11,000 pupils, as against 14 Governments colleges and English schools with 2000 scholars. The Bengal Government, following the older theory, had 30 colleges with 5000 pupils, but only 33 elementary schools. The despatch of 1854 was a justification of the Bombay policy. This difference of outlook was typical of a change which was taking place throughout the administration. As province after province came under British rule the new Governments took more direct responsibilities. The *ryotwari* system of direct assessment succeeded the zemindari method of farming out the land revenue. When the Government began to embark upon large development schemes, roads, irrigation canals, and buildings, these were constructed as far as possible by public departments. The whole of British India was divided up into districts, and subdivided into areas under Indian officials, *Tehsildars. Mamlatdors* etc. The district officer had an ever-increasing number of duties thrust upon him, especially in those early days in the Punjab, where sixty picked men, of whom Nicholson is the most famous, brought immense energy to their work. 'The sound of his horse's hoofs was heard from Attock to the Khaibar', as frontier tribesman said of Nicholson. 'The Englishman is at his best in dealing with a primitive people, and this ruthless progress and efficiency, imposed directly from above, was typical of Dalhousie's administration.

He came to an official world sunk in routine. The Commander-in-Chief spent the whole year in the hills, involving the State in heavy expense by his residence there and by 'the enormous quantity of transport which he required when he moved about';[51] the reader with Indian experience can fill in details. By personal example Dalhousie reformed those who could be reformed[52] and encouraged those who, in the Punjab and elsewhere, were moved by a zeal like his own. Though haughty and imperious, he was no stickler for sate; a note to his private secretary, at midnight of March 29, 1849, says:

> 'If you are up and have your breeches on come here. If not, without them'.

He worked unpausingly through the sorrow of his wife's death and his own deepening pain. An affection diagnosed as gout settled into malignant disease of the shin-bone, afterwards extended to his throat. He had to be much at sea or in the hills, and when he left India dragged himself on board with crutches. He had then long outlived any desire but for retirement, and praise and rewards were vanity to his spirit, which continued unflagging in unselfishness, in care for his friends, in uprightness and courage and witty vivacity. India has been the scene of abundant valour, but of none more moving than this man's. All things weighed, he was the greatest of the Governors-General after Warren Hastings; and as a man he has a place all to himself, his pluck and intellect making of steadfast conscientiousness a thing of exceeding loveliness,

> 'Not harsh and crabbed, as dull fools suppose,
> But musical as is Apollo's lute'.

REFERENCES

1. Sir William Lee - Warner, *Life of Lord Dalhousie*, i. 104 ff.
2. Cf. his letter to the President of the Board of Control, June 29, 1854: 'My experience has taught me that men who correspond over a space of 10,000 miles should watch their pens; for ink comes to burn like caustic when it crosses the sea. I therefore repress the inclination to say what I feel, and will merely reply that I am open to no blame; and will prove it'.

3. Life of Dalhousie, i. 353.
4. Life, i. 445 ff.
5. October 29, 1853.
6. Sir John Malcolm, who understood 'adoption' and the Indian attitude towards it better than anyone else, twenty years before Dalhousie's time (November 14, 1829) expressed this opinion: 'Adoptions, which are universally recognised as legal among Hindoos, are not a strict right (any more than direct heirs) where grants of land are for service....But while a few have been permitted to adopt, others are denied the privilege; and while we declare their direct heirs are entitled to succeed, we lie in wait (I can call it nothing else) to seize their fine estate on failure of heirs, throwing them and their adherents and the country into a state of doubt and distraction....The Bengal Government, influenced by, if not composed of, men bred in Calcutta, take a mere fiscal view of the subject, and be live, I imagine, our chiefs and Jagheerdars to be like the Baboos and Bengal Jemindars....' As this passage suggests, British-Indian history would have taken a very different, and probably far happier, course if Calcutta had not been the capital.
7. *Story of Satara* (*The Modern Review* Office, Calcutta, 1922)
8. Gleig,. *Life of Sir Thomas Munro*, iii 237.
9. Author of 'O warship the King all-glorious above' and other well-Known hymns.
10. Colebrooke, *Life of Elphinstone*, ii. 387 Elphinstone, in retirement, took a deep interest in the affair, having been so largely concerned in the re-establishment of Satara.
11. *op. cit.* ii. 387.
12. 674. It is worth noting that Kaye (*History of the Sepoy War*, i. 72) thinks his deposition justified.
13. Sir William Lee-Warner, *Life of Lord Dalhousie*, ii. 158.
14. *Life of Elphinstone*, ii. 388.
15. Minute of Colonel Low, February 10, 1854.
16. *Life of Dalhousie*, ii. 168.
17. *Op. cit.* ii. 178 ff.
18. See Kaye, *History of the Sepoy War*, Book 1, chapter 2; and for a partial defence, Lee Warner, *Life of Lord Dalhouise*, ii. 181.
19. Minute of March 30, 1853.
20. Treaty of May, 21, 1853

21. *Life of Dalhousie*, ii. 117 ff.
22. See Thompson, *Suttee*, 108 ff.
23. *Calcutta Review*, iii. 376.
24. W. Knighton, *The Private Life of an Eastern King*, 6, 5, 3, 5.
25. *Op. cit*. 9.
26. Sleeman, *A journey through the Kingdom of Oude*, 1849-50 (1858 ed), xviii.
27. Cf. Mary Webb's *Precious Bane*.
28. Sleeman, i. 275.
29. Sleeman in 1852.
30. *Journey through Oude*, ii. 68-9.
31. *Op. cit. i*. 334-5.
32. Sleeman, letter to Sir Erskine perry, February 2, 1850.
33. Sir William Lee-Warner, *Life of Lord Dalhousie*, ii. 317.
34. *Op. cit. ii*. 319 (Diary entry, December 30, 1851).
35. Lord Stanley, October 13, 1858.
36. January 9, 1856.
37. Court of Directors, November 21, 1855.
38. Mountstuart Elphinstone, May 4, 1856 (Life, ii. 395).
39. This, as we have seen, is mistaken. But it was the common belief.
40. The Court of Directors.
41. William F. B. Laurie. *Narrative of Events during the second Burmese war*, from August, 1852....., 89.
42. March 24, 1854. The Crimean War broke out, 1854.
43. He became Commissioner of Peshawar, October, 1853.
44. *Life of Dalhousie*, ii. 62 ff.
45. *Op. cit*. ii. 360.
46. Sometimes spelled 'Hearsay'. The Hearseys were a very famous Anglo-Indian family.
47. Sir Richard Temple, *Man and Events of My Time in India*, 45.
48. *Life of Dalhousie*, ii. 360.
49. William F. B. Laurie, *The Second Burmese War Pegu*, 280.
50. Grandfather of the Viceroy, Lord Irwin.
51. *Life of Dalhousie*, i. 113.
52. This did not include the military administration, whose head continued to live on heights.

2

Peasants Under the Company

With Lord Dalhousie's departure the Company's rule virtually ended. He had done much to transform its character, and his successor, Lord Canning, was soon embroiled in the Mutiny. Before describing that disastrous prelude to the formal introduction of Crown Government, it will be convenient to consider the influence of the British connection upon the manual workers. Unfortunately it was not until recently that any scientific enquiries were made into Indian economic and social conditions, and these have been limited in scope, referring to parts of the peninsula only. The historian searching for evidence of change, of improvement or deterioration over long periods, is driven to statistics of doubtful validity, to official reports which are seldom written from the required standpoint, and to chance observation of travellers and contemporary writers whose mental background and standards of comparison are difficult to estimate. There has been much tendentious writing about the condition of Indian villagers during the eighteenth and nineteenth centuries by authors who, consciously or unconsciously, have wished to suggest either that a golden age of peace and prosperity existed before the British came, or that the whole of India was plunged into anarchy and misery from which it was saved by the British connection. The honest historian must confess that, while it is easy to produce evidence to support either proposition, there is extremely little upon which to form a fresh and unbiassed opinion. A few preliminary generalizations may be permitted.

Throughout the period under consideration the measure of Indian prosperity was the condition of the peasantry. Not only did they form nearly three-fifths of the population, but the great majority of the rest worked for these directly, as farm labourers, or indirectly, as village servants, and as carpenters, smiths, etc. The rulers and the religious lived ultimately off the peasant's surplus produce. The *ryot's* first need is several acres of tillable land, containing sufficient phosphates, nitrates and potash. Probably fifteen acres of dry land, or five acres of irrigated, form a sound 'economic' family holding. The *ryot* also wants some draught cattle to help him cultivate. He is not much interested in other stock, partly because India is not a natural diary country, but chiefly because the population is largely vegetarian, and the pig, easy animal for the peasant to keep, is forbidden to Hindu and Muslim. Like most countrymen, he has no love for intensive farming, and slightly despises the *mali* or market gardener, grows vegetable near a town. His object is to grow enough food for his family, food which will keep for a year; and also something which he can exchange, or sell for cash, either grain, fibre, dye, or drug. His first two considerations are his acreage and the fertility of the soil. There is some evidence to show that the *ryot* was better off in both these respects a century and a half ago, though the deterioration which had already begun by the Mutiny, had only an indirect connection with the British occupation.

The first census was not taken till 1872, and the results, which surprised everyone, discount the value of rough estimates of population which were made previously.[1] It is, however, safe to assume a considerable increase in population between 1750 and 1850, especially in Southern India. During the latter part of the century it was the subject of frequent comment in official records. The spread of population was not relieved by any large-scale irrigation works until Dalhousie last years. It was due to the establishment of peaceful conditions amongst a people used to war, and possessing high natural fertility. The efforts to reduce female infanticide must also have had some influence. It is certain that the cultivators were becoming a larger proportion of the population. In the eighteenth century there were more aboriginal and outcaste tribes not settled on the land. Village servants and craftsmen were comparatively more numerous and far more men were in military service of some kind or another.[2] The cultivator was also less tied to the soil. In Bengal any *ryots* preferred to take their land on the seasonal or *paikasht* tenure, rather than on the permanent or *khudkasht*. With no great pressure on the land, occupancy rights had little value, and *royt* was freer to bargain with the *Zamindar*. He was also less exposed to the wiles of the money-lender, for he could only borrow money on his personal security, and in those lawless times the money-lenders plied a dangerous and uncertain trade. In the Deccan the drainage of men for military service was perhaps greater than in Bengal. The researches of Dr. Mann suggest that the average size of holdings was reduced to less than half during the seventy years preceding the Mutiny.[3] With a larger proportion of sons staying at home the evil of 'fragmentation' or 'morcellement' became more noticeable, each separate plot being divided up amongst the heirs of a dead man, until the village land was broken up into tiny irregular plots. Hindu and Muslim laws of inheritance both encourage this tendency. Efforts are now being made to counteract excessive subdivision, undoubtedly an important factor in lowering the standard of living.

The question of soil deterioration has been the subject of controversy. The official view is that 'most of the area under cultivation in India has been under cultivation for hundreds of years, and reached its maximum stage of impoverishment many years ago'.[4] Undoubtedly India is a very old arable country; the new areas brought under canal irrigation or reclaimed during the last century are a small fraction of the land normally cultivated. Wastage of natural fertility has probably gone on for centuries, for religious prohibitions prevent the use of certain excrements, and make it difficult to manage stock so as to produce farmyard manure.[5] It is, however, probable that the natural yields per acre were higher when the holdings were larger. Cropping would be less continuous, there would be more fallowing, and possibly more 'green manuring'. This would be enough to account for the tradition of greater fertility. There would have been rather higher returns per acre, with considerably fewer mouths to feed.

This is confirmed by some incidental references in early writers. Thus Tavernier, describing his journeys in seventheenth-century India, remarks that 'even in the smallest villages, rice flour, butter, milk, beans, and other vegetables, sugar and other sweetmeats, dry and liquid , can be procured in abundance'.[6] The general impression gained from such sources is of a village life in which the cultivators and craftsmen stood out more definitely than at present from a mass of unsettled and outcaste humanity. There was a larger 'kulak' element, to use a word familiarized since the Russian revolution. Female infanticide and frequent wars, raids, and disturbances helped to prevent any rapid increase in the population. It was a more dangerous, but probably a more interesting life. The *ryot*, with his larger holding, would not be so likely to suffer from that curse of modern village life, under-employment. His son, in those unruly times, might rise to almost any position if he left his village to join the army of some aggressive princelet. A shepherd's son might become a Holkar. A trooper, even in the nineteenth century, could rise to be ruler of Kashmir. The one chance in a milion may not interest the economist, but it would form the subject for endess talk, night after night, under the village pipal tree.

It was not a peaceful or well-ordered rural India through which the English spread from Calcutta, Madras, and Bombay. There were patches of moderately good government, but always under some ruthless and efficient prince, like Ranjit Singh in the Punjab, or Haidar Ali in Mysore. The whole area was covered by a network of semifeudal estates, but the feudal system was in the last stages of decay. The Mogul Emperors had used these territorial magnates, half landlords and half officials, as the easiest channels through which to collect revenue and armies, and had added largely to their numbers. As their rule relaxed, these *Zemindars, Talukdars,* Jagirdars and their like struggled to establish themselves as hereditary rulers, or at least as hereditary landlords. They seem to have been as incapable of organised action as the Polish nobility in the sixteenth century. The most they could inspire was feeling of personal loyalty amongst their tenants, or, in case of the important princes, amongst their feudatories. Nothing but a state of anarchy could explain the ease with which the English overran the country with ludicrously small armies. Only occasionally (as in Rohilkhand, or later, in the Punjab) did the English meet with men imbued with the feeling of local patriotism, and fighting for a country rather than an individual. Many villages, especially in the Deccan, had an ancient system of self-government by *panchayats,* or 'councils of elders'. These enforced caste rules, maintained village wells and 'tanks', and exercised some control over minor offences. Their authority, based solely on religion and tradition, seems to have weakened rather than strengthened the countryman's powers of resistance.

Princes and *Zemindars* proved themselves, as a whole, ineffective as leaders, but rapacious as collectors of revenue, providing nothing for the rent they received. As province after province came under British rule, the first problem was how to deal with all those superior holders whom we may lossely call *Zemindars,* claiming rights over the land apart from the cultivators themselves. Mention has already been made of this difficulty in Bengal. It arose in Madras, the Deccan and the North-West province, as these were absorbed by Lord Wellesley and Lord Hastings.

The two main questions were whether their vague territorial rights were to be acknowledged as equivalent to those of a landlord, and what financial arrangements were to be made with the *Zemindar* about land revenue, or with the *ryot* if the *Zemindar* was not recognized. Both were the subject of prolonged controversy in England as well as in India, and official practice has varied from one decade to another. In Bengal, the north of Madras, and later in Oudh and part of the North-West Province, the rights of superior-holders were admitted, and the revenue was collected from them. This is true *zemindari* system and is so styled. Over most of Madras and the west of India very few superior holders were recognized, assessment were made directly upon the cultivator. This is the ryotwari system.[7] In the *zemindari* areas many revenue farmers of no long standing were elevated into landlords. In *ryotwari* districts of Madras the Polygars, revenue officials 'whose actual condition had become changed to that of military rulers during the revolutions of power in the Deccan', were disregarded by Lord Wellesley.[8]

A change in the official outlook took place about the end of the eighteenth century. Sir John shore and Thomas Law, the Collector of Bihar, were in favour of encouraging 'a class of native gentlemen proprietors, who will gradually establish themselves in good houses, with the various comforts of life'.[9] Cornwallis shared theirview that agriculture needed landlords. To the Whig of that period it seemed right that land should be rack-rented, and that a landed aristocracy should be the leaders of the country. The keener officials of a later date, like Sir Thomas Munro, could see little use in a parasitic land-owning class, and since his time the tendency of the Civil Service has usually been towards a direct assessment on the cultivator or upon the village community. The *ryotwari* system entails harder work on officials, and requires a more intimate knowledge of the country. It fitted in better with the Europeanized and more efficient type of administration which was built up during the nineteenth century.

Other factors turned the balance against the *zemindari* system, except in those areas, like Bengal, where by reason of physical condition direct assessment was very difficult. Each year of ordered government proved more clearly the complicity of the *Zemindars* with the various robber and murder gangs which infested the country, and experience showed that it was almost impossible to give effective legal protection against a rapacious landlord. The joint family system also does not help the development of a landed aristocracy taking a direct personal itnerest in their estates.

Controversy about the *zemindari* and *ryotwari* systems had often been confused by the dispute over permanent and variable assessments. There is no connection, for *zemindari* or *ryotwari* assessments can either be made in perpetuity, or revised after a period of years. But it so happened that the one great permanent settlement was made by Lord Cornwallis in Bengal, the typically *Zemindari* area. It was also extended to a small part of Madras, but in the other provinces, as they came under British rule, the land revenue was left as a revisable charge, and remained so until to-day.[10] In most *ryotwari* areas each district is examined every twenty or thirty years, and the land revenue is reassessed by a 'settlement officer'. The arguments for and against permanent settlement have filled volumes of official and unofficial literature. The subject touches Indian administration at many points—thee need for a more elastic revenue, the financial relations between the provinces and the central Government, the connection between land revenue and the incidence of famine, the respective rights over land of the State, the landlords, and the *ryots*. The controversy broke out afresh after the Mutiny, and during Curzon's term of office. It is likely to be a political issue under the new Constitution, but during the period now under consideration the permanence of the assessment, though of interest to the *Zemindars* was less important than the amount demanded.

The origin of land revenue can be traced to the share of one-sixty of the produce taken by Hindu kings. In practice this was usuallh raised to a fourth. The Muslims claimed the conqueror's right to take the infidel's land though this was remitted on payment of a land tax the idea of the State's rights being limited to a fixed proportion of the produce had virtually disappeared before British administration began. The Moguls had farmed out the revenue, exercising little control over the relations between the revenue farmers and the cultivators. The English when they came to Bengal saw little difference, as we have noticed, between this and their own landlord system. They assumed that the State was supreme landlord, and that for every parcel or ground there must be someone vested with a proprietary interest in the land with whom the Government could settle. Land revenue was considered as a rent rather than a tax, and the eighteenth-century Englishman was obsessed with the idea that no harm could follow from taking the highest rent obtainable. The crude economic theories of the time justified the belief that the money raised in this way represented the difference between the best land and thee worst.

The history of thee pre-Mutiny assessments is a series of unsuccessful efforts to extract an 'economic rent', which was frequently identified with the 'net produce'. The original auctioning of the Bengal revenue farms was a attempt to get as large a share as possible of the 'net produce'. The failure of this system led to the Permanent Settlement. In Madras and Bombay the original assessments were usually based on four-fifths of the estimated 'net produce'. This proved far too high. The first attempt to assess the North-West Provinces failed in the same way, and was abandoned in 1832. A new system had to be introduced whereby 'fair' rent were ascertained by empirical methods. The modern settlement officer has to examine the previous history of the area, the type of soil, the rainfall, communications, and markets. The 'net produce' principle was never applied to the Punjab, or

Oudh, which came later un... doubt that much suffering was ... h rule. There is no and Bombay, by the heavy assess... both in Madras the first quarter of the nineteenth ... imposed during Government were striving to meet w... ary, when the revenue, and their staff was untrained, and ... enses from at Coimbatore) was also corrupt. Even in the Punj... etimes (as ... where the British assessments reduced the former Sikh demands, 'it would seem that cash payments and rigidity of collection largely set off the advantage to the cultivator.'[11]

English theories about land, the orderly collection of revenue in cash and on exact dates, were injurious to the *ryot* in several ways. The Whig idea that the payer of Government dues must have a proprietary interest in the land presented the *ryot* with a very embarrassing gift. Before the establishment of British rule he had no occupancy right, certainly none of which he could dispose. Under the new system, 'when a *ryot* has occupied and paid rent for land for two years, he is considered as its proprietor, and is, in fact saddled with the rent of it as long as he can pay'.[12] When there was plenty of waste land, this right was chiefly a liability, and the peasant in the ryotwari areas often had to pay for land he was not cultivating.[13] Later, as population increased, occupancy right grew more valuable, and became the basis of the money-lender's influence, and of the immense agricultural debt of modern India. The peasant gained a proprietary right which he could sell or mortgage for cash, at a time when the village was being placed on a monetary basis. The British system hastened what was probably an inevitable change, but it meant the ascendancy of the village shop-keeper who developed into a grain dealer and usurer. The ryot found himself in the position of the small peasant in nearly every part of the world. He was forced to dispose of part of his produce to meet a cash demand, and had only one channel through which to sell. He had to think of wealth in terms of money instead of as cattle or grain; money was a medium of which he knew little, which exposed him to the wiles of the shopkeeper demands of the priest, and the and silversmith robber. depredations ange in village life followed the

A subtl British law. The Cornwallis Regulations introductio from Bengal to Madras in 1802, and the were exte minal and civil code followed gradually behind British armies. Much of the physical brutality of the old the régime was eliminated.

'The Tehsildar was tripped of his *kitticole* or hand torture, the stone placed on the head in a burning sun, the stocks, and other of the former insignia of office, by the display and occasional use of which he had been enabled to saddle the ryots with the rents of such land as he deemed proper'.[14]

In theory the poorest Indian could seek redress in the courts. In practice it was some decades before this had much effect. Criminal law has little meaning unless enforced by an effective police force, or by organised public opinion. India had neither. Until 1820 British energies and most of the available personnel were absorbed in the Pindari and Maratha wars. It was only from about 1830 that organised efforts were made to deal with the robber and murder gangs, the dacoits and *thags*.

The evil traditions of eigtheenth-century disorder were to last for many years in the tyranny of the petty official, the criminal associations of many *Zemindars* and independent princes, and in the rough lawlessness of most employees and landlords, whether Indian or English. Thee possibilities of the new civil law only percolated slowly down to the villages, and then would mean little except to the money-lending shopkeepers and the *Zemindars*. The right of distraint on a debtor by order of court, the transferability of land, these were new ideas, and for many years they merely served as a cumbrous and expensive substitute for the '*ketticole* and the stocks. The Whig philosophy, which believed that ultimately no harm would arise from demanding a 'natural' rent, could foresee no hardship in applying the idea of free trade in land and commodities to India. It was some years, after the passing of the new Regulations, before the Government prevented a *Zemindar* in Bengal from distraining on the cooking pots and plough of a defaulting tenant. Complete free trade in land was to last for much longer, justified by the comfortable theory 'that the replacement of an owner who has shown himself to be thriftless and incompetent by one with superior intelligence and greater command of capital cannot be otherwise than beneficial', a theory which dominated English policy throughout the nineteenth century. From time to time it was modified by legislation intended to prevent the exploitation of the *ryot* by the money-lender, the inevitable result of the free disposal of land in a primitive agricultural community; but this quotation, taken from an official memorandum published in 1895, illustrates the persistence of a theory which made the rule of law a very doubtful blessing to the cultivator.

The landless countrymen—shopkeepers, craftsmen, labourers, village servants, and outcastes—still number about two-fifths of the rural population. In earlier days the proportion was higher. The British occupation affected them in different ways. The shopkeepers gained most from the introduction of the cash nexus and the rule of law. They reaped the reward of literacy and a sedentary life. Village servants and labourers, restricted by caste conventions which tie them to certain occupations, have never been much more than village slaves. The British Government has seldom intefered with the caste system, but a rule of law before which men are theoretically equal has done something to improve the status of the lower castes, though they are forbidden the use of village wells and temples. After 1840 the construction of canals, railways and roads absorbed many landless workers, who received cash wages comparing favourably with the returns from a peasant's holdings, but the growing pressure on the land blocked the easiest means of escape for menial castes. They had normally to follow their hereditary calling though their numbers might far exceed the demand for their services. The congestion which can occur in a prolific sub-caste may be brought home to the European reader by considering what would have happened if the smiths had been confined to their hereditary profession. The landless poor may have gained a little self respect, but not much material advantage from British rule.

Craftsmen may be divided into two groups; those making the simple commodities needed in the villages, and the far smaller section who produce luxury articles for the wealthy or for export. Weavers are still a feature of Indian village life, numbering over three millions, and making a full quarter of the cotton goods consumed. For the century before the Mutiny they had almost a monoply of the local market. Indian steam mills were just begining to compete, and imports from abroad were unimportant. Cotton goods of this rough class were exported by the East India Company, though in small quantities. From 1820 the current of trade was reversed. Piece goods from the longer-stapled American cotton were sent from England, but again the total amount was insignificant, and reached only a small part of the peninsula. After 1860 the position changed rapidly. By that time twelve mills had opened in Bombay; while foreign trade and overland communications were developing rapidly. The hand-loom weaver found himself competing with the foreign and indigenous machine made article at the moment when the American Civil War temporarily quadrupled the price of raw cotton. The decay of village weaving began under Crown Government.

The craftsmen engaged in making 'luxury' goods were affected in a different manner. They were concentrated in the larger towns, working in guilds, and each trade bore a close resemblance to the medieval 'mystery', in the manner of its regulation and insistence upon certain standards. Their customers were chiefly the princes and landed aristocracy, but there had been a certain export trade from the very earliest days of European civilisation. The delicate Muslims from Dacca, silk *bananas* from Murshidabad, brocades from Ahmadabad, shwals from Kashmir, brass ornaments from Tanjore, enamelling, damascening, and *bidri* work from the Punjab were all intended primarily for a leisured aristocratic class in India, and being exported to Europe helped to build up the unhappy European tradition of the 'gorgeous East'.[15] The anarchy of the eighteenth century, the partial monopolisation of foreign trade by the East India Company, the social changes in India due to British rule, were bound to influence these crafts, but it would seem that most of them were decaying even before the battle of Plassey.

The export trade suffered first. Information about the extent and character of the old caravan trade through Aleppo is not very reliable, but when the western European countries captured the Eastern trade in the seventeenth century the business consisted in the exchange of bullion, metals, and woollen goods, for spices, cotton and silk goods, indigo, and other tropical products. Bullion formed two-thirds of the exports from Europe, and manufactured articles about a third of the returning imports. The total trade was much affected by frequent wars in Europe, but towards the latter end of the seventeenth century English imports from the East averaged about half a million pounds, and England had become the *entrepot* for much of the European trade. About half the imports and nearly all of the manufactured goods were re-exported.

By 1700 the total imports from India to England amounted to £787,731, and the Dutch imports were rather over £100,000. The end of the seventeenth century marks the highest point in the export of silk and cotton goods. It was an extremely profitable business for the Company, and in 1672.

> 'several artificers such as throwsters, weavers, and dyers were sent over by the Company with great quantities of English patterns, to teach Indian weavers new methods of manufacturing goods suitable to English and European markets'.[16]

The export of manufactured goods began to decline during the first half of the eighteenth century. The fifty years which preceded Plassey were marked by a growing movement in all European countries against Indian imports. The most powerful argument, especially applicable in war-time was the 'mercantilist' objection to exporting bullion, but there was also a strong feeling, much exploited by the enemies of the Company in England, that good money was being sent out of the country in exchange for mere luxuries.[17] There were other factors, of which the most important was the growth of silk and cotton manufactures in Europe, but opposition to Eastern imports was based on the need for sumptuary laws as much as on the idea of 'protection'. From the beginning of the seventeenth century there was a struggle between the Company and the Government, which culminated in the total prohibition of Indian silks and painted calicoes in 1720. After about 1710 the greater part of the Company's Eastern trade which continued for may years after the English had become territorial rulers, but steadily declined as other countries developed their manufactures.

The ruin of this *entrepot* trade occurred rapidly towards the end of the eighteenth century, and during the early nineteenth century. Certain historians have given the impression that after the occupation of Bengal the export of manufactured goods from India was deliberately discouraged. This idea seems to be due to mistaken chronology. The British Government continued, but did not intensify, its old policy of protection and prohibition. The English consumption of cotton goods had never been an important factor. The cold climate and small population of eighteenth-century England prevented its being a good market. The Company did its best to encourage the lucrative re-export trade. There are even signs that it wished to hamper the English production of cotton goods, which had begun to compete in the foreign market. In 1786 orders were given that 'for prudential reason....no more cotton yarn was to be sent from Indian to England either as part of the Investment or in private trade'.[18] These efforts had little effect. The French revolutionary wars, which completely dislocated the European markets, were followed by a period of economic nationalism, of high tariffs and low purchasing power. The Company strove to combat these tendencies in England but was powerless abroad. Markets were lost in the New as well as the Old World, and the opening of the Eastern trade to private merchants in 1815 made no difference. Exports to America fell from 13,633 bales in 1801 to 258 in 1829, those to Denmark from 1457 to 150 in the same period. Indian exports to England were gradually reduced to certain tropical products, to spices, drugs, dyes, and fibres, the most important being tea and coffee, indigo and lac, cotton and silk. A similar tendency is to be found in the trade of the Danish Company throughout the period.

The movement of bullion eastwards decreased rapidly for a quarter of century after Plassey, though it began again towards the end of the century,[19] but it is difficult to estimate the effect upon the craftsmen. We have no real knowledge about the distribution of the bullion which came to India in the early eighteenth century, and very little about the condition of the weavers who worked for the export trade at that time. The Company in its earlier days merely bought through the usual agents, and when they substituted their own *gomastas* it would seem that this was more to get the type of article required than to drive a still harder bargain with the weaver. The Company's servants were not good master, but they only followed the existing custom when they got the weavers into their debt by means of advances, and then kept them working. They followed what had become the practice in India during its disorders, and were probably neither better nor worse than other Indian employers, though there was certainly some desertion of weavers from their factories. Verelst, in 1767 talks of weavers 'deserting their profession to seek for subsistence from a less precarious calling', but this was mentioned as a result of the decreasing demand for export which had already begun to operate.[20] There is no satisfactory evidence as to whether the English either lowered or raised the standard of treatment of the weavers by those who employed them or bought from them. It was not a subject which much interested their contemporaries. The Company did its utmost to keep alive a decaying industry, but it probably paid as little as it could for its commodities, and the type of covenanted servant in the eighteenth century was not likely to enquire too closely into the actions of his agents.[21]

Exports never absorbed more than a small fraction of the luxury trades. Changes in fashion and the anarchy of eighteenth-century Indian were far more potent factors in the decay of craftsmanship than the loss of the European and American markets. Industries which cater for the wealthy and for the courtier must be the first to suffer during such troubled times as followed the accession of Aurangzeb, and continued until the establishment of British rule. The specialised craftsmen of those times were dependent on a very limited market usually the patronage of a court, or the pilgrim traffic. The lack of roads and bridges, the prevalence of dacoity, and the multitude of internal customs discouraged the movement of goods, most of which were hardly known outside a small area. During the eighteenth century, when one State after another suffered a temporary eclipse or fell into the hands of some adventurer, the withdrawal of all patronage would damage many crafts irretrievably; and the process continued when courts such as that of the Nawabs of Oudh at Lucknow finally disappeared. Apart from these violent dislocations of industry there was a steady decrease in the demand for this very elaborate Oriental work, much of which was only suitable for a feudal method of living. The new types of wealthy Indian, the businessmen, the Europeanised officials, the successful money-lenders, were not good patrons, and even in those Indian States which have been least touched by European influence the ancient crafts have long been in a moribund condition. The British occupation hastened, but not very markedly, a process which had already taken place in Europe.

REFERENCES

1. The figure of 206, 162, 360 was much higher than was expected. See App. D.
2. In political criticism of military expenditure it is often forgotten that before the Mutiny the regular Indian army gave employment to a very small part of the population. The present proportion of about one in 200 is far less than in most parts of Europe. The extension of the Indian Empire led to the disbandment of large bodies of irregular soldiery.
3. H. H. Mann, *Land and Labour in a Deccan village*, 45.
4. Evidence of Agricultural Adviser to Government of India, *Report of Royal Commission on Agriculture in India*, 76.
5. The use of cow-dung for fuel in common throughout India. It is often claimed that this unfortunate habit has arisen form the difficulty of obtaining firewood owing to forest restrictions. This may be partly true, but the custom seems to date from long before the Forest Acts, and is prevalent where firewoods is plentiful.
6. *Travels in India* (Oxford University Press), 1925, i. 238.
7. The correct spelling is *raiyatwari*, but the words *ryot* and *ryotwari* have become familiar.
8. Fifth Report, 1812, p. 143.
9. Mr. Law to the President and Members of the Revenue Board, October 4, 1778. Quoted by Kaye, *Administration of East India Company*, 178.
10. In 1927-8, 52 per cent of the assessed area was held by *ryotwari* proprietors, and 18 per cent, by permanently, 30 per cent, by temporarily settled *Zemindars*. India, 1929-31, 128.
11. H. Calvert, *Wealth and Welfare* of the Punjab, 122.
12. Revenue letter from Court of Directors to the Government of Madras, January 22, 1822.
13. Buchanan, *Journey from Madras* (London, 1807) ii. 309. Dr. Buchanan was deputed by Wellesley to tour South India in 1800. He is very critical about the stringency of the early assessments.
14. *Report of Madras Board of Revenue*, quoted by Kaye, *Administration of East India Company*, 225.
15. Indian muslims found their way to ancient Greece, under the name of *gangetika*.

16. Bal Krishna, *Commercial Relations between India and England, 1601-1757*, op. 140. The reader is referred to this valuable monograph for further information.
17. This was a very old complaint against Eastern trade. Gibbon, writing of the later Roman empire, says, 'The objects of oriental traffic were splendid and trifling....As the natives of Arabia and India were contented with the productions and manufactures of their own country, silver, on the side of the Romans, was the principal, if not the only instrument of commerce. It was a complaint worthy of the gravity of the Senate, that in the purchase of female ornaments, the wealth of the state was irrecoverably given away to foreign and hostile nations'.—The *Decline and Fall of the Roman Empire*, chap. ii. He refers to a speech by Tiberius given in Tacitus, *Annals*.
18. Bengal public letter from Court of Directors, April 12, 1786. Further quotations from this important letter are given in Aspinall, *Cornwallis in Bengal*, 181.
19. Between 1758 and 1783 bullion from England amounted to just under £400,000, but from 1784 to 1807 over £8,000,000 was exported in bullion. India, of course, did not 'begin to pay for imports in food grains', as stated by R. C. Dutt in his *Economic History of British India*, 296. Except for small quantities of rice and sugar, no food was exported from India to Europe until the opening of the Suez Canal. This combined with the extension of irrigation in the Punjab, led to the development of the wheat trade from 1870 onwards. Previous exports of wheat had been less than 800 tons yearly. The journey round the Cape made it impracticable to send bulky and perishable articles.
20. Letter to Directors, March 17, 1767.
21. It is unfortunate that a story about the cutting off of weaver's thumbs has been used to typify the Company's treatment of those engaged in the silk trade. The matter is discussed in a recent work, Economic Annals of Bengal, by J. C. Sinha, where it is shown that the story takes two forms, neither of which can be justified by any evidence. The idea was probably originally based on a quotation from a contemporary book, *considerations on Indian Affairs*, by W. Bolts, who was dismissed from the Company's service and returned to England to carry on a campaign against its monopoly.

3

Nature and Origin of the Mutiny

An extensive literature has grown up round the Mutiny. Every incident has been described at length, the most minute engagements and the conduct of comparatively obscure individuals have been the subject of long controversies. The fierce light thrown upon each detail has put the whole struggle out of focus. Further distortion followed because most accounts have been written from the English standpoint after racial antagonisms had been aroused by accusations of atrocities and of treachery. The conventional view of the Mutiny was developed during an era when European ascendency and the superiority of Western civilisation were not seriously challenged, when many features of the Company's rule had been forgotten, and when few Englishmen had any experience of war. The present generation should be able to see the events of 1857 and 1858 in better perspective.

They were more important in their indirect results than in themselves. There was much hard fighting, including many exciting and some appalling incidents, but on a very small scale. It was a domestic affair. No seaport was seriously threatened, and no foreign Power intervened.[1] Afghanistan, under Dost Muhammad, was strictly neutral. Nepal allowed her Gurkhas to be freely recruited, and a Nepalese force, under the Minister Jang

Bahadur, joined Sir Colin Campbell before Lucknow. The frontier tribesmen remained comparatively quiet, watching the outcome of the struggle. Less than a third of the peninsula was seriously disturbed, though there was general excitement, due partly to the widespread belief that 1857—the centenary of Plassey—would mark a change in Indian history.

The Mutiny may be considered either as a military revolt, or as a bid for recovery of their property and privileges by dispossessed princes and landlords, or as an attempt to restore the Mogul Empire or as a peasants' war. From every aspect it was localised, restricted, and unorganised. Only one of the three provincial armies rebelled, and it is doubtful if a quarter of the sepoys were ever in arms against the Government. Estimates of rebel forces at Delhi and elsewhere suggest that, as each regiment mutinied, many sepoys drifted back to their villages. No important prince threw in his lot with rebels, and many, like Patiala, actively helped the Government. Of the thousands of landlords who had lost their property through the Inam Commission, or through changes in Oudh and the North-West Provinces, only the *Talukdars* of Oudh made any concerted attempt to help the mutineers, and they did not decide for some months. Of the fifty million Muslims in India only three men out of every ten thousand can have rallied to their restored Emperor. In a few areas, which had suffered from very high assessment, the villagers helped the mutineers, but nowhere was there anything approaching a *jacquerie*. The ordinary administration continued to function everywhere south of the Narmada, and in most of Bengal and the Punjab. Troops, Indian as well as British were sent from Madras and Bombay to join in the work of repression. In the recently annexed Punjab the Bengal army regiments mutinied or were disarmed, and the Cis-Satlej districts were affected; but a mobile column under Nicholson was spared to help in the siege of Delhi, and many Sikhs and Muslims were enlisted. Even in the North-West Provinces, where the severest fighting took place, only an insignificant section of the population took any active part.[2]

The Mutiny resembled some medieval civil war, or the early campaigns in Bengal. Minute armies operated amongst a population which was probably sympathetic with one side, but was disarmed and chiefly anxious to be left in peace. When the Meerut garrison mutinied and marched to Delhi there were scarcely 40,000 effective British troops in India[3]. When Havelock marched to the relief of Lucknow, through a country treated as hostile, he had under two thousand men, an army smaller than Clive had taken to Plassey.[4] Within four months a portion of the 40,000 British troops, with the help of some Madras regiments, a small force of Gurkhas, and the hastily raised Sikh and Muslim levies, had broken the back of the rebellion. Delhi was recaptured, Lucknow relieved, and all serious hopes of a successful revolution had been abandoned. Reinforcements from Europe arrived, and joined in hunting down those in arms against the Government, but they were not sufficient to alter the scale of the fighting.

It is not immediately obvious why the Mutiny should have had such a powerful influence upon later generations of Indians and English. Both races had seen fierce and even desperate fighting during the preceding half-century. Sixteen years earlier the Indian army had suffered an overwhelming disaster in Afghanistan. Subsequently the Government had been engaged upon the conquest of Sind, the two Sikh wars, and the second Burmese war. Nor were mutinies unknown in the company's army. As early as 1766 a regiment of the newly raised Bengal army rebelled, and twenty-four ringleaders were blown from guns. The outbreak at Vellore, in 1806, was more serious, and had certain analogies with 1857. There were the same rumours of India being forcibly converted to Christianity. Leather cockades[5] took the place of greased cartridges, and the intrigues of Tipu's children formed a parallel to those of the Nana Sahib and the King of Oudh. Three years later came the famous White Mutiny, one of numerous occasions when the Company's European troops set an example of organised insubordination. During the next fifty years there was periodic disaffection in the Indian army, chiefly due to disputes about pay and prospects, and about liability to serve either abroad or in those outlying parts of the country which were then being brought under the Company's rule. The first Burmese war led to the mutiny amongst high-caste sepoys at Barrackpur, who feared they would be sent overseas. After massacre by gunfire, the regiment was disbanded.

This severity discouraged such manifestations for some years, but the Afghan war was followed by a marked deterioration in discipline. Four Bengal regiments refused to march to Sind, and in 1844 two regiments mutinied on the Sikh frontier. Similar trouble, mostly about *batta* or allowances, occurred in the Madras army. After the second Sikh war Napier believed that twenty-four regiments were on the point of rising. In 1849 four regiments refused to draw their pay, and one regiment was sent to Multan in a state bordering on mutiny. In 1950 the 66th Infantry rebelled, but were crushed by some Indian cavalry, and the regiment was disbanded. The general feeling of insecurity was not lessened by the open dispute between the Commandeer-in-Chief and Lord Dalhousie, which ended in Napier's resignation and his alarmist statements about the condition of the army. Subsequently, in 1852, the 38th Regiment refused to march when ordered to Burma. These facts were possibly ignored in England. It was a point of honour amongst British officers of the sepoy regiments to resent vehemently any aspersions on the discipline of their troops, but the deep impression made by the Mutiny can hardly be ascribed to the unprecedented disloyalty of the native army.[6]

Two factors differentiated the Mutiny from the host of 'little wars' which the English fought in Asia and Africa during the nineteenth century. In most of these the final issue was never seriously in doubt, but for four months during the summer of 1857 it seemed that the Mutiny might develop into a real war of independence, which would make reconquest impossible.[7] By September it was clear that the Indians who were in revolt were incapable of working to any settled plan or of subordinating themselves to a national leader. Their prestige was waning, and their commanders had proved themselves incompetent except in guerilla warfare. The course of the revolt had, however, shown the weakness of the English hold on India. This aspect of the Mutiny was never forgotten, and its memory was to influence every branch of the administration. Even more important was the nature of the fighting. Colonial wars against disorganised levies and uncivilised governments are invariably conducted with considerable savagery and degenerate into something like the suppression of a servile revolt. Non-combatants, including women and children, are illtreated and occasionally murdered, their houses and villages are burnt. Prisoners are executed, and sometimes mutilated; or are tortured either by prolonging the agony of their death or by some act the religious significance of which might endanger their future immortality.[8]

Such disregard of the elementary rules of civilised warfare characterised nearly every campaign fought by European powers outside Europe. The English public knew little about these happenings. They had forgotten that wars, unless fought by highly disciplined troops obeying strict conventions, involve looting and house burning, much indiscriminate slaughtering, sieges which cause intense suffering to women and children, occasional rape and other bestialities. Information could only come from officers who might feel sufficiently strongly to risk their professional career, or from the few newspaper correspondents who might be present and were prepared to take the unpopular line of criticising their countrymen's conduct of a war.[9] The Indian revolt occurred in a settled country: English as well as Indian women and children were implicated; and the course of the Mutiny was closely followed by millions of educated Indians. From the first it was fought with peculiar savagery. The rebellious sepoys knew they would get no quarter if captured. Those in arms against the Government soon learnt that it was not only death they had to fear. The British troops were 'sewing Mohammadans in pig-skins, smearing them with port-fat before execution, and burning their bodies, and forcing Hindus to defile themselves'.[10] The mutineers rapidly lost their military discipline, and collected round them a rabble of Pathans, as well as the worst elements from the slums of Delhi, Cawnpore, and Lucknow, and from the criminal tribes. On the British side the Company's own British troops included some of the toughest and most hard-bitten soldiers in the world. The suggestion has been made in recent histories that the conduct of the fighting under-went a complete change after the massacre of Cawnpore. This event caused a great stir in England, and added to the ferocity with which the revolt was suppressed; but the lines along which mutineers and unfriendly non-combatants were to be treated had been decided within three weeks after the outbreak, and the war was from the first fought without any regard for the ordinary rulers of civilised warfare. It will be necessary to revert to this subject in the next chapter.

Apart from the feelings aroused by the nature of the fighting, the year 1857 is rightly considered as a turning-point in Indian history. By revealing the instability of the Company's rule, the Mutiny completely altered the system of government and the outlook of the administration. It is important therefore to consider not only the conditions which now appear to have engendered the revolt, but also the contemporary views of its origin. The end of Lord Dalhousie's administration had been marked by a vague but general feeling of unrest. Nearly every class had been affected by recent innovations, by social and administrative changes, by the expensive thoroughness of the Government, and by the impact of Western ideas. The princes and the landed classes had the strongest reasons for fearing this reformist spirit. The Englishman in India is often impelled by his conscience as a good administrator to advocate measures which would seem extremely socialistic to his compatriots in England. Few members of the Civil Service viewed with equanimity the congeries of feudal States which had been allowed to survive under inefficient and sometimes degenerate chiefs. Equally, obnoxious to the revenue officers were the landed estates within British territory, held on uncertain tenure by descendants of the Mogul revenue collectors. These men, though virtually landlords had little of the public spirit which might justify their kind in Europe. On such points Lord Dalhousie, the Liberal, was at one with John Lawrence. They had no wish to extend the frontiers of India, but they wanted within the peninsula a free peasantry directly under a unitary government standardized and homogeneous except for a few large States, which would remain nominally independent, but under some kind of tutelage.

With this ideal in view Dalhousie took every opportunity of mediatizing the smaller subordinate States and expropriating landlords with doubtful titles. For the first he used his legal prerogative of not recognising the right of adoption, and annexed Satara, Jhansi, Nagpur and other minor States, as already described. His second object he achieved by appointing the Inam Commission, which had the unpopular duty of investigating titles of landowners and confiscated some twenty thousand estates in the Decca. Theoretically the general policy was justifiable. Small States are an anchronism. India has suffered (and may suffer more) from the reversal of policy after the Mutiny which has perpetuated hundreds of tiny principalities. Indian agriculture cannot really support the parasitic millions, landlords and princelets, who have survived under post-Mutiny conditions. Dalhousie's action was, however, too drastic. The Government had certain disabilities for carrying out such reforms. It was foreign and expensive, and had been at no pains to enlist public support. Few Indians would feel that a measure of confiscation, though it brought revenue to the State, was necessarily a contribution to the common weal. The tradition of the 'tribute was to survive for many more decades. Innate conservatism and ancient loyalties, which delay agrarian reforms in Europe, were reinforced in India by racial feelings. The vast scale of these operations, the linguistic and legal complications, and the general illiteracy, led inevitably to individual cases of gross in justice which the Government did little to rectify. No attempt was made to mollify the feelings aroused. Much of the bitterness caused by the final and greatest annexation, that of Oudh, could have been avoided by adopting the advice of Sleeman and Henry Lawrence, who proposed that the land revenue should be devoted to local administration, and the balance given to support the royal family.

The effect of these dynastic and territorial expropriations was to leave, scattered over the country, a large number of princes and landowners who felt themselves deeply aggrieved, and whose followers and retainers saw themselves threatened by ruin. Some of the dispossessed were conspiring against the Government before the Mutiny, and supplied the only effective leadership after its outbreak. Chief amongst them were the ex-King of Oudh's very capable adviser, Ahmad Ullah, the Moulvi of Faizabad'; Dandu Pant, adopted son of the former Peshwa, who claimed unsuccessfully to allowed his father's pension, and became notorious as the Nana Sahib; Nana Sahib's nephew, Rao Sahib, and his retainers, Tantia Topi and Azimulla Khan; the Rani of Jhansi; the octogenarian Rajput, Kunwar Singh, whose estates had been lost owing to the unjustified severity of the Board of Revenue; Firoz Shah, a kinsman and dependent of the Moghul 'Emperor' Bahadur Shah. This list of the dispossessed and their followers contains the name of nearly every capable rebel leader, except Khan Bahadur Khan, who was a pensioner.

A larger section of the population had less specific grievances against the British. The higher castes saw a new civilization being introduced which lowered their standing and threatened their so dality. The Government was universally suspected of wishing to convert India to Christianity, the first step being the destruction of caste and of the traditional Hindu family life. Amongst the sedentary classes secular education, extended by then to both sexes, was undermining the influence of the family priest. Inventions, such as the railway and the telegraph, suggested to the lower castes that the foreigners possessed occult knowledge hidden from the Brahmin. Their old and holy land was being disturbed, and even the sacred Ganges was tapped for irrigation purposes. In the new factories and in railway carriages the castes were working and sitting cheek by jowl. The introduction of an efficient but common messing system into the goals was considered another attack on caste. The unwarranted optimism of certain missionaries lent some colour to this belief, which was sedulously fostered by active opponents of the Government. The abolition of suttee, though it had been in force for over twenty years, had never been accepted by the orthodox, and further legislation aroused their indignation. The Religious Disabilities Act of 1850 protected the civil rights of converts from Hinduism. The Hindu Widows' Remarriage Act of 1856 removed legal obstacles to these unhallowed unions. The Acts caused greater anger and alarm because they entrenched upon the customary Hindu law of inheritance, suggesting that the Government was prepared to destroy the civil law of the Hindu as it had previously disregarded their conceptions of criminal justice.[11]

Most contemporary histories, letters, and diaries dilate upon the racial bitterness displayed by the Muslims, who were usually assumed to be the real instigators of the Mutiny. It is difficult to explain the view, held almost universally amongst the British, that the 'mild Hindu' was suffering from some temporary aberration, but that the Muslim was our implacable foe. Undoubtedly the upper class Mohammedans had their grievances against a Government which had superseded the Mogul Empire, and then introduced educational standards favourable to the Hindu. Muslim domination in previous centuries had been based on a small number of Central Asian immigrants, backed by many million converts, drawn from the lower castes. Neither section found life too easy under the new regime. The Muslim *ryots* were the chief sufferers from the supremacy which English law gave to the Hindu moneylender. The disabilities of educated Muslims were enhanced by the religious ordinance which made their children spend some years in learning the Koran. It does not, however, seem that Muslims took a leading part in the Mutiny.

Possibly too much importance was attached to the machinations of the Wahabi sect, whose wandering Moulvis were active before as well as after the Mutiny. There is no evidence to suggest that the restoration of Bahadur Shah was part of an organised Muslim plot. Sepoys, Hindu as well as Muslim, seem to have regarded him as the rightful Emperor, though it is doubtful whether many seriously believed that the Company's 'treason' justified rebellion, though this was afterwards asserted.[12] From the first the mutineers treated Bahadur Shah with contempt. Firoz Shah, the most enterprising member of his household, was in Persia when the Mutiny began, and returned to lead only some of the revolted soldiery from Indore and Gwalior. Khan Bahadur Khan, a Government pensioner, set himself up as Viceroy at Bareilly, and established Muhammadan rule in Rohilkhand. Apart from these two, few Mohammedans of any standing were openly against the Government. Haidarabad, the leading Muslim State, was the scene of much intrigue, but under the guidance of the Nizam's Minister, Salar Jang, neither its inhabitants nor its troops took any part in the Mutiny. The bulk of the mutineers were Hindu.

India has always contained important groups with grievances against the Government, and too much weight can be attached to these vague causes for discontent, many of which could be paralleled at any period of the British occupation. Without a lead from the soldiers it is unlikely that any dissident group would have organised an armed revolt, though probably the grievances of the *Talukdars* and of the disbanded State soldiers in Oudh were sufficiently acute to have led to a local and easily suppressed rising.[13] Even when the mutineers won their first successes, and there were hardly any British troops between Calcutta and Delhi, the *Talukdars* held their hand for some months. On the other hand, discipline was deteriorating so rapidly in the Bengal army that, apart from the greased cartridges, almost any incident might have caused an outbreak.

The Bengal army was not recruited in Bengal, but in the North-West provinces, and in certain States. Oudh alone contributed 40,000 men. Many of the sepoys belonged to 'twice-born' castes, and were allowed a deference neither conducive to discipline nor compatible with military efficiency. In this, and also in retaining the rule of promotion by seniority, Bengal was more conservative than Bombay or Madras. The army was a survival of the sepoy force raised experimentally to overawe the Company's first neighbours, and its organization had never been brought up to date. It was totally unsuited for defending the new and turbulent North-West Frontier-for garrisoning distant and insalubrious parts of India like Sind, or for service in Burma and overseas. These limitations were recognised by the Government, but instead of reforming the old army they relied upon building up a new army drawn from Sikhs, Punjab Muslims, Gurkhas, and races not formerly available. The one departure from this policy was in 1856, when Lord Canning, finding it almost impossible to get regiments to serve in Burma, made a fundamental change. He insisted upon a General Service Enlistment Act, under which all future recruits had to undertake to march wherever ordered. The Bengal sepoys saw their privileged position being undermined, and they had other grievances arising out of the Government's new economy and efficiency. In valid pensions were no longer paid to those unfit for foreign service, and postal privileges were curtailed. The annexation of Oudh was doubly unpopular. Many sympathised with the ruling house, and sepoys from an Indian State had certain privileges not enjoyed by those from British India.[14] Those who came from the North-West Provinces were affected by the recent agrarian disputes, and by Thomason's heavy land assessments.[14]

As members of 'twice-born' castes the sepoys fully shared the general suspicion of European innovations and the supposed Christianizing enthusiasm of the Government. As professional soldiers they could not but be alarmed by certain developments in the Punjab and elsewhere. Formed at a time when the Company was only one of many 'war lords', the Bengal army had become a kind of military sub-caste, with exaggerated ideas of their own importance and of British dependence upon their aid. They strongly objected to being merely part of an imperial army, drawn from all the races of the peninsula, with no potential enemies except beyond the frontier. The temptation to mutiny before this new army came into being was intensified by the small number of British troops in Eastern India, and by ludicrously distorted ideas about the strength of England.[15] Throughout the vast area normally garrisoned by the Bengal army was hardly one British soldier to twentyfive sepoys. The remainder had been withdrawn for the Crimean was, or for service in the Punjab. No British regiment was stationed in Oudh, in spite of its disturbed condition, nor at Delhi, though the old Emperor still personfied the Mogul tradition and his palace, with its 5000 retainers, overlooked the magazine. This great ammunition 'dump' of Northern India was in the charge of two officers and six British sergeants. Between Calcutta and Allahabad the only British regiment was at Dinapur. The dissidents could point to this weakness, and play upon the sepoy's ignorance by suggesting that England could not spare any troops for reinforcements but was dependent upon the new Indian army, to which many of their keenest officers had been drafted.

At the end of 1856 the Bengal army was sullen insubordinate, and on the verge rebellion. 'A consciousness of power', wrote the Commissioner of Meerut, 'had grown up in the army which could only be exorcised by mutiny, and the cry of the cartridge brought the latent spirit of revolt into action'.[16] When the Government introduced the new Enfield rifle, its use which entailed biting a greased cartridge, provided exactly the type of grievance best calculated to being discontent to a head. The sepoys believed with some justification that the grease was made from cow or pig fat, and without any justification that this was a deliberate attempt to break the caste of the Hindus and affront the religion of the Muslims.[17] In spite of this incitement and the shadowy activities of emissaries of the King of Oudh and the Nana Sahib, the army only drifted slowly from insubordination to armed rebellion. The cartridges had been issued to several regiments before their use led to disturbances and incendiarism at Barrackpur. The agents of the King of Oudh, then living at Calcutta, probably helped to foment this trouble in the 34th, Infantry but the first refusal to obey orders occurred in the 19th Infantry at Berhampur on February 26, 1857. There were no British troops there, but the regiment marched quietly down to Barrackpur and was disbanded under the eyes of a British regiment, hastily brought from Rangoon. The 34th was also disbanded, but not till May 6, thought their offences had been far more serious. Lord Canning misled by the pathetic confidence which the British officers placed in their sepoys, treated this double outbreak as an isolated case, and allowed five weeks to pass before enforcing the order upon a regiment which had then got completely out of hand, the guard even refusing to help when their adjutant was shot and other officers were threatened by a sepoy—the Mangal Pandi, whose exploit gave the mutineers the nickname of 'a pandies'. The delay and mildness of the punishment may have encouraged to growing insubordination amongst the sepoys; but the first act, which converted spasmodic mutiny into armed rebellion, occurred at Meerut after a refusal to use the cartridges had been followed by a court-martial, and by the severe sentences of ten year's imprisonment upon eighty-five troopers of the of the 3rd Cavalry.

THE MUTINY

On Sunday evening, May 10, the day following the degradation and imprisonment of the Meerut troopers, the three Indian regiments at that station shot their officers, broke open the gaol, and after releasing their companions set out with their arms along the road to Delhi, some thirty miles away. The moment was propitious, and no serious attempt was made by the British troops to curt off their retreat.[18] The general confusion was increased by a crowd from the Meerut bazaar, which came, plundering and burning, into the cantonment. The next morning the first mutineers had reached Delhi. Some went to the palace and proclaimed Bahadur Shah Emperor. Others approached the three Indian regiments, which mutinied, murdered their officers, and joined in killing any Europeans they could find. An attack was made on the magazine, but the Englishmen in charge, finding themselves overwhelmed, blew up what they could. It was a courageous deed, which incidentally caused heavy loss to their enemy; but a considerable amount of ammunition remained undestroyed. Within twenty-four hours of the outbreak, Delhi was held by over five thousand armed soldiers. They had as their nominal leader the aged Bahadur Shah, whose name still conjured up to millions the past glories of the Mogul Empire.

The opening of the rebellion was remarkably successful, but it was soon apparent that no one opposed to the Government was capable of pressing home the advantage, though the British position in Northern India was sufficiently precarious. The hot weather had set in. Anson, the Commander-in-Chief, and his staff were at Simla. The available British troops were insignificant in number, and not mobilised. Neither transport nor supplies were ready. British forces in 1857 were little more mobile than a hundred years before. Communications were still rudimentary. Roads were few and bad, and not more than two or three hundred miles of railway had been laid. The Calcutta line ran 120 miles to Raniganj, the Bombay line only as far as Thana. The one recent improvement had been the linking up of the chief cities and garrison towns by telegraph lines. For some reason these wires—which sepoys afterwards allowed were 'the strings that hanged us'—were never systematically cut. If any able and energetic Indian had enjoyed the confidence of the sepoys he could have established a rebel government over most of British India between the Narmada and the Satlej; and destroyed or masked the few British troops in that area. This would have emboldened and attracted the dissident and wavering elements amongst the States and the neighbouring provinces. Three weeks elapsed, and then came a fresh crop of military revolts and civil disorder in every garrison town throughout the North-West Provinces, Oudh, and Central India. But there were still no signs of leadership or well-ordered plans. Over a large area the machinery of government was destroyed, but nothing set up in its place. The first instinct of the sepoys was to take the road to Delhi. Usually, but not always, they killed their own British officers, but they did not attack British regiments. In three or four cases a leader had sufficient force of character to win over the mutineers, and use them locally. The Nana Sahib called back the Cawnpore mutineers to surround Wheeler's little force of four hundred Englishmen, and at Lucknow the rebellious troops remained to fight and finally blockade Sir Henry Lawrence with a thousand British soldiers ad seven hundred 'loyal' sepoys. The Rani of Jhansi, widow of the Raja whose State had been annexed persuaded the mutinied garrison to accept her as leader and defend her capital. Khan Bahadur Khan at Bareilly set himself up as Viceroy. At a later date Kunwar Singh collected the Dinapur mutineers to carry on a guerilla warfare in Bihar. Over the rest of the area in revolt the sepoy either drifted towards Delhi or formed themselves into marauding bands.

The first weeks gave evidence of fatal weaknesses amongst those in arms against the Government. Regional and religious disunity showed itself in the absence of any co-ordination amongst the leaders. Even at Delhi, neither of the rival commanders, Mirza and Bakht Khan, were able to control the troops, which by the middle of June numbered some thirty thousand.[19] Even where a local leader asserted himself, religious differences caused trouble. Khan Bahadur Khan was soon involved in disputes with the Hindu landowners of Rohilkhand. The sepoys, freed from discipline, were joined by Gujars and other criminal elements. The general disorder did the rebel cause great harm by frightening the princes and the propertied classes. Another factor was the consciousness of inferiority which affected sepoys when opposing European troops. It did not prevent them fighting bravely, but showed itself in a lack of enterprise in attack. The advantage gained by the capture of Delhi was rendered nugatory by the delay which allowed two small British forces to combine and occupy the Ridge, overlooking the city. Anson had died on May 27; but his successor, Sir Henry Barnard, marched down from Karnal and was joined by Archdale Wilson from Meerut. The combined forces amounted to less than five thousand, but after a successful action at Badli Seria on June 8 they were able to establish themselves within gunshot of Delhi. The moral effect was incalculable. The rebel capital was nominally under siege, though there must have been more than six times as many men under arms in the city as on the Ridge. The presence of this small British force prevented any serious attempt to establish a rebel government, and it was soon apparent that the revolt, even if successful, would only lead to anarchy and the rule of 'war lords' of the type familiar in eighteenth century India or modern China. The withdrawal of British authority from any area. Such as the Doab, was followed immediately by the revival of old feuds, by outbursts of religious fanaticism, by the unrestrained activities of the criminal tribes.

The failure to establish a reputable authority on the rebel side was one powerful factor which prevented the spread of the rebellion. Another was the personal character of the Bengal sepoys. Their arrogance had made them cordially disliked in every part of India to which they had been sent. Troops which mutinied in the Punjab, or even in Southern Bengal, were attacked by the surrounding villagers. The peasant rising was confined to those parts from which the Bengal army was recruited, and there was no difficulty in enlisting men to fight again the mutineers from the areas in which they had been stationed. The most important as well as the most striking instance was the attitude adopted by the Sikh community. It was only eight years since the defeat of the *Khalsa* army and the annexation of the Punjab. Everything depended on this new province. Lord Canning could do little from Calcutta, except arrange for reinforcements from England, and indicate, not very effectually, the lines on which the campaign was to be fought and the general policy to be adopted south of the Narmada. If British rule in the Punjab had collapsed, as it had done in the North-West provinces, nothing could have prevented the troops on the Ridge from being isolated, and probably the whole of Northern India would have been submerged. The prospects of the Punjab going against the British seemed considerable. The new administration had been vigorous and efficient, but hardly popular. The attitude of the frontier tribes was uncertain. The garrison contained only ten thousand

European troops (most of whom were in the Peshawar valley), about thirteen thousand Punjab Irregulars, and thirty-six thousand sepoys of the Bengal army. The Sikhs might well have seen in the rebellion an opportunity of regaining their hegemony, or might, like the Pathans, have waited for the outcome of the struggle. So uncertain was the position that John Lawrence, the Chief Commissioner, was prepared to withdraw his troops from the Peshawar valley, and cede that area to the Amir, but the proposal was vetoed by Lord Canning. The fact that the initiative in the rebellion came from the Bengal army seems to have been decisive. Sikhs and Punjab Muslims joined the Government's hastily formed levies. The population generally supported the authorities in disarming and guarding the Bengal troops at Lahore, Peshawar, and Multan, and in pursuing those regiments, at Mardan, Jallandhar, and elsewhere, which succeeded in mutinying and absconding. The state of the province soon made it possible to send reinforcements to Delhi. Nicholson, in charge of a movable column, completed the disarming of Bengal troops at Jhelum and marched to the Ridge at the end of July.

The Government at Calcutta had the double task of keeping open the road to the north, and of relieving Cawnpore and Lucknow. The efforts which it made were on so small a scale as to be almost absurd, but however much it may be blamed for the peace-time distribution of forces, there is hardly sufficient evidence to criticise later policy. The affair was without precedent, and information, especially about the army, came through unreliable channels. Lord Canning's advisers succumbed at first to the official's temptation to minimize unpleasant facts. He himself was over-optimistic in refusing offers of volunteers from Calcutta, which might have enabled him to release British regiment, but he was deceived by the three weeks' lull which followed the Meerut outbreak and was naturally loath to assume that sepoys at Benares, Dinapur, and Allahabad would follow suit.[20] The second wave that swept through the Bengal army made him unwilling to move the few troops at his disposal without some definite objective, before he knew at what points the rebels were concentrating and how far the rebellion might spread.

The position in June was very obscure. Several princes, like Holkar in Indore, wavered when the troops garrisoning their States mutinied. Muslim fanatics were concentrating in Haidarabad, and it needed all the courage and astuteness of Sir Salar Jang to prevent an outbreak. One regiment mutinied as far south as Kolhapur, and disturbances occurred in Bombay and in the southern Maratha country. The valley of the Ganges was threatened at several points. Lack of decision prevented the disarming of sepoys at Dinapur, and three regiments escaped with their rifles to form the nucleus of Kunwar Singh's guerilla force. At Benares an attempt to disarm the Bengal regiment led to a confused struggle, but some Madras troops, which had marched from Calcutta under Colonel Neil, restored order locally. Neil then pushed on to Allahabad, where the Indian garrison had rebelled but the fort was still held by Captain Brasyer and a detachment of Sikhs. This became the advance base for operations from the south, and here Neill was joined, on June 30, by Havelock, with orders to relieve Cawnpore and Lucknow. Major Renaud was sent forward on the same day with four hundred British and four hundred Indian troops, Havelock and Neill following about a week later with 1000 British soldiers, 130 Sikhs, and twenty volunteers. In the interval news had come that Wheeler had surrendered at Cawnpore, and that his garrison had then been treacherously destroyed.

By the end of June the rebellion had spread over a large area, but the rebels had done little to consolidate their position. Large armed forces were collected at Delhi and Lucknow, but no attempt had been made to organise the civilian population, or to place the rebellious area in a state of defence. The British had now begun to take the aggressive, with Nicholson and Chamberlain in the north,

Havelock and Neill in the south; but the smallness of their forces shows how very narrow was the margin which enabled them to attack rather then defend. The comparative inertness of the rebel leaders is the more surprising because from the first the fighting was of a peculiarly brutal character, no quarter being given on either side. The post-war generation is wisely suspicious of 'atrocities', and it is necessary to discount much conscious and unconscious working up of a war atmosphere. The mutinous conduct of regiments prior to May 10 had been punished according to the normal peace-time procedure. The outbreak of armed rebellion coincided with the first murder of European civilians, men and women, at Meerut and Delhi. The British immediately replied by adopting similar standards, which were applied not only to the Bengal army, but to any known or suspected to be unfriendly. Mutineers if captured were executed, and also subjected to what the *Times* correspondent described as 'spiritual and mental tortures to which we have no right to resort, and which we dare not perpetrate in the face of Europe'.[21] After the abortive rising at Peshawar on June 10, forty prisoners were taken out and punishment for suspected mutiny.[22] Within a fortnight of the Meerut outbreak, and before the second group of mutinies, Nicholson in the Punjab was writing to Colonel Edwardes—'Let us propose a Bill for the flaying alive, impalement, or burning of the murderers of the women and children at Delhi. The idea of simply hanging the perpetrators of such atrocities is maddening'.[23] Lynching mentality as seen to-day in the Southern States of America, soon degenerates in a kind of racial mania. Every Indian who was not actively fighting for the British became a 'murderer of women and children'. Even the servants with the British troops at Delhi were treated 'with outrageous harshness....A general massacre of the inhabitants of Delhi, a large number of whom were known to wish us success, was openly proclaimed. Blood-thirsty boys might be heard recommending that all the native orderlies, irregulars, and other "poorbeahs" in our camp should be shot'.[24]

Townsmen and villagers near the centres of rebellion were victims of this lust for blood. Colonel Neill, after suppressing the mutiny at Benares on June 4, extended martial law into the surrounding district.

> 'Volunteer hanging parties went into the districts, and amateur executioners were not wanting to the occasion. One gentleman boasted of the numbers he had finished off quite "in an artistic manner", with mango trees for gibbets and elephants for droops, the victims of this wild justice being strung up, as though for pastime, in the form of figures of eight'.[25]

Similar events followed the capture of Allahabad a week later. Martial law was stengthened by the Act of June 8, which enabled the executive Government to proclaim any area to be in a state of rebellion, and to give capital powers to a Commission. By June 20, at Allahabad,

> 'soldiers and civilians alike were holding Bloody Assize, or slaying native without any assize at all, regardless of sex or age. It is on the records of our British Parliament, in papers sent home by the Governor-General of India in Council, that "the aged, women, and children are sacrificed as well as those guilty of rebellion!" They were not deliberately hanged, but burnt to death in villages—perhaps now and then accidentally shot'.[26]

Nill himself was not responsible, either at Benares or Allahabad, for the way in which his successors administered martial law, and only partially for the drastic manner in which Renaud, with the advance force, interpreted his instructions to 'attack and destroy all places *en route* close to the road occupied by the enemy, but touch no others'. Havelock's main force followed along a stretch of dreary waste, in which every village had been burnt, and from which every inhabitant had disappeared except those who had been caught and been caught and hanged by the roadside.[27]

It has been necessary to describe the nature of the fighting during six weeks following the Meerut outbreak in order to place in proper setting the terrible events at Cawnpore. These occurred later, about the end of June. General Wheeler had not expected that the mutinous sepoys would return to besiege the few European troops which he had, and he had collected the European and Eurasian population in an entrenchment poorly suited to withstand a siege. The epic story of the three weeks' defence, from June 6 to 27th, has often been told. It ended by General Wheeler's surrender on an ambiguously worded safe-conduct to Allahabad by river. The troops were attacked when embarking, and nearly all of them killed. The women and children were taken to the Nana Sahib's place. About a fortnight later the Nana Sahib, who had himself declared Peshwa, learnt that Havelock was rapidly approaching Cawnpore, and had defeated his troops at Fatehpur and in two other engagements. The two hundred and eleven women and children were then brutally murdered by some palace servants.

The two massacres must be considered separately in view of the importance which they acquired. The first was the work of mutineers, and, however reprehensible on general grounds, it was in keeping with a struggle in which no quarter was expected, and any trick seemed justifiable. It may be compared with the means by which Cooper, a Punjab civilian, captured and slaughtered some hundreds of unarmed sepoys belonging to a regiment which had been disarmed at Lahore. After escaping during a dust storm, these men were attacked by villagers, and took refuge of an island in the Ravi. About three hundred surrendered to Cooper and a few policemen, thinking they would be tried, but after being secured in a bastion they were taken out next morning and shot. Forty-five were already dead of suffocation.[28]

The massacre of the women and children at Cawnpore was a diabolical act, but it was not the work of the rebel troops, who refused to have anything to do with it. Nor is there the slightest evidence for the stories of rape and mutilation which were circulated at the time.[29] The slaughter seems to have been due to a panic, or possibly to a desire on the part of the Nana Sahib's retinue to compromise their half-hearted leader. It followed and was probably inspired by the savage punishments inflicted at Benares and Allahabad, and by Renaud's advance guard. Its results were altogether lamentable. In India and in England the news gave a welcome and almost religious sanction to any act of savagery which the Government troops might perpetrate. Townsmen were slaughtered wholesale at Cawnpore and later at Lucknow and Delhi.

> 'At the time of the capture of Lucknow—a season of indiscriminate massacre—such distinction was not made, and the unfortunate who fell into the hands of our troops was made short work of —sepoy or Oude villager, it mattered not—no questions were asked; his skin was black, and did not that suffice? A piece of rope, and the branch of a tree, or a rifle bullet through his brain, soon terminated the poor devil's existence'.[30]

In England, to quote a contemporary writer, 'everyone chuckled to hear how General Neill had forced high Brahmins to sweep up the blood of Europeans murdered at Cawnpore, and then strung them in a row without giving them the time requisite for purification'.[31] From Cawnpore can be traced the widespread belief that one European life, especially that of a woman or child, is worth the lives of innumerable Indians. Educated Englishmen came to India with ideas drawn from the Press of that period, invariably depicting the Indian cowardly slayer of women. How this was likely to appeal to the rank and file is illustrated by Trevelyan's story of an unfortunate incident amongst the drivers attached to a newly landed regiment. "I seed two Moors talking in a cart. Presently I heard one of 'em say " Cawnpore". I knowed what that meant; so I fetched Tom Walker, and he heard 'em say Cawnpore," and he knowed what that meant. So we polished 'en both off.'[31]

Another two months saw the end of the aggressive rebellion and the beginning of the punitive campaigns. Delhi fell after a series of operations carried through with marvellous courage. The siege train arrived on September 6; a week later the Kashmir Gate was blown in. The city and fort were then captured after six days' fighting. Nicholson, the moving spirit in a very hazardous enterprise, was morally wounded.[32] the rebels retreated, leaving Bahadur Shah behind. The ex-Emperor was arrested by Hodson, who also shot three of his sons. The city was sacked as ruthlessly as had been Cawnpore in July. Most of the male population, which had not already fled, were slaughtered, though many were known to have been friendly to the British cause, and few can have actively helped the rebel force. 'All the city people found within the wallas when our troops entered were bayoneted on the spot; and the number was considerable, as you may suppose when I tell you that in some houses forty or fifty were hinding'.[33] The rebel soldiers had purposely left behind large quantities of liquor, easily accessible to the incoming troops; and this ruse, while it facilitated their retreat, led to appalling excesses against their compatriots during the final stages of the capture of the city and fort.

Meanwhile Havelock, with his minute force, continued to win victories. After being joined by Outram he fought his way into Lucknow on September 25. These two events, the fall of Delhi and the relief of Lucknow, finally established the superiority of the Government's troops, even when at a great numerical disadvantage. The rebels never again showed the same vigour. Their nominal leader, Bahadur Shah, was captured, they had no headquarters and their last hope of ultimate victory disappeared as they found reinforcements were steadily arriving from England.

After September the British campaign became more orderly, while the rebels were divided into groups under such leaders as the Rao Sahib, Tantia Topi, Khan Bahadur Khan, Firoz Shah, Kunwar Singh, and the Rani of Jhansi. For another nine months these were systematically hunted down. Sir Colin Campbell operated in the North-West Provinces and Oudh, Sir Hugh Rose worked from Bombay through Central India. They were helped by columns under Colonel Greathed from Delhi and General Whitlock from Mhow. At first the hardest fighting fell to the share of Sir Colin Campbell. Lucknow had to be relieved for the second time in November, and he had only just succeeded in clearing the city and evacuating the non-combatants, when he had to hurry back to Cawnpore, where General Windham was hard pressed by some 20,000 men under Rao Sahib and Tantia Topi. Outram with 4000 men was left at Lucknow, where he successfully held the Alambagh against forces estimated at over a hundred thousand. Lucknow had therefore to be relieved for a third time, in March, 1858.

Tantia Topi's force was drawn from the Gwalior garrison. Sindhia's own State troops had remained loyal to their master, and still defended the treasury and arsenal, but the Government troops mutinied in June. This powerful army might have played a decisive part against the weakened British forces, but it did little for five months. It was now faced by Campbell's better equipped army and was defeated on December 6. Joined by a force of Gurkhas under Jang Bahadur, Campbell then returned to Lucknow, relieved Outram, and began campaigning in Oudh and Rohilkhand, driving Khan Bahadur Khan and his Ghazi followers out of Bareilly in May. These operations in Oudh continued until the end of the year. Ahmad Ullah and the Begum of Oudh fought with great determination round Shahjanpur, until the former was treacherously murdered by a brother of the Raja of Powain, from whom he was seeking help. The Begum ultimately fled to Nepal. This resistance in Oudh developed into a war of local independence. The *Talukdars*, who had previously adopted an attitude of benevolent neutrality towards the mutineers, were driven into active rebellion by a singularly injudicious Proclamation issued by Canning at the end of March, which declared that, except in a few specified cases, the *Talukdar's* lands would be liable to forfeiture .[34] This Proclamation was so opposed to the usually conciliatory attitude of the Governor-General that it is probable that he did not fully appreciate its significane, and merely wished to give the administration a free hand in the future settlement of Oudh. Ahmad Ullah was able to arouse the territorial patriotism which was so markedly lacking over most of India during the eighteenth and early nineteenth centuries; but his army had not the training of the sepoys who followed Tantia Topi and the Rao Sahib. The Moulvi fought with great courage, and fully deserved this tribute from a contemporary historian: 'He had not stained his sword with assassination, he had connived at no murders; and he fought manfully, honestly, stubbornly in the field against the strangers who had seized his country'.[35]

Interest in the Central Indian campaign turned on the siege of Jhansi and the combined activities of the Rani and Tantia Topi. Sir Hugh Rose, after capturing Ratgarh and relieving Saugor, reached Jhansi on March 21. He had not completed the investment effort he was called upon to meet a determined effort to relieve the city. Tantia Topi, after his defeat three months previously, had collected his forces at Kalpi and now marched on Jhansi. He was again defeated on the Betwa river, and Rose then stormed Jhansi, though the Rani managed to escape and joined Tantia Topi. Their forces were once more defeated at Kunch, but the indomitable Rani tried a final gamble, and marched with Tantia Topi into Gwalior, hoping that the State troops would at last join them. Sindhia went out to oppose them, but his army would not fight, and the rebels seized the town and fort, Rose saw the danger of a Maratha rising and, making a last effort, defeated Tantia Topi at Morar and Kotah, after which the Rani was killed when riding, dressed as a sowar, with her cavalry. Gwalior was retaken on June 20, and on July 8 Canning proclaimed peace, though nearly all the leaders were still at large. The Nana Sahib, the Begum of Oudh, and Firoz Shah escaped from India during the autumn of 1858. Tantia Topi was given up by Man Singh, a rebellious princelet who hoped to recover his fief by this betrayal. He was tried and hanged for waging war against the king.[36] The Rao Sahib was arrested and hanged three years later.

Thus ended an episode, lamentable in its origin, distinguished by great courage but by few other virtues during its course, and ending in a manner which left the seeds of much future trouble. On the British side the valour and endurance of soldiers and civilians were marred by crude racial passions, and by gross ingratitude to many Indians who assisted them. Indians must also recognise certain failings in the conduct of those who took arms against the Government, the indecision which kept large numbers inactive when they might have been most effective, the selfishness and lack of national pride which prevented their leaders working together or sacrificing their own personal ambitions.

REFERENCE

1. A possible exception was Persia, with which the Government had been at war until May 1856. Persian envoys, probably unofficial, visited Bahadur Shah at Delhi.
2. The North West Provinces, part of the modern Uttar Pradesh, must not be confused with the present North-West Frontier Province.
3. Immediately before the Mutiny the British troops, including invalids and some non-combatant services, numbered 45,522. Indian troops amounted to 232,224. The total population of India was probably about two hundred million.
4. Havelock's 'field state' before his first engagement was 1404 Europeans, 561 Indians.
5. The cockade of cow or pig skin might endanger the caste of a Hindu or affront the religion of a Muslim.
6. The absence of serious disaffection in the Indian army after its reorganisation has obscured the extreme dissatisfaction

with which most officers, especially of the British army, viewed the state of the Company's forces. This could not be expressed openly'. 'An officer would be persecuted, hunted down, ruined, who dared to tell the truth': Russell, *My Diary in India*, i. 267. Lord Dalhousie had no illusions on this subject. 'The discipline of the army, from top to bottom, officers and men alike, is scandalous', he wrote in a letter to the President of the Board of Control, and he repeatedly urged the need for more European troops. See Lee-Warner, *Life of the Marquess of Dalhousie*, ii. chap. viii.

7. Paradoxically it is an article of faith amongst Indian nationalists to describe the Mutiny as a war of independence. This may be due to the proscription of Savarkar's *War of Indian Independence of 1857*, a book which states the Indian case with force, but with little critical acumen. It is a poor compliment to Indian courage and ability to treat this revolt as an organised national movement. It was repressed by a minute force. Its leaders, when in a position to prove their competence as rulers, were a failure. Historical accuracy, as well as respect for Indian ability, makes it requisite to stress the small part taken in the revolt by the better elements in the country.
8. The Hindu is specially susceptible to this kind of suggestion, as he believes that dismemberment or ceremonial defilement ruin his prospects after death.
9. The second Afghan war illustrates these points.
10. Russell, *My Dairy in India*, ii. 43. The author was correspondent for *The Times*.
11. They must not be confused with the regular 'Queen's regiments' which were in India or were sent as reinforcements. The Company's European troops were specially recruited, no questions being asked so long as the men were physically fit. They had much in common with the French Foreign Legion.
11. As, for example, in refusing to allow a money payment in murder cases, or to recognise caste distinction in punishing offences. Few Hindus accepted the view, so contrary to the laws of Manu, that the murder of a Sudra by a Brahmin was an offence comparable with the murder of a Brahmin by a Sudra.
12. See F. W. Buckland's *The Political theory of the Indian Mutiny*, and subsequent controversy in the *Transactions of the Royal Historical Society*, vii.

13. The disbanded State army numbered about 80,000 men. They had already rioted in parts of Oudh before the mutiny at Meerut.
14. For these advantages see Kaye and Malleson, *History of the Indian Mutiny*, 254.
15. It was widely believed that most Englishmen had already migrated to India.
16. Letter to Colvin, dated September 24, 1857. *Enclosures to Secret Letters from India* 455-6.
17. The first cartridges sent out for instructional purposes were covered with lard. The mistake was recognised and mutton fat substituted, but explanations were complicated and delayed. Anson, the Commander-in-Chief, wrote to Canning, 'I am not surprised at their objections to the cartridges, having seen them. I had no idea they contained, or rather are smeared with, such a quantity of grease, which looks exactly like fat'. Lord Roberts himself refers to 'the incredible disregard of the soldiers' religious prejudices'.—*Forty-one Year in India*, i. 94.
18. There were two British regiments, one infantry and one cavalry, at meerut, and some British artillery. General Hewett, who was in command, has been much blamed for not despatching troops to Delhi before the mutineers had consolidated their position.
19. A countil of twelve, the 'Bara Topi', became the nominal rulers. In view of the controversy mentioned earlier it may be noted that Bahadur Shah was not directly or indirectly represented.
20. In replying to the first offer Lord Canning referred to 'the passing and groundless panic'. The news from Meerut did cause panic amongst Europeans at both Simla and Calcutta, two curious incidents which gave rise to later controversy.
21. Russell, *My Diary in India*, ii. 43.
22. Cf. a letter written by Lieutenant (afterwards Lord) Roberts to his mother, June 11, 1857: 'We have come along this far, doing a little business on the road, such as disarming regiments and executing matineers. The death that seems to have most effect is being blown from a gun', *Letters written during the Indian Mutiny.*
23. Kaye and Malleson, *History of the Indian Mutiny*, ii. 301.
24. See *The Chaplain's Narrative of the Siege of Delhi.*

25. The two quotations are from kaye and Malleson, *History of the Indian Mutiny*, ii. 177 and 203. The reference in the second extract is to papers presented to Parliament, February 4, 1858.
26. See note 5 on previous page.
27. There can be no doubt about the recklessness of these executions. *Parliamentary papers*, xliv. pt. i. 23. Also see Russell, *My Diary in India* ii. 402.
28. See Cooper's own account in his book *The Crisis in the Punjab*, 152, *et seq*: 'they were possessed of a sudden and insane idea that they were going to be tried by court-martial after some luxurious refreshment'. 'The doors were opened and behold. Unconsciously the tragedy of Holwell's Black Hole had been re-enacted.....Fortyfive bodies dead from fright, exhaustion, fatigue, heat, and partial suffocation, were dragged into light.
29. See Colonel William's valuable synopsis of evidence taken at Cawnpore. Printed in *Annals of the Indian Rebellion*.
30 Lieutenant V. D. Majendie's *Up among the Pandies*, 195. This ingenuous account of the Mutiny operations by a subaltern is of considerable importance in this connection.
31. G. O. Trevelyas, *The Competition Wallah*, 284.
32. The scale of the fighting round Delhi may be judged by the casualties. The siege cost 992 killed and 2795 wounded. This was more than the total casualties suffered during Havelock and Outram's campaigns, Sir Colin Campbell's relief of Lucknow, his subsequent action at Cawnpore, Sir H. Rose's campaign in Central India, and Whitlock's campaign in Bundelkhand.
33. Letter in the *Bombay Telegraph*. Quoted by Montgomery Martin, *The Indian Empire*, viii. 449. In view of these events the blame attached to Hodson for pistolling the princes seems hypocritical. They had been active members of the rebel army, and had surrendered without safe conduct.
34. This Proclamation brought a strongly censorious letter from Lord Ellenborough, then Secretary of State for India. He sent this without Cabinet authorisation, and resigned, but his condemnation, especially of the original draft of the Proclamation, was fully justified.
35. Kaye and Malleson, *History of the Indian Mutiny*, iv. 381.
36. Note, as frequently stated, for complicity in the Cawnpore murder. The justice of the sentence was severely criticised. See Kaye and Malleson, v. 265.

4

Siege of Delhi

1857 September

The time for resolute action had now come. In the last volume of this History, I brought down the narrative of the so-called "Siege of Delhi" to the ends of the month of August. But, up to that time, we had been the Besieged and not the Besiegers. Of the wonderful heroism and the consummate patience—of the gallant actions then performed, of the grievous suffering then bravely endured, no words can speak in language of sufficient admiration. It was, indeed, this waiting game that tried the metal of our people, all those long months, not of inaction, but of profitless activity—under burning suns, under heavy rains, under constant exposure; wasting human life, only to prove that we had lost nothing of our old vitality. But all this was changed in September. The dawn of that month saw our preparations nearly complete for the delivery of the final assault." John Lawrence had despatched from the Punjab the last of his succours, and, in the estimation of the general camp, the City of the Mogul was doomed—and all who held high carnival in it, in proud defiance of the English.

Neville Chamberlain

There were then, under the Chief Commander of the Delhi Field Force, three men in the very prime of life, who, holding high position in the Army, were working strenuously to accomplish, with the least possible delay, the great final consummation of the assault on the doomed city. There was Neville Chamberlain, who had been severely wounded, but who had lost none of his pristine energy. As chief of the Army Staff, he had been ever ready with sustaining and invigorating counsel; but his vigour was tempered by a clear, sound judgment, and a just appreciation of surrounding circumstances. If, looking from a distance at the work which lay before Anson and Barnard, he took up the Punjabee war cry, and was disposed to censure what seemed to be the weakness and reluctance of our leaders, a nearer view of the actual difficulties of the position convinced him that he hand greatly underrated them. Eager as he had been for the assault, he had not been long on Barnard's Staff before he confessed that, with the scanty means then at our disposal, it was a desperate enterprise. He was the man who first described it, in language often afterwards quoted, as the "gambler's throw." But nothing could have moved him an inch from the ground which we had taken up. The idea of a retrograde movement was an abomination in his eyes. He knew that we needed only a few more companies and a few more guns to make Delhi our own; and he never ceased to do his best, even when least capable of exertion, to persist in this course of action. It was a fortunate circumstance, too, that at this time, when Chamberlain's wound necessarily kept him much in his tent, he had the assistance of a young officer of the highest promise, whose great gifts were fast winning the confidence of his elders. In Captain Norman, of the Adjutant-General's Department, there was a rare combination of those qualities which make a wise counsellor and a man of strenuous action. He had all the enthusiasm and the enterprise of lusty youth, and all the staid intelligence of mature manhood; and there was scarcely a man in Camp who did not recognise in him one of its leading spirits.

Baird Smith

Then there was Baird Smith, Chief of the Engineer Department, who was also enfeebled by much sickness, and the distresses of a painful wound. He had been struck by the fragment of a shell, when superintending his work in the batteries, and he had been lamed by the blow; but, when he ought to have been on the sick-list, he was in the full swing of active employment; when he ought to have been in his tent, he was busy in the works. Worn to a skeleton by the most weakening of all ailments, he went about, when it was possible for him to go about at all, saturated with opium and brandy, dragging his maimed limb after him, with painful efforts; but never losing his high courage, or the habitual cheerfulness of his demeanour.[1] Like Chamberlain, he had an assistant, who was one of the younger heroes of the Camp. In Alexander Taylor, his second in command, he found a man capable of any amount of work, and ready for any heroic enterprise. His energies were unbounded, his spirit unfailing; and it was truly a fortunate circumstance, that when the frailty of the flesh restricted Baird Smith's personal activities, Taylor was ever ready and eager to pass from point to point, and to display his bodily presence, which was always inspiriting and encouraging. There was little or no sympathy between Wilson and Baird Smith. They were men altogether cast in different moulds. But the General fully recognised the great attainments of the Chief Engineer; and though rarely outwardly courteous or orally compliant, yielded to his opinions.

And now united with these Two, and in daily counsel with them, was John Nicholson, a born soldier, who seemed to have come down to Delhi with a special mission to take it. He had chafed under the long delay, which had left the vast and guilty city so long in the hands of the mutineers. Patience was not one of his virtues. With great ardour commonly some impetuosity is combined. John Nicholson had not the cool temper and calm judgment of Neville Chamberlain. He over looked all difficulties and ignored all responsibilities; and, perhaps, he did not always make allowance for those who clearly saw the one and were compelled to accept the other. He could not stand still. Active among the active, he was eager to execute any kind of work that might be entrusted to him, until the day of final retribution should arrive, when he coveted, and believed that he would obtain, the post of honour at the head of the storming party. No man doubted his power, and no man envied his reputation. All felt that a great soldier had come among them, full brained and lion-hearted; and they looked to him to lead them to victory.

Arrival of the last reinforcements

In the early morning of the 4th of September the siege guns, drawn by elephants, appeared upon the Ridge, with an immense assemblage of carts laden with ammunition—sufficient, it was said, "to grind Delhi to powder." On the 6th, the residuary Rifles from Meerut marched into Camp, strong, healthy, and jubilant, welcomed by the inspiriting notes of the band of the fifty-second and the cheers of their old comrades. On the morning of the 8th, the Jummoo Contingent, promised by Gholab Singh and sent down by his on, made their appearance, with Richard Lawrence at their head, and were greeted by the General and the Commissioner. Then the spirits of all men rose, for they saw the beginning of the end. The days of waiting and watching were spent. Every man, every gun, every shot, every shell that could be sent down for the final assault had now reached its destination. There was no pretext for further delay. The waste of a single hour would have been a crime, for our troops were dying fast, and the enemy were escaping. The "real siege of Delhi" was now to commence.

Question of assault

There are men now living, as I write, who will never forget that crisis; there are others, gone to their rest, who were stirred to the very depths of their natures by a grand enthusiasm, which made them cast aside every consideration of military discipline and decorum, and gird their loins up for that which would have been to them either total ruin or a grand reputation. They thought that the General was wavering; that even then he hesitated to issue the orders for the final assault; and had denial come they were prepared to appeal to the Army, to have put the Commander under arrest, and to have delivered the assault either under the direction of the Chief Engineer, or of a Commander selected by themselves. Eager among the eager was John Nicholson, whose strong impulses were not to be curbed, and who never scrupled to say what others ventured only to think. "The game is completely in our hands," he wrote to John Lawrence on the 11th of September; "we only want the player to move the pieces. Fortunately, after making all kinds of objections and obstructions, and even threatening more than once to withdraw the guns and abandon the attempt, Wilson has made everything over to the Engineers, and they and they alone will deserve the credit of taking Delhi. Had Wilson carried out his threat of withdrawing the guns, I was quite prepared to appeal to the Army to set him aside and elect a successor. The purport of his last memorandum, in reply to the Engineers, ran thus: 'I disagree with the Engineers entirely. I foresee great, if not insuperable difficulties in the plan they propose; but as I have no other plan myself I yield to the remonstrances of the Chief Engineer.' The above are almost the very words used by him." And, in truth, they were but little wrong.

But it is just that I should pause here for a little space to make clear and intelligible, by reference to documents before me, the facts out of which arose this pregnant talk of the Camp. On the 20th of August, Wilson, then in doubt with respect to the sufficiency of his force for the capture and occupation of Delhi, had written to Baird Smith saying:

GENERAL ARCHDALE WILSON TO COLONEL BAIRD SMITH

"My dear Smith,—A letter has been received from the

Governor-General urging our immediately taking Delhi, and he seems angry that it has not been done long ago. I wish to explain to him the true state of affairs: that Delhi is seven miles in circumference, filled with an immense fanatical Mussulman population, garrisoned by full 40,000 soldiers armed and disciplined by ourselves, with 114 heavy pieces of artillery mounted on the walls with the largest magazine of shot, shell, and ammunition in the Upper Provinces at their disposal, besides some 60 pieces of field artillery, all of our own manufacture, and manned by artillerymen drilled and taught by ourselves; that the Fort itself has been made so strong by perfect flanking defences erected by our own engineers, and a glacis which prevents our guns breaking the walls lower than eight feet from the top, without the labour of a regular siege and sap—for which the force and artillery sent against it has been quite inadequate; that an attempt to blow in the gates and escalade' the walls was twice contemplated, but that it was considered, from the state of preparation against such an attack on the part of the rebels, such an attempt would inevitably have failed, and have caused the most irreparable disaster to our cause; and that, even if we had succeeded in forcing our way into the place, the small force disposable for the attack would have been most certainly lost in the numerous streets of so large a city, and have been cut to pieces. It was, therefore, considered advisable to confine our efforts to holding the position we now occupy, which is naturally strong, and has been daily rendered more so by our engineers, until the force coming up from below could join to co-operate in the attack. That since the command of the force has devolved on me, I have considered it imperatively necessary to adopt the same plan as the only chance of safety to the Empire, and that I strongly urge upon his Lordship the necessity of his ordering General Havelock's or some other force marching upon Delhi as soon as possible. The force under 'my command is, and has been since the day we took up our position, actually besieged by the mutineers, who, from the immense extent of suburbs, and gardens extending nearly to the walls of the town, have such cover for their attacks, that it has been very difficult to repel them, and at the same time to inflict such a loss as would deter a repetition of them. They have frequently been driven back with loss, but they immediately take refuge under the grape fire of their heavy guns on the city walls, and, on our retirement, reoccupied their former positions; every such attack upon them has entailed a heavy loss upon our troops, which we can ill spare, and has done us little good. I shall be reinforced by a siege train from Ferozepore by the end of this or beginning of next month, when I intend to commence more offensive operations against the city; but I cannot hold out any hope of being able to take the place until supported by the force from below. As an Artillery officer, I have no hesitation in giving my opinion that the attack on Delhi, garrisoned and armed as it now is, as arduous an undertaking as was the attack on Bhurtpore in 1825-26, for which 25,000 troops and 100 pieces of artillery were not considered too large a force. I enclose a return of the original force which was sent down to capture this strong place, and also a return of the present effective force, including sick and wounded, from which his Lordship will see how desperate would have been any attempt to take the city by assault, more especially as the mutineers keep a large portion of their force encamped outside the city walls, who, on our assaulting the city, could easily attack and capture our camp, with all our hospitals, stores, and ammunition, unless a strong provision was made against it. Something of this sort I intend forwarding to the Governor-General, and shall be glad if you will return this with such remarks and emendations as your experience as Chief Engineer suggests.

"Yours sincerely,
"A. Wilson.
"August 20, 1857."

After the perusal of this letter, Baird Smith drew up a Memorandum stating his reasons most emphatically in favour of immediate action. He contended that although there was always hazard in an assault, the evils of inaction at such a time, were so great, and the chances in our favour were so many, that it would be better to risk the enterprise than to shrink from it. He demonstrated, on scientific grounds, that, although the material resources of the enemy were far greater than our own, the superior fore thought and skill, and the perfect union and combination, absent from the designs and operations of the enemy, would give us an immense advantage over them. He represented most urgently to the General that the breaches should be established and the assault should be delivered, with the utmost possible despatch, as the enemy once cognisant of our designs would strengthen their defences without and within the city and render its occupation impossible. To these arguments Wilson reluctantly yielded. The whole responsibility was thrown upon the Chief Engineer. The "ipsissima verba" used by the General were these: "It is evident to me that the results of the proposed operations will be thrown on the hazard of a die; but under the circumstances in which I am placed, I am willing to try this hazard—the more so as I cannot suggest any other plan to meet our difficulties. I cannot, however, help being of opinion that the chances of success, under such a heavy fire as the working parties will be exposed to , are anything but favourable. I yield, however, to the judgment of the Chief Engineer.—A. W." Baird Smith, transcribing the above, observed: "This, I think, every one would allow, places on my shoulders the undivided responsibility for the results of the siege. It would, doubtless, have lightened that burden greatly had I felt assured of the hearty support and concutrence of the General in command; but the withholding of these was no sufficient cause for hesitation, and I was too glad of even a qualified consent to immediate action to be careful as to the terms in which it was given."[2]

Baird Smith was not a man to shrink from the responsibility thrown upon him. To say that he cheerfully accepted it would be a faint recital of the fact; he engerly gransped it. And there was not an officer under him, whose heart did not bound with joyous exultation when he knew that the work was to be begun. But Wilson was not wrong when he said that to attempt to erect our batteries so near the city walls, in the face of the enemy's fire from their inexhaustible artillery, was a hazardous undertaking. The eager gallantry of the Engineers believed all things to be possible. And it is by this noble self-reliance that great victories are achieved. But the Engineers, as will presently be shown, had set them selves a task which they could not accomplish. In the midst of that awful by glorious crisis, men saw through a glass darkly. But time had brought them face to face with the Truth. Some of the Bravest and best of Wilson's officers, who, heated by the excitements and animosities of the Camp, had condemned this apparent reluctance to order the assault, looking back upon those troubles days, and calmly estimating the difficulties to be encountered and the responsibilities to be sustained, have since acknowledged that less then justice was done at that time to the Commandant of the Delhi Force. All the principles of warfare were upon his side. But these principles have not been much regarded in India. Everything has been gained by hard blows promptly delivered in defiance of all principles of war.

Having once resolved to stand the "hazard of the die," Wilson issued an Address to the Army, manly and spirit-stirring, and wise in the cautions it conveyed.[3] It spoke of the hardships and privations undergone by the Army, and of the gallantry which they had on all occasions displayed. It expressed a cheerful hope that their great trials were now wearing to a close, and that the grand reward was close at their feet. It called upon the troops of all arms to assist the Engineers in the arduous work that lay before them—in the digging of trenches and the erection of batteries. It appeared to the Artillery, who, it was said, would have "still harder work than they had yet had, and which had been so well and cheerfully performed." Then it spoke wisely and sagaciously of the precautions to be observed after the assault should have been delivered. It warned the soldiers against straggling—it warned them against indiscriminate plundering—it stimulated the worst passions of the soldiery by reminding them (or, as it is customary to say, "I need not remind them") of the atrocious murders and cruelties committed by the enemy, and told them to spare the women and the children, but to give no quarter to the men. And it concluded with the words, "The Major -General calls upon the Officers of the Force to lend their zealous aid and efficient co-operation in the erection of the works of the siege now about to be commenced. He looks especially to the regimental officers of all grades to impress upon their men that the work in the trenches during a siege is as necessary and as honourable as to fight in the ranks during a battle. He will hold all officers responsible for their utmost being done to carry out the directions of the Engineers; and he confidently trusts that all will exhibit a healthy and hearty spirit of emulation and zeal, from which he has no doubt that the happiest results will follow in the brilliant termination of all their labours."

And then began a work almost unparalleled in the history of modern warfare. That science, which has taught us how to make the siege of fortified places almost a certainty in the success of its results, was now of no service to us. The approach by parallels, so beautiful upon paper, and so effective in practice, was to us as if War and Science had been wholly divorced. The ring of fire closing in slowly, but surely, upon a doomed fortress, shutting up the garrison within its walls and reducing them to the necessity of surrender, was now to our English officers only a memory of the stirring pages of Napier and Jones. What they saw was an attacking force, scarcely one-third of the numerical strength of the enemy, who had still possession also of some important suburbs, without cover of any well-constructed trenches, bringing their guns within fire of the walls of Delhi, and pouring forth day and night an incessant shower of shot and shell, resolute to atone for the failure of science by gigantic physical efforts and an unexampled display of British pluck.

The plan of attack was that which Baird Smith had projected before he left Roorkee, and of the efficacy of which his convictions had never been shaken. It was the plan which had commanded itself to all our Engineer officers from the first establishment of our Army on the Ridge. Investment with our limited means being impossible, it was necessary to select a front of attack on which all our available breaching power could be brought to bear. The front to be assailed contained the Moree, the Cashmere, and the Water Bastions, with their connecting curtains. These works had, not many years before, been greatly strengthened and improved by our own Engineer officers, so that we well knew the force to be applied to their demolition. There were very important reasons for this selection—Firstly, because our left flank would be protected by the river, thus leaving us only the right flank to guard; secondly, because the flanking fire from the city would thus be comparatively harmless, as only the Moree Bastion commanded the ground in front of it; thirdly, because there was excellent cover to within a short distance of the walls.[4] The insurgents might have done more to increase both their offensive and their defensive powers, but they had failed to do so; and it was permitted to us, therefore, to take advantage of their neglect.[5] Some thought, however, that when the enemy should see that we were preparing our batteries in earnest so as to bring a crushing fire from a short distance upon their walls, they would raise cover for a larger number of guns wherewith to silence our batteries. It was manifest, therefore, that every hour was of the utmost importance to us; and so all our people went to work as if they had never had a day's fighting—never known a day's fatigue.

Then, night and day, worked the Artillery and the Engineers, as those services, with the lustre of long years of past activities upon them, had never, 'perhaps, worked before. The first thing was to construct the batteries behind which our guns were to work; the next was to get our heavy guns into position. Brownlow had charge of the Engineer's Park—Hogge of the Park of Artillery. Ever since his first appearance in Camp, Baird Smith had been collecting the materials of the batteries which were to cover the captors of Delhi. Immense supplies of gabions, and fascines, and sand bags had been prepared, with scaling ladders and all else required for the later operations of the attack. The first heavy battery was traced out on the evening of the 7th,[6] and all through the night the work was being pressed forward as silently as circumstances would permit; but silence was, indeed, impossible. The large number of camels that were bringing down the *materiel* of the batteries, and the bullocks which were dragging the carts laden with ordnance stores, followed by the heavy guns, each with a team of forty floundering beasts, made such confusion, and the drivers, who are nothing if not clamorous, made such a noise, that it is marvellous that the enemy did not discover our designs and pour an unceasing fire upon our toiling people. For a time all was secure; and things looked hopeful in the battery, when a heavy shower of grape came in from the Moree, and after a short interval another, too well-directed and too fatally destructive. Then the Engineers must have been much troubled in their minds, what would be the state of the working a parties in the morning, if the insurgents should continue thus to molest us all through the night. It was, indeed, a terrible question. But the painful expectation of the renewal of the fire from the bastion soon died away, for there was not another flash, another sound; and the work went on without any further interruption. The carriage, and the cattle, and the drivers, and the camp-followers were cleared away before the morning sunshine upon the scene. The ammunition was stored. The guns were ready for work. But all the exertions of the Engineers, under the vigorous direction of the inexhaustible Alec Taylor, had not sufficed to fix the platforms on which they were to be mounted. No men could have done more; but they had set themselves a task which could not be accomplished in a single night, and so far the doubts of the General were confirmed. He had rightly forecast the difficulty; and when it was reported to him that it had arisen, he was disposed to withdraw the guns. But the man in command was not one to go a step backwards. Let the Moree batteries roar as they might, he would not give the order for the withdrawal of the British Artillery. So they gallantly faced the fire and went on with their work.

The battery—known as Battery No. 1—was at a distance of seven hundred yards from the enemy's works. It was divided into two parts connected by a trench. The right portion, was constructed to cover five heavy guns and a howitzer, the special function of which was to demolish the Moree bastion—our most obtrusive assailant all through the siege. The left contained four guns, intended to keep down the fire of the Cashmere Bastion. This battery was under the command of Major James Brind, who had virtually, indeed, commanded the heavy Artillery throughout the greater portion of the operations before Delhi,[7] who had always been foremost where work was to be done, and who, whilst careful in the extreme of his men, had exposed himself in a manner which had called forth the remonstrances of his friends. If there was any fault to be found with him, it was the glorious fault of doing too much. His restless bravery never halted. He did not know what it was to "stand at ease."[8] But this very activity, though sometimes wasted, suggested, when there was real work to be done, that Brind was the man to do it. He had now the honour, coveted by every artilleryman in the field, of commencing the attack upon those works which had so long defied us. But on that morning, in that unfinished battery, it was a service of extreme danger. The morning light had fully revealed our designs to the insurgents, and laid bare our position. So they poured down from the Moree a pitiless shower of shot and shell, and sent out light guns with riflemen, to endeavour to take the battery in flank, whilst Brind's gunners, animated by his noble example, were working, unshaken and undismayed, to get their pieces into position. Only one gun was mounted when the fire commenced. Then "Brind dragged a howitzer well to the rear and fired over the parapet."[9] It was but a feeble response that he could return to the bellowing enemy; but he was resolute to give them something, and he knew that he would soon give them something more. Thus, ever as the sun rose higher and higher, the enemy fired and our people fell. But as gun after gun was mounted on its platform, the inequality of the conflict ceased; and then began that of which the insurgents behind their walls had no former experience—perhaps, indeed, no conception. They had laughed at our long shots. But the close quarters to which we now brought our heavy guns, and the admirable manner in which they were served, gave altogether a new aspect to the operations before Delhi. The insurgents stood manfully their guns. But the masonry of the Moree soon began to crumble; and ere the heat of the day had passed, the fire of the enemy had slackened, and before sunset it had feebly dwindled away into total quietude. But they had fired to some purpose. Our men were scarce, though our material was abundant, and the result of that first day's work was that there were some seventy casualties in our trenches.[10] Nor was it the fire from the Moree alone that distressed our people in the battery. They were, also, much molested by some light field-pieces and skirmishers of the enemy posted on our right. These enfiladed the battery and sometimes even took it in reverse. To meet these attacks and to protect our position Brind brought down two field guns from the rear. Moreover, the mutineers, inspired probably by our Sappers, who to the number of eight hundred had joined the insurgent force, ran a trench along the plain in front of both sections of the battery, about midway between the city walls and our position, from which they kept up a constant fire and did some damage to us, as the battery had been hastily erected without mantlets and with over-large embrasures.[11]

Whilst the eighteen-pounders were thus blazing away at the Moree, the twenty-four pounders in the left section of the battery were directing their fire on the Cashmere Bastion. This section of the battery was placed under the command of Major Frank Turner, one of the best Horse Artillery officers in the service. But previous exposure to the sun had broken him down; and an utter failure of his powers of endurance compelled him reluctantly to withdraw from the command. He was succeeded by Major Edward Kaye, who had taken an active part from the beginning in all the operations on the Ridge. Scarcely had the completion of the parapet enabled him to get his guns in position, when a round shot from the Moree shattered the skull of one of his subalterns—Lieutenant Hildebrand—and Riding-master Budd, of the Horse Artillery, was soon afterwards disabled by the fire of the enemy. But soon our guns were fairly in position, and right good service they did not only by keeping down the fire of the Cashmere Bastion, but by deluding the enemy into the belief that our assault was to be delivered entirely from the right. During the greater part of three days this left section kept up a continued fire on the enemy's works; but towards noon of the 10th its operations were brought to a close by the internal ignition of the battery. Hastily constructed of fascines, made of very dry brushwood, it caught fire from the blazing of our own guns. Every effort was made to suppress the flames; but the efforts were vain, for water was scarce and had to be brought from distance; and the water-carriers being much exposed, going and coming, suffered severely from the fire of the enemy. The Infantry on duty in the battery (some details of the Kumaon Battalion) were most zealous in their efforts, and suffered severely from the musketry-fire of the enemy. Several, including Lieutenant Lockhart, who commanded the party, were severely wounded. But, all to no purpose. The fire could not be mastered. So the guns were withdrawn—and made ready for their removal at night to No. 2 Battery. And thus the left section of No. 1 became a thing of the past. It was not, however, a disaster of any moment. For that part of the battery had done its work;

and both the guns and the gunners were wanted for service nearer to the real point of attack.

For by this time Battery No. 2 had been constructed — the left section immediately in fron of Ludlow Castle and the right about eighty yards to the right front of the former. How it happened that the enemy had allowed us to take up such a position, within six hundred yards of the city, no one could explain, except upon the supposition that the insurgents, though never wanting in courage, were greatly wanting in wit. It was expected that we should have a hard fight for the ground, but our occupation of it was never contested. And yet this battery was intended to have, and in effect did have, a most potential effect upon the issue of the war. It was designed to crush the Cashmere Bastion and the adjacent works, and so to breach the walls as to open an entrance for our assaulting columns. It was to comprise, in the right section, cover for seven heavy howitzers and two eighteen-pounders; and in the left for nine twenty-four pounders. The experiences of the first night had proved the impossibility of completing the battery and getting the guns into position before daybreak on the 9th; so the Engineers went more quietly to work, and there was not, during the darkness, much of a mischievous character from the enemy's guns to impede the operations of our working parties. On the second night the battery was completed and the guns brought into position. The right was to be commanded by Major Kaye; the left by Major J. H. Campbell.

When this Battery No. 2 had been completed,[12] it was not thought advisable immediately to unmask it. It was better to finish the other offensive works for the left attack, so that a simultaneous fire might be opened from both batteries. "The reason," said Baird Smith, "for delaying the opening of this battery until No. 3 has been armed, is that at present the siege works on the left are being carried on with very few casualties in consequence of the apparent ignorance of the enemy that any attack on that side is mediatated."[13] So the works of No. 3 went on apace with little interruption. This battery was erected behind one of the buildings of the Custom House, at a distance of not more than a hundred and eighty yards from the Water Bastion, upon which our guns were to play. It was to cover six eighteen-pounders, under the command of Major Scott, who had commanded No. 14 Light Field Battery throughout the siege. If the building did not much protect our working parties, it greatly obscured the nature of the work on which they were engaged. The enemy never clearly knew what we were doing, but they felt that something was going on that portended mischief, and they poured in such an incessant shower of musketry, with occasional discharges from their mortars, that it was difficult and dangerous to work even under the cover of the night, and impossible after the dawn of day. The workmen were principally Natives and non-combatants, but they faced death as bravely for their Christian employers as if they had been English soldiers.[14] There is nothing more true than that the calm courage of our native Adherents enabled us to recover India from their own Countrymen.

Of a different character was the courage displayed by our allies from beyond the border. Our working parties were composed of men of all races—of all sorts and descriptions of people—whom we could press into our service; for the labour was great and incessant, the heat was intense, and exhaustion soon came upon those who had to lift heavy weights. On the night of the 10th, no Sappers or Pioneers being available, Taylor had been compelled to employ the services of men drawn from two of our European regiments in the heavy howitzer battery. They worked heartily and effectively; but soon after midnight they were failing from sheer exhaustion, and then the Directing Engineer be thought himself of our newly-arrived Jummoo Contingent, and sent a hundred and twenty men down to the battery. Elated with the thought of some fighting, to be followed probably by plunder, they streamed down, armed to the teeth. But when the true nature of the service required from them was explained, they looked askance at the shovels, and the sand, and the sand-bags, and murmured among themselves. So Medley, the Engineer, who had charge of the work, with those immediately under him began cheerily and lustily to fill the sand-bags, and to do other coolies' work. Then the Commanding officer of the Jummoo Detachment, feeling some compunctions of shame, followed the lead of the European officers, and presently all his men piled their arms and laboured with the heartiest goodwill. All, for some time, was quiet, as they worked under the darkness of the night; but in the hour before the dawn, there came from the enemy's position in front a sharp shower of musketry, which so excited our Dogra friends, that they seized their matchlocks and discharged them with such impetuosity in the direction of their assailants, that they well-nigh shot down all our people who were before them in the battery. It was a mercy and a miracle that a bullet did not go through Medley's head. The danger was too serious to be repeated; so our impulsive allies were told that if they wished to fight they were to go out into the open, but theat they had been brought into the battery to work.

Whilst cover was being provided for our heavy guns and howitzers, a powerful mortar battery was in course of construction at the Koodsea Bagh, was one of the pleasantest places in the neighbourhood, shaded by orange and lemon trees, and odorous with the perfume of the fruit. Sheltered on three sides by a high wall, the position we had taken up, though but two hundred and fifty yards from the city, was but little exposed to the musketry fire of the insurgents. There was some hard work for our people in cutting away the trees; but the axe and the bill-hook were plied with hearty goodwill, and the ground was soon sufficiently cleared for the erection of the battery and the planting of the mortars. They were under the command of Major Tombs, and he was not one to lose a minute in doing good execution with his shells. Before the batteries were completed for the left attack, he was ready to open upon the lines between the Cashmere and the Water Bastions. But his orders were not to commence firing until the morning of the 11th, when it was expected that all the heavy guns and howitzers on the left would be fairly in position. Brind's battery all the time continued to pour in a destructive fire on the right, which so crippled the enemy, that the Moree Baston and all belonging to it had become little more than a name.

There was great joy throughout the Camp, when it was known that the batteries for the left attack were so far completed that the work of breaching could be commenced. The circumstances of our position were such as to engender impatience. Those who did not know the difficulties with which the Engineers were contending, were disappointed that the breaching operations along the whole line of the enemy's works had not sooner commenced. Doubtless, the first forecast, had been somewhat erroneous. Men, who are eager for the realisation of certain results, are wont to be over-sanguine in their calculation of the facilities of accomplishing them. But none could have worked with heartier zeal or more unflagging perseverance than the Artillery and Engineers engaged on that great work.

On the 11th of September, Scott's heavy guns[15] had been dragged into position, under such a fire of musketry as might have deterred men of fainter hearts; and then, although the battery, from causes to be presently displayed, could not be unmasked, there was no longer any reason why the final attack should be longer deferred. And well was it for us that there was no more delay. Mercifully the intellects of the besieged had been dulled for a time. But before our works were finished, they had woken up to a sense of the expediency of mounting heavy guns along the curtain between the Cashmere and the Water Bastions, from which such a fire could have been poured into our works on the left as to render them wholly untenable.[16] But God's providence arrested this calamity; the light had broken upon the enemy to late.

At eight o'clock, the fire from our twenty-four-pounders commenced. They were in the left section of No. 2 Battery, under the command of Major Campbell; and all the nine opened at the same moment with terrific effect upon the Cashmere Bastion. When the roar of this great first salvo had ceased, up went three ringing cheers of triumphant delight from the Artillery in the battery. We were now breaching in earnest. When the smoke cleared away, it was seen that the first discharge of our heavy guns had brought down vast masses of masonry, and that a few more such well-aimed blows would reduce their boasted defences to crumbling ruins. The guns on the Cashmere Bastion replied; and the enemy at least had some revenge, for they severely wounded the Commandant of the heavy guns, and sent him crippled from the battery. But a little more of our practice from both sections of the breaching battery, aided by Tombs's mortars on the Koodsea Bagh, soon reduced them to silence. Then it was a grand sight to see the walls of Delhi falling to pieces, as shot and shell rained heavily upon them; the breach widening and widening as the eight-inch shells bursting on it crest, brought down whole yards of parapet, the cruel signs of a future desolation becoming more apparent every hour. It was something which all can understand, apart from circumstances of time and space. But only those who had waited for the great opportunity—who, for months, had been insulted by an enemy behind the walls, who had seen their comrades falling around them, who had toiled day and night under burning suns and drenching rains, and had seemingly made no progress towards the reduction of the great Imperial City, can thoroughly appreciate the glorious excitement of seeing, opening out before them, day after day, the road that was to lead them to the re-occupation of Delhi. It was a turning point in the life of our Anglo-Indian Empire such as not even those who had seen the great crisis at Caubul had ever witnessed before.'

But there was heavier retribution yet to overtake the insurgents. An hour before noon, on the 12th of September, the advanced battery on the left (No. 3) was unmasked. It had been originally designed that it should open fire simultaneously with No. 2 on the preceding day; but it was found that this was impossible. The battery was constructed of sand-bags placed against the masonry of a part of the old Custom House. The walls had been so broken down as to admit of embrasures being made, through which it was intended that our guns should be pointed at the Water Bastion, only a hundred and sixty yards distant. These embrasures had been temporarily filled up with sand-bags, as a blind to the enemy, but, unfortunately, when our people began to remove them, it was found by the morning light that the embrasures, made under cover of the darkness, were so contrived as not to suffer our guns to be brought to bear upon the point intended. To Scott and Taylor this discovery was a bitter disappointment. It was necessary to reconstruct the cheeks of the embrasures, and thus to delay the opening of our guns upon the doomed city., Nothing could be more vexatious and embarrassing. Scott was eager to be first to open fires so as to dismount the enemy's guns at the very outset; but it was only too probable that if the battery were unmasked at mid-day, the insurgents would direct their heavy guns upon it before we could send in a shot. He was recommended to blow the sand-bags out of the embrasures, but this he refused to do, "being satisfied," as he said, "that the *debris* of the sand-bags would fall inwards, and seriously interfere with the accuracy of our fire." Whilst the question of the best made of procedure was under discussion, a Sikh sapper, with calm courage, quietly proceeded to throw outwards the sand-bags before his own gun. The example was caught up by the gunners behind the other embrasures, and so rapidly was the work of clearance effected, that our guns opened upon the enemy before they had discovered our designs. Then went forth such a stream of heavy shot from our eighteen-pounders, as within that easy range, even if less skilfully directed, must have soon smashed the enemy's guns and pounded the Water Bastion into ruins. The effect was almost instantaneous. The once symmetrical bastion became a shapeless mass of earth and masonry. Then, for the first time, the enemy learnt what was the cannonade we could keep up, now that, all our guns were in position, and the most sanguine must have despaired. All through the 12th and 13th the batteries on the left continued their breaching operations, under the direction of Kaye, Johnson,[17] Scott, and Tombs. The roar of fifty heavy pieces of ordnance was to be heard day and night without intermission. Never had our Siege Artillery a greater work before it. Never were guns more nobly served. Our trained gunners were few; but there was not a soldier in the camp who was not eager to handle a sponge-staff, or a portfire, or to being up the shot and shell to the cannon's mouth. Among these volunteers none were more active than the Lancers. They soon became serviceable gunners, and every officer in charge of a battery was right glad to have their help. It was a service of no little danger, especially in the advanced battery, which was exposed to the incessant musketry fire of the enemy. We could silence their batteries, but we could not stop this skirmishing, and our people were all day long dropping beneath the assaults of the hidden marksmen. The utmost care had been taken to protect the inmates of the battery. Scott had mantlets on all the guns, and he strictly enjoined officers and men to keep themselves well behind them. Thus many lives were saved; but notwithstanding these wise precautions one lamentable casualty in the battery caused a great spasm of grief throughout the whole camp. Whilst working one of the guns, Captain Fagan, of the Artillery, and officer of the highest promise, and, for his years, of great performance, was shot through the head. He had mounted a gun-carriage and was looking over the mantlet, when Scott went up to remonstrate with him. It was aid in camp, and Fagan himself thought, that he "bore a charmed life."

But scarcely had the words of caution been spoken when a musket-ball entered his temple, and he fell death-stricken at the feet of his commandant.[18]

It has been seen how, all this time, our Engineer officers worked, with unflagging perseverance, in the batteries. Alec Taylor was the heart and soul of every movement—always cheery, always active, never sparing himself—inspiring, aiding, animating all by his noble example. It was impossible not to admiration to endeavour to imitate him. He never complained; he never faltered; almost, it may be said that he never rested. He had the sole executive direction of all the Engineering department of the Siege Batteries, which opened the way to the interior of Delhi. The younger officers of the Engineers swore by him, and in truth there was something almost divine in his wonderful fertility of resource and the self-sacrifice which he continually displayed. He had studied the ground well, and he had seized, with quick soldierly eye, upon the exact points at which it would be desirable to erect our batteries. It was a happy stroke of genius to surprise and divert the enemy by running up a battery (No. 1) in a single night to play upon the Moree 'Bastion. It was Taylor's unaided idea—as was also the location of No. 3 Battery, the idea of which came suddenly upon him as an inspiration, and was worked out with wonderful promptitude and effect.

Among the many controversies which have grown out of this story of the Sepoy War, there is not one which it is more difficult to write of than the question as the whether the chief merit of the operations which resulted in the capture of Delhi is due to Colonel Baird Smith or to Captain Alexander Taylor. Such controversies are always painful; for it is not easy to extol the merits of one without seeming to detract from the claims of the other. I believe the real historic truth to be this. Neither could have taken Delhi without the help of the other. Alec Taylor was the necessary supplement of Baird Smith. The large brained chief of the Engineer Staff required just such a second-in-command to carry his plans into execution as he found in the noble-spirited Field-Engineer. The condition of Baird Smiths health was, as I have already said, such as would have sent most men to their beds. Lame from the effects of a painful and neglected would on the ankle—suffering acutely from one of the cruel scourges of the country, which compelled him to drench himself with opium and brandy, he could not move about from place to place, so as to become a badly presence, familiar to the eyes of men of all branches and all ranks of the army.[19] It has, therefore, sometimes been said: "We never saw Baird Smith." Taylor, on the other hand, though sometimes suffering from fever, was to be seen everywhere. He had great physical activity and powers of endurance to give practical expression to the zeal and courage which animated him. But the general directions for the conduct of our engineering operations, often even in minute details, emanated from Baird Smith. His thoughtfulness in respect of everything that could in any way contribute to our success is patent in the masses of manuscripts which lie before me. In his own handwriting may be read all his original conceptions and his amended designs; but these last were rare, for it was but seldom, except under pressure of altered circumstances, that he saw any good reason for modifying his first projects. But all these projects might have failed if there had been a less able, a less active, and a less courageous officer than Alec Taylor at the head of the executive officers of the Engineer Brigade. He was one who thought nothing impossible, and all men worked under him with the heartiest goodwill, for he in spired and animated all who came in contact with him in battery of in trench. Those who were above him were equally impressed by his noble exertions. "If I survive to -marrow," said John Nicholson, on the eve of the assault, "I will let all the world know that Alec Taylor took Delhi." This was characteristic of the brave impulsive man, who never lived to tell the story of the siege. But he erred, as he did on a previous occasion of which I have spoken, in not recognising the difference between a responsible and an irresponsible officer, whether at the head of a regiment or the head of an Army.

No one acknowledged Taylor's services more ungrudingly than Baird Smith himself; but he could not consent that History should accept the statement that the Chief Engineer had been in the background, doing nothing, whilst his first-assistant had gone to the front and done everything for the direction of the operations of the siege. "I think," he wrote to his wife some time afterwards, "that you may dismiss from your mind all sense of trouble about the injustice done to my work at Delhi. It is just as certain as that I am alive to say so, that from the day I joined, to the day I left, not a single vital act was done but under my orders and on my sole responsibility. And I know well that, but for my resolute determination, humanly speaking, there would have been no siege of Delhi at all; and even that assault which gave value by its success to all the exertions that were made would have ended in deplorable disaster, had I not withstood with effect the desire of General Wilson to withdraw the troops from the city on the failure of Brigadier Campbell's column. Nobody does heartier justice to Taylor's devotion, capacity, and zeal than I do. No personal consideration would, for one moment, induce me to detract, even in the faintest, degree, from them. But he was, throughout, my most able and most trusted subordinate, working wholly at my risk and on my responsibility in the one department entrusted to him—namely, the executive duties." And in another letter to a friend in the Royal Artillery he said: "I would not willingly do the very faintest injustice either to Captain Taylor or to any of the other junior officers of the brigade, to whose noble co-operation, given always without reserve and in the most cordial spirit, I was so deeply indebted, and for which I have done my best upon all occasions to express my gratitude. These feelings are especially strong in reference to Taylor, whom I found to be ever, not only the most energetic and competent of seconds, but in all relations a true and right-hearted gentleman. I should be ashamed of myself if I permitted any petty feelings to influence me in estimating his worth; and I feel assured that no credit which may be due to me will ever be really diminished by my doing the amplest and heartiest justice to every man who worked under my orders. But it was with myself alone that the entire responsibility for the conception, progress, and issue of the engineering operations in every essential point rested; and had we failed in our attack, this fact would have been recorded so often and so often and so emphatically, that I should have had none to share the fatal consequences with me."[20] It is better that, in such a case, Baird Smith should be left to speak for himself. On the subject of responsibility there could be no doubt; and whatsoever question might arise as to the design and execution of the detailed operations of the siege, Alec Taylor was not a man to deny, that as the risk of failure was his chief's, so also should be the credit of success.

But the chapter, which I have just completed, devoted mainly to the exploits of the Artillery. I have written in vain, if I have not shown what tremendous work lay before our gunners throughout that critical week; with what consummate courage they faced the unexampled dangers before them, and with what wondrous patience and calm skill they overcame all obstacles and opened the way for the entrance of the British forces into Delhi. I doubt whether there is any incident of History surpassing in the boldness alike of its conception and of its execution this bombardment of the Imperial City of the Moguls. But this was only the crowning work—the grand culmination of weeks and months of toil upon the Ridge, vexatious, harassing toil, rather demonstrative than effective, little tending to produce any immediate results upon the enemy, to attract the special attention of commanders, or to excite the admiration of comrades. In a little time the heavy-battery service came to be regarded as part of the routine work of the Camp. Its importance in keeping down the fire of the enemy and in arresting their frequent sallies upon our outposts by showing ourselves continually on the alert, could not be overvalued. To have slackened fire would have been to encourage and embolden the insurgents; by leaving them to believe either that our material resources were on the ebb, or that our personal strength was so reduced by death and disease that we were unable to man our batteries. Few but those with scant knowledge of the position talked of this untiring energy as "wasting our ordnance stores." Had our Rear been closed, it would have been wholly different; but as it was, we were never in any real want of ammunition, and we could afford to expend some powder and shot without every discharge from our batteries palpably producing any great material results.

It is among the accidents of the Service, which all good soldiers will cheerfully accept, that whilst one by the very nature of his employment has opportunities of distinguishing himself and finding a niche in some historical episode, by which his name, perhaps, may be remembered in later days, another is condemned to tail on unnoticed, doing equally good service to the State, but not of a nature to attract the regards of the Official Reporter or of the Military Annalist. So it was, emphatically, with the Bengal Artillery during the long so-called siege of Delhi. The Horse Artillery and the Light Field Batteries had opportunities of distinguishing themselves in dashing charges against the assailants of our outposts, but the Heavy Artillery on the Ridge had no occasion of displaying their high qualities save by their indomitable perseverance and endurance, until the longed-for summons came to go down below and to knock the main defences of the city to pieces. How they did that work, when the time came, I have endeavoured to show. That General Wilson, an old and good Artillery officer, did not appreciate—at least did not acknowledge—the magnificent services of his own branch, as might have been anticipated, alike from his sympathies and his experiences, was generally felt by the regiment. His honesty, if not his discernment, was conspicuous in this. But the omissions apparent in the

General's despatches caused much bad feeling in the corps and led to some painful controversy. Briad, with his wonted earnestness and directness of purpose, pleaded the cause of his comrades in language which men in authority were not accustomed to and did not approve. Some wrongs were righted, but others remained unredressed. It is enough to state that the Major Scott of these pages, who fought his Light Battery so nobly, before the day of assault, and then went down to the post of danger, to command the most exposed of the Breaching Batteries, still remains undecorated.

REFERENCES

1. See the following, from a private letter written by Baird Smith after the capture of Delhi: "an attack of camp scurvy had filled my mouth with sores, shaken every joint in my body, and covered me all over with livid spots, so that I was marvellously unlovely to look upon. A smart knock on the ankle, from the splinter of a shell which burst in my face—in itself, however, a mere bagatelle of a wound—had been of necessity neglected, under the pressing and incessant calls upon me, and had grown worse and worse, till the whole foot below the ankle became a black mass, and seemed to threaten mortification. I insisted, however, on being allowed to use it until the place was taken, mortification or not; and though the pain was sometimes horrible, I carried my point, and kept up to the last.... and to crown the pleasant catalogue, I was worn to a shadow by a constant diarrhoea, and consumed as much opium, with as little effect, as would have done credit to my father-in-law (De Quincey)".—MS. Correspondence.
2. Wilson's remarks are written in pencil on the copy of the "Memorandum by the Chief Engineer," which Baird Smith submitted to the General. It is now before me with Wilson's marginal notes.
3. It is said to have been written by Baird Smith.
4. MS. Memorandum by an Engineer Officer.
5. Medley, Page 73.
6. There had been a light battery previously (evening of the 6th) erected upon the plateau of the Ridge to the left hand of the Sammy House. The object of this was to keep the

ground clear and to protect the operations going on below. This battery contained eight light pieces—six 9-pounders and two 24-pound howitzers—under the command of Captain Remmington.

7. I have before said (vol. ii. pp. 594, 595) that the services of the Foot Artillery, during the period which preceded the actual siege, have been insufficiently recorded. It seems that there were some official misunderstandings as to the authority, whose duty it was to report them, which caused them not to be reported at all.

8. It was said of Major Brind that he "never slept"—and the statement was no great exaggeration. I am told that he more than once addressed his men, saying, as he shouldered a musket, "Now, you lie down and rest. Your Commandant will defend the battery." The same informant, himself an officer of the highest gallantry, often mentioned in preceding pages of this narrative, said to me, "The talk about Victoria Crosses—Brind is a man who should be covered with them from head to foot." See also the letters of Major Reid, now (1875) Sir Charles Reid, one of the foremost of the Delhi heroes: "battery No. 1 was commanded by my dear old friend, Major Brind, who had been constantly on duty with me on the Ridge, and who had given me most able assistance on the night of the Eed attack. Indeed, on all occasions the exertions of this noble officer were indefatigable. He was always to be found where his presence was most required; and the example he set to his officers and men was beyond all praise. A fiuer soldier I never met."

9. Medley.

10. "No. 1 Battery was unquestionably the key of the attack, and on its success depended the opening of Delhi to our assaulting columns. The progress of the other batteries depended essentially on its efficiency; and but for your moral courage, clear perception, and unwavering resolution in arming and working it, in spite of all obstacles consequences would have followed causing the greatest embarrassment."—*Colonel Baird Smith is Major Brind.—MS. Correspondence.*

11. MS. Memoranda by Engineer and Artillery Officers.

12. It was completed on the night of the 10th—11th, and the heavy guns from the left section of No. 1, then joined; others were brought down from the Park.

13. Baird Smith had recommended that No. 3 Battery should be commenced before No. 2. (*Memorandum by Chief Engineer*), but General Wilson had objected to this, saying, "The commencement of No. 3 Battery before No. 2 is, I think, objectionable, and will cause a fearful loss of life from the untouched batteries in the Cashmere Bations. It would be much safer to silence the guns on the left bastion before erecting No. 3." (*MS. Notes*). Wilson was right. I am told, however, that in point of fact, No. 2 Battery did open fire before No. 3—indeed, before it was completely constructed.

14. "They were merely unarmed Native Pioneers, and not meant to be fighting men. With the passive courage so common to Natives, as man after man was knocked over, they would stop a moment, weep a little over their fallen friend, pop his body in a row along with the rest, and then work on as before."—*Medley*, pp. 82, 83.

15. Norman says: "The establishment of Major Scott's battery within one hundred and eighty yards of the walls, to arm which heavy guns had to be dragged from the rear under a constant fire of musketry, was an operation that could rarely have been equalled in war." Under instructions received from the Chief Engineer, Scott had brought down his guns on the night of the 10th, but on reaching the site of the intended battery, after a difficult march, he found the works incomplete, or rather scarcely commenced. The ground had been cleared, but there were no signs of a battery. To have left the guns within such an easy distance from the enemy would have insured their destruction, so he was compelled to with draw them before daylight.

16. "So nearly were they being ready, that had the subsequent assault been delayed for forty-eight hours, I believe that we could not have assaulted at all, but must have been driven from our batteries, or had our men knocked to pieces there—*Medley*.

17. Captain (now Sir Edwin) Johnson, Assistant Adjutant-General of Artillery, had taken the place of Major Campbell, disabled in the left section of No. 2. Battery.

18. "When the enemy discovered the position and object of No. 3 battery, they at once placed heavy guns in position on the opposite side of the river to take No. 3 in flank and succeeded in dismounting one of the 18-pounders. Traverses were immediately constructed which saved the remainder,

but the continuous stream of shot shell, and bullets, directed on this battery by the enemy from front, flanks, and curtain proved the importance attached to it by them, and it was a matter of astonishment to all present that, thanks to the discipline and untiring devotion of officers and men, the battery was able to open the required breach so rapidly (less than thirty-six hours), so effectively, and at so small a sacrifice of life."—*MS. Memorandam by an Engineer Officer.*

19. Baird Smith says that brandy was his daily sustenance, and that it had no other effect upon him than had no other effect upon him than that of increasing his capacity for work. His brain was never clearer or more active. It carried him through the siege—but afterwards, rest and purer air enabled him to lay aside such dangerous diet.

20. MS. Correspondence.

5

Capture of Delhi

In the meanwhile, in Head-Quarters' Camp, upon the Ridge, Wilson and Baird Smith were taking counsel together as to the organisation of the assaulting columns, which were to move into the city, when the breaches should be pronounced practicable. Chamberlain was still confined to his tent, but he went out sometimes in a dhooly, and was every ready to put forth sound opinions on all military questions, both of principle and detail. One thing was certain—that the universal voice of the Camp had proclaimed John Nicholson as the man of men to lead the storming columns and to beckon them on to victory. He had come down to Delhi surcharged with the idea that he was ordained to plant the British standard on the proud Palace of the Moguls or to die the soldier's death at the head of his men. The decease of Sir Henry Lawrence had given an increased sobriety—indeed, solemnity—to his demeanour. If, before this, he had been possessed by any vain ambitions; if he had thought of the plaudits of his countrymen and the records of history, all this had passed away. He now thought only of the last words of his dying master—of the words which Lawrence wished to be engraved upon his tomb—and he also "tried to do his duty." He wrote that he wished to "get alongside" of Herbert Edwardes, that he might become more steadfast in his faith and tread more surely in the footsteps of his great exemplar who had died at Lucknow.

On the 13th, Taylor announced that the breaches were practicable. All was then ready for the delivery of the assault on the following day. The composition of the several columns had been minutely arranged. Their leaders were nominated. The precise direction which each column was to take, was laid down, and Baird Smith had mapped out on oil-paper for each commander a plan of the operations entrusted to him, and to the other leaders, to be taken with him for his guidance. A meeting of the principal officers was then summoned. All were present at the meeting, except Nicholson, who purposely or accidentally was down in the heavy batteries watching the effect of Scott's guns and Tombs' mortars.[1] He felt that his position was secured; and knowing that he was too prone to be intemperate in speech, he might have thought it better not to be present at a discussion, in the course of which he might express some divergencies of opinion without becoming moderation. Whatsoever the cause, the meeting was held without his animating presence. Wilson unfolded his plans. Nothing could exceed the clearness of the whole design or the minuteness, which left nothing to be guessed at or puzzled over by commanding officers. Baird Smith's charts, some of which are now before me, were guide posts which no one could misunderstand. But there were some inquiries to make surety doubly sure—and some minute explanations in reply. Though satisfactory to the inquirers the answers added little to the original information. And the officers upon whom their several responsibilities had been thrown, quieted Wilson's tent eager for the coming struggle, and full of grand expectations of triumphant success.

The force was divided into four columns and a column of Reserve. The First Column commanded by Brigadier General Nicholson, was to consist of—

Her Majesty's 75th Regiment	300 strong.
1st Bengal Fusiliers	250"
2nd Punjab Infantry	450"

Engineer officers attached, Lieutenants Medley, Lang, and Bingham[2].

This force was to storm the breach near the Cashmere Bastion and escalade the face of the bastion.

The Second Column was to be commanded by Brigadier Jones, C.B. It consisted of —

Her Majesty's 8th Regiment .... 250 strong.
"2nd Fusiliers .... 250"
4th Sikh Infantry .... 350"

Engineer officers attached, Lieutenants Greathed, Hovenden, and Pemberton."[3]

This column was to storm the breach in the Water Bastion.

The Third Column was placed under Colonel Campbell, of the Fifty-second. It was to assault by the Cashmere Gate after its explosion by the Engineers should have taken effect; and was thus constituted:

Her Majesty's 52nd Regiment .... 200 strong.
Kumaon Battalion .... 250"
1st Punjab Infantry .... 500"

Engineer officers attached, Lieutenants home, Salkeld, and Tandy.[4]

The command of the Fourth Column was assigned to Major Charles Reid of the Sirmoor Battalion, who had held so long and so gallantly the post at Hindoo Rao's house. It was to attack and to clear the suburbs of Paharunpore and Kishengunje and to enter the city by the Lahore Gate. Its components were:

Detachments of Enropean and
Native Begiments. — 860 men, not including
Sirmoor Battalion. — Jummoo troops.
Guides Infantry.
Detachment of Dograhs.

Engineer officers attached, Lieutenants Maunsell and Tennant.

The Fifth or Reserve Column was commanded by Brigadier Longfield, and was thus composed:

> Her Majesty's 61st, 250 men (Lieutenant-Colonel Deacon); 4th Punjab Infantry, 450 men (Captain Wilde); Wing Belooch Battalion, 300 men (Lieutenant-Colonel Farquhar); Jheend Auxiliaries, 300 men (Lieutenant-Colonel Dunsford)—Total, 1300; besides 200 of 60th Rifles, under Lieutenant-Colonel Jones, after they had covered the advance of the stormers.

But there was one thing more thing more to be done before the assaulting columns could be let loose. Captain Taylor had reported that the breaches were practicable. But it was expedient that they should be examined by some picked Engineer officers. It was a service of some danger; but there was not an officer in the brigade who would not have eagerly undertaken the duty. Lieutenants Medley and Lang were to explore the Cashmere breach and Greathed and Home were to examine the breach by the Water Bastion. It was a moonbless night, but clear under the broad starlight. And as the gallant subalterns went forth to their appointed work, taking with them a few picked riflemen of the Sixtieth, the guns and mortars from the breaching batteries were still playing upon the enemy's defences, making night hideous with their roar, and well-nigh bringing the services of our exploring parties to a disastrous close. But at ten o'clock there was a lull and the perils of the Engineers were then limited to the assaults of the enemy. "The enemy's skirmishers were firing away on our right," wrote one of the exploring party (Medley), "some thirty yards from us, and the flashes of their muskets lit up the air as if they had been fireflies. The shells and rockets of the enemy at one moment illumined the space ground, as they darted over our heads and then left us in total darkness." But the work was done; the desired information was gained and the results of the explorations were duly reported to the Chief Engineer. The breaches would have been better for a little more cannonading; but Baird Smith determined that this would not countervail the evils of further delay; so he despatched a note to Wilson urging immediate action. The General wisely endorsed the recommendation, and the order went forth for the delivery of the assault on the morrow's dawn.

Before daybreak the whole assaulting force had assembled near Ludlow Castle, with the exception of Reid's column, which was to advance from the post at Hindoo Rao's and to clear the suburbs of Kishengunje and Paharunpore. Not a man was absent from his post; and few were present who were not eager for the coming affray. After the muster and the dram, they would have rushed at the breaches, with a cheery English hurrah! But, as almost ever happens, there were unexpected causes of delay, and when all were ready for the advance, the signal was not given. No soldiers, seeing their work clearly before them, can bear to wait. Nothing is more depressing than that hour of the "shuddering dawn"—a time when the vital power is ever at its weakest—when men wonder over unexplained delays, and curse their commanders for keeping them waiting. This period of expectancy, as night kindles into day, takes the eagerness for fighting out of them grievously, unless it be sustained by stimulants; and the effect of these, if not renewed, is transient and dangerous.[5] The reaction may be worse than the first craving. The cause of delay was this. What Baird Smith had anticipated was now coming to pass. The insurgents having discovered our intentions had during the night, when our batteries were quiescent, filled up the main breach by which our columns were to enter Delhi. Skilled engineers were among them, who well knew the use of sand-bags, and moreover could improvise *chevaux-de-frise*. This had been done in the night; so orders went down, in hot haste, to the breaching batteries, to open fire again. This was done promptly and effectually; and soon the ramparts were cleared and our columns awaiting the appointed signal to advance.

Never, in the history of modern warfare, has an officer found himself in a position so environment and embarrassed with difficulties as that which General Wilson was now called upon to confront. The very thought of the responsibility before him had killed one general. A few weeks on the Ridge had sent another to his grave, and despatched a third for very life's sake to Simlah. But not one of them had attempted an assault. The two last had stood on the defensive; and even that was too much for frail humanity to bear up against. But Wilson, who had brought with him to Delhi all the enervating wear-and-tear of the first outbreak at Meerut, following closely upon a critical attack of small-pox, had toiled for months upon the Ridge, during the most trying season of the year, with all responsibilities upon him. His health, as time advanced, had failed him more and more; like Barnard, he was unable to obtain sleep, and some men, in like circumstances, would have followed Reid's example, and betaken himself to the nearest sanitarium. But Wilson, though feeling painfully, and bitterly deploring, his growing infirmities, determined not to abandon his post. With a candour most honourable to him, he confessed his physical prostration, and the mental disturbances which accompanied it. He was a man always of quick temper; but now, his irritability had become chronic, and he had none of that unfailing urbanity, that unceasing tenderness for others, which had glorified the last days of Sir Harry Barnard.[6] He was not, therefore, popular with the Army—not even with his own branch of it—and he was often thwarted by men in high places, who knowing his difficulties and responsibilities ought to have condoned his infirmities and supported him. The situation was cast upon him; he did not seek it. And with his high sense of duty and love of country, he would have given over the command to another, with all its high promise of honours and rewards and historical renown, if he had known one of sufficiently high rank equal to the work before him.

And now the critical moment had come when a great deed was to be accomplished or a desolating failure was to stain the annals of our country. The strongest brain might have been disturbed—the strongest nerves might have been shaken by the prospect which lay before Wilson on that September morning. With the Heavy Artillery at our disposal it had been no impossible work to breach the defences of the city. With the indomitable pluck of the British soldier it might be no difficult work to carry the breaches thus opened. The difficulty was to commence after the carriage of the defences of the city had been accomplished. It was said that Baird Smith knew Delhi well. And in truth he did. He knew the state of the defences thoroughly; but it was doubted whether he knew as much of the interior of the city—the great imperial capital of India, with all its vast piles of buildings, it numerous covered places, its streets, its lanes, and its bazaars. This, however, was a mistake. He knew Delhi well, inside and out.[7] But had he known the city as it was before the siege, how could he, even with the help of spies, know what changes had been wrought since in May we were expelled from Delhi? Of all our officers the man who knew most was Sir John Metcalfe,[8] our City Magistrate, ere the storm burst upon us and swept all authority away. His information was ever most reliable, and it was freely given. But even he could not say what might have been done, during those four months of Native occupation; what open streets might have been turned into blind alleys—what houses might have been raised for better command of observation and of fire—what spaces might have been cleared, what batteries erected, in prospect of the inevitable day of assault. We knew only that the enemy relied not on their moral, but on their material resources—not on the number and strength of their men, but on the number and strength of their men, but on the number and strength of their houses. Wilson saw that the crowning victory was to be gained only be overcoming these material resources. His columns had to fight their way to the Palace, to plant the British Standard on its walls, and to secure the person of the King. He knew that our troops had no appetite for street fighting, and he had a causeless lack of confidence in the officers and men of his Force. What wonder then that broken in body and in spirit, by the toil and exposure of months and the ever-present, wearing sense of the responsibility that lay upon him, he should have shuddered, as he looked down, through the grey dawn of that September morning, on the great city which lay before him; and that thinking of the paucity of troops told off for the assault and the scarcity of available fighting men left for the protection of his Camp on the Ridge, he should have painfully doubted the success of the enterprise on which he was launched.[9]

The general design of the attack was this: the Infantry, divided into four columns and a column of Reserve, each guided by Engineer officers[10] were to cross the ditch at different points by the aid of scaling ladders, to clear the outer defences of the city, taking possession of all bastions, guns, and gateways, and establishing defensible posts. This having been accomplished, it was to be left to the discretion of commanding officers, under the general direction of Nicholson, to determine whether, "dependent upon the circumstances of the moment, and the resistance of force," it would be advisable to direct the columns to clear the streets of the city in their front and vicinity, or to wait for the arrival of Artillery to aid them. The roads to the Palace and Selim Ghur having been rendered practicable, a vigorous bombardment of those places was to be undertaken with the least possible delay, every available mortar being conveyed into the city and placed in the Magazine or other suitable positions.[11] It was impossible to calculate the amount of resistance except upon the spot, so no one could say how much time it would occupy to clear the inner defences of the city, the streets and squares, and covered buildings, and to bombard the Palace of the Moguls. But it was the general conception that all this might be accomplished, and the person of the King secured, within three or four days from the time of our first delivery of the assault. It was thought, however, that much might be done on the first day; as the enemy, panicstruck and confused, dreading the terrible retribution which would descend upon them, might betake themselves to sudden flight, and clear the way for the advance of the English. Baird Smith's maps had indicated the points within the city at which the several columns, after clearing the outer defences, were to take post; and the Delhi Gate, beyond the Palace, was assigned to the First Column. It will appear, as the narrative advances, how erroneous was this forecast.

It was a fine still morning. As day broke and the columns took up their positions, awaiting the appointed signal, the heavy guns were still thundering at the defences, keeping down the enemy's fire, and enlarging the breaches for our entrance. Nicholson's column was on the left of the Koodsea Bagh. Jones, with the Second Column, was a little space to Nicholson's left. These two formed the Left Attack. Some way to the right on the road leading towards the Cashmere Gate was Campbell with the Third Column; and the Reserve were somewhat behind them. Eager was every man for the signal—the sight of the Sixtieth Rifles rushing to the front, and the sound of their bugle-call. For fast pound the shot from the ramparts of the enemy, and our people of the leading columns were ordered to lie down on the ground and wait. When the time had come for the advance, Nicholson, who directed the general attack, went over to Jones, and, placing his arm on the Brigadier's shoulder in token of comradeship asked him if he was ready to move. Having received a prompt answer in the affirmative, he rejoined his own column. Then the order was given, and the voice of our heavy guns, which had been roaring at their loudest, suddenly dropped into silence; the Rifles sounded the advance; the regiments up, and with a cry of exultation surged onward, and, in the teeth of a heavy fire from the enemy's works, steadily went up the slope of the glacis.

Whilst the First Column were thus establishing themselves, the Second under Brigadier Jones of the Queen's Sixty-first were doing their work gallantly and well. The fire of the enemy fell heavily upon them as they ascended the glacis, and the slaughter was terrible among the brave fellows of the ladder party, guided by the Engineers Greathed and Hovenden, who were the first to fall, wounded but not mortally, beneath the pitiless storm of the insurgents.[12] The column was divided into three sections. Colonel Greathed, of the Eighth Foot, commanded the first section, of which his splendid regiment formed the principal, part. Captain Boyd was at the head of the second; and Brigadier Jones brought up the Reserve. The stormers carrying the ladders were led by Captain George Baynes and Lieutenant Metje of the Eighth. When the signal was given for the advance they rushed forward from a covert of rose-bushes, behind which they had been partially hidden from the sight of the insurgents, who had gathered more thickly on the walls and were ready to sweep us down as we advanced. And awfully they did their work. The Grenadiers of the Eighth went forward manfully with the ladders on their shoulders, but so encumbered could not fire a shot; and they had no covering party.[13] Thus exposed naked to the fierce fire of the enemy, they fell fast upon the slope of the glacis or the edge of the ditch. One volley brought down five of our ladder-men. When Metje and some of his followers picked up the ladders and went forward they also were struck down and disabled. So fearful, indeed, was the carnage that when Baynes found himself opposite the Water Bastion, the seventy-five men who had started with him on their perilous mission were reduced to only twenty-five. For two days these twenty-five men, without a commissioned officer—for Metje had been carried wounded to the rear and Baynes had been disabled by sharp sickness—held their position in the Water Bastion under Sergeant Walker, and did excellent service.

Then came the difficulties of the escalade. On the crest of the glacis our men were falling fast. So furious was the fire of the enemy, and so heavy the shower of stones and bricks from the crumbling walls, which the maddened insurgents poured upon us, that it was difficult, for a little time, to plant the ladders in the ditch so as to ascend the scarp on the other side. Medley of the Engineers, who led the ladder party of the First Column, received a ball in the fleshy part of the arm. Fortunately the bone escaped; and his brave heart would not suffer him to halt in his work for mere bodily pain, however acute. He went on with the storming party. Two or three ladders, after this brief check, were thrown down into the ditch, and presently the wall beneath the breach was gallantly escaladed. The column was divided into two sections. One composed mainly of the Bengal Fusiliers under Jacob, was personally commanded by Nicholson himself. The other, of which the Seventy-fifth Queen's were the chief components, was led by Colonel Herbert of that regiment. Determined that his leadership should be not a name, but a fact, Nicholson went on in advance of his men, followed by Jacob and Greville of the Fusiliers, and was the first to mount the wall. The other section of the column pushed on with like eagerness. Lieutenant Fitzgerald, of the Seventyfifth, was the first to ascend, but he was shot down, in the moment of victory, and died the hero's death at the head of his men. Others not less gallant and, often, not more fortunate, took his place; and soon both sections of the First Column had gained the ramparts, carried the breach near the Cashmere Bastion, and taken up their position at the Main Guard.

The main body of the Second Column went steadily on, and having made good its entrance by the breach in the, Cashmere Curtain, went forward, at the double, across the open space, inside the Cashmere Bastion, where they inclined to their Right. Then seeing some men rushing into the city on his Left, Jones cried out to them to "bear away to the right along the ramparts." They were at that time running at the topmost of their speed, the men with jones being partly of Nicholson's column and partly of his own. As they were proceeding along the road leading to the Caubul Gate, the Brigadier's bugler cried out that the enemy were firing down the streets. This fire was speedily answered, and the insurgents left remaining on the ramparts ran like hares before us and so escaped the fire of our eager soldiery. In the Moree Bastion the gunners made bold resistance; standing to their guns with a gallantry worthy of the great school in which they had been taught. But our English Infantry went in amongst them, bayoneted them as they stood, and cast them dead or dying from the ramparts into the ditch below. Then our people leapt up exultingly on the parapet of the Moree Bastion—that grand defence of the enemy, from which for months an unceasing shower of shot had been poured in upon the besiegers; and waved their caps rejicingly to their comrades on the Ridge. Thence they had a prevision of what was going on elsewhere. They saw the Sepoys in their white dresses, huddling on confusedly from Kishengunje, and they saw the Cavalry and Horse Artillery forming up, under Hope Grant, and sustaining a heavy fire from the insurgents in the suburbs. The column then advanced to the Caubul Gate, where Jones having ascended to the summit of it, ordered a party of his men to fire down the streets on each side of the Canal. The order was promptly obeyed, and one of the enemy's deserted guns was turned on the Lahore Gate, from which the enemy had been keeping up a galling fire, whilst the houses adjacent to the Caubul Gate and along both sides of the Canal, were occupied by our own people. The Caubul Gate was now secure, and it remained for us only to plant the British flag on the summit of it. This was done under Jones's orders, by a private of the Sixty-first, whom he rewarded in the presence of his comrades.[14] The regimental bugle-calls were then sounded; the different corps were gathered together; and men shook hands with and congratulated each other and somewhat marvelled that any were alive. The light of these first congratulations was soon darkened by the gloomy thought of their diminished ranks. They had done their work nobly and well; but how many brave men and good soldiers had been left, dead or dying behind them; how many friends and comrades had been lost to them since the dram had been served out in the early morning. The enemy fought well to the last, and the bloody instructions which we had taught, were returning to plague the inventors. Alas! for our shattered columns.

It was not until after the flag had been planted on the Caubul Gate that Nicholson joined the Second Column. He had diverged from the intended line of advance to suppress a brisk fire of musketry, from some houses on his left flank, between the Cashmere and the Moree Bastions, which was severely harassing his people. Having turned aside for the reason stated, as men must at times under heavy pressure of circumstances, and entered the town, he did not meet Jones at the Caubul Gate until more than an hour after the Second Column had reached it. The enemy then observing our inactivity, regained somewhat of their courage and began to pour in a sharp fire of musketry and cannon-shot.[15] The men of the Second Column were then resting from their work. Misunderstanding the quietude of their demeanour, the young Brigadier-General exclaimed, "The men are not in hand." Upon this Greathed fired up and said, "What do you want done? Tell me and I'll soon show you that they are in hand." Nicholson then, whose words had conveyed a meaning beyond what he had probably intended, made some wise suggestions as to the positions of the enemy and the disposition of our troops and then went back to join the First Column. Jones had received orders to remain at the Caubul Gate until he might hear tidings of the fall of the Jumma Musjid; so he got his men well lodged in houses commanding the approaches and waited for the signal to advance.

Meanwhile, a sad misadventure was befalling us in the First Column. Still annoyed by the fire from the Lahore Gate, Nicholson determined to take it, and got together a number of men of different regiments to follow him on this enterprise. It has been said that there were officers without their men and men without their officers, so that they were a "mere rabble." It was a hazardous duty that loomed before them; for the way from the Caubul to the Lahore Gate lay through a narrow lane swept by artillery and commanded by houses occupied by the enemy. If there is one thing to dishearten the British soldier more than all else it is the thought of street fighting. He can receive a charge of Cavalry with a loud hurrah. He can march steadily on the enemy's blazing batteries and scale their ramparts, or enter the breaches in their walls, as though it were mere play-work. But he is not used to street-fighting. He does not know what barricades may have been suddenly thrown up; he does not know what masked batteries may be erected: and he fancies that every house is full of a hostile soldiery, and that every window is an embrasure, at which a skilled marksman may be placed, and with aim steadied by the sense of his own security. And so it was now. Nicholson's column having entered the outskirts of the city, found itself in a long narrow lane lined with marksmen on both sides, and commanded by some more distant positions of the enemy. It was soon obvious that some of the enemy's guns had been brought forward to scatter confusion in our ranks, and, in our helplessness, to send back the advanced columns to the Ridge. The men were falling fast. Major George Jacob of the First Fusiliers, an officer of distinguished gallantry, received his death-wound; but refused to be carried to the rear[16] Captain Greville and Lieutenant Speke doing duty with the Fusiliers, were struck down,[17] and other officers fell disabled and helpless under the enemy's fire. Then there was something of a wave—a pause. The British soldier found himself in the position which he most hated. It was not fair fighting. He was in a trap. Nicholson saw it all—saw what was depressing the hearts and checking the onward movement of our fighting men. So he drew himself up to his full height, and with his sword raised high above his head, called upon his men to follow him. To some at least of the defenders of Delhi, that face and figure must have been familiar. Others saw a man of commanding presence, whose position at the head of the column, and whose gestures of command, indicated that he was a great chief. His lofty stature rendered him so conspicuous, that if he had been' a private soldier, some rifleman at a window or on a housetop would have taken deadly aim at him, and he would have sent one more hated Feringhee to his account. But it was not a single life that he took; it was the life of a whole army.

Nicholson was shot through the body. He knew at once that he had received his death-wound; but he begged that he might not be carried back to Camp until the capture of Delhi were secure. This, however, was impossible, and he was gently removed to the Hospital on the Ridge. The surgeons who attended him were doubtful of the final issue, for the ball had not touched the lungs. But he had got the death-chill upon him—the worst sign of all; and there was really no hope for him. He could not help chafing, too, under the miserable infliction which had taken him away in the very hour of the grand fulfilment of his hopes, and rendered him helpless as a child. It was a sad addition to his own suffering to know that his brother, Charles Nicholson, who had commanded the Punjabees, in the First Column, had been brought into Camp with a shattered arm, and that nothing but amputation could save him. He was a fine gallant soldier of high promise, but his lofty stature had made him a sure mark for the enemy, and the promise could never be fulfilled.[18]

It was the apportioned duty of the Third Column to enter the city through the Cashmere Gate; and to this end a party of Engineers was told off to blow in the gate with powder-bags. The officers appointed for the performance of this hazardous duty were Lieutenants Home and Salkeld. The non-commissioned officers were Sergeants Carmichael, Burgess, and Smith. With them went a party of Native Sappers. It was broad daylight when they started. Leaving Ludlow Castle at the double, headed by a party of the Sixtieth Rifles, they reached the road leading to the Customs House, where they opened out: the Sappers under Lieutenant Home, and the carrying party with the powder-bags under Lieutenant Salkeld—Sergeant Smith bringing up the rear. Forward they went, at first unseen by the enemy, straight upon the Cashmere Gate, followed by the Sixtieth Rifles and the other components of the column under Colonel Campbell, awaiting the explosion and prepared for the deadly work before them. Home, with his bugler, was first down into the ditch. The danger of the enterprise was then upon them. The designs of the exploding party had been perceived by the enemy; and as they crossed over the broken drawbridge leading from the outer to the inner gate a brisk shower of musketry was poured upon them. But they made good their hazardous march to the point at which the explosion was to be effected. Many were the brilliant episodes of adventure which illustrated the siege of Delhi; but not one more heroic than this. Home had planted his bag, but on Carmichael advancing with his powder on his shoulder, he was shot down by a death-dealing musket-ball. Smith then went forward and placed his dying comrade's bag in position, having also placed his own, and prepared the fuzes for ignition. Salkeld stood ready with a slow match[19] in his hand, but as he was lighting it, he was struck down; a bullet in his arm and another in his leg had sent their death messages to him. In falling, he held out the match and called on Smith to take it. Burgess, who stood nearest to Salkeld, took the match but could not ignite the charge. Smith then was in the act of giving him a box of Lucifer-matches, when Burgess was shot down by a bullet through the body. Smith was now alone, or thought he was alone, for he had lost sight of Home for some time. The moment was a critical one; but he had succeeded in striking a light and was applying it, when a portfire, which it was thought had been extinguished, went off in his face. There was a confusing fog of smoke and dust as he scrambled down into the ditch, and presently a roar and a crash, significant of a deed accomplished. The gate had been shattered by the explosion, but not with the destructive effect that had been anticipated by the assailants or by those from whom the design had emanated. It was enough, however, for the Third Column, which awaited this signal to advance, and the stirring sounds of the bugle sent them forward to do their work, the Rifles leading the way.[20]

Sliding down into the ditch, his back to the wall, and groping his way amidst the obscuring dust and the masses of falling masonry, Smith placed his hand on some one whom he could not discern and cried out, asking "Who are you?" He was answered by Lieutenant Home, who said he was unhurt. When the dust had somewhat cleared away they went together to minister to Salkeld; but as there was a fire of musketry then bearing upon them, the gallant sergeant told his lieutenant not to expose himself, as he would remain behind to tend the wounded. Having full confidence in Smith and being all eagerness to go forward, Home, after giving some brandy from his flask to Salkeld and Burgess, joined the column and went ahead. Salkeld at first refused to be moved; so Smith and the bugler, who had remained with him, placed the dying officer's head upon a powderbag and bound up his wounds, as best they could, with improvised bandages torn from a puggery. Smith then went to the rear to obtain some stretchers, and not without threats and the display of a drawn sword succeeded in obtaining the use of two, a third having been taken from him by an officer of the Rifles. Upon one of these Salkeld, now too feeble to resist, was placed, and sent to Camp under charge of the bugler, with strict injunctions not to leave him until he should have seen the wounded man in the hands of a surgeon. But human skill could do nothing for him, and after lingering for a few days the fine young soldier was laid in the grave. Burgess was placed upon the other stretcher and sent under care of a Naick to the hospital, but they had not proceeded far before he died. For these achievements Home, Salkeld, Smith, and the Bugler Hawthorne were promptly rewarded by General Wilson with the Victoria Cross. Neither of the two gallant subalterns lived long to enjoy their honours. Salkeld had passed away from the scene of mortal strife, before Home, on the 1st of October, was killed by the premature springing of a mine, after the capture of the fort of Malagurh. And the explosion well-nigh cost us, in the sequel, another life, which would have been greatly mourned. George Chesney, who was Brigade-Major of Engineers, and one of the most promising of the younger officers of that noble Engineer Corps[21] went, after the explosion, with a party of Sappers to restore the broken bridge, of which mention has before been made. Whilst making for the gate, a heavy shell from one of the enemy's batteries at Kishengunje burst in the air, some twenty yards off, severely wounding Chesney, who received a shrapnel bullet through his right side and in his arm.[22] Renny of the Artillery, whose Native troop had withstood all trials and temptations and shone forth with conspicuous loyalty from first to last,[23] met the Engineer as he was returning. Then he and Fulton of the Artillery finding that the wounded man with some assistance could walk, helped him on to Ludlow Castle, whence he was conveyed to Camp, and by the skill and care of the surgeons saved to do good service to the State.

Having carried the Cashmere Gate, Campbell's column, followed by the Reserve, streamed onward towards the city. It was a grand sight to see their compact masses, moving forward, like hounds in the hunting-field, and carrying everything before them[24] The point to be gained was the Jumma Musjid, which Campbell had been commissioned to take. The capture of this place was to have been the signal for the further advance of the First and Second Columns. But it was a duty of far more difficult accomplishment than it had been thought to be. Campbell, a right-good soldier, intrepid and well-skilled, had the inestimable advantage of the personal guidance of Sir John Metcalfe, who knew neither fear nor pity and was ever eager to push forward in the great work of retribution. He had the plan of the city with all its turns and windings at his fingers' ends; and now he knew well how to lead the column, by a devious way, so as to encounter little opposition on the road. It passed on unharmed until the great street of the Chandna Chouk was reached and the Kotwallee seized by our people. Then fast fell the fire of the insurgents upon them, and it was found impossible to take the Jumma Musjid without such heavy loss as we could ill endure; so the column fell back to the vicinity of the Church and joined the Reserve, which had followed it through the Cashmere Gate and was pressing forward into the heart of the city.

Up to this time, if the success of our operations had not been complete, there had been no disastrous failure. But the fortune of war was now turning against us on the Right, in a manner little expected. The Fourth Column, commanded by Major Charles Reid, whose gallant and most serviceable exploits in command of the important position at Hindoo Rao's house have been already narrated in this work, was struggling with unforeseen difficulties. It was to have cleared the suburb of Kishengunje and entered the city by the Lahore Gate.[25] It was an enterprise of no little difficulty and danger. But he had a detachment of the Sixtieth Rifles; a detachment also of the Sixty First and of the Bengal Fusiliers. He had some of Daly's guides, and he had great reliance on his little Goorkahs. Their indomitable spirit was something beautiful to be hold. They had expended themselves so freely, during months of fearless fighting, at the post which they never quitted, that there were but few efficient men, at Hindoo Rao's, on the eve of the assault. The improvised hospital in the back rooms of the building was full of sick and wounded, and all who could move were eager to take part in the coming assault. When Reid went in amongst them, lying, as they were, on the floor, for there wee no cots for them, and told them what was to be done on the morrow, sorrowfully adding that he could muster scarcely a hundred of his Goorkahs for service, all sprung up as if the word of command had been given to them and volunteered to follow him into the field. Some were wholly unfit for such rough work; but of the hundred and fifty men, who had been reported ineffective, ninety-five mustered for active service on the morning of the assault. So Reid's heart was gladdened by the thought that he was taking with him two hundred of the sturdy little Goorkahs who had clung to him so nobly from the first.

At five o'clock the column was mustered and moved forwards in high spirits. Unfortunately, however, it was over weighted with Jummoo troops. John Lawrence had said that they might be trusted, and in ordinary circumstances they might have been. But their ways were not as our ways; and the great principle of cohesiveness was unknown to them. The original conception of the General had been that this Contingent might act independently, as a substantive force, carrying the Eed Gate and suburb of Paharunpore and spiking the enemy's guns in position there, whilst Reid with his picket was to support this attack, after leaving a sufficient number of men for the defence of Hindoo Rao's house. But Baird Smith saw at once the error of this and asked, "Is the Jummoo Contingent to make this attack as a Principal and not as an Auxiliary Force? It consists of untried troops with no interest in our cause. It is not a Native Fashion to take guns, and I greatly fear the results. If Major Reid leads and the Jummoo troops support the attack, I should expect it to be quite successful.[26] The good sense of the General yielded to this suggestion and the original programme was reversed. But even in this secondary position our allies soon demonstrated their deficiency in those very qualities which we most needed in such a conjuncture. There was a hitch. Reid had been promised three guns, but when the time came there were only gunners enough to man one of them. He was not now going in defiance of the principles of warfare to take a single gun into action, so he ordered the Artillery officer to make inquiries and to endeavour to obtain more gunners. Whilst he was awaiting the result he heard musketry fire to the right, and learnt that the Jummoo troops, on their way down from Camp, had become engaged with the enemy. Any further delay then would have been hazardous in the extreme. So Reid determined to advance without the promised artillery.

The enemy had prepared themselves for his reception. When within a short distance from the canal bridge, Reid discovered that the insurgents had erected a breastwork across the road and another running parallel to it. Trained in our English schools of discipline, they knew well the advantage of reserving their fire; so they did not open upon us until our people we rewithin fifty yards of their cover, when they poured in a heavy well-directed volley of musketry from the foremost breastwork. Thus assailed, Reid at once sent forward the British Riflemen and the Sepoys of the Sirmoor Battalion, who headed his column, and dislodged the mutineers from the breastwork and, drove them into the road. For some time the enemy stood irresolute, uncertain of the next movement, seemingly hesitating as to whether they should fall back on the further breastwork or should attack our Jummoo allies on the right. Then was seen the result of the miserable accident or mismanagement that had caused the column to go forward without guns. If Reid had been able to open upon the enemy with grape from the Horse Artillery pieces, he could have cleared the road at once and would have hurled back the reinforcements which were pressing onwards to the aid of their comrades. As it was, he presently found himself opposed to some fifteen thousand men, of all kinds, surging on to overwhelm him. In the crisis, which then threatened the gallant leader of the Fourth Column, Reid was making his dispositions, firstly for a false attack upon the enemy, in the front of the Kishengunje batteries, and secondly, for a real one, in front, flank, and rear, when he was smitten down by a bullet, which struck him on his head, and incapacitated him from further command. The officer next in rank was Major Lawrence, who had brought down the Jummoo troops, ten days before, to Delhi. As Reid was being carried to the rear, he met the Punjabee officer, made over the command to him, and explained his plan of attack. "Up to this time," he wrote afterwards, "all was going on admirably; the troops were steady and well in hand, and I made sure of success. I was not a little surprised to hear, about an hour afterwards, that the columns had retreated—that the Jummoo troops had lost their guns and were flying back to Camp.[27]

But although this was a disastrous failure, it was not an ignominious one. There was no better soldier—no braver gentleman, in all the Camp than Charles Reid. Nothing could have been more skilfully devised than his plan of attack, which was unhappily only half developed. Circumstances were against him. He had failed to obtain the light field-pieces, which would have so greatly promoted his success; he had been grievously thwarted by the eccentricities of his Cashmere Allies; and the enemy were not only mighty in numbers but were posted so strongly and so judiciously as to have all the advantages of ground on their side. But our own troops—European and Native—the European detachments, the Goorkahs, and the Guides fought splendidly; and there was more than one of those acts of heroic personal enterprise, which are seldom wanting in such episodes as this, to lighten up the surrounding darkness. One of these incidents, a mournful one, may be narrated here. A party of the enemy sheltered by a breastwork were firing heavily upon our people, when some officers with a handful of men made a rush upon the work to take it. Foremost of these was young Murray of the Guides,[28] who had been wounded in June and July, who had gone to the Hills to recruit and had returned to Delhi a few days before the assault. Speeding onward with impulsive bravery, the grim message of death met him, in the pride of his youth and the flush of his daring. He was shot through the chest and fell dead upon the field. Almost at the same moment, Captain M'Barnett, attached to the Fusiliers, a good officer, ever eager for work was shot down never to rise again on this side of the grave—altogether the loss on our side was heavy. Europeans, Guides, and Goorkahs all suffered severely. The sturdy little fellows of the Sirmoor Battalion left forty of their comrades behind them.

The enemy fought well—never better than on this occasion. They were in truth no contemptible opponents. Our finest soldiers are ever the most prompt to acknowledge the merits of their adversaries. On that morning of the 14th of September two of our greatest warriors, crippled in previous fights, and all-eager for the battle, were condemned to be onlookers only in this momentous crisis. Neville Chamberlain and Henry Daly were at Hindoo Rao's house. Both had carried their wounds thither, thinking that they might be of more service to the State than they could possibly be in Camp. Day had not broken, when Chamberlain went down to the famous Picket to see Reid's column started and to be a present help, if any time of trouble should come. When the operations against the enemy in the suburbs were fairly commenced it was broad daylight. Chamberlain, Daly, and Khan Singh, Rhosa,[30] went to the top of Hindoo Rao's house and watched the progress of the conflict. From this elevated position a stirring scene was visible below in the early daylight; and Chamberlain, whose quick soldierly eye took in all the details of the struggle below, could not but admire the dashing manner in which the Native officers rode in among the ranks of the mutineers, urging them and leading them on to the battle against the British and the Jummoo troops. Nor was his admiration, in this conjuncture, without some feeling of anxiety. For it seemed at one time that the enemy might break through our subzee-mundee defences, carry the undefended battery below Hindoo Rao's house, and take possession of the post itself, with its Hospital and its magazine. So critical, indeed, was the aspect of affairs that Chamberlain summoned the Native guard to the roof of the house, that it might better defend the entrance to the Magazine. And the three wounded officers prepared to take post with muskets in their hands. Happlily Reid's people held on, when they reached the Subzee-mundee line of defences and the present danger was averted; so Chamberlain and Daly descended from their plateau and strenuously exerted themselves to keep order among the excited assembly of mixed races below.[31] It is not questioned that about this time, our position on the Right was in great danger. Reinforcements of any sufficient strength could not be sent from the Camp,[32] and the Picket at Hindoo Rao's was itself called upon to afford assistance to others in this emergency. It was plain that we had received a severe check, which might have been turned to terrible account against us, and would have been, but for an incident which must now be narrated in detail.

The siege of a fortified city rarely affords much opportunity for a display of the great qualities of the Cavalry branch of an army. It is mainly the work of Engineers, Artillery, and Infantry. But when a city cannot be invested, and therefore the enemy are not shut up within the walls—when, as in this case, they can come out at one end of the place to fight, and go out at the other to escape, the mounted branch may do excellent service.[33] Seeing clearly the need of our troopers, especially for the protection and support of Reid's column Wilson had called upon Hope, Grant; and Grant, than whom there was no better soldier in Camp, eagerly donned his sabre and his spurs and prepared himself for the battle. The Brigadier took with him two hundred men of the Ninth Lancers, and four hundred Sikh horsemen, and awaited orders from the General. The orders soon came, and Grant marched his men down to a position under the walls of the city, covering the whole of our batteries, which before had been unprotected. At this time the enemy at Kishengunje had just defeated Reid's column, and elated with success were raging furiously against us. Availing themselves of the cover afforded by numerous houses and gardens in the vicinity, they poured in a brisk shower of musketry upon our line of Cavalry and strove mightily to dislodge us. So Tombs's troop of Horse Artillery was ordered up, to open fire on these mischievous insurgents. This was done, promptly and well, at a range of two hundred yards, and the occupants of the sheltering houses were compelled to fall back. But there was a still more dangerous enemy. The Lahore Gate, which had been a source of such grievous trouble to our Infantry, was still untaken, So the enemy, at a distance of some five hundred yards, turned a twenty-four-pound gun, charged with grape, upon our horsemen, and soon had cause to exult in their success.[34]

It must have been a grand sight then to have seen these troopers and their officers, drawn up in battle array, stern and immovable, to face the deadly fire of the enemy. There they sate, firm in their saddles, "ghastly motionless as if they slept," whilst the unerring grape-shot streamed upon them and made dreadful openings in their ranks. There was scarcely a man, who had not caught the noble spirit of their commanders, Hope Grant, Drysdale of the Lancers,[35] Tombs of the Artillery, Watson and Probyn of the Punjab Horse. The courage of the Ninth Lancers was never surpassed. Net only were they under the immediate command of an intrepid soldier, but their own Colonel commanded the brigade. When Grant commended their sturdy gallantry under fire, they replied that they were ready to take as much more of it as he liked. Forty-two men and six officers were struck down. Rosser of the Carabineers, who had been so eager to carry to Delhi the first tidings of the revolt at Meerut, and who now was acting as Hope Grant's aide-de-camp, fell with a bullet in his forehead, which all regarded as his death-wound. Others were slightly wounded. Eleven officers of the Lancers had their horses killed under them. Nor were the Artillery under Tombs less exposed or less steadfast under their exposure. Animated by the noble example of their commander they were equal to any daring and ready to face any danger. The Punjabees, to whom the situation was new, for they were not familiar with grape-shot, lacked nothing of the steadfastness of their white comrades, and never flinched from the merciless fire. Watson's Cavalry lost few men, for they were clothed in slate coloured uniform, and the neutral tint was of good service to them, placed as they were between the white jackets of the Lancers and the scarlet uniform of Probyn's Horse. For two long hours the brigade stood firm as a rock, and as one after another fell riddled with grape or canister there was no wavering in the ranks. Every man pressed his knees more tightly on his saddle and took a firmer grip of his reins. There was nothing else in their demeanour to distinguish this grand scene of defiance and endurance from an ordinary Cavalry parade. I may be wrong, but I think that this Heroism of Patience is grander far than the active gallantry displayed in a perilous charge. It is far easier to rush at an enemy in the fine enthusiasm of battle, than to stand steadfast on a given spot, for an ungiven period waiting for the order or the opportunity to move, whilst swept by the fire of a hidden enemy. It is the waiting that tries the man. And never were men more tried, or more patient under trial, than the troopers of Hope Grant's Brigade.

After a while the enemy's fire began to slacken. Those within the works were, perhaps diverted by other emergencies, and those in the open were kept back by the guns of Tombs and Campbell, afterwards reinforced by Bourchier. The Brigadier had made a requisition for some infantry to aid him; but only from the Picket at Hindoo Rao's house could any footmen be obtained. A party of two hundred and eighty of the Guides and Goorkahs—staunch as Europeans—were then placed at his disposal, and his nephew, Frank Grant, brought them down to the points where they were most needed.[36] But there was not much for them to do. The enemy were ceasing to prevail against us, and the General gave orders conditionally to the Cavalry Brigadier to withdraw to the neighbourhood of Ludlow Castle. Grant had done a good morning's work. The presence of the Cavalry Brigade alone prevented the enemy, who had driven back the Fourth Column, from advancing along the open ground between the Ridge and the City, and taking the whole of our Left Attack in flank.

Little more could be done by Infantry or Cavalry against the enemy on that day. Our assaulting columns, though not wholly successful, had done some good work. They were much exhausted by fatigue, and much depressed by the mortality that surrounded them. They saw the dead gathered up and the dying carried off in long strings of doolies to the hospitals in the Camp. Never were our medical officers more saddened by the sights brought before them; never have they shone more brightly in all the best manifestations of professional skill and manly devotion; never have they striven more mightily in the God-like work of alleviating human suffering. The result of that morning's fighting was that sixty European officers and nearly eleven hundred men were either laid in the grave, where burial was possible, or carried disabled to the hospitals.[37] But among those who remained after that day's carnage, although the desire to avenge their slaughtered comrades was strong, nothing could be done, for exhaustion had disabled them; and they were not fit to undertake the perilous work of penetrating deeper into the city. It would not have been wise to attempt any further offensive operations at such a time; but on the morrow, refreshed and recruited, they might force themselves into the heart of Delhi and plant the British standard on the proud Palace of the Moguls. The Artillery, however, to whom the morning had been comparatively one of inactivity, were eager to lay their mark upon the city itself, as they had before done upon its defences. And Brind, Salt, Remmy, Hamilton, and others, under the direction of Wilson, who had fixed his head-quarters in Skinner's house,[38] turned all their available means to account, in shelling or battering the buildings which it was most important to take or destroy, or in edeavouring to disperse such of the enemy as were still eager to act on the offensive.

To a General, strong-bodied and strong-minded in such a juneture, there would have been in the aspect of affairs, which presented itself to his eyes and to his understanding, after the assaults of that memorable morning, much to cause the most profound anxiety. To Wilson, feeble as he was at that time, from circumstances already narrated, the half-success of the enterprise was disheartening in the extreme. When he rode down, with his Staff, to the city and, map in hand, learned distinctly all that had happened, his first thought was that the only hope of preserving his army from utter destruction, was to withdraw his columns to their old position on the Ridge. Baird Smith had also gone down to the city. He was at Wilson's elbow, near Skinner's house, when the General put the critical question as to what was then to be done—asking whether he thought we could hold what we had taken. The answer of the Chief Engineer was prompt and decisive, "We *must* do so."[39] The General, who had before bowed to the decision of a man whose genius he could but recognise, although personally he disliked his "obstinacy," did not now oppose the suggestion. The Chief Engineer had taken, so far as he could take it, the responsibility on himself, and if the aspect of affairs had been still worse, he would not have shrunk from upholding the counsel, which he had tendered when he was more hopeful of immediate success.' It is possible that other officers, at a later period, may have urged similar opinions upon the General. Neville Chamberlain from Hindoo Rao's house, sent down a strong appeal in favour of continued action. But it was to Baird Smith's opinion that Wilson deferred, and the merit of the "holding on" is due to the brave pertinacity of the Chief Engineer.[40]

The morrow was a miserable blank. Delhi was full of spoil—of gold and silver and precious stones and all the rich fabrics of the looms of the East. All these things had been promised to the army as "Prize." Upon the action of the first two days depended, in no small measure, the value of the booty to be divided; for the people were huddling out of the city with all the property they could carry off and burying the rest, with a distant hope that some day they might recover it. But there was one kind of property which all were fain to leave behind and to which our soldiery after that long waiting on the Ridge and the excitement of that fierce assault upon the defences of Delhi was more alluring than all. A black or a green bottle, filled with beer or wine or brandy was more precious than a tiara of diamonds. The enemy knew this too well; and with the subtlety of their race had purposely left the immense supplies of intoxicating liquors, stored in the city, open to the hand of the spoiler. The result was more terrible than strange. The Europeans fell upon the liquid treasure with an avidity which they could not restrain. And if the insurgents had then seized the opportunity as cunningly as they had made it, it is hard to say what calamity might have befallen us. But the good Providence, which had so often confounded their wisdom, frustrated their plans, and turned their victories into defeats, now again strangled this pet project in the womb. With the great suburb of Kishengunje still in their hands; with the Lahore Bastion and numerous strongholds within the city still held in force by them, whilst our Camp on the Ridge was occupied by a scanty body of troops, many of them invalids or convalescents, a stroke of generalship on the part of the enemy far below genius point, might, at that time, have caught our whole army in the toils, and left the Mogul triumphant. On that miserable Fifteenth of September, a great cloud hung over us. It was the hour of our sorest peril and our extremest need. For the first and last time during this great struggle the destinies of the English in India trembled in the balance; and no human wisdom could foretell the issue.

It was not strange, therefore, that Wilson, who had doubted, from the first, the expediency of the assault without further reinforcements, and who, on the preceding day, after the failure of the Third Column and the Reserve to penetrate the city, followed by the repulse of Reid's troops, had thought of withdrawing his forces to their old position, should now have felt burdened with a weight of anxiety enough to crush him to the ground. He could scarcely have gone more nearly to the act of withdrawal without positively accomplishing it; for he had made arrangements to cover the retreat of the assaulting columns. But having once recognised the wisdom of the adverse councils tendered to him, he flung away all thought of receding, even if greater disasters should overtake him. It seems to have been little more than a petulant utterance; a hasty inception; the growth of an irritable and nervous temperament wrought upon by hostile circumstances. A little mature thought convinced him of the disgrace and humiliation of going back to be again besieged. What Clive had said a hundred years before, of our position in Indian, was in this crisis eminently true, "To stand still is danger; to recede is ruin." There was nothing for us, in such a conjuncture, but to go on.

But there could be no going on with any good hope of victory, whilst so many of our fighting men were wallowing like swine in the filth that had been set before them. No sustained efforts could be made for the reduction of the city, until they had been delivered wholly from the temptation of the intoxicating liquor. In a similar emergency Havelock, at Cawnpore, had made over all such stores to the Commissariat. But Wilson could not follow this example. It was necessary to act promptly, and the Commissariat had other duties to perform. It must have been sorely against the grain that the General issued an order for the destruction of the liquid fire, which, if often a baneful enemy, is not seldom a most serviceable friend. But there was clearly no alternative. So the streets ran with spirits, and wine, and beer; the dust licked up the stimulants so much needed for our hospitals,[41] and a large amount of valuable Prize was sacrificed to the necessities of the hour.

The great object was gained. The troops shook themselves free from the humiliating debauch, which, prolonged for another day, might have sent many to the grave and many to the hospital. But there was still the omnipresent thought that, at almost every turning, new stores might be found, as we advanced further into the city; and the fear of such a result sat heavily upon the mind of the General. But on the 16th, though he was obviously suffering under much depression of spirit, he recognised some hopeful appearances in the general aspect of affairs. During the preceding night the enemy had evacuated Kishengunje, and now the great magazine was falling into our hands. Wilson personally superintended the operations. His experience as an Artillery officer must have been very serviceable at a time, when the chief work was to be done by the scientific branches of the Army. And it must have gladdened his heart to see the immense supplies of Ordinance stores which now came into his possession. The grand exploit of the Artilleryman Willoughby[42] was none the less grand, because the material wealth of the Delhi Arsenal had been but little diminished. It was chiefly the small-arm magazine that had suffered by the explosion in May. It was thought in the British Camp that the insurgents must have been sorely put to it for copper-caps; but large quantities were still in store when the English entered the city. It was no profitless morning's work that placed all these guns and mortars and ammunition again at our disposal; but it did not seem to rouse Wilson, who wrote still in great despondency:

16th September, 2 p.m.

"We took possession of the Magazine this morning, with the loss of only three men wounded. This advances us a little, but it is dreadfully slow work. Our Force is too weak for this street fighting, when we have to gain our way inch by inch, and of the Force we have, unfortunately there is a large portion besides the Jummoo troops in when I can place no confidence....What gives me, however, most trouble, even more than the enemy, is the immense quantity of wines, spirits, and beer which is discovered, and which our fellows, European and Native, get hold of before we can destroy it and make beasts of themselves and incapable of doing their duty. I find myself getting weaker and weaker every day, mind and body quite worm out. The least exertion knocks me down. I walk with difficulty and fully expect in a day or two to be laid altogether on my bed. This is very sad and frets and worries me... . The rebels who so long attacked Reid's Picket from Paharunpore, evacuated the place last night, leaving their heavy guns behind. How I wish Reid could have driven them out on the 14th and joined in the attack on the city... . We have a long and hard struggle still before us. I hope I may be able to see it out".

It was in the very nature of things that it should be a long and a hard struggle. Nothing else could be reasonably expected. To think of the great city itself, with all its impediments—of the teeming population, of the military and religions elements, of the still pervading sentiment of loyalty to the House of Delhi even in its decline, was to be convinced of the difficulty of the enterprise. It is a sentiment as old as heroism itself, that the difficulty of an enterprise makes it pleasurable excitement in the hour of action, is glory in the hour of accomplishment. And few men would have felt this more than Wilson, if it had not been for that great failure of the body, to which the mind of every man, great or small, is compelled to succumb. Still, little by little, though his dejection was great at the outset, he began to look more hopefully upon the aspect of affairs. Time was his best ally. There was no sign of any offensive action on the part of the enemy to cause serious inquietude. On the other hand, it was plain that they whose evacuation of the city had been arrested by our inactivity after the assault, had begun to discern the wisdom of flight. A few desperate men, not madmen or "fanatics," but brave soldiers and loyal subject of the Throne of Delhi, might hold out for a time and die at their posts: but large bodies of soldiers and citizens were flocking out of the city, some with much property and others with only their lives in their hands; whilst sour Artillery and Engineers were putting forth their strength, in strenuous endeavours to bombard all the great buildings of Delhi, and to occupy the houses which afforded cover to the enemy and impeded our progress into the city. But what seemed the easiest operation of all was in reality a most difficult one—the bombardment of the chief buildings of Delhi. Mortars, and shells, and fuzes were abundant, and there was no lack of experienced gunners; but it perplexed our best artillerymen to determine the elevations, as they could only vaguely surmise the distances, and there was some fear of dropping a loaded shell in the midst of an assembly of our own people, or sending it clean over the building on which it was intended to lodge[43].

Ever to the front, ever active, ever fertile in resources, the Engineer Brigade had much work to do, and did it well in this conjuncture. It had been terribly shattered during the assault. One after an other the subalterns attached to the different columns had fallen beneath the fire of the enemy. Few had escaped the perils to which they had been exposed[44]. But happily Alexander Taylor was alive, though not unhurt, for a bullet had struck him painfully on the chest on the morning of the assault[45]. And there was work of his active brain in devising the best means of securing what we had gained and in superintending their execution. All the professional resources of "those who were left," were brought into play, to intrench the different commanding positions, as they fell from time to time into our hands. The outer openings, as in the College premises, were closed with sandbags, leaving loopholes for our fire. Barricades were through up across the roads, leading to posts likely to be attacked. Houses were garrisoned and loopholes. Implements and stores of all kinds, necessary for immediate use or of probable requirement were furnished, and nothing was left undone that the sagacity of science could suggest, for the retention of the posts which we had captured, but which might be wrested from us[46].

On the evening of the 17th, the general state of affairs was this. Our troops and endeavoured to advance up to the streets towards the Palace—the grand object of all our movements—but in almost every instance they had been repulsed. There was still some heart left in the insurgents. Many had evacuated the city by the gates of egress, either in search of the personal safety of the moment, or with some ulterior designs of mischief in other parts; but enough were still left in the city to render the advance of our weak force a work of difficulty. The Magazine and the Bank had been captured and occupied. But the Lahore Bastion[47] was still in the enemy's hands. No advance had been made in that direction since Nicholson had fallen. It was evident that the appetite of our troops for this kind of fighting had not improved, and that our attempts to gain our ends by open force must be superseded by some more insidious system of attack. The exposure of our few fighting men was by all means to be avoided. They had seen enough of it already. They courted no more; and if they consented, it was with manifest reluctance.

So Taylor, who had returned to the city after his two days' rest in Camp, suggested at Head-Quarters that each brigade should be ordered to work, under the guidance of the Engineer officers attached to it, not along the open streets, but through the sheltered houses, during the advance; using them as means of communication; fortifying all commanding buildings as soon as they could be secured; and placing garrisons in them. The project met with willing concurrence and consent; and Taylor and his subalterns went about their work with the thoughtful activity that had characterised all their proceedings. But the progress was not rapid. On the evening of the 18th they were little further advanced than on the morning. The cause was not very remote; nor was it very unintelligible. The veterans of the different brigades did not fall in very readily with the views of the young Engineers or cheerfully recognise their temporary supremacy. So situated, Taylor, with the concurrence of the Chief Engineer, went to the General and drew from him an order to the Brigadier commanding at the Caubul Gate to place at the disposal of the Field Engineer a force of some five hundred men, European and Native, to carry out the above-mentioned design; and early on the 19th the advance began in earnest. This was not one of the least of the great services of the Alec Taylor. Some thirty houses, important both by their size and their position, fell into his hands, and were duly barricaded and garrisoned. Nothing could have been more satisfactory than the result, especially as it was attended with but trifling loss on the part of the assailants. The houses thus taken were principally detached houses with surrounding premises, very favourable to our operations, for the occupants were exposed to a flanking and cross fire from the troops occupying the houses which we had already taken in the rear. Working onwards in this insidious but most effective way, our people towards nightfall found themselves in possession of a building, behind the gorge of the Lahore Bastion, which so entirely commanded it that the enemy, seeing their danger, were fain, after firing a few shots, to escape under cover of the night; and so the Bastion became our own. But so great was the terror, which the very name of this formidable work had inspired in the hearts of our men, that although the bastion had fallen thus easily into their hands, and there was no opposition, there was a manifest reluctance on the part of our soldiery to hold what we had taken. It was hard to restrain them from leaving the Bastion.

In the meanwhile an attempt had been made to carry the Lahore Gate by assault. Edward Greathed, of the Eighth, who had worked cordially with the Engineers in their house-to-house visitations, was eager to carry the Lahore Gate, which had so long defied us. It appeared that this might be done, without encountering the dreaded opposition of the Lahore Bastion, by a route of a less hazardous nature. Greathed was appointed by Brigadier Jones to command the attack, and Colonel Pelham Burn, who had been selected to be Military Governor of Delhi after its occupation by the English, was requested to accompany the detachment.[48] Greathed took with him a party consisting of some details of the Eights and Seventy-fifth Queen's and of the Bengal Fusilier Regiments, accompanied by a couple of guns. It was arranged that, on the sound of firing being heard, supports should be sent on from the Caubul Bastion by a narrow lane under the ramparts. The force made good its way without difficulty to the narrow street leading into the Chandna Chouk, but the enemy were posted in force behind a gate at the end of it, which was unexpectedly flung open, for we thought that our movements were unknown, and a six-pounder gun was brought to bear upon our advancing detachments.[49] On this Greathed ordered up a gun under Lieutenant Harington and directed the men of the Seventy-fifth to charge under cover of the smoke, when the gun should be fired. But the Seventy-fifth did not charge. The Eighth were then ordered to the front, but they also refused to charge; and the Artillery were left to be fired at by the insurgents, who exhibited more gallantry than our own people. The noble example of our officers could not induce their men to display that fine onward feeling—that regulated impetuosity—which alone can command success under such trials as this. They hated the kind of work which they were called upon to spring at, and they shrunk back when they ought to have flung themselves upon it. Greathed saw at once the temper of his followers—if followers they could be called who would not follow: he saw the Artillery suffering from the musketry of the enemy; he knew the value of life at such a time too well to needlessly expend it, and wisely, though most reluctantly, he determined to withdraw his men from the unequal encounter before they had sustained any heavy loss. But a new difficulty confronted him, for the men seemed equally unwilling to advance or retire. To give assurance to the rest by covering their advance. Burn had taken the detachment of the First Fusiliers to occupy the houses in the narrow street. So with this aid Greathed was able to withdraw his men in an orderly and creditable manner. It was another illustration of the national character in its soldierly aspects. They did not know what they were fighting against, and the unseen danger assumed, in their imaginations, proportions, the reality of which would have been contemptible in the open field.[50]

There was nothing to exhilarate or to encourage the General in all this. Indeed the crowning misery of all was the thought of the backwardness of the troops under his command. He need not have thought much about numbers, if the hearts of the few were in the right place. Had Wilson been assured of the temper of his men, he might have taken a more cheerful view of the prospect before him. But how this last failure saddened him his letters clearly evince:

> "We are still in the same position in which we were yesterday. An attempt was made this morning to take the Lahore Gate, but failed from the refusal of the European soldiers to follow their officers. One rush and it would have been done easily, but they refused to make it. The fact is our men have a great dislike to street fighting; they do not see their enemy, and find their comrades falling from shots of the enemy who are on the tops of houses and behind cover, and get a panic and will not advance. This is very sad and to me disheartening. We can, I think hold our present position, but I cannot see my way out at all. I have now only 3100 men (infantry) in the city—with no chance or possibility of any reinforcement. If I were to attempt to push on into the city they would be lost in such innumerable streets and masses of houses, and would be annihilated or driven back. It is true that a great

number of the enemy have bolted, but they have still a large camp out between the Delhi and Ajmere Gate, and those who have bolted may possibly return when they find we cannot make any progress. Again in our favour we have possession of nearly all their guns, shot and shell, except those they have in the bastions still in their possession, and we are bombarding from an easy distance, Selimgurh and the Palace.... "It has been a hard task imposed upon me, almost too hard; both mind and body are giving way. Since the night of the 13th I have certainly not had five hours' sound sleep, and nature cannot stand it. I trust, however, and think, I have done my duty. May Almighty God still support me in doing so.... This is a very doleful letter, but the state of my mind and body perhaps make me more depressed than I should be....."

"Camp before Delhi, 19th September.

".... I came up to Camp last night in hopes of getting a good night's sleep—I was not, however, very successful. Brain, nerves, and body have been too much strained to quiet down so quickly. I am going back to the city immediately, but shall try to get back here to-night to sleep.... We are progressing more satisfactorily—bombarding the city and gradually seizing strong posts in advance of our present position. The King evacuated the Palace yesterday afternoon with most of his followers, finding it too hot to hold him; report says very few are left in it. He is gone to a place near the *Poorana Killah* (Old Fort), outside the city. We have met with a very heavy loss in taking what we have done. I have not yet seen the returns, but hear the total loss in killed and wounded is full 1150 men, including 46 officers. The killed are only about 250. Brigadier-General Nicholson is a very great loss to me—I have no one who can supply his place. I am very much afraid we shall lose him. He was not going on at all favourably yesterday....."

But when Wilson returned to his Head-Quarters in the city, glad tidings awaited him. Taylor reported the success of his operations, in working from house to house and making grand progress with little loss. The occupation of the Lahore Bastion was an important step in advance; and the General, determined not to lose what we had gained, sent some officers of his Staff to spend the night in the Bastion, or to remain there as long as might be necessary to secure its continued occupation. But there was no attempt on the part of the enemy to recover it. The night passed peaceably away. When day dawned on the 20th, arrangements were made to resume the tactical operations, which had so far been crowned with such complete success. But those who were on the look-out were struck by the deserted aspect of the streets. Some adventurous explorers then went out to ascertain more certainly the position of affairs in the city, and they found that the place was well nigh abandoned.

The Lahore bastion being secured, the fall of the Lahore Gate speedily followed. A body of the Sixtieth Rifles rushed at it; and its defenders, finding that "the game was up" with them, from one end of the city to the other, evacuated the work which had so long defied and frustrated the best efforts of our troops. The story of the Lahore Gate is a curious one. It is the story of a lost opportunity. After the first onslaught of the Second Column, the Brigadier, scarcely knowing the importance of the position, found himself on the Lahore Bastion. A bold front, in the confusion and half-Panic which had then set in among the defenders, might have carried everything before it and saved all after-trouble and disaster. But Jones had received his orders. He had gone beyond the point at which he had been directed to await tidings of the fall of the Jumma Musjid; so in obedience to orders he fell back and lost the golden opportunity. Emboldened by our inaction at such a time the enemy clung to the work with desperate pertinacity, and for six days held it to the infinite discomfiture of the besiegers. Nicholson had been the only leader of a column, who had, previous to the assault, personally gone down to the breaching batteries, studied the effect of their operations and taken a comprehensive ocular survey of the breaches through which we were to push our way on to victory. But, it may be doubted whether even that "born General" know much of the position or the designs of the enemy within the ramparts, which Brind, Scott, and others with their heavy guns were battering with such wonderful effect. There were few to whom the advance into the city had not appeared to be a much easier operation than after-events proved that we were justified in anticipating. In affairs of war, it is hard to say what great issues may depend upon some accident of the moment. Had this cruel Bastion and the Lahore Gate, with or without orders, fallen to our arms on the 14th of September, when the Second Column first advanced on these works, Delhi would have fallen sooner; and Nicholson might have survived the siege.

But, whatsoever the misadventure may have been at the outset, the capture of the defensive works of Delhi was now complete. There was an almost general rush inwards. The cry was "To the Palace! To the Palace!" The occupation by British troops of the great home of the Moguls was the only genuine proclamation of victory. Our scouts had brought us intelligence that the Royal Family had forsaken their old asylum, and had become fugitives and outcasts huddling together in the suburds, not knowing what to do. The Reality of Indian warfare was now at an end in Delhi; we were about to see the Romance. Hope Grant sent Hudson to the General to convey to him the glad tidings that the city was evacuated.[51] Wilson sent at once a party under Jones of the Sixtieth Rifles to blow in the gates' of the Palace and of the Selimgurh. The powder-bags aided by our guns, did the work with but little difficulty. A few desperate men remained, moved either by religious enthusiasm or by military devotion, to die at their posts in the Palace of the Moguls. It is related that a sentry was found at each gate, with his musket on his shoulder, grim and immovable, prepared for his doom[52] No one found in the imperial premises was left alive. The British standard was hoisted. And the Englishman celebrated his victory by ordering dinner to be laid in the Elysium of the Dewan-Khas, with its lustrous marble walls and lovely arabesques, triumphs of that barbaric art, beside which the best effort of the nineteenth century Englishman is but as a Caliban to an Ariel. I know not whether any harmonious spirit, "tired of war's alarms," celebrated and enlivened the occasion by a burst of song, with the well-known adaptation of the words, which our people now saw around the cornices of the Dewan-Khas, but they Knew that the famous "Elysium on Earth" was their resting-place and the enemy who had mocked us was no more.[53]

To the weary warriors of Delhi the best Elysium at that time must have been Rest. There was little or nothing in the material environments of the place strongly to impress the captors with a sense of its splendour or its beauty. We saw it at the worst in the hour of its decadence and humiliation, with the well-remembered pollution of half a century upon it. But since the early days of May, the Mogul, before a puppet, had become a potentiality; and Delhi, one of our greatest civil and military stations, where the old imbecile King and his multitudinous family had so long lain prostrate at our feet, for four long months, had snorted defiance at us, garrisoned by our own army. But now Delhi again was occupied by our British troops. The usual accompaniments of retribution and spoliation could not be wholly absent from such a siege as this. But if there had been no failures, no checks; if our legions had entered the imperial city, which had so long defied us, with a grand rush, sweeping everything before it, the results would have been terrible. Hatred of the inhabitants and greed for the spoil would have borne their accustomed fruits. But the delays to which we had been compelled to submit gave altogether another character to the first partial and then complete occupation of the city. When on the 20th of September Delhi fell into our hands it was little more than a vast solitude. The cry of *Væ Victis* therefore, was never raised. It was the desertion of the enemy that made us victors at all. There could, happily, therefore, be no wholesale retribution. But during that week of incertitude, when our half-successes were almost counter-balanced by whole failures, and no man knew what might be the issue of these vicissitudes, opportunities arose for the assertion of our retributive strength; and the temptations, if not irresistible, were most difficult to resist.

Seldom, if ever, since War began, had there been so much to exacerbate and infuriate an army, as then inflamed the brains and fevered the blood of the men, who found themselves in the blood-stained city. No reader of this narrative needs to be told what were these exciting influences. But when we come to weigh the heavy burden of unutterable guilt, of which our women and children were the victims, against the cruelty and inhumanity of the avenging power, we see how light were our reprisals. Still it must always happen, both in the West and the East, that the miserable consideration still remains that the innocent must suffer for the guilty. Many who had never struck a blow against us—who had tried to follow their peaceful pursuits—and who had been plundered and buffeted by their own armed countrymen, were pierced by our bayonets, or cloven by our sabres, or brained by our muskets or rifles. In this instance, I have said, there were aggravations, which have not stirred the hearts of our western warriors. From western warfare there had been absent that which in the East has been most perilous of all, the difference of colour. The very sight of a dark man stimulated our national enthusiasm almost to the point of frenzy. We tolerated those who wore our uniforms and bore our arms, but all else were, in our eyes, the enemies and persecutors of our race. So it sometimes happened that during the first days of our occupation of

Delhi, many innocent men were shot down or otherwise massacred. Some of the best and bravest of our officers sanctioned, if they did not take part in these outrages; and it is doubtful whether they could have controlled the excesses of their fighting-men, especially when they were maddened by much drink.

I know only one instance of slaughter on a large scale, which was made the talk of the Camp. Major James Brind, Brind of the Batteries, was sent into the city on the most ungrateful duty of burying the rotting carcases which were polluting the atmosphere of certain parts of Delhi. He took with him a detachment consisting of Artillery and Infantry, mainly, if not wholly, Natives of the country. Among them were forty Sikh artillerymen. The duty thus fixed upon him was of a sanitary, not a retributive character. But it happened that, as he was proceeding to his unsavoury work, news was brought to him of "a brutal attack" which had been made upon a party of Muzbee Silks, in one of the lanes between the Delhi and Ajmere Gates. At this time he fell in with Brigadier Jones, who had commanded the Second Column of Attack, and he asked to be reinforced, if needed, by some European Infantry, that he might dispose of the men who had committed these outrages and others which Jones reported. The Brigadier promised to aid Brind, and approved of retributive action. A wounded Sapper was with difficulty persuaded to lead the way to the spot where these "murderers" were located. When Brind got among them he made short work of the chastisement to be inflicted upon them. Among the traitors were "Syuds and various classes of debauchees." Many of the enemy were slaim on the spot, and others, "against whom blood-proofs, as also relics of our murdered countrywomen, children and other Christian residents" were to be found on their persons or in their houses, were reserved for more humiliating punishments. Following the example set by Neill at Cawnpore, he kept these men "to labour in cleansing our polluted lines before their final punishment." The number slain by Brind's detachment ranged from a hundred and fifty to two hundred men. As a pleasant set-off to this, Brind had the satisfaction of reporting that he had "sent out of the city many hundreds of women, children, and helpless male inhabitants—blind and decrepit."[54] It is not clear whether the men thus "slain" were our revolted Sepoys or civil inhabitants of Delhi. It does not appear to me, however, that the fact of their having certain articles in their possession was any proof of their having murdered the English people, to whom they had belonged., The goods might have been purchased at a prize-auction, or might have come into their possession by some very innocent accident. It was not the first or the last time, when mere possession has been treated as a roof of forcible spoliation attendant on "treacherous murder."[55] There was not a kinder-hearted, as there was not a braver man in the Delhi army than James Brind; but he was a man of an excitable temperament, and he had been working day and night in the batteries under a fierce sun, seldom or never sleeping all the time. And he had ever before him the memory of the fact that his brother had been killed at Sealkote by the treacherous connivance of his own servants[56]

There is other testimony, which, though not so officially authentic as this, is very strong and reliable, to the effect that many innocent men were destroyed, after the occupation of Delhi, by our infuriated troops. An officer, who served throughout the siege, and who has given us the best account of its chief incidents now before the public, says, "Our men " treated these (the women and children) with kindness and sympathy, but many of the citizens were shot, clasping their hands for mercy. It was known, too, that a large proportion of them had all along wished us well.[57] And Colonel Bourchier of the Artillery, in his published narrative says: "Some men were caught going out of the Cashmere Gate disguised as women and were hung; whilst several bheesties, or water-carriers, detected in bringing in drugged liquor for the troops, were likewise disposed of."[58] The enormity of endeavouring to escape the fury of the assailants by huddling out in petticoats in not very clear. The device was one not altogether unknown, or unpractised, in like emergencies, by our own officers. It might have been better to have given these epieene creatures the benefit of the doubt. It is a pleasure to the Historian to be able to add that from the mass of manuscript documents before him he can clearly derive the one gratifying fact, that the women and children were almost uniformly respected. A stray shot might, now and then, inadvertently have carried death with it; but no intentional outrages were committed. A distinguished officer of the Eighth, which formed part of the Second Column, writes: "The Eighth took possession of a large house, the basement and court of which was filled with women and children, evidently of a respectable rank of life, who were naturally much frightened.[59] But they had no reason to be so, for our good fellows treated them as if they had been their sisters and passed them out carefully and kindly on their way to the Cashmere Gate, which was all, indeed, we could do for them." I could add many other proofs of the forbearance of our soldiery; but this may be taken as a sample of the whole.

The reign of unlicensed plundering had begun at an early period. The Sikhs, among whose traditional day-dreams the sack of Delhi had ever been prominent, now found themselves within reach of the realisation of their fondest wishes. No scruples restrained them. They had no conception of a Prize Agency beyond the grand cardinal principle that it was the duty of every man to gather up what spoil he could get and to keep it as long as he could. Their natural astuteness, aided perhaps by some experiences elsewhere, had taught them how to discern the lurking-places of concealed treasure. It might be buried beneath the floors of their houses or bricked up in their walls. In the former case it might be ascertained by pouring water through the crevices, for if the space below were excavated it would soon filter down; if not it would return to the level of the floor. In the latter, the wall might be sounded, as a physician sounds the chest of a patient; and the results of this process of auscultation were very convincing to our Sikh comrades. To what extent their surmises were justified can only be conjectured. But nothing was more patent than the energy of their endeavours, for almost everywhere battered walls and wrenched up floors told plainly what they had done. It was clearly ascertained, too, that large quantities of plunder were handed over the walls to their brethren below, and that afterwards numbers of laden carts passed out at the opposite gates of the city. It has been stated, indeed, that their countrymen would not believe in the fall of Delhi until they had ocular demonstration of the "loot." But it is not to be thought that the Sikhs were the only recipients of unauthorised Prize. Sepoys of other nationalities and camp followers of all, went in remorselessly for what they could clutch. And our own European soldiery in a lesser degree took part in the unlicensed spoliation. But they had not the same discriminating eye for booty as their Sikh comrades, and they were seldom richer in the end for their contempt of the Prize Agents and their evasions of the Provost-Marshal.

The Head-Quarters' Staff, Military and Civil, were now fixed in the Palace. But there was one absent from the party, whose work at that time had developed into peculiar interest and importance. It was truly a sad thing that just at this point, when all things were working on, surely if not rapidly, to the complete occupation of Delhi, the subversion of the Mogul, and the proclamation of the Queen's authority, the man who, from the very beginning, had superintended all the political and civil transactions connected with our position at Delhi was suddenly stricken by cholera. The Pestilence that walketh in the darkness had laid the cold hand of death upon Hervey Greathed. He was a man in the prime of his life, with the flush of health on his cheek; with strength and activity in every movement. The published extracts from his family correspondence show how cheerful he was throughout the long months of the siege, how friendly and sociable he was with his comrades, especially his old friends from Meerut, and how lovingly he dwelt with his brothers. It was a luxury during that long dreary period of waiting to have an old friend or relative of any degree with whom to converse and to exchange sympathies. But the Greatheds had no such scanty consolation; for the three brothers, Edward, Hervey, and Welby were all in Wilson's camp, performing different duties, but seldom, for a day, apart.[60] Nothing could be more cheery than the manner in which the civilian wrote of this pleasant family intercourse. And as it did much to sustain the spirits of the Triumviri, so also it must have sustained their health. But the brightest and the lustiest are often those to succumb first to the approaches of cholera; and on the 19th of September, whilst full of hope, eager for the crowning action, and never doubting the final issue of the great contest, all that was mortal of Hervey Greathed lay in the pale stillness of death. He was buried in the graveyard near Ludlow Castle—the first to find a resting-place there.

The English had now captured the Palace; but where was the King? If any man in our Army could track him down, that man was Hodson of Hodson's Horse—the famous partisan leader, who had the fierce courage of the tiger unsubdued by any feelings of human compassion—who might have grown into something good and great, had years, which bring the philosophic mind, taught him the might of mildness and the glory of forbearance. As it is, viewed by such light as is cast by his antecedents on his character and conduct at this time, he appears as a man labouring under a strong sense of intolerable wrong, excited and exasperated by what had befallen him, feeling that he was under a cloud, but firmly resolved to blaze through it, with the light of some heroic enterprise that would cause the past to be for gotten. He had nothing but his character as a fighting man left to him; but this was of the finest temper. He had been dismissed from political employment in the Punjab for truculent injustice to a Native chief and had been pronounced wholly unfit ever to exercise any civil power.[61] Another grave charge had been brought against him, which I am not competent to discuss. But there was not a stain upon the brightness of his sabre. In critical conjunctures such men are of eminent service to the State. They will do deeds which some would shrink from in fear and others would abstain from on principle. Wilson was not unwilling to give him *carte blanche* to deal with the Royal Family as he might think fit—with the single reservation that the life of the old King was to be spared.

Hodson, who had been appointed executive Chief of the Intelligence Department, had done his work right well with the aid of some notable native spies, the chief of whom was Rujjub Ali, who rendered excellent service to the English by the intelligence and sagacity with which he obtained and communicated information regarding the movements of the enemy throughout the siege. But we owed much also to a traitorous, or as it was the fashion to say a "loyal" member of the House of Delhi, the Meerza Elahee Buksh, who was the father-in-law of the late heir-apparent. This man, who was said to be more "respectable" than the majority of his kinsmen, was also more sagacious. He had no dream of the restoration of the lost honours of the House of Delhi. Believing that the English would triumph in the end, he saw clearly that his own interests would be best served by covertly aiding the Infidels, whilst assuming the part of a friendly adviser of the Mogul. The game which he played was distinguished by no little Oriental astuteness. The leaders of the Army were eager to carry off the King with them. They pleaded that although want of provisions compelled them to leave the city, outside the walls, they could, if it were necessary, ravage the country, supply themselves, and make a great war against the English. And they had well-nigh succeeded, when the wily Meerza, who had persuaded the poor old man to accompany him to his house, where they spent the night, had not used all his efforts to keep the King from joining the Insurgents. He was satisfied that "a real fidelity required him not to let the King go with the Army." So with "great effort" and "extreme endeavour," when Bukht Khan and other chiefs of the Imperial Army met Behaudur Shah and the Princes at Hoomayoon's Tomb, the Meerza "made so many good arrangements that neither the King nor his sons did ever listen to them, and none of them have ever gone with the officers of the ungrateful regiments."[62] All this and much more was communicated to Hodson principally through the Moonshee Rujjub Ali. It was plain that the wily Meerza had got the whole Royal Family in his toils, and that it needed now only that the bold heart and the strong had should be brought in aid of this crouching treachery. By specious representations Elahee Buksh held them in gentle bondage at the Tomb of the Emperor Hoomayoon with its surrounding structures, a suburb in itself, beyond the modern city. It was the way out of Delhi, and large numbers of the Insurgents were still flocking there for safe egress, carrying off what property they could, but glad to escape even with their lives. It was thought that amidst this crowd of people, the King and his family, swayed by later counsels, might escape. So Hodson galloped down to head-Quarters and obtained reluctant permission from the General to take a party of his own men to Hoomayoon's Tomb and bring in, without injury or insult, the last of the Mogul Emperors. Taking fifty of his troopers he rode off, elated with the success of his mission, and passing the ruins of the ancient city of Delhi, made his way to the asylum of the prostrate monarch. There was then little risk either of escape or resistance; for the King, under guidance of Zeenut-Mehal, was already treating for his surrender. Still it was hard to say what terrible crisis might not be evolved at such a time, out of the desperation of those about him. It was necessary to move cautiously; so Hodson concealed himself and his men in some ruined buildings near the gateway of the Tomb; whilst he sent his emissaries on to convey his instructions to the royal fugitives. Two weary hours dragged away—hours of painful suspense—before they brought back an answer. The King consented to give himself up to Captain Hodson, on assurance received from that officer's own lips that his life would be spared.

So Hodson went forth from his resting-place and stood out before all, in the open space near the beautiful gateway of the Tomb, a solitary white man, among so many, awaiting the surrender of a King and the total extinction of a dynasty, the most magnificent that the world had ever seen. It was then but a title, a tradition; but still the monarchy of the Moguls was a living influence in the hearts of the Mahomedans of India. And, truly, a grander historical picture was rarely seen than that of the single British subaltern receiving the sword of the last of the Mogul Emperors in the midst of a multitude of followers and retainers grieving for the downfall of the House of Tamerlane and the ruin of their own fortunes. Grand as was the central incident in itself, it was rendered still grander and more impressive by its gorgeous historical background—"the magnificent gateway with the milk-white domes of the Tomb towering up from within'[63]—the gateway through which, preceded by the Queen and her son, for whom the wretched old man had endured so much and was now perishing, passed the palanquin containing the last poor remnant of royalty on its way to a living tomb. Hodson pricked on with drawn sword, to meet it and called upon the King to give up his arms. The old man asked if he was "Hodson Behaudur," and asked for a renewal from the Englishman's own lips of the promises made by his herald. This was done; and Hodson formally guaranteed the personal safety of His Majesty and of the son of Zeenut-Mehal. The Imperial arms were then surrendered to the Englishman, who made them over to his orderly, observing that if any attempt were made to rescue his prisoner the King would be shot down like a dog. Then the procession to the city commenced. It was a slow and dismal march along five miles of road; and it might have been a critical one, for a vast crowd followed the palanquins and their escorts during the greater part of the Journey. They seemed hushed and overawed—rather wondering then excited—and gradually slunk away as they neared the Lahore Gate. Hodson and his captives then passed up the great street of the Chandna Chouk to the city. Meeting Saunders, the principal civil officers left to us at Delhi, Hodson made over the prisoners to him and went to report himself to the General. Wilson received him in his usual way, with a sort of bluff heartiness, which few in Camp understood, for there was more kindness in his heart than appeared upon the gritty surface; and said, "Well, I am glad you have got him, but I never expected to see him or you again!" But when the royal arms were given up to him Wilson told his subaltern to select any that he wished to possess as memorials of the adventure. One of the swords which he took had adorned the side of Nadir Shah, the other had been worn by the Emperor Jehanguire.

I wish that the record of Hodson's exploits had ended with this narrative of the capture of the King. It would have gladdened the heart of the daring subaltern to have been ordered or permitted to shoot Behaudur Shah like a dog or to strike him down like an ox in the shambles. But this congenial occupation was not conceded to him. His captive was a miserable, infirm old man, much wrought upon by evil advisers; the slave rather than the master of circumstances, the shadow of a name turned to evil purposes.[64] To have used brutal violence towards such a poor feeble creature would have been little more manly than the slaughter of a woman. But the game of royalty-hunting had not yet been played out. Some of the King's sons, or near relatives, who were believed to have taken an active part in the insurrection and in the massacre of our people, were still to be tracked down. They were in the prime of life—if life, spent in that great reeking stye of the Delhi Palace could ever be said to have a prime—and no pledges or promises had been made to them. They were lawful game and Hodson knew where to find them. So he got Wilson's permission to hunt down the Shahzadahs and sent to his Second-in-Command, M'Dowall, to bring up a hundred troopers. He promptly obeyed the summons, and Hodson mounted, eager for the affray. The princes were at Hoomayoon's Tomb where the King had been captured on the preceding day. With them were some thousands of followers, including a number of Mussaulman fanatics, who called upon them in the name of the Prophet to resist the infidel intruders; but they thought it better to sue for terms—hoping at least that their lives would be spared. Hodson would grant them no terms—would make no promises of any kind. He commissioned his emissaries[65] to say that "he had come to seize the Shahzadahs, and intended to do so, dead or alive." After two hours spent in useless negotiation—mere idle talk leading to nothing—the delegates of the British Government as it was then represented by Hodson, reported that the Princes were coming out in covered bullock-carts. Soon the wretched captives appeared, made one last despairing appeal for their lives, and were sent on towards Delhi guarded by our troopers on both sides of the way.[66]

Having seen his prisoners fairly started, Hodson, with his remaining Sowars, passed the precincts of the Tomb, and in a loud voice, called upon the people assembled there to surrender their arms. It is true that the multitude were but the "scum of the Palace," weak, nerveless, heartbroken people, who had seen their King carried off from the midst of them, and yet in their pitiful prostration had not courage to strike a blow in his defence. Still there were at least six thousand of these miserable creatures within the precincts of Hoomayoon's Tomb, and a rush of the surging multitude might have overwhelmed the little body of Hodson's Horse. But the commanding attitude and authoritative utterance of their intrepid leader overawed the congregated numbers; a great fear fell upon them; they felt that it was hopeless to endeavour to resist the power of the White Man, now that he had shattered their defences, dispersed their fighting men, and established himself in the Palace of the Moguls. So they submitted almost without a murmur; and in less time than Hodson had dared to anticipate, they were quietly collecting their arms, their horses and carriages, and under the supervision of the troopers gathering them together in the centre of the square.

Up to this time all that had been done by Hodson was worthy of a Christian Warrior. He had captured the Princes; he had disarmed their followers; and in doing so he had confronted great dangers, from the thought of which most men would have shrunk appalled. But, whether he had gone out with any foregone intentions to kill his captives, or whether any sudden emergency arose, which rendered it necessary for the public safety that they should be forthwith executed without the formality of a trial, Hodson resolved that he would shoot them down like dogs. When he left Hoomayoon's Tomb, fearing that some misadventure might have befallen the escort on the road to Delhi, he galloped forward to overtake them. As he neared them a little way outside the city he saw that a crowd was pressing on the guard and he thought that a rescue would be attempted.[67] Upon this Hodson rode in amongst them, and addressed his troopers, so as to be heard by the multitude, saying that the prisoners were the butchers who had murdered our women and children, and that an outraged Government had now ordained their punishment. So he ordered the Shahzadahs to quit the cart in which they had been placed and strip themselves to their under-vestments. They tremblingly obeyed and were ordered back to the cart. Then either thinning that his Sowars might not obey him, or rejoicing in the work of carnage, he took a carbine from one of his troopers, and deliberately, with his own hand, shot to death his unarmed and unresisting captives. This done, he rode with his prey into the city, and ordered the corpses of the Princes to be flung out and exposed to public view in front of the Kotwallie. And there they remained till the bodies rotted and stank, and it was necessary, for health's sake, to bury them.

I have told this story, briefly and plainly, as it is narrated by the only two European witnesses, who were present at this terrible execution—Hodson himself and his Second-in-Command, M'Dowall. I cannot, for a moment, question the truth of their evidence. But after a full consideration of the incident, as thus recorded and accepted, I cannot resist the conviction that Hodson, in thus stripping and shooting the Princes, committed an act which no good man can, at this distance of time, approve. That the men so suddenly sent to their account were members of the House of Delhi, was shown upon the testimony of that loyal kinsman of the King, who had been bought over, and who had accompanied Hodson for the purpose of identifying his prisoners. But that these identical men were promoters or prime agents of the massacre of our women and children, Hodson seems to have had no satisfactory proof, to justify his summary execution of the suspects. Their trial, probably, would have educed some pregnant truths illustrative of their conduct and of the conduct of other members of the Imperial House—facts now, perhaps, lost to us for ever. It was no uncommon thing in those days to execute the wrong man. I have heard terrible stories of these "mistakes"—stories not to be told unless supported by overwhelming evidence. Hodson was the last man in the Camp to trouble himself much about evidence. He believed that it was his mission to take an active personal part in the infliction of dire retribution upon the House of Delhi. On the last day of August he wrote: "If I get into the Palace, the House of Timour will not be worth five minutes' purchase, I ween; but what my share in this work will be no one can say"—and on the 23rd of September he wrote again with exultation; saying, "In twenty-four hours. I disposed of the principal members of the House of Timour the Tartar. I am not cruel, but I confess that I did rejoice in the opportunity of ridding the earth of these ruffians." He said that he would sooner have brought in the old King dead than alive. He would fain, indeed, have ridden into Delhi with the head of Behaudur Shah at his saddle-bow.

It is not to be questioned, therefore, that Hodson, as portrayed by himself, was a man of a truculent and sanguinary disposition, delighting in such deeds as this. He was gratified by the execution and proud in the remembrance of such exploits. There is no sign of his having been pained by the thought of them. He scarcely supposed that they required any justification. But as they were altogether of an abnormal character, he felt that the propriety of such an act as the massacre of the Princes might be questioned by men in authority more scrupulous than himself. He set forth therefore, firstly, that the General had told him that he did not wish to be troubled with the prisoners; and, secondly, that if he had not killed them, their adherents would have killed him. But it is not fairly to be assumed that Wilson hinted at the summary execution of the prisoners. He probably meant only that they should be made over at once to the civil authorities. The other plea has certainly much weight, if the emergency was as great as is stated. But at that time the people were so prostrate, and the Princes themselves so powerless for evil or for good, that it is little likely that any serious effort at rescue, resistance, or retaliation would have emanated from such a body, in the presence of Hodson and his well-mounted, well-armed troopers. They had not heart for such an encounter. The fact that so large a body of men had succumbed to Hodson and readily surrendered their arms at Hoomayoon's Tomb, shows the hopeless imbecility to which the adherents of the Imperial House had been reduced. And if Hodson thought that with his heroic band of horsemen he could not have guarded his prisoners and dispersed the mob, with a great slaughter, he must have thought more meanly of his own prowess and of his splended regiment than did any other man in camp.

But what was thought of this achievement by his comrades? "I cannot help being pleased," wrote Hodson, on the 25th of September, "With the warm congratulations I receive on all sides for my success in destroying the enemies of our race. The whole nation will rejoice." But in the February following he wrote in a different strain. "I made up my mind at the time to the abused. I was convinced I was right, and when I prepared to run the great physical risk of the attempt I was equally game for the moral risk of praise or blame." The truth is that, at the time of the capture of Delhi, when men's blood was fevered with anger and hatred, and their faces flushed with shame and indignation at the thought of the measureless cruelty of our enemies, some of the best and wisest of our countrymen in India looked with excited approval upon what they came afterwards to regard with calm regret. And although Hodson at one time believed that the "whole nation" would rejoice, I may aver without hesitation, that the general feeling in England was one of profound grief, not unmingled with detestation. I never heard the act approved; I never heard it even defended.

All danger was now at an end. All doubt was now at an end. The King was a captive. The city was a wreck. It had been a week of ceaseless anxiety—of tremendous care. Whatever might have been said or thought at the time, Wilson did not exaggerate the difficulties of the situation. I repeat here at the end, what I said at the beginning, of this narrative of the Siege[68]—for Justice may reiterate itself without offence—that after the excitements and impetuosities of the hour had passed away, after the eager irresponsible audacities of the younger heroes of the siege had been calmed down by the subduing influence of Time, and that great crisis in our national history had become a tradition, many of the best soldiers of the Delhi Army frankly declared that, the longer they lived, the more convinced they were, that justice had not been done to the General, who had commanded them. Men, whose blood was at fever-heat, looking only from certain fixed standpoints at details within their circumscribed view, and not seeing even the whole significance of those details, were not in a position, neither were they in a temper, at the time, to take a calm and comprehensive view of the great expanse before the General. I have observed during a period of many years the progress of this reaction. Sooner or later Time will ever bring in its revenges.

But the fact that he had taken Delhi did not seem much to rouse him from his depression. He was profoundly thankful to the Almighty for the great deliverance; but he scarcely seemed to rejoice in his victory. There can be no stronger proof of the heavy clouds of gloom which enfolded him, that no thought of honours or rewards—of the realisation of fame or fortune—as the captor of Delhi, seems to have possessed him at this time. He was too much broken down to long for anything but perfect repose. In his private letters he said little of himself. Not a particle of ambition or greed entered into them. Seldom has a man in such a position been so little egotistical:-

"The Palace, Delhi, 22nd September, 2 P.M.

"The plot thickens. Yesterday evening the King and his favourite Begum, Zenut-Mehal, gave themselves up and are now my prisoners. I have not allowed them to return to the Palace, but they are in honourable confinement in Zenut-Mehal's house. To-day Hodson and his Horse surrounded Hoomayoon's Tomb, in which some of the princes had taken refuge with nearly all the women of the Palace. Three of the Princes, Mirza Moghul, Mirza Abboo Bakr, and Mirza Rezi sultan, were taken and shot. The two former have been the most virulent against us. Hodson as a partisan officer has not his equal. To-morrow morning a movable column of about 2800 men move in the direction of Muttra, under Colonel Greathed, in pursuit of the flying rebels. If Havelock could only relieve Lucknow and move up this way, the whole rebellion would be put down I believe at once. I have sent a party of Irregular Cavalry in the direction of Meerut to my old battle-ground on the Hindun River to reconnoitre in that direction. I have not a single moment that I can call my own and cannot write you a long letter..... Hodson has presented me with the King's sword, dagger, and matchlock .... I have just heard the party I ordered to the Hindun (the Mooltanee Horse) have refused to march. You see what materials I have to work with!

"23rd September, Palace, Delhi.

"..... We are, I hope, going on smoothly. Order is getting gradually restored, though the discipline of the troops has, I am sorry to say, got sadly disorganised. Such a heterogeneous force as I command was certainly never before collected together—Beloochees, Afghans, Sikhs, Pathans, Dograhs—all of whom have been bred and taught to consider plunder of an enemy legitimate, and will not be restrained. The Europeans are so badly commanded from the loss of most of their old officers, as to be quite as bad, if not worse. I hope, however, it will soon quiet down. Burn is Military. Governor of the city and is exerting himself well...I am completely done and can't carry on much longer. I have written to J. Lawrence to tell him I am quite unequal to the task now before me and that I wish some younger and more competent man may be sent to relieve me....That fine fellow Nicholson died to-day at one o'clock; if he had been spared what an assistance he would have been to me."

During nine days John Nicholson lay dying in the Camp upon the Ridge. He had been removed to a bungalow for greater comfort and quiet. Now and then , it was said, upon medical authority, that he was a little better. But he chafed under the great misfortune that had fallen upon him. He could not rest for thinking of the doubtful issue of the final struggle. He was continually inquiring how the attack was going on—and was very readily excited by the news that was brought to him. On one occasion the vehement impetuosity of his passionate nature broke through all restraints. When told that there had been some talk of retiring, the dying hero exclaimed, "Thank God, I have still strength enough to shoot that man."

If he had lived, calmly to review all the events of this momentous siege, with its chances, its perils, its responsibilities, he would never, to himself or to others, have justified such words. And if he had ever got beside Herbert Edwardes, both men would most earnestly have condemned them. But the passionate vehemence of the natural man overbore all restraints, and there may have been something of the delirium of fever which rendered him scarcely responsible for his words. There were few of the more earnest spirits in Camp who were not moved by like seething indignation, at the thought of with drawal from Delhi; but they did not express their anger and shame in the same truculent language.

These outbursts greatly enhanced his fever and increased his pain, and it was found necessary to give him large doses of morphia to secure him temporary rest. When not under the influence of the drug,' he continued to inquire after the progress of our offensive operations, tidings of which Chamberlain, who had gone into the city with Wilson, frequently sent to his dying friend, through the "good Surgeon Mackinnon." And whenever he could leave the city he was beside his friend, gentle as a woman in his ministrations, and ever speaking words of hope and encouragement, to cheer him on his dying bed. Once or twice, as time wore on, warmed, perhaps, by the cheering intelligence which he received from the city, he rallied a little; and again his friends entertained some faint hopes of his recovery. But there was really no hope. He was wearing away to his rest.

And so days passed, and the complete occupation of the great imperial city was every day approaching the final issue. The tidings brought to Nicholson's bedside were, every day, more and more assuring. He lived to hear that the palace of the Moguls was occupied by British troops. He lived to hear that Behaudur Shah was a prisoner in our hands. He lived to hear that Hodson had, with his own hands, shot down the Princes like dogs. He lived to hear that Edward Greathed had been ordered to command the column of pursuit—a command which he himself had coveted. But he felt now that the world was passing away from him, and he thought much of those whom he was leaving behind; especially of his aged mother at Lisburne, and of Herbert Edwardes and his wife. "Tell my mother," he said, "that I do not think we shall be unhappy in the next world. God has visited her with a great affliction, but tell her she must not give way to grief." And of Edwardes he spoke, "Say that if at this moment a good fairy were to give me a wish, my wish would be to have him, here, next to my mother." This was on the evening of the 22nd of September. On the morrow morning he rendered back his soul to his Maker.

Thus died John Nicholson, in the prime of his life, amidst a great wail of the universal Camp. He was a man *sui generis*. There were features of resemblance in his character to some characteristics of other heroes of the time. He had much of the high sense of duty—the stern conscientiousness of Henry Lawrence, with something more of the impetuosity of temper which that great man so often deplored. There was much also of the fearlessness of responsibility and the contempt of authority that sometimes made Neill a thorn in the flesh of those above him. But the whole massive manhood of Nicholson had no perfect resemblance, in Camp or in Council, present or past. And the reason was this; his character was not yet fully developed. He was growing into something other than he was when he fell—something more perfect, more complete, more harmonious in its consistency. Some qualities might have been toned down and others might have ripened—each and all for the better. But before the fruit was ripe it fell to the ground. It is not difficult, however, to perceive what would have been the ripening effect of time. The very desire to get nearer to Herbert Edwardes and to think more of Henry Lawrence reveals clearly to us what would have been the growth of the future—what India lost in that final encounter. He had been so much associated with the affairs of Afghanistan and the Punjab, that his comrades and others in Lower India knew but little about his worth. They had a general idea that in the Punjab there was a man of great promise named Nicholson. It has been said that the Queen's officers were jealous of his high reputation. But there were brilliant exceptions to this. Hope Grant said of his as Nicholson lay dying that he was "like a noble oak riven asunder by a thunderbolt.[69] It must have been painful to the senior officers of the Force to be superseded by so young a man; but there were no complaints, for all admitted the grandeur of his character and his fitness for the work on which he was employed. But it is true that the Punjab was the home of his renown. The native of the district which he had governed, regarded him almost as the embodiment of an Avatar—as something little short of Godhead itself—as a hero-saint to be adored and worshipped. When he chastised his followers, they regarded it as an honour—for he could do nothing wrong in their eyes. It has been said that such is the prodigal growth of English manhood of the noblest type, in Camp and in Council, that when one great man passes away from the scene, his place is soon filled by one of equal worth. I do not think that it is so. As I write, eighteen years have passed away since Henry Lawrence, Neill, and Nicholson fell beneath the fire of the enemy; but I do not know the men who have replaced them. Nurtured by the grand old East India Company—knowing nothing of purchases and exchanges and Civil Service Commissioners, they went to the front by the unaided force of their own personal heroism. They flung aside, as if it had been a feather, the dead-weight of the seniority system. They knew little, if anything, of the art of war. But they knew how to do the right thing at the right time, and gained victories, when, according to all scientific principles, they ought to have been ignominiously and disastrously beaten.

Then from city to city, from cantonment to candonment went the chequered tidings; Delhi had fallen, the King was a captive—but John Nicholson was dead.

REFERENCES

1. A few days before he had written to the Punjab: "The Engineers have consulted me about the plan of attack though Wilson has not. They tell me they proposed to him that I should be consulted, and that be maintained a chilling silence. I imagine it is as I supposed, that he is afraid of being thought to be influenced by me. I care little, however, whether he receives my suggestions direct or through the Engineers. Like Barnard, he talks about the 'gambler's throw.' I think, however, we have a right to hope for success, and I trust that are another week passes, or flag will be flying over the Palace minars. Wilson has told me that he intends to nominate me Military Governor, for which I am much obliged, though I would rather he had told me that he intended to give me command of the column of pursuit."—*MS. Correspondence.*
2. Lieut.-Colonel Herbert commanded the Seventy-fifth, Major Jacob the Fusiliers, and Captains Green the Punjabees.
3. Lieut.-Colonel Greathed commanded the Eighth. The Fusiliers were under Captain Boyd, and Captain Rothney led the Sikhs.
4. The Fifty-Second, were under Major Vigors, the Kumaon Battalion under Captain Ramsay. Charles Nicholson Commanded the Sikhs.
5. A double dram was served out to them.
6. Vol. II., pp. 541, 542.
7. Hear Baird Smith himself on the subject: "I mentioned to you in a former letter that I had been personally familiar with the localities about Delhi for fully sixteen years. Two of the canals under my charge terminate there, on flowing through the heart of the city and throwing out branches in different directions through Delhi. In connexion with this work different plans of improvement or extension had been submitted to me and I made it part of my duty to examine the localities carefully. It was only in the mouth of September preceding the mutiny that I spent ten days at Delhi, and almost every day was occupied in examining parts of the city. My camp was pitched upon the ground

we carried our operations over, and on the whole I had, before I joined the force at all, a tolerably minute knowledge of the important features of the ground both inside and outside the place."-*Litter to General Lefroy, MS.*

8. Generally known and described as Sir Theophilus. Theophilus was a family name borne also by Sir Charles and Sir Thomas.

9. I find in the Laureate's last work, "Queen Mary," the following words, much to my purpose:

   "Stupid soldiers oft are bold. Poor lads, they see not what the general sees,

   A risk of utter ruin."

10. Nicholsons had recommended that two or three Artillery officers, with some gunners, should accompany each of the leading columns to work the captured guns (*MS. Mem*). The suggestion appears to have been a good one, and it was turned to account.

11. MS. Memorandum in handwriting of General Wilson.

12. Welby Greathed, when wounded, hid himself among the rose-bushes that his brother might not see him.

13. There was a sad mistake about this. One of the leading officers of the column thus explains it. "The supporting party of the Second Bengal Fusiliers instead of following the leading stormers to the left towards the Water Bastion, bad gone straight over the breach in the Curtain. This was the result of the divided command in the storming arising from a mixture of regiments. Thus the storming party was left without any support, and their situation would have been very critical, if the company of the Fifty-second Light Infantry, which was sent by Colonel George Campbell to clear his left flank, after he had got into the town, had not cleared the bastion of its defenders, and allowed the remnant of the Eighth stormers to make their way in."—*MS. Memorandum.*

14. Unpublished letter from Major-General Jones to Sir Archdale Wilson, March, 1864. This was written, at the suggestion of Colonel (now Sir Edward) Greathed, in consequence of an error in Wilson's Delhi despatch, in which he says: "The firm establishment of the Reserve rendering the assaulting columns free to act in advance, Brigadier-General Nicholson, supported by Brigadier Jones, Swept the ramparts of the

place from the Cashmere to the Caubul Gates, occupying the bastions and defences, capturing the guns and driving the enemy before him." Wilson sent the letter to me (for which purpose, indeed, it was written) and confirmed the truth of it. Greathed, who commanded the Eighth under Jones, wrote to the latter: "As I was close to you from the time we got up to the top of the breach together, until you had finally caused the troops to re-form and rest at the Caubul Gate, I am perfectly aware that the clearing of the walls, ramparts, and bastions was performed solely under you orders, and that Nicholson did not join us until some time after at the Caubul Gate, when the work had been accomplished."

15. "The Lahore Bastion kept up a steady fire on us from a twelve-pounder, which we could not silence, and a couple of guns were brought to bear on us from a side street; but fourteen men of the Seventy-fifth ran down and took one of them; the other was taken away, and we received no further molestation from that quarter. A gun was also brought to bear upon us from the end of the long straight street which led down directly to our position at the Caubul Gate: and this pelted us throughout the day with round shot and grape. In short our position was a ticklish one."—*MS. Memorandum by an Officer of the Eighth Foot.*

16. See a very interesting letter from an officer of the regiment, quoted in Hodson's "Twelve Years of a Soldier's Life": "again the word was forward, and leading on the men, my glorious friend George Jacob was mortally wounded; he, poor fellow, was shot in the thigh, and died that night. As he lay writhing in agony on the ground, unable to stand, two or three men went to take him to the rear, but a sense of duty was superior to bodily pain, and he refused their aid, desiring them to go and take the guns."

17. The writer above quoted says of Speke that he was "gentle everywhere but in the field." Speke never recovered from his wounds. Greville happily was spared.

18. Charles Nicholson survived the operation, but he never altogether recovered from the effects of his wounds, and soon passed away. Sir Hope grant speaks of him as one of three young officers worthy of especial mention—Probyn, Watson, and Nicholson.

19. Most accounts state that it was a portfire. It was really a slow-match as stated in the text.
20. Lieutenant Medley writes:–"The bugle sounded the advance, and then with a loud cheer the Fifty-second charged through the broken gateway." I wish I could accept this statement unreservedly. But I am bound to add that Sergeant Smith, in an unpublished memorandum given "in the Appendix, says: "They did not go fast. Their bugler had sounded fifty times at least, and some ten minutes elapsed before any one came." It was not only known at Head-Quarters, but throughout the army, that there had been some backwardness.
21. Now Lieutenant-Colonel Chesnev President of the Engineering College at Cooper's Hill.
22. It is stated in MS. accounts that some men of the party were killed. I believe that this was a mistake. Chesney was in advance of his party when the shell burst.
23. In pursuance of the principle and practice of the time, the guns were taken away from Renny's troop and restored after the fall of Delhi. The gunners were all Hindostanees, but they were as ready to fight against the Poorbeah rebels as if the enemy had been of a different colour and a different rece. It is a remarkable illustration of the scant justice done to the Artillery, that no mention was made of Renny's troop in any of the despatches.
24. An officer of the Second Column, who saw the advance says: "The sight at this moment was beautiful. We could see the two columns on our right up the breach and the Cashmere Bastion; like a swarm of bees, or rather like the horses of the Sun all abreast—then like hounds topping the fence into a gorse cover they disappeared into the town."—*MS. Journal.*
25. In a letter to the Reverend Mr. Rotton, Chaplain and Historian, Reid says that he was to have entered the city by the *Caubul Gate.* But Norman, who was Deputy-Adjutant-General, has recorded that the Fourth Column was to enter by the Lahore Gate (*ut supra,* 583). The two statements are not irreconcilable. The fact appears to be that the enemy held the Lahore Gate in force and were not disposed to evacuate it. It would have been a dangerous experiment for Reid, weakened by much fighting in the suburbs, to attempt to carry it.
26. Autograph notes by General Wilson and Colonel Baird Smith.

27. Norman says that "the Cashmere Contingent (Jummoo troops) were so sharply attacked by the insurgents, who were in great force, that, after losing a great number of men, and four guns, they were completely defeated and fell back to Camp. Major Reid's column met with the most strenuous opposition, greatly increased, doubtless, by the failure of the Cashmere Contingent, and the enemy were so numerous and so strongly posted, that after the loss of many men and officers, the Commander, Major Reid, having been carried away severely wounded, Captain, Muter, Sixtieth Rifles, the next senior officer, judiciously withdrew the troops to their former post at Hiudoo Rao's and the Subzemundee." The variance between these two statements is obvious. It may, perhaps, is some measure, be explained by the fact that Major Lawrence came to Delhi, not in a military but in a political capacity. I find no mention of this affair in Mrs. Muter's interesting volumes.

28. The Commandant of this distinguished corps, Major Henry Daly, was then at Hindoo Rao's recovering from his wounds. He was able to take charge of the Picket for a time, though , as he said, able neither to ride nor to run.

29. Captain M'Barnett was an officer of the Fifty-fifth Native Infantry.

30. This man was a Sikh chief, who had fought against us at Chillian wallah. He offered his services to us, when the mutiny broke out, and went to Delhi with Daly and the Guides.

31. Among the troops at Hindoo Rao's house were a part of the Kumaon Battalion. They were in a somewhat disorderly state, when chamberlain, reproving them for their noise and confusion, addressed them as a *Pultan* (regiment) and called forth an indignant, half-insolent rejoinder: "We are not a regiment, but a battation" Chamberlain's answer was prompt and to the point: "Then show yourselves worthy of the distinction." Order was at once restored.

32. I believe that the Belochee regiment were first to arrive. They were steadfast in their loyalty and fought well. Captain Bannerman was killed.

33. There was a skirmish on the 11th, in which the Punjab Horse greatly distinguished themselves. The enemy's Cavalry in the Kishenganje suburbs had suddenly attacked one of our pickets; seeing this, Watson, the heroic commander of the

First Punjab Cavalry, turned out at once, with his troopers and a few of the Second, and went at the insurgents at "tip-top speed." It was a wild helter-skelter affair; but the enemy could not stand the rush of our horsemen. Some forty of them were left dead on the field. Our own loss was slight, but Watson himself encountering one of the enemy's most intrepid swordsman in hand-to-hand fight, received a swashing sabre-cut on the head, which glanced off his helmet, and clove his left cheek and upper lip. He was also slightly cut on the shoulder. But he was not a man to take heed of anything much less than a death wound; so he had his face sewn up, and went about his work as before. The sear will go with him to the grave.

34. It was at this time that Sir Hope Grant says that he saw Nicholson on the ramparts and exchanged greetings with him. "He called out to me that fighting was going on well for us in the town, and that he was on his way to attack the Lahore Gate." I am informed, however, that it was not Nicholson, but Colonel Greathed, who spoke to Hope Grant from the ramparts. Both, however, may have spoken to him.

35. Captain Drysdale commanded the detachment of Lancers. Hope Grant says of his that he was "a gallant officer and a thorough Scotchman."

36. Sir Hope Grant ("Incidents in the Sepoy War") writes: "Though the officer in command of that post, Chamberlain, who had partially recovered from his wounds, was himself short of men, he placed at my despoils two hundred and eighty men of his little force."

37. It would be a very close approximation to the truth to say that the casualty list on the 14th was this: *Europeans*, eight officers killed, fifty-two wounded. Rank and file: one hundred and sixty-two killed and five hundred and ten wounded. *Natives*: Killed, one hundred and three; wounded, three hundred and ten.

38. A life-like picture of Wilson and his Staff, at this time, is given in the following extract from the Journal of an Artillery officer: "Towards evening, Frith" (of the Artillery—Wilson's brother-in-law) came to me and said, 'The General wishes you to fire some shells just over the top of Skinner's house (in which the General and Staff were), as the enemy had just got into the houses there close by. I pointed out that I had no regular scales and weights and that it was a ticklist

operation, because I knew not what posts were held by us beyond, in the direction of the Moree Bastion. I, therefore, went with him to Skinner's house, and in a large hall I found Johnson, Norman, Anson, and the rest of the Staff and told them I wished to speak about the order I had got. They told me that in that case I had better speak to the General myself, for they had rather not go near him, and pointed to him at the other end of the hall, where he sat balancing himself in a chair, with his face to the wall, on which his feet rested. I told him my errand and he said 'Come, and I will show you what I want, and I followed him to the flat roof of the house, where, creeping to the edge, we looked down on the houses beyond, where we could see the enemy firing at our field guns and a strong picket in the street at the gate, who even came and fired upon us. After looking at the state of affairs and hearing what I had to say, he told me I had better leave it alone; and going back to the hall resumed his old contemplative position."—*MS. Records*.

39. I have the clearest possible proof of this in a memorandum, written for me by a Field Officer, who heard the conversation: "I got some men together," he writes, and cleared the way for the guns to enter. General Wilson and his Staff passed through the gate soon after this. I joined them, and accompanied them to the vicinity of Skinner's house. Whilst standing there reports were brought to the General that some of the attacking columns had been checked in their advance.... Wilson appealed to Colonel Baird Smith, asking him if he thought we could hold what we had taken. The reply was clear and decisive that we *must* do so."

40. *See ante*, page 575, for Baird Smith's own statement. I have read in print, some fabulous accounts, with fancy pictures, of the General propped up by Chamberlain and Seaton, in the city, and forced by them to do what was right. Chamberlain was at Hindoo Rao's house, and Seaton, whose irrepressible desire to see what was going on, took him down to the scene of our operations, was soon sent back to Camp, by the infirmity of the flesh, "so sick and faint that he was more than two hours returning, and when he got to his tent he felt if he should never rise again from his bed."

41. "It was deplorable to see hundreds of bottles of wine and brandy, which were sadly needed for our sick, shivered, and their contents sinking into the ground. Wine Which had

fallen to threepence the bottle soon rose again to six shillings."—*History of the Siege of Delhi by One who was there.*

42. See vol. ii., pp. 90, 91.

43. *Ante*, page 617, note.

44. "I found our Doctor at the General Hospital," writes Medley, "and then heard, as he exclaimed on seeing my bandaged arms, 'what, another of you!' That I was the eighth Engineer officer that had already claimed his good offices today." Salkeld and Tandy were killed—the former, as already related; the latter on the withdrawal of the Third Column and Reserve from the attempt on the Jumma Musjid.

45. As Field-Engineer he had accompanied the Brigadier - General and the First Column of Attack, and when Nicholson, as above related, visited the Second Column, he left the troops immediately under him and all operations that might be necessary to the charge of Captain Taylor, in case the signal were given, during the absence of his chief, for an advance—a contingeney which actually occurred. The assault on the breach was delivered under the direction of the Field Engineer.

46. This refers to what was done on the day of the assault. After the assault, as already shown, Baird Smith removed his Head Quarters to the City. He found that his Lieutenant had anticipated all that he desired to be done. Taylor, then worn out with exhaustion from the preceding eight days' hard work in the Batteries, and suffering much from his wound, was compelled to betake himself to his bed until the latter part of the 17th, when he returned to fling himself into his work with all his old energy unabated.

47. This is called by some writers the Burn Bastion. It led to the Lahore Gate. I have adhered to uniformity by calling it the Lahore Gate throughout the narrative.

48. Burn, who had distinguished himself in Afghanistan, and who had afterwards approved himself as an excellent administrator in one of the great Public Departments at the Presidency. He was a general favourite with the Bengal Army. At Delhi he appeared only as a volunteer, and having no fixed position could not avail himself of his rank, But he war very useful as a field officer, and General Wilson spoke of him as one of his best officers. He accompanied Nicholson's column on the morning of the assault.

49. In this attack Lieutenant Bristowe of the Seventy-fifth was killed.
50. In a letter before me this is described as the "sagacious instinct of the British soldier, which teachers him what can be and what cannot be done." But the *Audace, audace—toujours audace*! is better than this.
51. Whether this was the first intimation that reached Head-Quarters I do not know. I follow here only the statement of the Cavalry Brigadier. Sir Thomas Seaton also says that he reported it himself at Head Quarters. Many others, doubtless, did the same.
52. Aitkin of the Artillery shot one of them. See in Appendix, an interesting account of the capture of the Palace and Selimgurh.
53. Moore's poetry is better than his authorities. Quoting Franklin, he informs his readers that around the exterior of the Dewan-Khas in the cornice are the following words in letters of gold on a ground of white marble: "If there be a Paradise on earth, it is this, it is this." The inscription is in letters of *black marble inside* the hall; and I can find no other account of its having been otherwise.
54. Major James Brind to Colonel Gaitskill, commanding Artillery.—*MS. Correspondence.*
55. There has been a story, long time current, to the effect that a number of wretched villagers were hung up, because they had some new *pice* in their possession (a neighbouring treasury having been looted); but it appeared afterwards that the copper coins had been paid to them, for milk, vegetables, grain, & c., by a detachment of our own people. I have no authentic evidence of the truth of this story—so I merely relate it as something very like truth. In the language of the day every Native of the country was a traitor—if he turned against us. The Sepoys, who had received our pay, and had been drilled and disciplined by us, were, in some sense, rebels and traitors—but all the other inhabitants of Delhi who did *not* strive mightily, against us were, assuredly, rebels and traitors. All their loyalty was due to the Mogul.
56. *Ante*, Vol. ii. p. 629-631.
57. "History of the Siege of Delhi by an officer who served there."—This very able writer observes: "Helplessness ought to be respected in either sex, especially in those who have

never done us wrong. It is as unmanly for an officer to drive his sword through a trembling old man or a soldier to blow out the brains of a wounded boy, as to strike a woman."

58. "Eight Months' Campaign in India against the Bengal Sepoy Army, by Lieutenant-Colonel Bourchier, C.B."-Afterwards Sir George Bourchier, K.C.B.

59. This was Jung Behaudur's house. The Eighth had afterwards to evacuate it, as the building was required for other purposes.

60. Much mention is made of Welby Greathed, the Engineer, and of his bold projects for a *coup-de-main*, in Barnard's time, will be found in the second volume of this History. He was severely wounded in the assault (*ante* page 592). Edward Greathed was Lieutenant Colonel of the Eighth Foot. Wilson, at no time very prodigal of praise, spoke of him as one of his best officers of his force. His subsequent career in India will be detailed in the last volume of this history. He was created a Knight-Commander of the Bath in 1865. Hervey Greathed himself was a man of high promise. He had passed out from Haileybury first of his term, and was held in great estimation by all under whom he served, especially by Mr. Colvin, who was in confidential communication with him almost to the day of the Lieutenant-Governor's death. He was at Meerut, when the mutiny broke out, and went to Delhi with Wilson's force. See vol. ii., pages 68 and 183.

61. See *ante*, vol. ii. p. 182.

62. These are a translation of Elahee Buksh's own words as given in a manuscript statement before me.

63. "See a letter addressed to Hodson's brother in "Twelve Years of a Soldier's Life." The writer is probably Captain M'Dowall, of the Bengal Fusiliers, and second-in-command of Hodson's Horse, who could use his pen as well as his sword.

64. Hodson himself spoke of the Behaudur Shah as a mere puppet, a "ruse," "He is old and well-nigh impotent, and is only used as an authority for all the acts of rebellion ad barbarity committed by his sons." Yet he admits that he would rather have brought in the king dead than alive.

65. These delegates were the notorious Moonshee Rujjub Ali, who was the very life of Hodson's Intelligence Department, and the "loyal" member of the Delhi Family, willing to betray his kinsmen for his own ends.

66. Meerza Elahee Buksh had a principal hand in this. "At night," he says, "when I went to Hodson Sahib he told me to bring to him the Meerza Khazar Sooltan, Meerza Mogul, and Meerza Aboo-Bakr. I Answered that I had already made arrangements for that. He might find them any time he liked. . . . Then (22nd September) according to the order of Hodson Sahib, I brought those three above-mentioned from the sepulchre to him. Having taken them with the King's property with him, he returned, and was very pleased with me."--*MS. Records*.

67. It is not stated whether these, or any of these, were armed men.

68. *Ante*, pp. 554-555.

69. Incidents in the Sepoy War," by General Sir Hope Grant.

Note:- Much that I wished to say in this chapter has unavoidably been left unsaid. But it is proposed to return to Delhi in the first chapter of the next volume. It is but an episode in this story: but it is a very important episode; and demands more than common consideration.

6

British Policy

SECT. I—HOME GOVERNMENT

It will appear from the preceding summary that the government of British India is administered in England by two distinct departments:—

1. By the East India Company as represented by the Court of Directors; and 2. By the Crown as represented by the Board of Control.

Constitution of East India Company—Court of Directors.

The Court of Directors, as reconstituted in 1853, consists of eighteen Members, of whom it is provided that twelve shall be elected by the votes of all Proprietors possessing the requisite qualification of 1000/- East India Stock, while the remaining six Directors are to be appointed by the Crown—the qualification of all Directors being fixed at 1000/- East India Stock. All the Directors appointed by the Crown, and six of those to be elected by the Proprietors, must have been civil servants of the Company in India of ten years' standing.

The Chairman and Deputy Chairman of the Court of Directors are elected by that body from among themselves annually by ballot, the usual practice being that the Deputy Chairman of one year is elected Chairman at the commencement of the succeeding one, and retains that office also for one year.

In the Court of Directors is vested the power to originate all measures for the Government of India, and all grants of money, both at home and in India; also the patronage of all military, naval, and ecclesiastical appointments, in respect to the primary nomination of candidates, except those to the civil service, which has been, since 1853, opened to public competition under conditions hereafter to be noticed. The mode of distributing the patronage still reserved to the Court of Directors is as follows:—An estimate of the probable requirements of the service in the various departments having been framed, the appointments are distributed among the Directors in proportions arranged between themselves, the Chairman and Deputy Chairman having the largest share, and certain appointments being placed by courtesy at the disposal of the President of the Board of Control.

The patronage of certain superior appointments in India also rests with the Court of Directors. These appointments are as follows: General Officers on the Staff for the Company's Army, the Superintendent of the Indian Navy, the Master Attendant in Bengal and in Madras, and volunteers who are appointed by Directors in rotation for the pilot service, Assay-Masters for the Mint, who are generally, though, not always, members of the services in India, but appointed at home, because it is necessary that they should qualify in this country; the law-officers of the Government at each of the Presidencies, and the Members of Council, as well that of India as those of Madras and Bombay, with the exception of the fourth or legislative Member of the first-named Council, whose appointment is subject to the approbation of the Crown. With respect to appointments to vacancies among Members of Council, the ordinary course is for the Chairman and Deputy-Chairman to select three or four individuals from among the civil servants of the Company of twenty-five years' standing. The records are searched for an account of their services, of which statements are drawn up and notice is given that those documents will be laid before the Court with reference to filling up the vacancy. It is open to any Member of the Court to ask that a statement of the services of any other eligible person should be prepared. On the day of election the merits of the several parties are discussed, and the appointment is determined by ballot.

The Court of Directors possesses also the following further rights of patronage, subject to the approval of the Crown, signified through the Board of Control, that is to say, the power of appointing the Governor-General (who has, in practice, been usually selected by friendly arrangement between the Chairman of the Court and the President of the Board of Control, from the public men of the day, who supported the existing Administration); also the Governors of the subordinate Presidencies, the Commanders-in-Chief, and the fourth Member of the Supreme Council (the remaining Members being appointed by the Court absolutely).

In the event of a nomination to any of the offices subject to veto not being approved by the Crown, the Court must proceed to make another and if this be not made before the expiration of two months, the Crown may appoint. The Court has the power of recalling or removing any of the officers or servants of the Company (except those appointed by the Crown, on default of the Court), and this power is absolute and uncontrolled.

Secret Committee

The Court of Directors meets weekly at the East India House for the transaction of business, the ordinary details of which are discharged by three Committees, designated:—1. Finance and Home. 2. Political and Military. 3. Revenue, Judicial and Legislative. There is also a "Secret Committees," with peculiar functions altogether different from those of the three ordinary Committees. The office of the Secret Committee is purely ministerial. It receives from India all dispatches on matters with respect to which secrecy is deemed important—including those which relate to war, peace, or negotiations with Native powers or States within the limits of the Charter, or other States or Princes; and forwards such dispatches to the Board of Control. The Secret Committee also transmits to India, after signature, dispatches prepared by that Board, which it is bound to do, under oath, prescribed by statute 3 and 4 Will. IV. cap. 85, s. 35, "without disclosing the same". The Secret Committee is composed, as prescribed by Act of Parliament, of three Directors. The Court may elect whom they please, but the Chairman, Deputy-Chairman, and senior Member of the Court are almost invariably appointed.

The papers of the Secret Committee are in charge of the Examiner at the East India House, who is clerk to the Committee.

The Directors of the East India Company receive salaries (fixed in 1853 by statute 16 and 17 Vict. c. 95, s. 34), as follows:—

The Chairman and Deputy-Chairman 1000/-, all the other Members of the Court 500/- each per annum.

Court of Proprietors

The Court of Proprietors, or "General Court," consists of all holders of a certain prescribed amount of East India stock. All holders of 500/- stock are entitled to attend the Court, and to speak. 1000/- stock is the qualification for voters, of whom there are now about 1800.

The General Court, which is held quarterly, possesses no longer its ancient powers, which were coextensive with those now exercised by the Court of Directors.

The remaining powers are as follows:—

1. Of electing twelve out of the eighteen Directors, subject to the qualifications above-mentioned.
2. Of making bye-laws not inconsistent with the laws of the land.

3. Of making money-grants, and of controlling those proposed by the Court of Directors in favour of their servants in India, exceeding 600/- in a round sum, or 200/- per annum to one person.
4. Of calling for the production of dispatches, except those in the Department of the Secret Committee.

The establishment of the East India House consists of four departments,[1] and is maintained at a cost of about 120,000/- per annum.[2]

Board of Control

The Board of Commissioners for the affairs of India, commonly called the "Board of Control," is practically a corporation sole—the duties of which devolve on a Cabinet Minister, who is designated "President" of a Board which has, for purposes of business, no real existence.

The present theoretical Constitution of the Board is defined by statute 3 and 4 Will. IV. cap. 85, by which the Crown is empowered to appoint as Commissioners for the affairs of India any number of persons, whether of the Privy Council or not; and it is enacted that the Lord President of the Council, the Lord Privy Seal, the First Lord of the Treasury, the principal Secretaries of State, and the Chancellor of the Exchequer shall, by virtue of their offices, be Members of the Board;—two to form a quoram, and the Commissioner first named in the patent to be President.

The Commissioners never now sit as a Board, though it appears that in former times they did so, and minutes of the attendance of Mr. Dundas, Mr. Pitt, and others exist. Subsequently, when there were two paid junior Commissioners, there were occasional meetings; but since the only paid Commissioner has been the President, no Board has been held. The President is regarded as acting on his own responsibility.

The fiction of a "Board" is however still kept up, by the signature of one of the ex-officio Members, being, in conformity with the law, attached to all documents recording the decisions of the President.

The chief powers of the Board are now as follow:—

1. The supervision of all financial measures of the Courts of Directors.
2. The revision of all their correspondence.
3. The exercise of veto, in the name of the Crown, on the patronage of certain appointments above specified, and the absolute patronage of certain other appointments, as of the Indian Bishops and the Judges of the Supreme Courts.
4. The right of recalling or dismissing, in the name of the Crown, an officer or servant of the Company in India.

Two Secretaries were, by statute 3 and 4 Will. IV. cap. 85, attached to the Board; one of whom is a Member of the House of Commons, and liable to lose his office when the Administration by whom he was appointed lose theirs—the other Secretary being a permanent official.

The business coming before the Board is divided among six Departments:—

1. Revenue, embracing all matters relating to the assessment and collection of the revenues of India.
2. Finance and accounts, taking cognisance of the public expenditure, remittances, and the management of mints in India.
3. Military.
4. Marine and Ecclesiastical.
5. Political.
6. Judicial and Legislative.

These departments are all placed under the supervision of the two Secretaries, three being committed to each Secretary and to each of the Departments are attached a senior clerk, an assistant clerk, and junior clerks. There is also as Secret Department in the Board of Control for the purpose of carrying on written and oral communications with the Secret Committee of the Court of Directors. The latter class of communications are for the most part carried on through the President personally; in the former he is assisted by a senior clerk, and occasionally by the Secretaries of the Board.

It appears that on the arrival of secret dispatches from India, the copy intended for the Board is sent to the senior clerk in the Secret Department, who prepares a precis of all the letters and enclosures, which he lays before the President, who thereupon gives him instructions, oral or written, for the preparation of an answer, or sometimes drafts one himself. It is then copied in official form and transmitted to the Secret Committee at the East India House.

The salary of the President (having been changed five times since the first constitution of the Board in 1784,) now stands at 5000/- per annum. The establishment consists (in addition to the two Secretaries) of about thirty clerks, and is maintained at an average annual cost of about 30,000/- per annum.

The present Constitution of the Court of Directors and that of the Board of Control having been thus briefly described, it remains to explain the mode by which the powers given to the latter over the proceedings of the former are exercised.

Mode of transacting business adopted by the Court of Directors and the Board of Control.

In the ordinary transaction of the business of the Home Government of India, for the purposes of that intercommunication which takes place between the Court and the Board, the former are represented ordinarily by the Chairman and Deputy Chairman, the latter by the President.

This complicated system of mutual check and intervention is nowhere more clearly described than in the evidence given by Mr. Waterfield and Sir James Melvill before the Parliamentary Committees of 1852. That evidence, as condensed in the analysis subsequently printed, is as follows:—

Each dispatch from India is laid before the Court of Directors, to which body all dispatches are addressed. They arrive in duplicate, one copy being fro the Court, one for the Board. When a dispatch comes from India it is accompanied by a collection of papers bearing upon the subject, which collection contains the former correspondence relating to it, and the present proceedings of the Government upon it. The dispatch comes to the Secretary's office, and from it is immediately transferred to the department to which it relates. In that department an abstract of the contents of the dispatch is made; this is lithographed, and copies of it are sent to the Chairman and Deputy-Chairman, and the members of the Committee having the superintendence of the department to which the dispatch relates. The officer in charge of that department then communicates with the Chairman and Deputy upon the dispatch, and, in cases in which the subjects are not mere routine, receives instructions as to the tenor of the reply. A draft answer is then prepared, and submitted with the collections to the Chairman and the Deputy; they confer together, and with the officer, upon the subject; and when the draft conforms to their views, they place their initials upon it as the authority for its being sent to the President of the Board, in what is technically called "P. C.;" that is to say, previous communication. When the "previous communication" is received from the India House, it is referred, with the accompanying "collections," to the senior clerk of the department to which it may belong. It is his duty to make himself acquainted with the contents of the papers, and the "previous communication" is then, with the notes and comments of the clerk, laid before the Secretary under whom the particular department has been placed. He reads these papers, and, if not satisfied with them, he refers to the "collections". Having formed his opinion, he expresses it in writing; and the papers are, with that opinion, submitted to the President.

The President in like manner reads the "previous communication," and the notes and comments, and, if necessary, refers to the "collections". Having considered these various papers, he gives his decision; that decision may be entire approval of the "previous communication;" the cancelling of it, on the ground that it is not advisable to give any opinion on the subject; the substitution of other paragraphs in place of those proposed; or the partial alteration of them, in greater or less degree. The "previous communication" is returned to the clerk, in order that the President's decision may be carried into effect, and it is then sent back to the Chairman, together with the "collections". The "previous communication," in fact, is merely a suggestion of the way in which the Chairman and Deputy think that the dispatch or letter should be answered; so the alterations made in the "previous communication" by the President are merely suggestions back again to the Chairman and Deputy of the way in which the President thinks that the draft should stand. There is nothing authoritative till the proposed dispatch is in the form of a draft; what passes is considered on both sides merely a suggestion. If the "previous communication" be returned unaltered, the draft is immediately submitted to the Committee of the Court having superintendence of the department in which it is. If altered, the officer communicates with the Chairman and Deputy-Chairman, who either allow wholly or partially, or reject entirely, the alterations. Differences are generally settled in conference between the President and the Chairman and Deputy at the weekly meeting which takes place between them. If they do not succeed in convincing each other, or in effecting a compromise, it remains for the Chairman and Deputy to consider whether they should adhere rigidly to their opinion or not. The draft is finally arranged by the, and is then submitted to the Committee. Drafts generally lie on the table of the Committee for a week, during which time both the draft, and any papers bearing upon the case, are perused by the members of the Committee. The Committee then discuss the draft, and adopt or alter it as they think fit, after which it is submitted to the Court, who usually take a week for consideration, and then the draft comes on for discussion. Every Director has an opportunity of expressing his sentiments, and, if he differ from the majority, of recording a dissent. When the draft is approved by the Court, the Secretary sends it officially, with all the papers, including the dissents, if any, to the Board of Commissioners, and the Board return it always within two months, the period limited by law, approved or altered; and if altered, with a statement of their reasons for making the alteration. The unaltered drafts are immediately transcribed, and fair copies, signed by at least thirteen Members of the Court, are despatched to India. The altered drafts are referred to the proper Committee, upon whose report the Court decide, either that the alterations shall be adopted, in which case the draft is signed and despatched to India, or that a remonstrance shall be addressed to the Board against the alterations, in which case the draft is retained until the decision of the Board is communicated. Instances are known where, on the Board adhering to its original opinion, a second letter has been written by order of the Court, and even a rejoinder to a second reply. Ultimately the dispatch is sent out as approved by the Board; and the instances are not numerous in which the Board overrule the Court.

The Court, after remonstrance, have the power of recording a protest against a decision of the Board from which it finally dissents; and under a bye-law such protest is to be laid before the next General Court. But it is only in a case believed to be of very serious importance that the Court would have recourse to such a proceeding, and no instance of the exercise of this right has occurred since 1834.

By the 3 & 4 Will. IV. cap. 85, if the Court doubt whether any instructions of the Board be consistent with law, a case may be framed, which, when approved by the Board, is to be submitted to three judges of the Court of Queen's Bench, whose decision upon the point at issue is to be final. But neither has this right ever been exercised. Of the drafts that go to the Board in "P.C." (previous communication), more than one-half come back without any alteration at all. It appears, however, that in the Political Department (to which the statement is limited) there are not many previous communications returned without some alterations, but these are usually adopted by the Court. Of the altered drafts, a large proportion consist of alterations that are little more than verbal, and are generally acquiesced in by the Chairman and Deputy-Chairman before the draft goes to the Committee; and of the drafts that, being approved by the Committee and the Court, go to the Board officially, and are returned by it, not more than five per cent contain any alterations.

Since the last Act came into operation, no case of irreconcilable difference between the Court and the Board has arisen. Previously there were one or two instances in which the resistance of the Court to the views of the Board was so determined, that the latter threatened to enforce their purpose by *mandamus*.

Previous communications have sometimes been returned from the Board in one or two days. Usually they are returned within three months, but oftener much sooner. In 1851 there was only one in the Political Department which remained in the office a month. There have been cases in which such communications have been detained a year or more.

The origin of the practice of making previous communications seems not distinctly trace, though a record of such papers is retained. It is thought to have arisen about the year 1793. At an early period it was restricted to questions of principle, but gradually extended itself to details. The title P.C. used to be regarded as something mysterious, until Mr. Canning made known its meaning in a speech made by him in the House of Commons, on a motion of Mr. Creevey. Some sort of communications probably took place between the President and the Chairman and Deputy before these more formal ones.

The ordinary interval between the return of the previous communication to the India House and the sending up the draft is about a month or five weeks.

Previous communication being entirely a matter of private understanding between the Court and the President, and there being no law to prevent a proposed dispatch being sent up in the first instance as a draft, this occasionally takes place. Drafts come up at once *as* drafts, sometimes because they treat of more matters of course, sometimes because they relate to matters of a pressing nature, and a mail may be on the point of departure; but if a long dispatch were required, the previous communication would not be dispensed with.

Dispatches are addressed to the Governor-General of India in Council, to the Governor in Council of Madras, to the Governor in Council of Bombay, and the Governor of Fort William. None are addressed to the Lieutenant-Governor of the North-West Provinces, the whole of that correspondence being conducted with the Governor-General.

The Court has the initiative in the preparation of dispatches: of the board of Control think any subject neglected it can call upon the Court to frame a dispatch in regard to it; and, in the case of the Court's non-compliance within fourteen days, the Board has the power to frame such dispatch, and send it to the Court to be forwarded to India.

SECT. II.—LOCAL GOVERNMENT

The Supreme Local Administration of India (which was formerly distributed between the three co-ordinate Governments of Fort William, Madras, and Bombay,) is now centred in the "Governor-General of India in Council," the seat of the Supreme Government being now at Calcutta, but removable at the will of the Governor-General.

Governor-General in Council—his powers and duties

The Governor-General is, as has been stated, appointed by the Court of Directors with the approbation of the Crown. The Supreme Council consists of four ordinary members, three of whom must have been civil or military servants of the Company in India of at least ten years' standing, and the fourth a person not previously in the service of the Company. The Commander-in-Chief of the forces in India is also always admitted an extraordinary member of the Council, which thus consists altogether of five members. To these were added in 1853, six Legislative Members, empowered only to sit and vote on the framing of Laws and Regulations; of these, four are civil servants of the Company of ten years' standing in Bombay, Madras, Bengal, and the North-West Provinces respectively, and the two remaining members are the Chief Justice and one other Judge of the Supreme Court of Calcutta. Two other members may be appointed by the Governor-General, under section 22 of statute 16 and 17 Vict. cap. 95.[3]

The Council of India may thus be said to consist, for general purposes of Executive Government, of six members, including the Governor-General and Commander-in-Chief, and for Legislative purposes of twelve members—seven to be a quorum.

The powers vested in the Governor-General are extensive. They are as follows:—

He has a veto on all legislative measures proposed in Council, and an independent prerogative of initiating and carrying out measures irrespective of the Council. He has also the patronage of nearly all appointments designated as "political" throughout India; these comprise the Residents in native States and the Commissioners in the Non-Regulation Provinces. In the Governor-General is also vested the appointment of the Lieutenant-Governor of Bengal and the North-West Provinces, also that of the Judges of the Sudder Courts and the military patronage in Bengal and the North-West Provinces.

The Governor-General in Council has also a direct control over all those districts of British India comprising the Punjab, Cis-Sutlej States, Oude, Berar, Pegu, the Tenasserim Provinces and the Straits' Settlements, which are not included within the limits of any of the four subordinate Governments. His authority extends also to the territories of all native princes with whom we have contracted subsidiary or protective relations, and to the exercise of such influence as Great Britain may possess by treaty over those independent States which have accepted of our mediation.

Official Staff of Governor General

The official staff of the Governor-General in Council consists of four Secretaries of the four following Departments:—

1. The political or so called "Foreign" Department, to which is committed all correspondence arising out of British relations with native States.
2. The Home Department, which is charged with the judicial and revenue correspondence.
3. The Financial Department.
4. The Military Department.

There is also a Secret Department of both the Political and Finance Secretariats, to which all secret dispatches are entrusted.

Mode of transacting business

The mode of transacting the business of the Council is as follows:—All papers involving questions for discussion or projects of law are circulated, going first to the Governor-General and then to all the Members of Council.

The Council meets at the Government House once or twice a week. At or before the Meeting, the Governor-General writes orders on the backs of the papers, in which, if the Members of Council concur, they subscribe their initials, and letters in conformity therewith are despatched from the Secretary's office. If a member of Council dissent, he writes "reserve," and the case is then brought before the Council for discussion. In other matters the Governor-General reserves the case for discussion, or minutes upon it, when the Members of Council do the same; or a Member of Council may record a minute at once, while the papers are in circulation. The mode of conducting the correspondence between the Government of India and the Court of Directors is the following: Upon questions requiring a reference to the Court's authority, and in matters of more than ordinary importance, separate letters are prepared and written; but upon the whole record it is usual that a report should be sent every quarter, which reviews the whole proceedings of the Government, and is called a quarterly general letter; that is, every letter of any importance on the record, and the substance of the reply, are abstracted and reported in paragraphs of this general letter, and these general letters are sent home now with the collections of papers referred to in each paragraph. Three copies of the government proceedings used to be sent quarterly, the whole proceedings being completely copied out in triplicate for the purpose; but when collections were sent home, one copy was dispensed with. The letters thus transmitted are replied to by the Court with the same detail, every paragraph having us paragraph of reply. The dispatches of the Court of Directors, immediately upon their arrival in India, are circulated among the Members of the Government, as above stated, and the Secretary takes the orders upon them, paragraph by paragraph. It is then the duty of the Secretary to write the resolution upon every paragraph *seriatim*, which resolution is the foundation of orders, if such are required, to the subordinate authorities, and at the same time gives the substance of the reply, when the time comes to make the reply to the Court of Directors. The time occupied in transmitting a communication and receiving a reply varies according to the nature of the matter contained in the dispatch; sometimes orders may be required to be sent to a subordinate Board, calling for an explanation, before a full reply can be sent; those orders appear in the record as issued on the day when the Court's dispatch is read, and the reply is entered on the record on the date when it arrives, and is laid before the Council. In replying to the Court, these letters are all referred to, and the substance of the specific statements is given, but the receipt of the dispatch is always separately acknowledged. Under the present system, collections have to be made in India for every paragraph, and sent home in duplicate.

It is necessary to place everything on record; no discretion is vested in any member of the Government, or in the Secretary, of changing or withholding from the record anything which is addressed to the Government, and the exact nature of the reply to it.

In regard to the subordinate Governments, it was determined, in place of the transmission of proceedings *in extenso* (which these Governments continue to transmit to the Court of Directors), to call from each of the Presidencies below for abstracts of their proceedings, which abstracts, on coming to the different departments, it is the business of the Secretary to overlook, to put a cross upon any matter which he deems of more than ordinary importance, and then to take the orders of Council as to whether the papers shall be called for. There are other matters which the Governments themselves refers, because of the incompetency of their own powers. Their references include all questions of salary or new appointments, and all questions relating to legislation; indeed, all important subjects.

Every appointment is made by a minute of the Governor-General in Council. If the Members of Council concur, of course the appointment is made; if they do not, the dissentients record their disapproval. If a majority objected, the appointment would not be pressed, and it is said that the Governor-General would not in general propose an appointment unless he knew it would be carried in Council. If, however, it should be put and negatived, the appointment could not take place, except under the Governor-General's special power of overruling the decision of his Council. It appears to be held, without qualification, that this power maybe exercised in regard to appointments, and if the Governor-General considered the appointment essential in a political point of view, it certainly would. If the Governor-General's nominee were withdrawn, another man would not be proposed by the Members of Council, but it would be left to the Governor-General to propose another.

No new office can be established without reference to the home authorities; and the Government of India cannot expend more than 50,000 rupees upon public works without their sanction.

An increase in the military establishment being generally a matter of emergency, is, in such case, made by the Governor-General in Council at once, but when not matter of emergency, the question must be referred home.

The Governor-General ordinarily holds office for five years, and receives a salary of 25,000/-, and each Member of his Council 10,000/- per annum.

The absolute authority vested in the Governor-General in Council extends, not only over those provinces which, by lapse or annexation, have fallen under his direct control, as the Punjab, Oude, Berar, the Burmese Provinces, and the Straits Settlements, but also over the four subordinate

Governments of British India, and applies to all powers, legislative and executive, subject only to the limitations specified in section 43 of statute 3 and 4 Will. IV. cap. 85.[4]

Subordinate Governments

The subordinate Governments are, subject to such general control, administered as follows:—

The Presidencies of Madras and Bombay are each under Governors and Councils of three Members (the Commander-in-Chief being one)—both Governors and Councillors being appointed by the Court of Directors.

Bengal and the North-West Provinces are each under Lieutenant-Governors, appointed by the Governor-General.

These Governments have no powers of legislation, nor can they create any new office, or even "grant any salary, gratuity or allowance without the previous sanction of the Governor-General of India in Council". This provision being found to involve the necessity of a formal reference of every petty detail to the Governor-General, the rule has been established of making periodical reports of these minor matters. The Governor-General, for instance, does not require the employment of each additional menial servant in a public office to be separately reported; but every quarter, reports are made, in the form of a statement, of the additions and changes of the establishments made in the quarter, and these are so passed under the review of the Governor-General in Council. This practice, though not in strict accordance with the letter of the law, is generally adopted; everything passes under the review of the Government of India, and ultimately is sanctioned by it; while the inferior Governments are not fettered in the nomination of petty officers—as of customs or excise, by the necessity of a previous reference, but rely upon obtaining the sanction of the Government of India when they make the quarterly report. In regard to expenditure on Public Works, there is an order from the Court of Directors that no work requiring an expenditure of more than 10,000 rupees should be undertaken by any of the Governments, neither the Government of India, nor the Governments below, without their sanction first obtained; but the Court of Directors enlarged the discretion in the case of the Governor-General in Council: and now the rule is understood to be, as laid down by the Governor-General in Council to the subordinate Presidencies, that they are to refer to the Governor-General in Council all works requiring an expenditure of more than 10,000 rupees, according to the estimates. But the Home authorities often sanction expenditure for Public Works without reference to the Government of India.

Though the mode of transacting business adopted by the subordinate Governments is not uniform, it may be stated generally, that at Madras and Bombay where there are Councils, there is also a staff of Secretaries by whom the business brought weekly before the Governments is despatched in their distinct departments; and the Governors of these Presidencies exercise, with the concurrence of their respective Councils, all the ordinary local patronage which, in the case of Bengal and the North-West Provinces, is also, with the exceptions above noticed, vested in their respective Lieutenant-Governors.

The Governments of Madras and Bombay have the privilege of corresponding direct with the Court of Directors. They send their proceedings to the Court, and furnish abstracts only to the Government of India. They have also their separate services, civil and military. A question arose very early, as to whether, in the case of a servant being suspended, or removed from office by one of the subordinate Governments, the appeal should lie to the Court of Directors or to the Government of India; and it was determined that, in consequence of the existence of separate reports to the Court from the subordinate Presidencies, and of the fact that the servants there were the Company's servants, placed under the authority of those Governments by the Court of Directors, the appeal should lie to the Court.

The power of selection for political appointments is exercised very largely in favour of military officers, who are, equally with civilians, qualified to hold those situations. Certain military appointments are considered the patronage of the Commander-in-Chief; others are the patronage of the Governor. The right of nominating to offices connected with finance, such as the Military Auditor-General, the Military Accountant, Paymasters and Commissariat Officers, is vested in the Governor. To those connected with the discipline of the army, such as the Adjutant-General and the Quartermaster-General the Commander-in-Chief appoints, but his appointments require the confirmation of the Governor in Council.

These statements apply to the subordinate Presidencies; the rights of patronage, civil and military, vested in the Governor-General of India in Council have been already explained.

REFERENCES

1. The Secretary's, the Examiners', the Military, and the Statistical.
2. Exclusive of Charities. Pensioners, and Annuitants.
3. It does not appear that the power given to the Count by s. 22 of statute 16 and 17 Vict. c. 95, to authorise the nomination of two additional legislative councillors, being civil servants of the Company of ten years' standing, has as yet been exercised.
4. The limitations to the powers of the Governor-General in Council are those which preclude any alternations of the Act of 1833, or any subsequent Imperial statute relating to India, or from promulgating laws affecting the prerogatives of the Crown, or the allegiance of British subjects.

7

Instruments of Indian Government

The Services—Civil (Covenanted and Uncovenanted), Military, Naval, Ecclesiastical

SECT. I—THE CIVIL SERVICE

The two great functions of the Civil Service, and of all who are concerned in the Civil Government of India, are,—The collection of the Revenue, and the Administration of Justice.

It is either in a fiscal or a judicial capacity, or in a combination of both, that all Civil Officials, from the highest to the lowest, are employed.

The Civil Service in India consists of two classes:—

1. Those who, having passed an examination in England, and subjected themselves to a certain degree of training in India, have entered into the covenant prescribed by ancient custom, "That they "shall obey all orders; that they shall discharge all "debts; and that they shall treat the natives of India "well". This select body, consisting of Europeans only, by whom the higher class of Government duties are performed, are termed the "Covenanted Service".

Those Europeans, Natives, and half-castes, to whom subordinate duties, fiscal and judicial, are committed, and who are not subjected to any preliminary training, and do not enter into covenant with the Company, and are consequently designated as the "Uncovenanted Service".

Covenanted Civil Service

The Covenanted Civil Serviced in India, which none could formerly enter but those who, at the nomination of Directors, had been admitted to a preliminary two years' training at the Company's College at Haileybury, is now open by as prescribed system of examination, to public competition.

B s. 36 of statute 16 and 17 Vict. cap. 95 (which applied not only to the Civil Service proper, but to all candidates for employment as Assistant–Surgeons to the Company's forces in India), the Directors' rights of patronage to primary appointments were extinguished. And by statute 18 and 19 Vict. cap. 53, Haileybury College was prospectively abolished. The Board of Control was also, by the first-mentioned Act, empowered to appoint Examiners, and to frame Regulations for conducting Examinations to be laid before Parliament. Doubts having arisen as to the mode in which the powers conferred by the Act should be exercised, the question was referred by the Board of Control to a Committee, who were requested to take the subject into consideration, and who subsequently reported thereupon.[1]

Regulations[2] prescribing the mode and subjects for the examination of candidates for the Civil-Service were promulgated by the Board of Control, in January, 1855, by which it was provided that two examinations of all such candidates should take place: the first in ancient and modern languages, mathematics, Arabic, and Sanskrit; the second, which was to be held at an interval of a year after the fist, in law, Indian history, and political economy. The second examination, which, on the special ground of an immediate demand for recruits for the Civil Service in Sinde was waved in 1856, has never in fact taken place.[3]

The present practice is, to send out all youths who shall have passed the single examination now required, to those parts of India where they may be wanted. Those intended for the Civil Service in Bengal, the N. W. Provinces, and those districts which are directly under the Supreme Government, are sent to Calcutta, where they are subjected to a further course of study, concluded by an examination in the native languages at the College, Fort William. At Bombay and Madras there are no establishments for preparing young Civil servants (or writers, as they were formerly called) for their duties, by the study of the native languages. It is pursued under certain teachers appointed for the purpose. It may be stated, as a general rule, that every member of the Civil Service is entitled to *some* office, though not at once nominated to any particular office. During the probationary period, from the time of their arrival in India, all receive a certain rate of pay, called the "out of employ allowance".

In Bengal, after passing the necessary examination, they are sent into the Mofussil (the country, as distinct from the Presidency), and become assistants to collectors and magistrates. Assistants are subjected to two examinations, before they can rise to superior grades in the service: the first, chiefly to test their familiarity with the vernacular languages; the second, to ascertain their further proficiency therein, and also their knowledge of criminal and fiscal law and practice. These examinations are conducted by Divisional Committees at certain large stations, under a Central Committee at the Presidency. The Divisional Committees consist of the Commissioners of the division, the Judge of the district, and others. These report to the Central Committee, who report to the Government.

On first entering the Public Service, the civilian is occupied with magisterial and fiscal duties simultaneously. In his magisterial capacity he takes the depositions of witnesses, and prepares cases for the decision of his superior, or he hears and determines, subject to revision, cases specially made over to him by the Magistrate. His power of punishment extends to two months' imprisonment, a period which, when he is entrusted with special powers by the Government, is enlarged to twelve months. As assistant in the revenue department, he decides petty claims relating to arrears or exactions of rent.

After an apprenticeship of several years, the assistant is regarded as a candidate for promotion. He is then subjected to a further examination, with the view of testing his knowledge of the languages and laws of the country; and his promotion depends on the success with the which he passes the test. A successful candidate is then deemed qualified for the office of Collector or Magistrate. As Magistrate he directs the police operations of his District, and takes cognisance of all criminal matters. The law provides for his dealing with certain classes of offences, but limits his power of punishment to three years' imprisonment. Appeals from his sentences, or from those of his assistant, when vested with special powers, lie to the Sessions Judge.

As Collector he has charge of the district treasury. He superintends the collection of the Government rental; puts in execution coercive measures against defaulters; sells estates for arrears of revenue; and manages those escheated or bought by Government. He superintends the partition of estates, and regulates the distribution of the Government Assessment among the several sub-divisions. He also exercises judicial powers in settling, by summary process, disputes among the agricultural community regarding rents.

The gradations of the Service differ in some respects in the different Presidencies.

In Bengal, the offices of Judge, Magistrate and Collector are held by three distinct persons. In Madras, Bombay, and the North-West Provinces, the functions of

Magistrate and Collector are discharged by one individual, the office of Judge by another. In the Non-Regulation Provinces, which are under the direct control of the supreme Government, all the three offices are united in the person of a single representative of the local Executive Government.

To a certain extent, advancement in the Civil Service is regulated by law, but there is also opportunity for selection. The mode of proceeding under the supreme Government (and the same general rule is acted upon throughout British India) is as follows:—When an appointment is vacant, it is the business of the Secretary to lay before the Governor-General a statement of all those who can be considered to have any claim, with his own opinion as to their relative fitness, and also his opinion whether the office requires peculiar fitness. The Governor-General thereupon makes his selection. He is not bound to regard seniority, and if it be an important office, he will choose the most competent. Seniority, however, has large influence in advancement. The Covenanted Service is by law a seniority service, every member of which, in consideration of his having been specially, and expensively, trained up for the service, is supposed to possess certain prescriptive rights, which can only be forfeited by misconduct or gross incapacity, and cannot be withheld *quamdiu se bene gesserit*: here, with some exceptions, the office of the local Government is merely to distribute. In practice, however, the superior appointments, such as Secretaries to Government, Judges of the Sudder Adawlut, Revenue Commissioners, and a few others, are filled by selection.

Military men are employed to a considerable extent in Civil duties, chiefly in the Political Department, or in the Civil Administration of districts not brought regularly under the existing laws of British India. They are especially selected for particular duties, and the practice has prevailed since the time of Lord Cornwallis. Instances have occurred, under the Presidency of Bombay, of their being appointed

Collectors in the Regulation Provinces; but such instances are few, and it is believed that a deficiency of Civil servants led to the appointments being made. The officers selected are generally appointed young, and with especial reference to their knowledge of the native language without which important qualifications no officer can be removed from his regiment to Civil duty. The proportion of military employed in diplomatic duties is conjectured to be one-third of the whole, but this estimate is restricted to high appointments: if inferior situations be admitted, the number of military men employed, as already described, has a great preponderance; and if Sinde be included, the proportion to Civilians is stated to be as twelve to seven.

The Members of the Covenanted Civil Service receive salaries graduated according to the nature and duties of their respective offices, from that of the lowest Assistant Collectors to the Members of the Supreme Council, and ranging in amount between £500 and £10,000 per annum, payable in rupees per mensem.

Uncovenanted Civil Service

The Uncovenanted Civil Service comprises that large class of Indian officials who are appointed by the local Governments, and who do not, as their designation implies enter into covenants with the Company, and who, though subjected to certain prescribed examinations on promotion, are not placed under any preliminary training.

There is no precise line drawn as to the offices which Covenanted Servants alone may fill, and those which are open to Uncovenanted Servants also. The distinction exists with regard to the Services only; the appointments to the Covenanted Service which are made at home, forming one class, and those left in the hands of the local Government the other—the former being entitled on vacancies to promotion, the latter not. The Covenant is in fact an old form, having its origin at a time when the East India Company was a Commercial body, but it now indicates a separate and exclusive Service.

Of the Uncovenanted Civil Servants, some are Europeans—some of mixed origin, European and native—some—and by far the largest proportion—pure natives.

The European Uncovenanted Servants consist chiefly of persons who have gone out to India in some other calling, and of sons of commissioned officers who have obtained Government employ. Though they do not ordinarily attain the higher offices, and are not entitled to furlough, exceptions to this rule have arisen. Pensions also have been granted to them on retirement.

The total number of Europeans, and of persons belonging to the half-caste population in the Uncovenanted Service in India, appears to have amounted in 1853 to between two and three thousand individuals.

The employment of native agency in the Uncovenanted Service, which may be said to have commenced about thirty years ago, under Lord William Bentinck, and was promoted in 1834 by s. 85 of statute 3 & 4 William IV. cap. 85, removing all disqualifications for office on account of descent, creed or colour, has been since so largely extended, that at this time almost the whole of the Judicial Administration of the lower Courts is in the hands of natives. Not only the Vakeels or Pleaders, but the three grades of Judges called Principal Sudder Aumeens, Sudder Aumeens, and Moonsiffs, numbering altogether about 700 in all India, are now natives. The subordinate Revenue Collectors in the Salt, Opium and Customs Departments, with the Land Revenue Officers, called Tehseldars, in which various duties about 1200 functionaries are employed, are also natives. There is also a class of Medical Officers, called Sub-assistant Surgeons, which consists entirely of natives; and every regiment has a native Doctor to assist the Surgeon. Added to these, their is a large number of natives employed in subordinate police and revenue duties, and drawing less than twenty rupees per month, amounting in Bengal alone to upwards of 40,000 in number, exclusive of the village watchmen, of whom there were said to be, in 1853, more than 170,000 in the lower Provinces. Natives are admitted to all offices in the Uncovenanted branch, for which they are deemed qualified in point of trustworthiness, and the principle now in progress throughout the Civil administration of India, is native agency and European superintendence.

The salaries received by the higher officials employed in the Uncovenanted Civil Service range from £100 to £900 per annum. It appears that a native who recently held the office of Judge of the small Cause Court, at Calcutta, received no less than £1560 per annum. The Judicial appointments are held chiefly by Mohammedans, but many Hindoos are employed, and at the head of the factory at Bombay a Parsee presides, who has Europeans placed under his authority.

SECT. II.—THE MILITARY SERVICE

The army ordinarily used for the defence of British India is (or rather as before the recent revolt) composed of four elements:—

1. The East India Company's native Forces officered by Europeans.
2. The East India Company's European Forces.
3. The Queen's Forces, which at the request of the Court of Directors are furnished for the Indian service, the cost of their conveyance and extra pay being provided by the East India Company.
4. The contingent Forces, which are at the command of the British Government under Treaties with native Princes.

The total number of the East India Company's native Forces of all arms, including commissioned and non-commissioned native officers and men, up to the latest period received before the recent revolt, was as follows:-

	Regiments.		Officers and Men
Engineers.—Native Commissioned and Non-commissioned, Rank and File			3,158
Artillery.—Horse	Brigades	5	1,073
Foot	Batts.	8	7,676
Cavalry.—Regular and Irregular'*	Regts.	50	26,129
Infantry.—Regular and Irregular *	Regts.	196	189,008
Veterans.—Native Officers and Men			3,374
Native Medical Establishment			858
	Total	269	231,276

Giving a total number of 269 native regiments of all arms, and of 231,276 native offices and men. A large portion of this force, comprising about one-half of the whole, has by mutiny and disarmament ceased to exist, leaving a total number of native Forces of all arms practically available of about 120,000 men.

The total number of the East India Company's European Forces now in India (not deducting losses arising out of the recent revolt, of which no complete authentic return has been received), is as follows, and presents a total of 22,047 European officers and men:-

Engineers.—European Officers and Men		434
Artillery.—Horse and Foot, do (of which there are 12 Battalions of European Foot.)		6,585
Cavalry *—European Officers and men		509
Infantry.—Do.	do	13,032
Veterans.—Do	do	436
Medical Establishment.—Europeans, including European Warrant Officers		1,051
	Total	22,047

* The Irregular Forces have four officers to each Regiment.

The total number of Queen's troops now in and on their voyage to India amounts to about 63,500 men.

The contingent Troops of the native States commanded by British officers, and bound under Treaties to serve the British Government, amounted, before the mutiny of 1857, to about 32,000, viz.:-

Hyderabad (Nizam's) Auxiliary Force	8,094
† Gwalior (Scindiah's) Contingent	8,401
† Kotah Contingent.	1,148
Mysore Horse (officered by Natives)	4,000
Guzerat (Guicowar's) Contingent.	3,756
† Bhopal Contingent	829
† Malwa United Contingent	1,617
Malwa Bheel Corps	648
† Joudpore Legion	1,246
Meywar Bheel Corps	1,054
Colapore Local Horse	907
Sawunt Warree Local Corps	611
	32,311

Holkar is bound by Treaty to furnish a contingent of 1000 horse; but these troops are not commanded by British officers.

The Commander-in-Chief of Her Majesty's Forces in India is *ex-officio* Commander-in-Chief of all the Company's Forces there; and any officer who may be appointed by Her Majesty to be Commander-in-Chief of Her Forces in any Presidency in India is, by virtue of such appointment, also Commander-in-Chief of the Company's Forces in such Presidency.

* Four additional Cavalry Regiments are now in course of formation.

† The Contingents which have mutinied are marked with an obelisk.

Ruler for admission to the Military Service, Addiscombe

The officers of the East India Company's Forces are primarily nominated to the service by the Directors, and those who receive "direct appointments" are examined (See Appendix B) and sent out at once—the rest are trained for two years at Addiscombe.

The seminary at Addiscombe is for the preparation of youths for those branches of the Military service where scientific attainments are indispensable,—the Engineers and the Artillery; but as the establishment will accommodate a larger number than is required for those branches, others are admitted. There is a preliminary examination. At the final examination the most distinguished obtain appointments in the Engineers,[4] and those next in merit in the Artillery. These are the prizes of the institution. The Cadets who fail to obtain them go into the infantry. Those receiving cavalry appointments in no case pass through Addiscombe, but proceed direct to India, as do a large portion of Infantry Cadets. These, however, are subjected to an examination, and are eligible up to twenty-two years of age. The number of Cadets at Addiscombe is 150. There are four terms, which extend over a period of two years; and the age of admission is from fourteen to eighteen. The payment to the Company is 100/. a year; the total expenses of a Cadet may be stated at 120/. or 130/. a year. The Company's charge was formerly much lower. It is the same to all. The only Oriental language taught is Hindostanee.

SECT. III—THE NAVAL SERVICE

The East India Company maintain an independent Marine, under the orders of the Government of India.

The chief branch of that service is the Bombay Marine, the officers of which are primarily appointed by the Directors (the patronage being allotted between the members of the Court), and sent out from England. From 15 to 18 is the age for Naval Cadets.

The duties of the Bombay Marine consist of Surveys on the coast of Arabia and the Red Sea, and the coast of Sinde. The Force is also used for the prevention of piracy in the Persian Gulf.

The total present strength in vessels and men of the Bombay Marine, consists of 53 steam and sailing vessels, and 4286. European and Native men,—according to the latest returns.

The general correspondence relating to this force is carried on with the Home authorities, and not with the Government of India. In regard to the expenditure, it is partly managed from home and partly by the Government of India. The Indian Navy is connected with the overland communication; and therefore, on many points, such as the building of ships steam-factories, and docks, instructions are received from England. But as regards the repair of ships and the establishments in those ships, any increase is referred to the Government for India, like any other increase. As an example of the control exercised by the Government of Indian, if repair of a vessel be wanted, and the expense is estimated to exceed Rs. 10,000, it must be referred for the sanction of that Government.

There is a small Marine force under the Bengal Government. Those acting as officers have no commissions, and the force is not subject to the Articles of War or the Mutiny Act. They have been employed in the China war, and are constantly employed in the Eastern Archipelago.

SECT. IV.—THE ECCLESIASTICAL SERVICE

The Ecclesiastical establishment is maintained at the charge of the Indian revenue for the exclusive benefit of the servants of the Company, and without reference to the population of India generally, with whose religion the Government profess not to interfere. The present establishment consists of three Bishops—of Calcutta, Madras, and Bombay, respectively; and 135 Chaplains, English and Scotch, who are covenanted servants of the

Company, and are placed on the same footing, as to furlough and other privileges, with other classes of European servants.[5]

There are also three Roman Catholic Bishops, and 78 Roman Catholic Priests, who participate in an annual grant from the Indian Government of about 5000/- per annum.

The three Anglican Bishops receive salaries from the Indian revenues as follows:—The Bishops of Calcutta, 5000/- per annum; the Bishops of Madras and Bombay, 2560/- each per annum. The jurisdiction of the Bishops extends, not only over the Chaplains, but over all the clergy of the Church of England within the limits of their respective dioceses. The present metropolitan jurisdiction of the Bishop of Calcutta extends over all the British territories, from the Punjab to Sigapore. In addition to his salary he has, while on his tour, an allowance of 1000 rupees per month for his expenses, besides which the means of travelling, either vessels or carriages, are provided for him by the Government.

The total aggregate amount charged on the territorial revenues of India for ecclesiastical salaries, exclusive of travelling allowances, is 111,030/- per annum.

REFERENCES

1. The Committee consisted of Lord Ashburton, Mr. J. G. Shaw Lefevre, the Rev. H. Melvill, the Rev. B. Jowett, and the present Lord Macaulay. For their Report, *vide* Parliamentary paper 34, 1855.
2. The first Regulations issued by the Board of Control, under the Statute of 1853, are printed at length of Appendix C.
3. *Vide* Parliamentary paper 317,1856.
4. The Engineers are afterwards trained for a year at Chatham.
5. Candidates for the Office of Chaplain must have been two years in Orders, under forty years of age, and approved by the Archbishop of Canterbury and the Bishop of London.

8

Administration of Justice

SECT. I—LAWS IN FORCE IN BRITISH INDIA GENERALLY

In the legal and judicial Administration of India, the uniform principle of British policy in respect of Territories acquired by conquest or cession, has been adopted.

The laws and system of jurisprudence, Mahomedan or Hindoo, to which we have succeeded, have, in every case, been recognised as valid, until superseded by the supreme authority of the British Government. The circumstance that this authority has, in the case of British India, been in some degree delegated to a chartered Company, has occasioned no difference in the practical application of the rule.

In the territories of the East India Company, as in all British dependencies similarly acquired, and not possessing Representative Institutions, the dominant country has exercised its legislative powers, either by order in Council, or by Act of Parliament.

At the present time, both the Imperial Parliament and the Governor-General in Council have the power of legislating for India; but there are certain exceptions to the power of the latter authority, by one of which it is restrained from interfering with any Act of parliament passed subsequently to 3 & 4 Will. IV. cap. 85, and applying to India. Acts not so made applicable by the British Parliament are sometimes, made so by the local Legislature.

All laws passed by the Governor-General in Council extend, unless specially limited in their application by the Acts themselves, to all inhabitants, whether British or Native, or all territories within the Company's Charter.

Drafts of all laws, previously to being enacted, are published in the newspapers at all the presidencies, in order that any parties thinking themselves likely to be affected by them, may apply to the Government. The publication does not take place at any fixed time before the enactment is passed; but it is usually from six weeks to two or three months. This practice of preliminary publication originated with the Court of Directors, and was adopted with the view of preventing precipitate legislation, by interposing a delay between the proposing and passing of a legislative Act.

The laws themselves, when they become such, are published in English—in Oordoo, a higher dialect of Hindustanee—and in other Native languages, according to the part of India to which they may apply.

Power is reserved to the Imperial Parliament (before which all such laws are to be laid) to alter or repeal them.

SECT. II.—LAWS AND JUDICIAL PROCEDURE APPLICABLE TO BRITISH-BORN SUBJECTS IN INDIA—THE SUPREME COURTS.

British-born subjects and their descendants, resident in India, whether in the service of the Company or otherwise, are, with certain exceptions,[1] amenable only to British law, as administered by the Courts called the Supreme Courts, now existing at Calcutta, Madras, and Bombay. The history of this exemption, from the ordinary tribunals of the country, is described in the appendix to the first report of the Indian Law Commissioners, wherein also the present constitution and jurisdiction of the three Supreme Courts is minutely described.

The first Charter of the East India Company which contained any provision for the administration of justice was that of the 13th Charles II., which empowered the Company to appoint Governors and other Officers to govern their plantations, forts, fortifications, factories, or colonies, and authorised the Governor and Council so appointed to "judge all persons belonging to the said Governor and Company, or that should live under them, in all cases, whether civil or criminal, according to the laws of he kingdom, and the execute judgment accordingly."

By the 35th Charles II. The Company were empowered to erect Courts of judicature, "consisting of a person learned in the civil laws, and two merchants, who were to decide according to equity and good conscience, and according to the laws and customs of merchants." And similar provisions were contained in the subsequent Charters down to the period of the union of the old and new Companies.

By the first Charter granted to the United Company which was that of the 13th George I. in 1726, a Mayor's Court was established at each of the settlements "to be a Court of Record, to try, hear, and determine all civil suits between party and party that should arise within the towns of Madras, Bombay, and Calcutta, or within any of the factories subject thereto, between all persons there residing, or who, at the time of action accrued, did reside or be within the said towns, or the precincts, districts or territories thereof, and to determine according to justice and right."

From the decisions of this Court an Appeal was given to the Governor and Council, whose decision was declared to be final in all suits under 1000 pagodas;[2] but if the suit exceeded that amount a further appeal was given to the King in Council. The criminal jurisdiction was given to the Governor and Council, who were appointed Justices of the Peace, with power to hold Courts of Quarter Sessions, and Oyer and Terminer and Goal Delivery, for the trial of all offences except treason, committed within the said towns, or within any of the factories subordinate, or within ten miles of the same. They were also empowered to grant probates of wills.

By the Charter of the 26th George II. upon the surrender of the previous Charter, the Mayor's Court and the Court of Oyer and Terminer and Gaol Delivery were again established at the three settlements, and similar provisions made—with this difference, that the native inhabitants of the respective towns were excepted from the civil jurisdiction of the Mayor's Court, unless with their own consent; and the criminal jurisdiction of the Court of Oyer and Terminer was limited to the trial of offences committed within the said towns, or within any of the factories of places subordinate thereto, the words "or within ten miles of the same" being left out.

A Court of Requests was also established, to which natives were liable for suits under five pagodas.

By the Act 13th George III. c. 63, so much of the said charter as related to the establishment of the Mayor's Court at Calcutta was cancelled, and His Majesty was empowered to grant a Charter or Letters Patent for the erection of a Supreme Court of Judicature at Fort William in Bengal, to consist of a Chief Justice and three other Judges, being barristers of England or Ireland, of not less than five years' standing. And the Supreme Court was accordingly constituted by Royal Charter, dated the 6th March, 1774. By the 37th George III. c. 142, s. 1, the number of Judges was reduced to a Chief Justice and two other Judges, and the Court now consists of that number, the qualification of the judges being the same.

The Court exercises civil and criminal jurisdiction, the former under the different heads of Common Law, Equity, Ecclesiastical, and Admiralty, and the latter as a Court of Oyer and Terminer. The Judges are also Commissioners of the Court for Relief of Insolvent Debtors, established by the Act 9th George IV. c. 73.

The Supreme Court appointments own ministerial officers; and the same persons may hold offices on different sides of the Court at the same time. The officers are paid by salaries. The whole annual expense of the Court is 471,248 rupees, of which 208,367 rupees are for the salaries of the Judges, and 262,880 for the salaries of the officers and other expenses attending their establishments. This is exclusive of the emoluments of the Registrar, who is paid by a commission on the estates of persons dying intestate.

The Court is also authorised by its Charter to admit, and enrol such and so many advocates and attornies as shall seem meet; and no other persons but such advocates and attornies are allowed to plead or act for the parties.

The general qualification for an advocate of the Supreme Court is, that he shall produce a certificate of having been called to the bar in England or Ireland, or of being entitled to practise as an advocate in the principal courts of Scotland, except the Judges shall see fit to dispense with the same.

The qualification for admission as an attorney is, that the applicant has been admitted an attorney of one of Her Majesty's Principal Courts of Record in England or Ireland, or a writer to the Signet in Scotland, or a member of the Society of Solicitors practising before the Court of Session there, or that he has served a regular clerkship of five years, under a contract in writing to some attorney practising in the Court, or that he is or has been a principal clerk to one of the Judges.

The advocates and attornies practise on all sides of the Court, under the same professional designations as in England.

The local jurisdiction of the Supreme Court is limited to the town of Calcutta, which for this purpose is bounded on the west side by the river Hooghly, and on the other sides by what is called the Mahratta Ditch. Within these limits the Court exercises all its jurisdictions, civil and criminal, over all persons residing within them, with the exception of its ecclesiastical jurisdiction, which has not been applied to Hindoos and Mahomedans beyond the granting of probates of wills.

The persons residing within these limits, and therefore subject to the local jurisdiction of the Supreme Court, are computed, according to the latest information, at about 400,000.

Secondly. In like manner the Court exercises all its jurisdictions over all British-born subjects, that is, persons who have been born within the British islands, and their descendants, who are resident in any of the provinces which are comprehended within the Presidency of Bengal, or the North-Western Provinces. The number of persons so subject to the jurisdiction of the Court, including the members of the Covenanted Services, civil and military, but exclusive of the Queen's troops and their families was, on the 30th March, 1851, according to the Parliamentary census returns, 22,387, and is now probably larger.

Thirdly. All persons resident at any places within the said provinces, who have a dwelling-house and servants in Calcutta, or a place of business there where they carry on any trade, through their agents or servants, are held to be constructively inhabitants of Calcutta for the purpose of liability to the common law and equity jurisdictions of the Court.

Forthly. Natives of India, within the said provinces, who have bound themselves upon any contract or agreement in writing with any British subject, where the cause of action exceeds the sum of 500 rupees, to submit to the jurisdiction of the said Court, are subject to its jurisdiction in disputes relating to the said contract.

Fifthly. In like manner, persons who avail themselves of the Courts's jurisdiction for any purpose, are held liable to its jurisdiction in the same matter, even on other sides of the Court than that of which they have availed themselves; as, for instance, persons who have applied for and obtained probates of wills, are held liable to the Court's equity jurisdiction for the due administration of the estate.

Sixthly. All persons who, at the time of action brought or cause of action accrued, are or have been employed by, or directly or indirectly in the service of, the East India Company, or any British subject, are liable to the civil jurisdiction of the Court in actions for wrongs or trespasses, and also in any civil suit by agreement of parties in writing to submit to the jurisdiction of the said Court: and all persons who, at the time of committing any crime, misdemeanor, or oppression, are or have been employed, or directly or indirectly in service as aforesaid, are liable to the criminal jurisdiction of the Court.

Seventhly. The admiralty jurisdiction of the Court extends over the provinces of Bengal, Bihar, and Orissa, and all other territories and islands adjacent thereto, which at the date of the charter were or ought to be dependent thereon, and comprehends all causes, civil and maritime, and all matters and contracts relating to freights, or to extortions, trespasses, injuries and demands whatsoever between merchants or owners of ships and vessels employed or used within the jurisdiction aforesaid, or other persons, contracted, done, and commenced in or by the sea, public rivers, or creeks, or within the ebbing and flowing of the sea about and throughout the said three provinces and territories. The criminal jurisdiction extends to all crimes committed on the high seas by any person or persons whatsoever in as full and ample a manner as the jurisdiction of any other Court of Admiralty in any colony or settlement belonging to the Crown.

Lastly. The Supreme Courts at Calcutta, Madras, and Bombay have criminal jurisdiction over all British subjects for crimes committed at any place within the limits of the Company's Charter, that is, any part of Asia, Africa, or America, beyond the Cape of Good Hope to the Straits of Magellan, or for crimes committed in any of the lands or territories of any Native Prince or State, in the same way as if the same had been committed within the territories subject to the British Government in India.

The law administered in all cases, except as hereinafter mentioned, is as follows:

First. The common Law as it prevailed in England in the year 1726, and which has not subsequently been altered by Statutes especially extending to India, or by Acts of the Legislative Council of India.

Secondly. The Statute Law which prevailed in England in 1726, and which has not subsequently been altered by Statute especially extending to India, or by the Acts of the Legislative Council of India.

Thirdly. The Statute law expressly extending to India, which has been enacted since 1726, and has not been since repealed, and the Statutes which have been extended to India by the Acts of the Legislative Council of India.

Fourthly. The Civil Law as it obtains in the ecclesiastical and Admiralty Courts.

Fifthly. Regulations made by the Governor-General in Council, previously to the 3rd and 4th Will. IV. c. 85, and registered in the Supreme Court, and the Acts of the Legislative Council of India made under the 3rd and 4th will. IV. cap. 85.

The exceptions are Hindoos and Mahommedans in the following cases:

First. Actions regarding inheritance and succession to lands, rents, and goods, and all matters of contract and dealing between party and party in which both parties are Hindoos. Such cases are to be determined by the laws and usages of Hindoos.

Secondly. Actions of the same kind where both parties are Mahommedans, and in these the case is to be determined by the laws and usages of Mahommedans.

Thirdly. Actions of the same kind where only one of the parties is a Mohommedan or Hindoo; and these are to be determined by the laws and usages of the defendant.

The procedure on the different sides of the Court is similar to the procedure of the corresponding Courts in England, with this difference, that, as directed by the Charter, the *viva voce* examinations of witnesses are taken down in writing, and the depositions are signed by the witnesses. The new rules in law and equity passed from time to time in this country are quickly adopted by the Judges in India, as far as circumstances will admit, and applied with the requisite modifications to their own practice.

The suits are generally of the same description as in England; those on the common law side being very similar to the cases at *nisi prius*. They are tried, however, without a jury, the judges determining both fact and law; though the latter, when points are raised, is commonly reserved, as in England, for further argument. Calcutta is a commercial town, almost all the European inhabitants, with the exception of the Company's servants and professional persons, being engaged in commerce. The common law suits are therefore much of the mercantile character, the equity suits are most commonly between natives, and then generally relate to wills, or the succession to intestate estate, or the partition of joint property, and frequently involve questions of Hindoo law, and matters of account.

In all suits, where the property in dispute is of the value of 10,000 rupees, there is an appeal to Her Majesty in Council. When a suit is appealed, it is the practice for the appellant to take two examined copies of the whole proceedings, including the depositions of the witnesses, which are committed to some trustworthy person, usually the master of a ship, to be delivered to the proper officer in this country.

So much of the Charter of 1726 as related to the Mayor's Court at Madras, or to the President and Council, as a Court of Appeal therefrom, or of Oyer and Terminer and Gaol Delivery, was cancelled by the Act 37 Geo III. c. 142; and by virtue of letters patent, issued in pursuance of the Act, a Court of Record was established within the settlement of Madras, called the Court of the Recorder of Madras, with such civil, criminal, and ecclesiastical jurisdiction, and with such powers and authorities, as in the said letters patent mention.

The Recorder's Court at Madras was abolished by the Act 40 Geo III. c. 79; and by letters patent, dated the 26th December 1800, and issued in pursuance of the Act, the Supreme Court of Judicature at Madras was established, to be a Court of Record, and consist of a Chief Justice, and two other Judges, who should be Barristers in England or Ireland of not less than five years' standing.

The Court has generally the same powers, and its jurisdictions are generally the same, within the settlement of Madras, as those of the Supreme Court of Judicature at Fort William within the territories attached to the Presidency of Bengal and the North-West provinces.

The local jurisdiction of the Court is confined to the town of Madras, which for this purpose is held to be bounded by the sea on the east, the Saint Thomé river on the south, the banks of the Long Tank and the Nungumbaukum Tank, with the villages of Kilpaukum and Peramboor on the west, and a line from the latter village to the sea on the north, and to comprise all the lands included in the villages of Chettapet, Kilpaukum, Peramboor, and Tandear. The inhabitants of Madras within these limits are computed at about 720,000.

The British subjects residing within the provinces attached to Madras, and subject to the jurisdiction of the Supreme Court, were, on the 30th March 1851, according to the Parliamentary Census Returns, 15,133, including the civil and military members of the Covenanted Services, but exclusive of the Queen's troops. The Court's civil jurisdiction extends to British subjects within any of the dominions of the native Princes of India in alliance with the Government of Madras.

So much of the Charter of 1726 as related to the Mayor's Court at Bombay, or to the President and Council as a Court of Appeal, or of Oyer and Terminer and Gaol Delivery for the town and island of Bombay and the limits thereof, was cancelled, by the Act 37 Geo. III. e. 142; and by virtue of letters patent issued in pursuance of the Act, a Court of Record was established within the settlement of Bombay, called the Court of the Recorder of Bombay, with the civil and criminal jurisdiction in the letters patent mentioned.

The Recorder's Court at Bombay continued till the 4th Geo. IV. c. 71, when it was superseded by letters patent, bearing date the 8th of December 1823, and issued in pursuance of the Act, constituting the Supreme Court of Judicature at Bombay to be a Court of Record, and consist of a Chief Justice and two other judges, who should be Barristers of England or Ireland of not less than five years' standing.

The local jurisdiction of the court is confined to the Island of Bombay, the inhabitants of which are computed at 566,119.

The British-born subjects who reside within the provinces comprised in the Presidency of Bombay, including the Covenanted Servants of the Company, were, on the 30th March 1851, according to the Parliamentary Census Return, 10,704, exclusive of the Queen's troops.

The Supreme Courts at Madras and Bombay have generally the same powers, and their jurisdictions are generally the same within the settlements of Madras and Bombay, as those of the Supreme Court of Judicature at Fort William within the territories attached to the Presidency of Bengal and the North West provinces.

SECT. III.—LAWS AND JUDICIAL PROCEDURE APPLICABLE TO THE NATIVE POPULATION OF INDIA—CIVIL COURTS—CRIMINAL COURTS AND POLICE

The native population of India is now under a system of judicial administration, Civil and Criminal, which has been organized by the Anglo-Indian Government, founded on pre-existing native systems of jurisprudence. On the Hindoo and Mahommedan stock have been grafted, from time to time, modifications resulting from legal precedents and constructions, which have been, in the Regulation Provinces of India, embodied into a system by successive enactments, though at present no uniformity exists. "The Courts profess to administer to every man the law of his own religion, country, or tribe, and, where the plaintiff and defendant are of different tribes, to decide according to the custom of the country, or the law of the defendant."[3]

An exception must here be noted in respect to the Presidency of Bombay, which has a special code of its own, compiled during Mr. Elphinstone's Government, and called after his name. It affects natives only, and is both Civil and Criminal. Its chief operation is in regulating Civil procedures. The Mahommedan law may be said to the unkonwn in the Bombay Presidency, except as to inheritence and similar matters among Mahommedans.

Civil Courts

The Constitution and Procedure of the East India Company's Courts of Civil Judicature are in their main features alike throughout India, though in the practice of the Courts and titles of the functionaries differences are observable in the judicial machinery now existing in the different Presidencies.

The inferior Civil Courts of Justice are, as has been stated, almost entirely in the hands of Native Judges. The lowest and most numerous class of these is that of Moonsiffs,[4] to each of whom a small district is allotted, and who have power to try all causes affecting real or personal estate in which the amount in dispute does not exceed 30/-[5]. Candidates for Moonsiffships are annually examined, and those qualified receive diplomas, which render them eligible for appointments. These diplomas are generally obtained by the pleaders practising in the Courts, called Vakeels.[6]

There are two grades of Moonsiff: 10/- per month is the usual allowance for the lower, and 15/- per month for the superior grade, to which they are promoted according to merit.

The next rank of Civil Judges above Moonsiffs is that of Sudder Aumeens,[7] also Native, who have power to try all causes between 30/- and 100/- in amount, and who receive salaries of 25/- per month each.

Immediately above the Sudder Aumeens comes the third and highest grade of Native Judges, called the Principal Sudder Aumeens, who try suits from 100/- and upwards to any amount. Of these Judges there are two grades; 40/- per month is the usual allowance of the lower, 60/- of the superior grade, which is the reward of merit.

The next Court of Civil Justice above that of the Principal Sudder Aumeen, is that of the Zillah[8] Judge, who is a European functionary belonging to the Covenanted Service (and who is invested, besides his powers as Civil Judge, with criminal jurisdiction hereafter to be noticed). To the Zillah Judge an appeal lies from the decisions in original suits of the Moonsiffs and sudder Aumeens, also from the decisions of the Principal Sudder Aumeens up to 500/-; but the Zillah Judge has power to refer to the Principal Sudder Aumeens appeals from the Moonsiffs and Sudder Aumeens, and of this power he makes large use. The Zillah Judge tries all original suits above 500/- if he had not referred them to his Principal Sudder Aumeen, which he may do.

In the trial of civil suits, original or appeal, it is competent to the European Zillah Judge to avail himself of the assistance of natives in one of the three following modes:

1. By a Punchayet,[9] or Court of Arbitrators (generally five) chosen by the parties, who conduct their inquiries on points submitted to them apart from the Court, and make their report to the Judge.

2. By native Assessors who sit with the Judge, make observations, examine witnesses, and offer opinions and suggestions.
3. By a July who attend during the trial, and, after consultation, deliver in their verdict.

Under all these modes of procedure, the decision is, however, vested solely and exclusively in the Judge.

It may here be remarked that the mode of procedure adopted in all the Courts above-mentioned is generally the same. All pleadings are in writing. The Plaint must be lodged on a stamp of a value proportioned to the sum claimed. Attached to the "declaration" is a power of attorney naming a licensed pleader. A formal notice is served on the defendant, or stuck up in the village where he is supposed to reside, and he is required to file answer and defend the cause within a certain number of days. The pleadings, all of which are on stamped paper, then go on till all the points of law and fact being raised for decision, issue is joined. The witnesses who may be called on either side are not subject to cross-examination. In carrying out the process of the Courts, execution is enforced either by distress of personal property, or sale of landed rights, which latter are at once sold to the highest bidder in satisfaction of the decree.

From the decisions of the Zillah Judge, by whichever of the processes above indicated they may be arrived at, an appeal lies to the High Court of Civil Justice, called the Sudder Dewanny Adawlut.[10] There are four of these High Courts of Civil Justice in India, possessing co-ordinate jurisdiction within their respective limits. At Calcutta for Bengal, at Madras and Bombay for those Presidencies respectively, and at Agra for the North-West Provinces. In the Calcutta Court there are five Judges, in that at Bombay four, at Madras three, a member of council being added as President of the Court at the two last-named presidencies. In the Court at Agra there are three Judges.

In all the Courts the Judges are selected from members of the Covenanted Civil Service of considerable standing in the judicial department.

The Sudder Dewanny Adawlut exercises no original jurisdiction. It is the Court of final appeal in each Presidency, and controls all the subordinate civil tribunals. Besides regular appeals from the original decisions of the European Zillah Judge, and in certain cases from those of the Principal Sudder Aumeen, the Court is competent to admit second or special appeals from decisions of the Courts below. The grounds for special appeal are, when the judgments shall appear inconsistent with law or the practice and usage of the Courts. The power thus given to the Sudder or High Civil Courts of hearing special appeals, extends their means of supervision, and brings judicially before them the proceedings and decisions of all classes of judicial offenders, and affords opportunity for correcting errors, it being one of their duties to regulate the practice and proceedings of the lower Courts, each judicial officer of which is required by law to record his decisions and the reasons for them in his own vernacular tongue. This process is supposed to afford the Sudder Court means of judging correctly of the individual qualifications of their subordinates. In the trial of appeals, the proceedings of the lower tribunals are read before one or more Judges. A single Judge is competent to confirm a decree. Two or three sitting together must concur for its reversal, whether the appeal be regular or special. The Sudder Courts sit daily, except during the Dusserah[11] and the Mohurrum,[11] when all civil proceedings are suspended. The salaries of the Judges of the Sudder Courts are not uniform, but none receive less the 4200/- per annum.

From the decisions of the Sudder Courts an appeal lies to the Queen in Council in cases where the amount in litigation is not less than 1000/. The petition for an appeal must be presented to the Sudder Court within six months from the decree, and accompanied with security for the respondent's costs, now fixed at 500/-, which may be either money, or Government securities, commonly called 'Company's paper's or a *Mal Zaminy* or land mortgage.

Pending the appeal the Sudder Court may either cause their judgment to be executed provisionally, or suspend it, according to their discretion.

Criminal Courts

The administration of the Criminal Law in India differs materially in the different Presidencies. But it may be said generally, that its basis is the Mahommedan Law, modified by the Acts and Regulations of the British Government.

Before noticing the higher departments of Criminal Administration in India, it may be observed that the powers of Magistrates appointed by the Government in the Presidency Towns have been defined from time to time at Calcutta, Madras, and Bombay, by the provisions of Imperial Statutes and local Acts and Regulations.

The gradations in the authority of the Magistrates and Criminal Courts are for the most part alike in all the presidencies. In the Mofussil, or Country Districts of Bengal, the system of Criminal Administration is as follows:— "Each district is committed to a Magistrate, and contains fifteen or twenty subdivisions or "Thanahs," each of which is placed under a subordinate officer, called a Thanadar or Darogah. Each of these last-named functionaries has under him the following establishment:— a Clerk or writer, a "Jemadar" or sergeant, and twenty or thirty policemen. The Darogahs are generally Mahommedans or Hindoos. Besides this machinery for the apprehension of criminals, there are also a large number of village police or watchmen, appointed by the village Committees, or by the Zemindars. These functionaries, who are not generally supposed to be very efficient, amount, in Bengal proper, to the large number of 170,000. The Darogahs, or Inspectors of Police, are invested with a certain measure of summary authority in cases of affrays, disturbances of the peace, & c., but are bound to bring all other matters under the previous cognizance of the Magistrate, who has the power of punishment to the extent of imprisonment for two years in certain cases, in some others for three years; but ordinarily his power extends to imprisonment for six months, and a fine of 200 rupees, and if the fine be not paid, to a further imprisonment of six months. Corporal punishment was abolished by Lord William Bentinck, but has since been revived in case of theft, where the property stolen does not exceed fifty rupees in value, and for juvenile offenders, as well as in certain crimes committed by convicts.

The Sessions Judge is the officer next in the ascending scale of rank, and appeal lies to him in certain cases from the Magistrate. He is the same individual who acts in a Civil capacity, as before mentioned, as "Zillah" judge. In Bengal his original jurisdiction is limited to offenders committed by the Magistrate to take their trial at the Sessions.

In Madras, the Sessions Judge is aided by a subordinate Judge, who acts as Committing officer instead of the magistrate. In Bombay, the Sessions Judge is aided by an officer called the "Assistant Sessions Judge."

The Sessions Judge has the power of punishment to the extent of nine years' imprisonment, and, in certain aggravated cases, of sixteen years. All cases involving punishments above those limits are referred to the Sudder Court, which is composed of the same Judges as the Supreme Court of Civil Appeal, and is called the Sudder Nizamut[12] Adawlut, in Bengal, the Foujdary[13] Adawlut, in Madras and Bombay. This Court decides on the record and report of the Sessions Judge. It never hears oral evidence; but if the case requires more elucidation, sends it back to the Sessions Judge, with orders to take further evidence on particular points; and its ultimate decision is final.

If the Judges of the Nizamut concur in the verdict of the Lower Court, and the prisoner be considered deserving of a higher degree of punishment than could be awarded by the Session Judge, he may be sentenced to suffer death, or to undergo imprisonment for twenty-one years; but if sentenced to imprisonment for life, then transportation for life either to the penal settlements of Singapore, Penang, or Malacca, the Tenasserim Provinces, Arracan, or Aden, would be substituted; but no native of India can be transported beyond the Company's territories. If the case be not capital, it is decided by the sentence of a single Judge. Sentences of death require the concurrence of two Judges. The government has the power of pardon or mitigation, but it is seldom exercised.

There are in Bengal two modes of trial, in one of which a Mahommedan law officer, or assessor, expounds the law; but if the prisoner is not a Mahommedan, he may refuse to be so tried, and for such cases there is a system of Juries, or Assessors, or Punchayet. The Sessions Judge may reject the opinion of the Mahommedan law officer, on points expressly provided for by the Regulations, and that opinion may be overridden altogether by the Sudder Court. When the case is tried with a Jury, or Punchayet, the decision may be overruled, and sentence awarded to the extent of the Judge's competence. Cases tried by the magistrate are generally prosecuted by the party injured.

With respect to Madras and other parts of British India, except Bombay, it may be stated generally that the system of criminal administration, though differing in some particulars, is based on the same general principles as that existing in Bengal. The police, who are, in Bengal and Bombay, placed under the command in chief of a superintendent, specially charged with that duty, are, in Madras, placed under the Governor in Council, and in the North-West provinces under the Commissioners of Revenue. In the Punjab there is a military preventive Police of foot and horse, who furnish guards for jails, treasuries, frontier-posts, and escorts of treasure.

It may also be noticed that, with respect to the professional criminals peculiar to India, and called Thugs and Dacoits, a special Police invested with summary powers, is organized under one superintendent for all India.

SECT. IV.—THE INDIAN LAW COMMISSION

Reforms in the Laws, Judicial Establishments, and procedure of British India, have been now under the consideration of the imperial Parliament and of the Indian Government for a quarter of a century. Though no practical result has been yet attained, a brief notice of the origin, progress, and present stage of these investigations seems an essential appendix to any sketch of the existing system of Judicial Administration in British India.

In 1833, by s. 53 of statute 3 and 4 William IV. cap. 85, the Governor-General of India in Council was empowered to appoint a Commission, not exceeding five members, to inquire into and report upon the Jurisdiction of the existing Courts of Justice, and the operation of the Laws in India, with a view to their consolidation and amendment. The sections of the statute relating to the appointment of this Commission are as follows:

> S. LIII. Whereas it is expedient that, subject to such special arrangements as local circumstances may require, a general system of Judicial Establishments and Police, to which all persons whatsoever, as well *Europeans* as natives, may be subject, should be established in the said Territories at an early period, and that such laws as may be applicable in common to all classes of the inhabitants of the said territories, due regard being had to the rights, feelings, and peculiar usages of the people, should be enacted, and that all laws and customs having the Force of Law within the same territories should be

ascertained and consolidated, and as occasion may require amended: be it therefore enacted, that the Governor-General of India in Council shall, as soon as conveniently may be after the passing of this Act, issue a Commission, and from time to time Commissions, to such persons as the said Court of Directors, with the approbation of the said Board of Commissioners, shall recommend for that purpose, and to such other persons, if necessary, as the said Governor-General in Council shall think fit, all such persons, not exceeding in the whole at any one time five in number, and to be styled "The Indian Law Commissioners," with all such powers as shall be necessary for the purposes hereinafter mentioned; and the said Commissioners shall fully inquire into the Jurisdiction, Powers, and Rules of the existing Courts of Justice and Police Establishments in the said territories, and all existing forms of judicial procedure, and into the nature and operation of all laws, whether civil or criminal, written or customary, prevailing and in force in any part of the said territories, and whereto any inhabitants of the said territories, whether Europeans or others, are now subject; and the said Commissioners shall from time to time make Reports, in which they shall fully set forth the result of their said inquiries, and shall from time to time suggest such alterations as may in their opinion be beneficially made in the said Courts of Justice and Police Establishments, forms of Judicial procedure and laws, due regard being had to the distinction of castes, differences of religion, and the manners and opinions prevailing among different races and in different parts of the said territories.

LIV. And be it enacted, that the said Commissioners shall follow such instructions with regard to the researches and inquiries to be made and the places to be visited by them, and all their transactions with reference to the objects of their Commissions, as they shall from time to time receive from the said Governor-General of India in Council; and they are hereby required to make to the said Governor-General in Council such special Reports upon any matters as by such instructions may from time to time be required; and the said Governor-General in Council shall take into consideration the Reports from time to time to be made by the said Indian Law Commissioners, and shall transmit the same, together with the opinions or resolutions of the said Governor-General in council thereon, to the said Court of Directors; and which said Reports, together with the said opinions or resolutions, shall be laid before both Horses of parliament in the same manner as is now by law provided concerning the rules and regulations made by the several Governments in India.

LV. And be it enacted, that it shall and may be lawful for the Governor-General of India in Council to grant salaries to the said Indian Law Commissioners and their necessary officers and attendants, and to defray such other expenses as may be incident to the said Commissioners shall be according to the highest scale of remuneration given to any of the officers servants of the India Company below the rank of Members of Council.

In pursuance of the powers thus conferred, an Indian Law Commission was, in the year 1834, appointed. It consisted of five Members—the Legislative Councillor appointed under the Act of 1833 (Mr. Macaulay), another English barrister, and three Civil Servants from each of the three Presidencies.

The question with what part of the Law the Commissioners should begin, was determined by the Government. Their first work (which occupied about two years) was to prepare a single penal Code for all British

India. By this Code (known as Macaulay's Code) the Mahommedan Criminal Law was to be swept away, and that substituted was to apply to all classes of persons without exception; but the penalties were to be varied according to the diversities of birth, class, and circumstances. This Code was afterwards recast under this auspices of Mr. Bethune, who subsequently held the office of Legislative Councillor, but, in consequence of differences of opinion at home and in India, has never received authoritative sanction.

Other suggestions relating to the Administration of Civil Justice were made by the Law Commission, as for a Model Civil Court and a plan of civil procedure, under which the administration of law and equity was to be united, and the whole case brought under the cognizance of one judge, while small-cause judicature was not to be committed to inferior Judges, but all causes, whatever their amount, were to be cognizable in the same Courts. In regard to Appeals, the scheme of the Law Commission was, to have a General Court of Appeal in each Presidency, consisting of the Judges of the Supreme Courts and the Judges of the Sudder Courts, which should receive appeals both in civil and criminal cases, and from all the Courts in the country. The Mohammedan law was to be codified; the Hindoo law was to be codified, and a third civil code, the *lex loci,* was to be applicable to all but Mohammedans or Hindoos.[14]

The conflict of opinion both in England and in India as to the various suggestions offered by the Law Commission having rendered its inquiries practically inoperative, the vacancies arising in it from time to time by death or resignation were not filled up, and it was thus permitted to become gradually extinct.

In 1853, by s. 28 of statute 16 and 17 Vict. cap. 95, Her Majesty was empowered to appoint Commissioners in England to consider and report upon the Reforms proposed by the Indian Law Commissioners, appointed under the provisions of statute 3 and 4 will. IV. cap. 85.

The section of the Act of 1853, relating to the appointment of this second Commission, is as follows:

> XXVIII. Whereas by the Act of the third and fourth years of King William the Fourth it was provided, the Commissioners to be appointed thereunder, and to be styled the Indian Law Commissioners, should inquire into the jurisdiction, powers, and rules of the existing Courts of Justice and Police Establishments in the said Territories, and all existing Forms of Judicial procedure, and into the nature and operation of all Laws, whether civil or criminal, written or customary, prevailing and in force in any part of the said Territories, and should from time to time make reports, in which they should fully set forth the result of their inquiries, and should from time to time suggest such alterations as might in their opinion be beneficially made in the said Courts of Justice and Police Establishments, Forms of Judicial Procedure, and Laws, due regard being had to the distinction of castes, difference of religion, and the manners and opinions prevailing among different races and in different parts of the said territories. And whereas the Indian Law Commissioners from time to time appointed under the said Act have, in a series of Reports, recommended extensive alterations in the Judicial Establishments, Judicial Procedure, and Laws established and in force in India, and have set forth in detail the provisions which they have proposed to be established by Law for giving effect to certain of their recommendations, and such Reports have been transmitted from time to time to the said Court of Directors; but on the greater part of such reports and recommendations no final decision has been had:

It shall be lawful for Her Majesty, at any time after the passing of this Act, by Commission under the Royal Sign Manual, to appoint such and so many persons of England as to her Majesty may seem fit to examine and consider the recommendations of the said Indian Law Commissioners, and the enactment proposed by them for the reform of the Judicial Establishments, Judicial Procedure, and Laws of India, and such other matters in relation to the reform of the said Judicial Establishments, Judicial procedure, and Laws, as may, by or with the sanction of the Commissioners for the affairs of India, be referred to them for their consideration, and to authorise and direct the persons so appointed, or such number as may be limited by their commission in this behalf, to report their opinion to Her majesty on the matters afore said, and especially to report from time to time what Laws or Regulations should be made or enacted in relation to the matters aforesaid, but so that every such report be made within three years after the passing of this Act; and for the purposes of such examination it shall be lawful for Her Majesty to authorise the persons so appointed, or the number limited by the Commission in this behalf, to call before them and examine in England such persons in the service of the Crown and the said Company respectively, and to require the production of such official documents in the possession of the Board of Commissioners for the affairs of India, or of the Said Company, as they may think fit.

In pursuance of the powers thus reserved to Her Majesty, a Commission was issued under the Royal Sign Manual, dated November 29, 1853, appointing Sir John Romilly, Sir John Jervis, Sir Edward Ryan, C. H. Cameron, J. M. Macleod, J. A. F. Hawkins,[15] T. F. Ellis, and R. Lowe, Esquires, to be members of the said Commission, and authorising them, or any three or more of them, to make a diligent and full inquiry into and to examine and consider the recommendations of the Indian Law Commissioners, and the enactment proposed by them for the reform of the Judicial Establishments, Judicial procedure, and Laws of India, and such other matters in relation to the reform of the said Judicial Establishments, Judicial procedure, and laws, as might, by or with the sanction of the Commissioners for the affairs of India, be referred to them for their consideration. And full power and authority was granted to the said Commissioners to call before them, or any three or more of them, such persons in the service of the Crown or of the East India Company, and all such other persons as they should judge necessary.

Also to cause all or any of the officers and clerks in the service of the Crown or of the East India Company to bring and produce before them all records, orders, books, papers, and other writings in the possession of the Board of Commissioners for the affairs of India or the East India Company. And within three years after the twentieth day of August, one thousand eight hundred and fifty-three, or as soon as the same could conveniently be done, to certify under their hands and seals, what they should have done in the premises.

In fulfilment of the duties thus devolved onthem, the Commissioners have since presented four Reports, the last of which bears date May 20, 1856.

These Reports recommend an amalgamation of the Supreme and Sudder Courts now existing at Calcutta, Madras, and Bombay, respectively, into one Court at each of those Cities, to be designated the "High Court." They also recommend the establishment at Agra, where no Supreme Court now exists, of a "High Court" for the North-West Provinces, similar to those proposed for the three Presidencies.

They also propound uniform Codes of civil and criminal procedure, applicable both to the High Courts so to be formed, and to all inferior Courts within the limits of their respective jurisdictions.

They further recommend that the High Court at Calcutta shall consist of not less than eight Judges—those at Madras and Bombay respectively of not less than five, and that at Agra of not less than four Judges. A proportion of the Judges in each Court to be appointed by the Crown, the others by the Governor-General in Council at Calcutta and Agra; and by the Governors of Madras and Bombay at those presidencies respectively. The Judges to be appointed by the Crown, to be selected from Barristers of England and Ireland, and members of the Faculty of Advocates in Scotland, of not less than five years' standing. The Judges to be appointed by the Governor-General or other Governors, to be members of the Covenanted Civil Service, of not less than ten years' standing. All the Judges to hold their officers at the pleasure of the crown.

Further detailed suggestions were also offered as to the civil and criminal jurisdiction, both original and appellate of the High Courts, and as to the area to which the proposed Codes of civil or criminal procedure should extend.

The Commissioners also advised that in order to harmonize the system of Civil Law at the capitals and in the provinces of India, a body of substantive Civil Law should be constructed on the basis of the law of England to be the Law of India on all the subjects it embraced.[16]

No Legislative Measure has been founded on these Reports, all of which have been sent out to India. The first on December 12, 1855 the second on February 20, 1856, the third and fourth on June 25, 1856, and are reported to be now under the consideration of the Legislative Council at Calcutta.

REFERENCES

1. The exceptions are cases of oppression of the natives, or judicial malversation, cognizable by the ordinary tribunals, which also try civil suits between natives and British subjects.
2. A pagoda is about eight shillings.

3. *Vide* Compbell's "India as it is," p. 535.
4. Arabie, Judge, from *insaf*, justice; literally, dividing in half.
5. In Madras and Bombay the Moonsiffs have larger jurisdiction, extending to 100/- in the former, and 500/- in the latter Presidency.
6. Arabic, general word for agent or attorney.
7. Arabic, literally "Chief trustees."
8. A Zillah is a large division of country.
9. From *Punj* or *Panch*, the Persian or Hindoo word for five.
10. The words are Arabic. *Sudder* means chief or first of anything; Dewan, a seat, or tribunal; and *Adawlut*, justice. *Dewanny* is generally used in India to signify the civil government.
11. The great Hindoo and Mohammedans anniversaries.
12. Nizamut is an Arabic word, which means "arrangement, or reducing to order," and governors of provinces under the Mahommedan Government were sometimes designated by names derived from the same root, as the Nazim and the Nizam.
13. From *Foujder*, the General, or holder of a *Fouj* or army.
14. Certain parts of the *lex loci* Code, which protect converts from Mahommedanism and Hindooism from loss of ancestral or other property, which they previously incurred, have since become law.
15. By a subsequent Commission, dated march 17, 1854, the name of F. Millet, Esq., was substituted for that of Mr. Hawkins, who became Secretary to the Commission.
16. The Commissioners were not unanimous in their recommendations, Mr. Lowe and Chief Justice Jervis dissenting from the 3rd Report, and the latter having refused to sign both the 3rd and 4th Reports, and after their presentation having formally retired from the Commission.

9

Revenue System of British India

SOURCES OF REVENUE—LAND—SALT—OPIUM—CUSTOMS—MISCELLANEOUS

The territories comprised in the East India Company's Charters form the only portion of the British Dependencies which have hitherto borne the entire cost on their own Civil and Military Administration.

This result has been attained under a Revenue System, inherited from our Mahommedan predecessors, engrafted by them on ancient Hindoo customs, and modified from time to time, under British rule, by a series of Regulations, by which the system, as it now exists, has been constructed.

The estimate of the total revenues of British India, for the year ending April 30, 1857 (without deduction for costs of collection, allowances, and drawbacks), is as follows:

Land Revenue	£16,682,908
Opium	4,487,269
Salt	2,362,308
Customs	2,018,270
All other Sources of Revenue (comprising Stamps, Post-Office, Sayer, Abkarry, Mint, Marine, Pilotage, Judicial, Electric Telegraph Receipts,	

Subsidies from Native States, and other Miscellaneous Revenues	3,605,702
Total Revenues	£29,167,457

The collection of these revenues forms, as has been already stated, one of the most important duties of the Civil Service in India. These duties are discharged under the general superintendence of Boards of Revenue, of which there are three in India: namely, for Bengal, the North-West Provinces, and Madras. The Bengal Board consists of three members, that at Agra, for the North-West Provinces, of two, that at Madras of one Member of Council as president, and three ordinary members.

In Bombay there is no Board of Revenue, but two Revenue Commissioners divide the whole territory, and are immediately under the Government. Subordinate to these Boards of Revenue, there are also throughout India in all the Revenue "Divisions," officers charged with all details and petty appeals, who were first appointed by Lord William Bentinck, and who are, in some cases, exclusively revenue functionaries; in others entrusted also with magisterial and other duties.

SECT. I—LAND REVENUE

The Chief source of revenue in India is the land. This revenue (which as now levied under various systems in the presidencies of Bengal, Madras, and Bombay, in the North-West provinces, and in the Punjab, yielded by the latest returns, previous to the recent disturbances, more than sixteen millions sterling) is sometimes designated as a tax, sometimes as a land-rent, but is practically an annual payment, levied by the Anglo-Indian government, and payable (subject to certain exceptions hereafter to be noticed) by all who hold land within the territories of the East India Company.

To trace the origin of this tax, or to discuss the various theories relating to it, is beyond the province of these pages; but in order to a correct apprehension of the existing system, it will be necessary to take a brief review of the modifications to which it has been subjected.

The various systems of Administration in respect to the Land Revenue of India, which have from time to time been adopted, and of which distinct and varying samples are now to be found throughout the different Presidencies, have all their foundation in a state of things which existed anterior to the British or even the Mohammedan Conquest.

The ancient village[1] communities which almost everywhere existed in form, more or less perfect—sometimes managed by a single head-man—sometimes by a committee of their own number—sometimes by Zemindars,[2] hereditary Hindoo Chieftains, or Bailiffs of Mogul Emperors, were, wherever those communities existed, the foundation of the Revenue System of India. Where they did not exist, attempts were made to construct imitations of them, in order to provide a convenient machinery for levying that share of the produce of the land which the successive sovereigns of India have claimed; and which, under our present system of commutation, is said to amount to nearly one-fourth of the gross produce,[3] or, taking an average of the cultivated lands throughout India, about 3s. 6d. per acre in English money.

It was not until a century and a half after the establishment of our first factories in India, that any territorial rights devolved on the East India Company.

In 1765, with the grant of Bengal, Bihar, and Orissa, to the Company, by the Mogul, the necessity of providing some Revenue System arose. For four years the system was carried on by the Native Officers who had been employed in the same service by the Nawab of Bengal. The Zemindars, aided by District-Registrars called Canongoes, contracted with the Government on behalf of the villagers—the revenues being dependent on the produce, and, in some cases, subdivisions of the villages, called "*Pattees*," being chief tenants in a corporate capacity, gave the name to an intermediate tenure called "Patteedaree."

In 1769, Supervisors, being covenanted servants of the Company, were appointed in each district to report on the existing Revenue System, with a view to its amendment.

In 1772, by Proclamation, dated May 11, the Company asserted their authority under the Mogul's grant to the "Dewannee," or Civil Government, and by Regulations dated May 14, a system of lease for five years to the highest bidder was in augurated.

In 1776, instructions were issued by the Directors, authorising the sale of lands, in default of payment on the part of the Zemindars, or landholders, with whom the Government contracts were made.

In 1781, Regulations were framed and passed by the Governor in Council, establishing a plan of annual leases; preference to be given, in all cases, to the Zemindars.

In 1789, by a Minute of the Governor-General (Lord Cornwallis), a Settlement, involving a fixed payment of Revenue for ten years, was announced.

In 1793, by Proclamation, dated March 22, the decennial settlement was declared to be permanent and irrevocable for ever, and regulations were framed for carrying it out.

In 1799, an Act was passed relaxing the stringent power of sale given theretofore to the Government over the estates of defaulting Zemindars.

In 1802, the permanent Revenue System of Bengal was extended to a portion of the Madras Presidency, in which, under the auspices of Munro, a system had been established of direct dealing with individual cultivators, on yearly agreements, with allowances for irrigation or other improvements, and providing also for the liability of villages for individual defaults.

In 1803—4-5, the district called the Barahmal, in Madras, was mapped out into Zemindarries, and disposed of on fixed permanent terms.[4] After many changes and modifications of system, we find—

In 1817, three different systems existing in different parts of Madras. 1. The Cornwallis or Zemindarry System. 2. The Ryotwar or Munro System, above described; and 3, the Village System of leases for years of all the lands comprised in the village, together with all the profits; the liability for rent, and the duty of internal management being committed to the leaseholders collectively.[5]

It 1820, the Ryotwar System was made general through all parts of the Madras Presidency not already permanently assessed.

In 1821, a Commission was appointed to investigate and report upon alleged abuses in the Revenue System of the North-West Provinces, and in 1822, by Regulation VII., a system, of which Mr. Holt Mackenzie was the author, was promulgated, the leading object of which was to combine the advantages of the Ryotwar System with that of village leases.

In 1827, by the Bombay Code of Regulations, the work of Mr. Mountstuart Elphinstone, a system was established which, with subsequent modifications hereafter to be noticed, still exists.

In 1833, by Regulation IX. (under Lord William Bentinck) the Settlement of the North-West Provinces was further carried out, and in 1842 it was completed. In the working of this system native functionaries were largely employed. In the North-West Provinces, Madras, and Bombay, the offices of Collector and Magistrate were at this time united in the same person. In Bengal they were kept distinct.

In 1844, Sinde (in which territory a plan of collecting Land Revenue under military superintendence had been attempted by Sir C. Napier) was annexed to Bombay, and partly subjected to the same system with that presidency.

In 1847, a system of thirty years' leases of "Fields" (the name given to so much land as one man and a pair of bullocks could cultivate) was established in part of the Bombay Presidency—the boundaries of the fields to be marked by stones—portions of the territory being also annually let for grazing grounds. Under this system the dealings of the Government were (on the Ryotwar plan) with the individual cultivators and the fields were to be sold in default of payment.

In 1849, the Punjab system of decennial contracts with the village communities for the Land Revenue was established by Lord Dalhousie.

In attempting to reduce into chronological order the various changes which have taken place in the Land Revenue System of India, the transitions from one district to another are necessarily so frequent and so rapid, that it is difficult to present the net result of these changes, and the system as it now stands, in an intelligible form. It will nevertheless, be seen that (notwithstanding the sub-divisional rights and titles brought under our notice in any historical survey of Indian territories, partly by the introduction of Middlemen[6] or collectors of revenue for the Government, partly by the various nomenclatures adopted in different districts for the proprietary body[7] the hand tenures of India fall, in fact, under two great classes.

1. The Zemindary, where the ground is cultivated by tenants under a landlord standing between themselves and the Government—that landlord being sometimes an hereditary chief, sometimes a mere district officer, sometimes a village corporation.
2. The Ryotwar, where, under all its various modifications, the cultivator and the proprietor are identical, and are brought into immediate tenant-relations to the Government.

The actually existing Land Revenue Systems in Bengal, the North-West Provinces, Madras, Bombay, and the Punjab, are thus described in a Return recently made in pursuance of an order of the House of Commons:[8]

Existing System in Bengal

In the Lower Provinces of the Bengal presidency, the land is held by Zemindars, on payment of an annual sum fixed in perpetuity in 1793 by Lord Cornwallis, the estates being liable to be sold in default of payment, under the provisions of Act 1 of 1845. The only land at the disposal of government consists of estates which have been thus sold, and purchased on the public account. The rate of land tax is believed to amount, on the average, to about half the rental. Between the actual contractors of the soil in Bengal, and the Zemindar who pays the revenues to the Government there are several (Sometimes three or four) intermediate renters or farmers.

Existing System in the North West Provinces

The system pursued in the North-West Provinces is briefly described in the following extract from the "Directions for Revenue Officers," promulgated under the authority of the late Lieutenant-Governor, Mr. Thomason.

First. All the inhabited part of the country is divided into portions with fixed boundaries, called Mehals or estates; on each Mehal a sum is assessed for the term of twenty or thirty years, calculated so as to leave a fair surplus profit over and above the net produce of the land; and for the punctual payment of that sum the land is held to be perpetually hypothecated to the Government.

Secondly. It is determined who are the person or persons entitled to receive this surplus profit. The right thus determined is declared to be heritable and transferable, and the persons entitled to it are considered the proprietors of the land, from whom the engagements for the annual payment of the sum assessed by the Government on the Mehal are taken.

Thirdly. All the proprietors of a Mehal are, severally and jointly, responsible in their persons and property for the payment of the sum assessed by the Government on the Mehal. When there are more proprietors than one, it is determined according to what ruler they shall share the profits, or make good the losses on the estate. If the proprietors are numerous, engagements are only taken from a few of the body, who on their own parts, and as representatives of the rest, undertake to manage the Mehal, and to pay the sum assessed upon it.

The rate of assessment was in the first instance limited to two-thirds of the net produce[9] of each Mehal or estate, but, on the revision which is about to take place on the expiration of the thirty years which formed the first term of settlement, it has been determined to restrict the demand of the State to one-half of the average net assets.

In some districts, such as Goruckpore, the Deyrah Dhoon, and Kumaon, there are large tracts of land in which no private rights exist and which are consequently at the abolute disposal of the Government. These are granted to applicants on favourable terms, such as those mentioned in the following Notification, which was issued in September, 1855:

1. Grants of land for the tea cultivation in the Kumaon and Ghurwal districts of the Kumaon province, will be made on the following conditions, on application to the Senior Assistant Commissioner of the district.
2. Each grant will be of not less than 200 or more than 2000 acres; more than one grant may be taken by one person or company, on the applicants satisfying the local authorities, acting under the usual control in the Revenue department, of their possessing sufficient means and capital to undertake an extended cultivation and manufacture of ten.
3. One- fourth of the land in the grant will be given free from assessment in perpetuity, on fulfilment of the conditions below stated.

4. The term of first lease will be for twenty years; for the first four years the grant will be rent free; in the fifth year, one anna per acre will be charged on three-fourths or the assessable portion of the grant; two annas per acre in the sixth year; three annas in the seventh year, and so on, one more anna being added in each year, till, in the last year, the maximum rate is reached of one rupee per acre. The full assessment on a grant of 2000 acres will thus not exceed 1500 rupees per annum.
5. The following are the prescribed conditions of clearance: At the close of the fifth year from the date of grant, a twentieth part of the assessable area; at the close of the fifteenth year, half of the assessable area; and at the close of the last year three-fourths of the assessable area is to be cleared and well stocked with tea plants.
6. In the twenty-first year, on the fulfilment of the above conditions, the proprietary right in the grant and the right of engagement with Government shall yest in the grantee, his heirs, executors or assignees, under the conditions generally applicable to the owners of estates in Kumaon; and the rate of assessment on the lands in the grant, in whatever manner cultivated, shall never exceed the average rate on grain crop lands in the same locality.
7. On failure of payment of the prescribed assessment in any year, or of any of the above conditions (the fact of which failure shall, after local inquiry, conducted by the Senior Assistant Commissioner, be finally determined by the Sudder Board of Revenue), the entire grant shall be liable to resumption at the discretion of the Government, with exception of the portion of the assessable area which may be *bond fide* under tea cultivation, and a further portion of

land which shall be allowed in perpetuity free of assessment to the extent of one-fourth of such cultivated area. The portions so exempted will remain in the possession of the grantee, subject to the usual rates and rules of assessment in the district.

8. Grantees shall be bond to erect boundary pillars at convenient points round the circuit of a grant within six months from its date; failing which, such pillars will be put up by the Government officers, and the cost thereof shall be recoverable from the grantee in the same manner as the regulated rate of assessment.
9. No claim to the right and interest in the grant on any transfer by the original grantee, will be recognised as valid unless on registry of the name of the transferee in the office of the Senior Assistant Commissioner.
10. So long as Government establishments for the experimental growth and manufacture of tea shall be maintained in the Provinces, supplies of seeds and plants will be given gratis to grantees, on application to the Superintendent Botanical Gardens, North-Western Provinces, as far as may be in his power.

Existing System in Madras

The tenures of land under the Madras Presidency are thus described in a Report recently received from that Government.

The Revenue Systems in force in the Madras presidency are the Zemindary, Village joint rents, Ryotwar, Oolungoo.

The Zemindary System is also termed the Mootahdary,[10] the former designation being usually applied to old ancestral estates, and the latter to those created under the Regulations of 1802.

Under this system estates, of greater or less extent according to circumstances, are held by the proprietors direct from the Government, on payment of a fixed annual sum, or "peishcush." This payment was fixed on the creation of the estate by a calculation of its actual proceeds at the time, and for some years previously, a deduction, generally of from 33 to 15 per cent., being made there from to cover the expenses of management, and to constitute (with the future revenue of the whole of the culturable lands then waste), the emoluments of the Zeminder or proprietor.

The Zemindary tenure prevails chiefly in the Northern Circars, though there are large proprietary estates in other districts, as Madura, Nellore, North Arcot, &c.

In the Village-renting System the villagers stand in the Zemindar's position, and jointly hold from the Government. The village is rented to the whole body, or a section of them, for a term of years, and they make their payments direct to Government, managing their affairs independently, and allotting the lands for cultivation among themselves.

Under the Ryotwar System every registered holder of land is recognised as its proprietor, and pays direct to government. He is at liberty to sub-let his property, or to transfer it by gift, sale, or mortgage. He cannot be ejected by Government so long as he pays the fixed assessment, and has the option annually of increasing or diminishing his holding, or of entirely abandoning it. In unfavourable seasons remissions of assessment are granted for entire or partial loss of produce. The assessment is fixed in money, and does not very from year to year, except in those cases where water is drawn from a Government source of irrigation to convert dry land into wet, or one into two-crop land, when an extra rent is paid to Government for the water so appropriated; nor is any addition made to the assessment for improvements effected at the Ryot's own expense. The Ryot, under this system, is virtually a proprietor on a simple and perfect title, and has all the benefits of a perpetual lease without its responsibilities, inasmuch as he can at any time throw up his lands, but cannot be ejected so long as he pays his dues; he receives assistance in difficult seasons, and is irresponsible for the payment of his neighbours.

The assessment if fixed on each field, and the mode in which this was done is as follows: a certain portion of the produce was first set aside from the gross produce as a joint contribution of the Ryot and Government for the pay of village officers, and the remainder divided in certain proportions, the share allotted to Government being commuted into money at the average value of the produce for a period of years antecedent to the settlement.

The "Annual Settlements" under Ryotwary are rendered necessary by the right accorded to the Ryot of diminishing or extending his cultivation from year to year. Their object is to determine how much or the assessment due on his holding the Ryot shall pay, and not to re-assess the land. In those cases where no change occurs in the Ryot's holding, a fresh Puttah or lease is not issued, and such parties are in no way affected by the annual settlement, which they are also not required to attend.

The greater portion of the Presidency is under Ryotwary.

The Oolungoo-renting System prevails only in Tanjore and Tinnevelly, and is not general in either; its peculiarity consists in the Government demand being dependent on the current price of grain. On the introduction of the system, a standard grain assessment was fixed on each village, and also a standard rate, according to which the grain demand was to be commuted into money; but it was, at the same time, arranged, that if current prices in any year rose more than 10 per cent, above the standard commutation rate, or fell more than 5 per cent, below it, the Government, and not the Ryot, was to receive the profit and to bear the loss. The profit up to 10 per cent, remains with the landowners, who also bear all loss by fall of price as far as 5 per cent. The advantages of the system are, that the Government participates with the Ryot in the benefit of high prices, while the latter is relieved from loss when prices are much depressed; its disadvantage consists in the difficulty that is experienced in obtaining accurate and fair returns of the current prices which are taken throughout the year.

Existing System in Bombay

Under the Bombay presidency, "the revenue management" may be described in general terms as "Ryotwary," implying that , as a general rule, the occupants of government lands settle for their land revenue, or tax, with the Government officers direct, and hot through a Middleman. It should be understood, however, that throughout the Presidency, instances not unfrequently occur in which the Government revenues of entire villages are settled for by individual superior holders, under various denominations, or by a co-partnery of superior holders; as instances of the former, the Khotee villages of the Konkan, and the Talookdaree[11] estates of Guzerat may be adduced, while the latter are exemplified in the Bhagdaree[12] and Neerwaderee tenures of the Broach and Kaira Collectorates.

In Sinde, not many years ago, the revenue throughout was collected in grain by actual division of the crop: the grain was then sold by reserved auction, at artificially high, and sometimes even at famine, prices by the Government, as the great grain dealers of the country. Great progress has been made in superseding this system by cash assessments, which have been already introduced into several districts of the province. In the Shirkarpore Collectorate generally, and in Larkhana particularly, the principle of cash-assessments had been successfully adopted.

A revision of assessment is now is progress throughout Bombay, by which the amount payable on each field is determined according to its quality, and the amount so fixed is not liable to alteration for a term of thirty years.

Existing System in the Punjab

In the Punjab one and the same man is usually absolute proprietor and generally the sole cultivator, though he may occasionally lease out a few fields to tenants. He is saddled with no rent. He has to provide for the cost of cultivation and for the Government demand; the rest of the produce he may devote to the maintenance of his family and the accumulation of his capital. But these men, while maintaining their individuality, do yet belong to Village communities. A village is not inhabited by a certain number of Ryots, each unconnected with the other, but by a number of persons of common descent, forming one large cousinhood, having their own headmen, accustomed to joint action and mutual support.

The British Government has from the first decided on levying the tax by money payments assessed for a term of years. The peasant proprietors compound with the State for a fixed period, such assessment and compounding being technically termed a Settlement. But the proprietors do not engage individually with the Government, but by Villages. The brotherhood, through its headmen or representatives, undertakes to pay so much for so many years; and then, having done this, they divide the amount among themselves, assigning to each man his quota. Primarily each man cultivates and pays for himseif, but ultimately he is responsible for his co-parceners and they for him; and they are bound together by a joint liability. The Punjab System, therefore, is not Ryotwary, nor Zemindary; but the *Village System*. In the hills, and occasionally elsewhere, the Zemindary System, and near Mooltan, something approaching to the Roytwary System, may be found. But the Village System is the prevalent one, especially in the most important districts.

The average rate of assessment per acre, per annum, in the Cis-Sutlej States is, in English money, 2s. 3½d.; in the Trans-Sutlej States, 3s. 11 $\frac{3}{8}$ d. ; in the Upper Baree and

Rechna Doabs, 2s. $9\frac{5}{8}$d.; in the Upper Chuch Doab, 2s. $3\frac{7}{8}$ d. It will be observed that the rate diminishes as the settlement progresses westward, the country being poorer; the same result will occur in the southern districts. It is estimated that a peasant proprietor cultivates, on an average, eight acres, and, at a mean rate of assessment, would pay 1l. 4s. per annum to State. From searching and accurate inquiry in the Settlement Department, showing the exact yield and value per acre of every kind of crep, it has been ascertained that the Government demand does not exceed one-fifth of the gross value of the produce in rich tracts, and one-sixth, or one eighth, in poor tracts.

Revenue free Lands

Large tracts of land in various parts of India are exempted from the payment of any Land Revenue.

These lands, known by various designations, but called generally Lakhiraj,[13] lands, consist principally of those, the revenues of which were originally assigned by the Mogul Emperors to holders of officers in payment for their services, which lands are called Jaghires, or sometimes Maaffees.[14]

There is also another class of revenue-free lands, originally assigned either by the State, or by the Villages, or by opulent Mohammedans and Hindoos, for the keeping up of temples, shrines , and mosques, and for various other purposes, without any conditions. These exempted Grants are called *"Inams,"*[15] and are subdivided into many classes.

There are also lands which have been the subjects of a permanent assessment, called Mocurreree[16] or Istamraree,[16] not liable under any circumstances to be increased.

The above-mentioned exemptions, which originated with the native Governments which preceded us, have since been confirmed by the British authorities.

The amount of Land-Revenue actually received by the latest Government returns in each Collectorate in Bengal, the North-West Provinces, Madras, Bombay, the Punjab, and in those Provinces of British India directly under the Governor-General in Council, which are for revenue purposes borne on the Bengal books, will be found in the statistical tables appended to the revenue map which accompanies this volume.

Opium Revenue

The Opium Tax, which forms the most considerable source of revenue in British India next to that derived from and, is levied in two forms:

1. By an exclusive system of cultivation and sale carried on by the Government in Bengal.[17]
2. By a high export duty lived in Bombay on opium grown in the native States of Malwa and shipped from Bombay.

In Bengal the revenue from opium is realised by means of a Government monopoly. It is grown exclusively for the Government, under severe penalties, for any infraction of the laws.

The cultivation of the poppy was prohibited in Bengal by Regulation VI. of 1799, sect. 3, and in the North-West Provinces by Regulation XLI. of 1803, sect. 2.

The system now pursued in Bengal is as follows: Annual engagements are entered into by the Government with the Ryots in certain selected districts, to sow a certain quantity of land with the white poppy, under a system of pecuniary advances, the produce to be delivered in the form of opium to the Government at a fixed rate.

In the month of August contracts are entered into with the Ryots, and an advance of four rupees per beega (nearly two-thirds of an acre) granted by the Government. The sowings commence in November, when another advance is made of three rupees per beega. Again in January and February, when the crop arrives at maturity, a third advance of about three rupees per beega takes place to assist the cultivator in gathering the produce. The crop is collected by the end of March, when the poppy heads are cut or scratched with a sharp instrument, and a milky juice exudes, which becomes brown in colour and thick in consisteney by exposure to the sun and air.

The opium in this crude form is delivered by the Ryots to the Agents of the Government, whose chief depots are at Ghazeepore and Patna for the Benares and Bihar Provinces respectively.

The opium is prepared by the Government Agents for the China market by rolling it into large balls covered with a coating of opium paste and poppy leaves, so as to exclude the air; it is then packed in chests—forty balls to a chest —and transferred to the Government warehouses in Calcutta, where it is put up to auction at the Government sales, of which there are four each season at intervals of a month, commencing with January. At these sales the opium sells at prices varying from 700 to 1600 rupees per chest containing 116 lbs. weight, and its is estimated that after deducting cost of production, charges of transport, and commission, a revenue is yielded to the Government by these sales of from 40/- to 120/- per chest. The merchants in India purchase the opium either on their own account or for mercantile houses in China, and it is then shipped for the Chinese coast or Hong King, in vessels capable of carrying from five hundred or one thousand chests.[18]

The total net receipts from the opium monopoly in Bengal amounted in 1856 to 2,767,136/-.

A large additional revenue is derived from the transit of the opium of Malwa through the British territories to Bombay for exportation to China. Previous to the year 1831 the British Government reserved to itself, by separate treaties with the Native princes of Central India, subsequently cancelled, a monopoly of the articles, which was purchased by the British Resident at Indore, and sold by auction, either at Bombay or at Calcutta. But in that year it was deemed advisable, chiefly on account of the large quantity of opium smuggled to the Portuguese settlements of Demaun, &c., on the coast, to relinquish the monopoly, to open the trade to the operations of private enterprise, and to substitute, as a source of revenue, in place of the abandoned system, the grant, at a specified rate, of passes to cover the transit of opium through the Company territories to Bombay. In determining the amount of transit duty, it was proposed to be guided by a comparison of the cost of transit direct to Bombay, with that of the transmission of the drug to the coast by the cheapest of the more circuitous routes through the territories of Native States; and on the basis of such a comparison it was fixed at Rs. 175 per chest of 140 lbs. each. In 1835, the results of the preceding official year being unfavourable, the shipments of opium from Bombay having largely declined, while those from Demaun had greatly increased, the rate was reduced to Rs. 125 per chest.

The subjugation of Sinde afforded opportunity for the levy of a higher rate. Down to the period of that event, a large portion of the opium of Malwa had been conveyed through Sinde to Kurrachee, and thence onwards to the Portuguese ports of Diu and Demaun. That route was now closed, and it was reasonably expected that an advance might be made in the charge of passes, without risk of loss to the revenue from a diminished demand for them. The rate was accordingly increased, in October, 1843, from Rs. 125 to Rs. 200 per chest. Upon the principle that it was desirable to fix the price at the highest amount which could be lived, without forcing the trade into other channels, a further increase was made in 1845, when-it was determined that the charge should be Rs. 300 per chest. On the same principle it was, in 1847, raised to Rs. 400 per chest.

It appears from recent returns, that from Pass Fees on Malwa opium exported through Bombay, a net revenue (after deducting all costs and charges) was received, in the financial year ending in the spring of 1856, of rather more than a million sterling.

The total gross revenues derived by the Government of India from this tax, in the two forms in which it is lived, amounted, by the last returns, to about four and a half millions sterling.

The Salt Tax has been, like the Land Revenue, inherited or instituted by the Government of British India from their predecessors in power. It was an ancient source of revenue to the Sovereigns of Asiatic countries. It was first applied by Warren Hastings, in 1773, to the payment of certain departments of the Civil Service.

Salt Revenue

The Salt Tax now yields in India (exclusive of all Customs' duties on salt imported) about two and a half million sterling, and is levied by different means in the different Presidencies.

All the salt produced in India, whether that obtained from the sea-water in Bengal by boiling, or in Madras and Bombay by a process of solar evaporation, or that obtained from the salt mines in the Punjab, or from the salt lakes in Rajpootana, is subject to tax in one or other of the following forms.

In Bengal the Government have establishments for the manufacture of salt, the monopoly of which they retain in their own hands. It is manufactured by a system of advances to the Natives (about 100,000 of whom are thus employed in the Sunderbands), and who, by contract, are bound to deliver at a fixed low price, all salt manufactured, which is sold by Government at public sales, at six principal agencies in Bengal. The price at which salt is sold, by the Government, is thus regulated. To the actual cost of producing the salt is added an amount equivalent to the duty levied on imported salt, which is now two and a half rupees per maund, or three farthings per lb., which makes the average retail price to the consumer about a penny per lb. The private manufacture of salt is permitted round Calcutta, subject to an excise of the same amount with the Customs' duty levied on imported salt. The system which has been adopted since 1837, in pursuance of the recommendations of a Select Committee of the House of Commons in the previous year, has been one of fixed prices, and open warehouses, at which the sales, instead of being as before periodical, are constantly going on. The duty on imported salt has been since three times reduced, and with such effect, that in 1853 half the salt consumed in Bengal appears to have been supplied from the port of Liverpool.

It is calculated that, taking the average annual consumption of salt, and the average earnings of the Bengal Ryots, the salt consumed by each absorbs about five days' wages per annum.

The salt agencies in Bengal are located along the head of the Bay; namely, at Hidgelee, Tumlook, Chittagong, Arracan, Cuttack, Balasore, and Khoredah.

The supply of salt to the North-West provinces is furnished partly from the Lower Provinces of Bengal, and partly from the Sambhur Salt Lake,[19] in Rajpootana, and other localities on the western side of India. The salt of Bengal, having paid the excise or import duty of Rs. 2 8a. per maund, passes free into the North-West Provinces. The Sambhur and other salt, on crossing the north-western frontier customs' line is subjected to a duty of two rupees per maund, and to a further duty of half a rupee[20] per maund, on transmission to the eastward of Allahabad, thus coming into competition with the salt of Bengal, under an equal duty of Rs. 2 8a. per maund.

At Madras salt is manufactured on account of Government, and sold for internal consumption at one rupee per maund, or under one farthing per lb. The duty on imported foreign salt was three rupees per maund, but it had been recommended by the home authorities that the import duty should (as in Bengal) be equal only to the difference between the selling price and the cost of manufacture; the difference between the cost price and the price at which the salt is given out for consumption being the duty to be realised.

In Bombay the manufacture of salt is carried on by individuals, but subject to an excise duty of Twelve annas

(1s. 6d.) per maund, a similar duty being imposed on imported salt. In the Punjab the salt-mines are worked by the Government. Salt is sold at the mines at two rupees per maund. Facilities are also afforded for the export of salt to Malabar, Travancore, Cochin, and other places.

Customs

The Customs' duties, which now amount to about two millions sterling per annum, are levied (not as formerly after the fashion of the native Indian States, in the shape of inland and transit tolls[21]), but under one generally uniform system throughout British India.

The Customs' duties now arise from two sources.

1. The Sea Customs on imports and exports—the latter chiefly on silk and indigo.
2. The Land Customs, levied on certain articles of produce passing the frontier lines between native States and British Territories

Subsidies from Native States

The Revenues received from tributes and subsidies payable under existing treaties between the British Government and native States in India, amount, altogether, to about half a million sterling, per annum, as will appear from the following extract from the accounts of the territorial Revenues, for the year, ending in April, 1856.[22]

Bengal:	£	£
Tributes from the under mentioned States:		
Kotah	7,056	
Odcypore	18,516	
Mundy	9,375	
Jhalwar	7,500	
Banswarra	2,568	
Doongerpore	2,568	
Jeypore	37,500	
Serohee	1,269	
Various Petty States	4,320	
Nizam's Government on account of Mahratta Choute	10,133	100,805

Bengal:	£	£
Madras:		
Peisheush and Subsidy:		
Mysore Government	229,687	
Travancore ditto	74,666	
Cochin ditto	18,750	323,103
Bombay:		
Subsidy from the Cutch Government	15,795	
Kattywar Tribute	56,105	
Various Petty States	3,096	74,996
		£498,904

The remaining sources of Indian Revenue, not particularized above, are as follows.

Stamps, with reference to which it may be observed that in India stamped paper is required, not only as in England for bills of exchange, agreements, receipts and deeds, but for all judicial proceedings, petitions, and papers of all kinds filed in Court.

The gross Revenue derived from this source amounts to about half a million sterling, per annum.

Abkarree

Another considerable item in Indian taxation is Abkarree,[23] the name given to the Revenue derived from the sale of monopolies to vend spirits. These licences are, in every large town or district, farmed yearly to the highest bidder, who sells his wares at his own price, but under Government regulations as to the position of his store and hours of business. From this Alkarree, and from another tax of the same nature on the (Sale of certain drugs not strictly classed as spirits), and called Sayer,[24] a gross annual Revenue of about a million sterling, is obtained.

The total residuary amount of the Indian Revenue is made up from the following various sources:

Miscellaneous

Post Office,[25] Mint, Marine, Pilotage, Judicial, Electric Telegraph receipts, and other miscellaneous items[26] adding altogether about a million sterling to the aggregate annual Revenue of British India, the gross amount of which (as estimated for the year, ending April 30, 1857) is 29,344,960/-.

The detailed statistics of the income and expenditure of India are given fully in the accounts of the Territorial Revenues, annually laid before Parliament.

It may, however, be stated generally, that the chief items of expenditure of the Anglo-Indian government, on an average of four years, preceding the mutiny of 1857, have been, in round numbers, as follows:

Charges incident to the Collection of the Revenue	about	£6,000,000	sterling.
Military and Naval Charges	"	11,000,000	
Civil, Judicial and Police	"	5,000,000	
Public Works	"	1,500,000	
Interest on Bond Debt in India	"	2,000,000	
Charges defrayed in England (including Interest on Home Bond Debt, Dividends to Proprietors of East India Stock[27] Payments on account of Her Majesty's Troops, and Establishment:— Charges of the East India House and Board of Control	"	3,500,000	
Allowances and Assignments to native Princes under treaties and other engagements	"	1,000,000	
Total about		£30,000,000	sterling

In order to meet the exigencies from time to time arising from the excess of expenditure over revenue, two distinct modes of raising money in England and in India have been adopted by the Government.

In England the only mode in which money can be raised by the East India Company is by the process usually adopted by Corporations similarly circumstanced, namely, on bond. About one-fifth part of the debt now existing has been so contracted.

In India a different mode of borrowing money has been adopted by the Government, as follows.

When the Government wants money, it advertises that the Treasury is open to receive money upon loan, at certain rates specified in the advertisement, and upon the conditions there contained. So long as the loan remains open, parties are admitted to make what payments they please, and to receive what are called loan notes in acknowledgment, and this to any amount. The money raised on loan is all raised in India.

The aggregate amount of the India Debt, as contracted in these two modes, is now about 60,000,000/- sterling.

In the accounts of the Territorial revenues of India for the four years preceding the mutiny of 1857, Bengal alone presents an uniform local deficit; the North-West Provinces alone an uniform local surplus.

The excess of expenditure over income on the estimate of the revenues, and charges of all the Presidencies and Provinces of British India, for the year ending April 30, 1857, is 1,981,062.

REFERENCES

1. A 'village" is not a collection of houses, but a tract of land, bounded and named, and occupied by hereditary cultivators.
2. Zemindar—A Persian Word, signifying "landholder," originally applied to hereditary Hindoo Chiefs, afterwards to functionaries appointed by the Mogul Emperors to collect revenue, receiving a percentage.
3. "It is desirable that the Government should not demand more than two-thirds, of what may be expected to be the net produce to the proprietor during the period of settlement, leaving to the proprietor one-third as his profits and to cover the costs of collection. By net produce is meant the surplus which the estate may yield, after deducting expenses of Cultivation."—*Directions to Revenue Settlement Officers, North-West Provinces,* Section 52.
4. A full account of the Land Revenue System, as it existed in 1812, will be found in the Fifth Report of the House of Commons of that year.

5. The first of these systems, the Zemindarry, prevailed in Ganjam, Vizagapatam, Rajahmundry, Masulipatam, Guntoor, Salem, Chingleput, Cuddalore, and the Pollams.

   The second of Ryotwar—in Malabar, Canara, Coimbatoor, Madura, and Dindigul.

   The third or Village System—in the Ceded Districts—Nellore, Arcot, Palnaud, Trichinopoly, Tinnevelly, and Tanjore.

6. These Middlemen of India are found under various designations as the Polygars and Mootadars of Madras; the Dessayes and Moinmdars of Gujarat; the Deshmooks of the Deccan and Bombay; the Talookdars of the Moguls &c.

7. Proprietors and Headmen are variously called Zemindars in Bengal and the North-West provinces; Bhumyar in Rajpootana Potails in Malwa, Gujarat, and the Deman; Merrassidars in the Carnatic; Vellalers in the Southern Peninsula, and Patteedars in the Punjab.

8. *Vide Return*, " Showing under what Tenures, and subject to what Land Tax, Lands are held in the several presidencies of India."—*Parliamentary Paper*, 1857, 112.

   Also, "A Selection of papers illustrative of the Character and Results of the Revenue Surveys and Assessments, which have been introduced into the North West provinces and Bombay, since the year 1833—*Parliamentary Paper*," 1853-999.

   Also "Paper relating to the Revised Survey and Assessment of the Madras Presidency."—1857-51.

9. By net produce is meant the surplus which the estate may yield after deducting the expenses of cultivation, including the profits of stock and wages of labour.

10. From *Mootah*, the name given to the subdivision of a district in the northern Circars.

11. So called from Talook, a proprietary estate, generally smaller than a Zemindary, but held on the same tenure.

12. From *Bhagdar*, a sharer or partner.

13. *Lakhiraj* signifies no tribute.

14. *Maaffee* signifies forgiven, or remitted.

15. *Inam* signifies a gift or benefaction.

16. Both these words signify "established or agreed upon".

17. Opium Farms are also established at Penang, Singapore, and Malacca.
18. *Vide* "What is the Opium Trade ?" a pamphlet by Mr. Donald Matheson.
19. The Sambhur Lake belongs to the native States of Joudpore and Jeypore.
20. The Allahabad special duty was fixed by Act 14 of 1843 at one rupee per maund; but in 1847, and again in 1849, when reduction of duty on Bengal salt was effected, corresponding reductions were made in the Allahabad duty.
21. Transit or inland duties formerly levied at every town and on every road were abolished, in Bengal by Act 14, of 1836; in Bombay by Act 1, 1838; and in Madras by Act 6, of 1844.
22. The amount given in the estimate for 1857 under this head is 510,166/-.
23. *Abkarree* singifies a tax on "waters."
24. *Sayer* Signifies the "remainder," or unclassified taxes.
25. The postal rates are uniform throughout India from Cape Comorin to Peshawur. There is also a Book post.
26. The Moturpha, a tax on shops, &c., was abolished in 1856.
27. Amounting in the last estimated Returns to 627,893/-.

10

Administration of Native States

The system of Government above described must be understood to apply to that portion only of British India, which is comprised within the Presidencies, and those Provinces which are directly subject to the Governor-General of India in Council.

The native States of India are not included in this system of administration; but are bound by treaties and engagements varying in their provisions, but generally entitling these States to British protection on the condition either of payment of tribute or providing a Military Contingent, except in those cases in which a communication for other conditions has been arranged by cession of a portion of their territory to the British Government.

The stipulations contained in the various treaties are not uniform. The Rajah of Nepal, for instance, though bound by the Treaty of 1815 to cede certain territories, undertook simply to accept British mediation in event of any differences arising between himself and the neighbouring Rajah of Sikkim.

In other cases again, as in that of the State of Mysore, and the smaller States of Kolapore, and Sawunt-Warree, engagements involving an absolute surrender of independence have been contracted, and the entire internal administration of these States has been assumed by the political agents of the British Government.

Summary of the Native States of India, and of their Relations with the British Government.

	Residencies and Political Agencies.	Area in Sq.Miles	Estimated Population	Existing relations with the British Government.
The Nazam's dominions in the Deccan	Hyderabad.	95,337	10,666,080	Bound by treaty to maintain a contingent force.
Scindia's dominions in Central India	Gwalior.	33,119	3,228,512	Ditto, Ditto.
Holkar's dominions in Central India	Indore.	8,318	815,164	Bound by treaty to furnish 1000 horse (not commanded by British Officers).
Bundelcund States (Central India)		7,404	824,000	Undervarious tributary and protective treaties.
Bhopal (Central India)	Sehore.	6,764	663,656	Bound to furnish a contingent force.
Mysore (Southern India)	Bangalore.	30,886	3,460,696	Mysore is administered by a Commissioner, two Assistants, and four Superintendents, exercising the powers of Judge, Magistrate, and collector, at Bangalore, Ashtagram, Chitterdroog, and Nuggur, respectively. The Revenue, after defraying the expenses of the Commission, the Subsidy payable to the Company, and the fixed Stipend (one-fifth of the revenues) allotted to the Rajah, is appropriated to the purposes of the Mysore State.

Kolapore (Western India)	Kolapore.	3,445	500,000	Under direct British management, similar to that of Mysore. Carried on through the Bombay Government.
Sawunt Warree (Western India)		800	12,000	
Travancore (Southern India)	Trivandrum.	4,722	1,011,824	Under a Subsidiary Treaty. The management of Travancore and of Cochin is carried on through the Madras Government.
Cochin	Cochin.	1,988	288,176	
Gholeep Sing's dominons in Kashmir		60,000	3,000,000	Bound to pay tribute, but no returns.
Nepal (Northern India)	Khatmandoo	54,500	1,940,000	Bound to accept British mediation in certain cases.
Bahawulpore (Northern India)		25,200	925,000	Under a protective treaty.
Bhurtpore (Northern India)		1,978	600,000	Ditto, Ditto.
The Guicowar's dominions (North-Western India)	Baroda.	4,399	325,526	Bound by treaty to maintain a contingent.
Rajpoot States (North-Western India)	Aboo	114,391	7,370,326	Jeysulmere and Alwar under protective—all the rest under Subsidiary Treaties.
Various States in Northern India — including Dholpore, Bhurtpore, Cis and Trans-Sutlej States, the Cuttack Mehal, and certain petty States contiguous to the Presidencies of Madras and Bombay		174,296	12,752,257	The Cuttack Mehals and Cis-Sutlej States, with few exceptions, are bound to pay tribute. The smaller States are, for the most part, simply entitled to British protection. Total—Area and Population of Native States
Total—Area and Population of Native States		627,910	48376,247	

Subject to such exceptions, it may be stated generally, that the Native Princes of India are bound by their respective treaties to act in "subordinate cooperation" with the paramount power, some by maintaining a military force, others by the payment of a subsidy: and an article almost universally introduced into such treaties is one restraining the Native Contracting powers from the employment of Europeans or Americans, in their respective services.[1]

The relations of the British Government with the Native States of India are generally maintained through the medium of functionaries (who may be either civil or military officers), who are styled "Residents,"[2] and who are stationed at the metropolis of the State to which they are respectively delegated. The degree of interference actually exercised by the "Resident" in the internal affairs of each State (precluded, in some instances, by the terms of the treaties) depends, not so much on the instructions received from head-quarters, as on the personal energy and policy of each "Resident".

The Native States are, in their relations with the British Government (with certain exceptions hereafter to be noticed), placed under the Supreme Authority of the Governor-General in Council, in whom the appointment of British Representatives at their several Courts is vested.

The aggregate military resources of all the Native Princes of India are estimated at about 400,000 troops, and their aggregate revenues at about thirteen millions sterling per annum. The obligations of these Native Princes to the British Government involve altogether a nominal military contingent of 32,000 troops, and an aggregate annual subsidy of about half-a-million sterling per annum.

The actually-subsisting relations between the Native States of India and the British Government will appear from the following summary:

List of Treaties or Engagements

Between the British Government and the Native Princes and States of Asia, from the earliest period to the present time, arranged chronologically.

1739, July 12th, Treaty with the Mahrattas.

1756, October 12th, Treaty with the Mahrattas.

1756, Treaty with the Prince of Cherrikal (Malabar).

1757, February 9th and 12th, Treaty and Agreement with Serajah Dowlah.

1757, March 31st, Perwannah from Serajah Dowlah.

1757, Treaty with Jaffier Ali Khan.

1757, Perwannah from Jaffier Ali Khan, for the Mint.

1757, Perwannah from Jaffier Ali Khan for Saltpetre of Bihar.

1757, Sunnud from the Company's Zemindary, for lands given under the Seal of Allow-o-Dowlah, Meer Mohammed, Saddk Khan Bahadur Assud Jung, Dewan of the Sobah of Bengal.

1757, July 15th, General Sunnud from Jaffier Ali Khan.

1757, December 20th, Perwannah from Jaffier Ali Khan for the granted lands.

1758, Sunnud for the free tenure of the town of Calcutta, &c., to the Hon'ble East India Company, given under the seal of the Nawab Allow-o-Dowlah, Meer Mohammed Saddk Khan Bahadur Assud Jung, Dewan of the Sobah of Bengal.

1758, Articles of the Firmaund granted by the Bringah Raja (Malabar), for granting to the Company the exclusive privilege of purchasing Pepper, &c. in his dominions.

1758, September 22nd, Perwannah, &c., from the Prince of Sinde, relative to the rate of

Customs and Duties to be paid by the Company.

1759, March 4th, Articles of Agreement made with Meah Atchund, at Surat, for the confirmation of Faris Khan in the Naibship.

1759, May 14th, Treaty with the Nizam for the Cession of Masulipatam to the Company.

1759, August 23rd, Articles of Agreement, offensive and defensive, relative to certain commercial arrangements with the King of Cotiote (Malabar).

1759, Perwannahs, &c relating to Surat, &c.

1759, December 6th, Treaty and Accommodation and Ratification between the Dutch and English.

1760, August 23rd, Treaty between the Nawab Jaffier Ali Khan and the Dutch, guaranteed by the Governor and Council of Fort William.

1760, Sunnud under the seal of the Nawab Nusseer-ul-Mulk, Inteaz-o-Dowlah Nessaret Jung Meer Mohammed Cossim Ally Khan Behauder.

1760, December 24th, Firmaund from the Raja of Loundah (Malabar), for the purchase of Pepper in his country for one year.

1760, September 9th, Royal Grant of King Baddacalameur, Regent of Colastria (Malabar), for the trade in Pepper, and agreement for the payment of certain debts.

1760, September 27th, Treaty between the Nawab Meer Mohammed Cossim Ally Khan and the Company, assigning to them the lands of Burdwan, Midnapore, and Chittagong.

1761, January 3rd, Articles of Agreement with Seiddee Hillal of Jinjerah, on the part of himself and the inhavitants of Jaffrabad, relative to commerce.

1761, April 22nd and 23rd, Three Perwannahs from the Prince of Sinde, relative to certain commercial privileges.

1761, September 14th, Articles of Agreement made with Seuram Punt Tatiah, in behalf of Madaroo Balajee son of Balajee Badjeerow, of Poolah.

1761, December 30th, Articles of Agreement made with the King of Cartenadder (Malabar), for the purchase of Pepper in his country, and for mutual aid and assistance.

1763, April 12th, Articles of Agreement made with Shaik Saddoon, of Bushire, for the establishment of a Factory and other commercial privileges.

1763, May 27th, Articles of a Firmaund granted by the Nawab Hyder Ali Khan Bahadur, for the establishment of a Factory at Onore, and other privileges.

1763, July 2nd, Royal Grant from Kureem Khan of certain privileges of trade.

1763, July 10th, Articles of a Treaty and Agreement between the Governor and Council of Fort William on the part of the East India Company, and the Nawab Shujah-ul-Mulk, Hossain-o-Dowlah, Meer Mohammed Jaffer Khan Bahadur or his restoration to the Sobahship.

1763, October 16th, Sunnud from the Nawab of Arcot, for the Seven Magans dependent upon the Soubah.

1764, September 16th, Nawab Meer Mohammed Jaffier Ali Khan's note for Rupees 500,000 per month, for the expenses of the army.

1764, November 22nd and December 6th, Proposals made and Articles executed by the Mogul, granting to the Company the Zemindary of Benares.

1765, February 20th, Articles of a Treaty and Agreement concluded between the Governor-in-council of Fort William, on the part of the English East India Company, and the Nawab Nudjum-ul-Dowlah, on his accession.

1765, March 23rd, Agreement with the Prince of Cherrikal (Malabar), for the grant of the Province of Randoterrah to the Company.

1765, April 7th, Articles of Agreement of peace and friendship with the Boonshla, concluded at the Fort of Karee.

1765, August 12th, Firmaund from the King Shah Aulum granting the Dewannee of Bengal, Bihar and Orisssa to the Company.

1765, August 12th Firmaund from the King Shah Aulum for the Dewannee of the province of Bengal.

1765, Augusst 12th, Firmaund from the King Shah Aulum for the Dewannee of the Province of Bihar.

1765, August 12th, Firmaund from the King Shah Aulum for the Dewannee of the Province of Orissa.

1765, August 12th, Firmaund from the King Shah Aulum confirming the grants of Burdwan, and the rest of the Company's possessions in Bengal, to them.

1765, August 12th, Firmaud from the Mogul for the Northern Circars.

1765, August 12th, Firmaud from the Mogul, being a confirmation of Nawab's grants to the Company in the Carnatic.

1765, August 16th, Treaty between the Nawab Shujah-ul-Dowlah, the Nawab Nudjum-ul-Dowlah, and the English Company, executed at Allahabad.

1765, August 19th, Articles of Agreement between the King Shah Aulum and the Company for the tribute of Bengal.

1765, August 28th and 30th, grant from the Nawab of Arcot for the Company's Jaghire.

1765, September 30th, agreement between the Nawab Nudjum-ul-Dowlah, and the Company for his stipend.

1765, Grants for Lord Clive's Jaghire and the Sunnuds for the reversion of the Jaghire to the Company.

1766, January 12th, Articles of Agreement made with the Ranee of Kattywar for the restoration of Fort Augustus and in regard to commerce.

1766, February 23rd, Grant from Hyder Ali Khan Bahadur of certain commercial privileges in Malabar.

1766, May 19th, articles of a Treaty and Agreement concluded between the Governor and Council of Fort William, on the part of the English East India Company, and the Nawab Syef-ul-Dowla on his accession.

1766, November 12th, Treaty with the Nizam for ceding to the Company the northern Circars.

1768, February 23rd, Treaty of perpetual friendship and alliance with the Nawab of the Carnatic and the Sobah of the Deccan.

1768, November 29th, Treaty between the Company and the Vizier Shujah-ul-Dowlah, for the reduction of his army.

1769, April 3rd, Treaty of perpetual friendship and peace with Hyder Ali.

1770, March 21st, Articles of a treaty and agreement between the Governor and Council of Fort William, on the part of the English East India Company, and the Nawab Mobarek-ul-Dowlah, on his accession.

1770, August 8th, Treaty of peace with Hyder Ali.

1771, October 20th, Translation of a paper containing the articles agreed to by the Raja of Tanjore, for the discharge of the Peshcush.

1771, October 22nd, Agreement with the Nawab of Cambay for the eventual grant to the Company of a Factory at Gogo.

1771, Treaty with the Nawab of Cambay for the cession to him of the Fort of Tarrajah, taken from the Coolies.

1771, November 30th, Treaty of peace and friendship with the Nawab of Broach.

1772, Treaty with the Raja of Coach Bihar.

1773, January 12th, Treaty with Futteh Singh, for a participation of the Revenues of Broach.

1773, September 7th, Treaty of Subsidy with Shujah-ul-Dowlah.

1774, April, Articles of a treaty of peace with Deb Raja of Bootan.

1774, October, treaty under the hands and seals of Nawab Shujah-ul-Dowlah Bahadur and Col. Champion.

1774, October, Treaty under the hands and seals of Fyzulah Khan and Col. Champion.

1775, March 6th, Treaty with Ragobah for placing him in the Peshwaship.

1775, May 21st, Proposed Articles of the Treaty with the Nawab Asuf-ul-Dowlah, for the cession of Benares to the Company.

1776, April 12th, Agreement with the Raja of Tanjore for Subsidizing a body of the Company's troops for the protection of his country.

1776, April 15th, Sunnud granted to Raja Cheyt Singh for the Zemindary of Ghazeepore, Benares, &c.

1776, May, Treaty of peace between the Hon'ble the English East India Company and the Mahratta State.

1778, November 24th, Treaty with Ragobah for conducting him to Poonan, with a view of placing him in the Peshwaship.

1779, Convention of Wurgaon.

1779, April 27th, Treaty of alliance with Bazalet Jung, for renting the Guntoor Circar to the Company, and for receiving into hiss service a body of the Company's troops.

1779, December 2nd, Draft of a treaty proposed between the company and Maha Raja Luckindar Bahadur, Rana of Gohud.

1780, January 26th, Treaty of alliance and defence with Futteh Singh, Gwicowar, by General Goddard.

1780, January 26th, Treaty of alliance and defence with Futteh Singh, as amended and ratified by the Governor-general in Council.

1781, September 14th, Copy of the Pottah granted to Raja Mehipnarain Bahadur of Benares.

1781, September 19th, Agreement concluded by the Governor-General with the Vizier of Oudh, for the removal of the temporary Brigade.

1781, October 13th, Translation of a Copy of the Treaty entered into by Mobariz-ul-Mulk, Iftiker-ul-Dowlah, Colonel Muir, Behauder Mahabul Jung, on the part of the English East India Company, and the Maha Rajah

Sahib Madhajee Rao Scindia Bahadur Sobahdar.

1782, May 17th, Treaty of peace with the Mahrattas.

1784, March 11th, Treaty of perpetual peace and friendship with the Nawab Tippoo Sultan Bahadur.

1785, June, Preliminary Treaty and Agreement with the Nawab Mohammed Ali, for his proportion of the charges for the defence of the Carnatic.

1786, Agreement with the King of Queda for the cession of Prince of Wales' Island.

1787, February 24th, Treaty with the Nawab Mohammed Ali, for settling his proportion of the expenses for the protection of the Carnatic and for the adjustment of his private debts.

1787, April 10th, Treaty with the Rajah of Tanjore for settling his proportion of contribution towards the defence of his country, and for adjusting his private debts.

1787, April 15th, Treaty with Asuf-ul-Dawlah, Nawab of Oudh, fixing the whole of his payments at 50 lacs of rupees

1788, August 12th, Agreement with the Raja of Travancore for two battalions to be stationed within his dominions.

1788, September 1st, Treaty of Commerce with the Nawab Asuf-ul-Dowlah.

1788, September 18th, Translation of the Nizams Order to Seyf Jung, for the surrender of the Guntoor Circar to the Company, delivered to captain Kennaway, the Resident at the Nizams Durbar.

1789, July 7th, Copy of a letter from Earl Cornwallis to the Nizam deemed equal to a Treaty, being preliminary to that of 1790, June 5.

1790, June 5th, Treaty of Alliance between the Company, the Peshwa and the Nizam, against Tippoo Sultan.

1791, February 2nd, Treaty of Alliance with the Raja of Cochin.

1791, May 1st, Treaty with the King of Queda for an annual quit-rent for Prince of Wales Island.

1792, February 22nd, Preliminary Treaty with Tippoo Sultan.

1792, March 18th, Definitive Treaty with ditto.

1792, March 1st, Treaty of Commerce with Raja of Nepal.

1792, July 12th, Treaty with the Nawab Mahomed Ali, with a modification of the Treaty of 24th February, 1787, assigning certain districts as securities for payment of sums stipulated.

1793, January 28th, Agreement with the Raja of Travancore, commonly called the Pepper contract.

1793, February 28th commercial agreement with the Raja of Assam.

1794, June 12th, Agreement between Commodore Mitchell and' Johannes Seberg, Councillor and Director of Batavia, for furnishing and equipping a vessel as a cartel ship to Mauritius.

1794, December 13th, Treaty with the Nawab Asuf-ul-Dowlah and the chief of the Rohillas, with appendix.

1795-6, Captain Syme's Commercial Arrangement with the States, king of Ava.

1797, March 20th, Agreement with the Nawab Vizier Asuf-ul-Dowlah, for the pay of an additional regiment of cavalry.

1797, April 9th, Paper of Declarations for the management of Turrakabad.

1797, May 18th, Treaty with the Raja of Travancore, as originally proposed by the Government of Bombay, and afterwards amended, and finally concluded and ratified by the Governor-General of India in Council.

1798, February 7th, Engagement executed by the Nawab Saadut Ali Khan to the Bow Begum (mother of the late Nawab Asuf-ul-Dowlah), under the guarantee of the Company.

1798, February 21st, Treaty of Alliance and subsidy between the Nawab Vizier Saadut Ali Khan Bahadur and the Hon'ble East India Company.

1798, September 1st, Treaty of Alliance, Defence, and subsidy, with the Nizam, and for the dismission of the French Troops from his service, and the reception of a body of British troops in lieu of them, with two separate articles.

1798, October 12th, Treaty with the Imaum of Muscat.

1799, June 22nd, Partition Treaty of Mysore for strengthening the alliance and friendship subsisting between the company, the Nizam, and the Peshwa, and for effecting a settlement of the dominions of Tippoo Sultan.

1799, July 8th, Subsidizing Treaty with the Raja of Mysore.

1799, October 25th, Treaty with the Raja of Tanjore for transferring the sovereignty of his country to the company.

1800, January 18th, Treaty of Friendship with the Imaum of Muscat.

1800, May 13th, Treaty with the Nawab of Surat for the cession of the City of Surat and the circumjacent country to the Company.

1800, August 26, Articles of Agreement for the adjustment of the Desh Cavelly and Talem Cavelly of the province of Tinnevelly.

1800, October 12th, Treaty of Alliance and Defence with the Nizam, and for the cession of territory in commutation of subsidy.

1801, January, Political Treaty with the King of Persia.

1801, January, Commercial Treaty with ditto.

1801, July 31st, Treaty with Azeem-ul-Dowlah for settling the succession to the Sobahdarry, and for vesting the administration of the Civil and Military Government of the Carnatic in the Company.

1801, October 30th, Treaty of Alliance with the Raja of Nepal.

1801, November 10th, Treaty with the Nawab Vizier Saadut Ali for ceding to the Company in perpetual sovereignty certain portions of His Excellency's territorial possessions in commutation of Subsidy.

1802, February 15th, Final arrangement with the Nawab Vizier Saadut Ali Khan.

1802, March, Articles of Convention between General Duncan and Rowjee Appajee, for and on behalf of Anund Rao Gwicowar Senakasskell Shumshere Bahadur, for the security of the dominion and government of the Gwicowar in Guzerat.

1802, April 12th, commercial Treaty with the Nizam.

1802, July 6th, Treaty of Alliance and Subsidy with Anund Rao Gwicowar.

1802, July 24th, Treaty with the Nawab of Furruckabad for ceding to the Company, in perpetual sovereignty, the Province of Furruckabad and its dependencies, in Commutation of Tribute.

1802, July 29th, Agreement concluded between the Resident at Baroda and Anund Rao Gwicowar.

1802, November, Treaty with the King of Queda for cession of territory on the coast of Queda.

1802, December 31st, Treaty of Alliance and Subsidy with the Peshwa, commonly called the Treaty of Bassein.

1803, January 25th, Agreement with Anund Rao Gwicowar, supplementary to the Treaties of March and June, 1802.

1803, August 14th, Treaty with Amrut Rao of Poonah.

1803, August 24th, Instrument under the signature of the Governor General in Council, delivered to the Nizam (Secunder Jah) on his accession to the Musnud, recognising all the former treaties and engagements with Nizam Ali decreased.

1803, September 4th, Agreement with Raja Himnut Bahadur.

1803, September 29th, Treaty of Alliance and Friendship with the Raja of Bhurtpore.

1803, November 14th, Treaty of Alliance and Friendship with the Raja Macherry.

1803, November 14th, Treaty with the Raja of Lunaward in Guzerat declaratory of his allegiance to the Company.

1803, December 12th, Treaty of Amity and Alliance with the Raja of Gyepore (or Gyenagur).

1803, December 15th, Treaty with the Raja of Soonth in Guzerat, declaratory of his allegiance to the Company.

1803, December 16, Treaty of Amity and Alliance with Raja Umbajee Rao (Gwalior and Gohud).

1803, December 16, supplementary Article to the Treaty of Bassein.

1803, December 17th, Treaty of Peace and Friendship with the Raja of Berar, commonly called the Treaty of Deogaum.

1803, December 22nd, Treaty of Amity and Alliance with the Raja of Joudhpore.

1803, December 29th, Supplementary Treaty with the Rajah of Mysore, for adjusting an exchange of certain districts, dated 29th December, 1803, with reference to thee 15th Article of the Treaty of Mysore, concluded in 1799.

1803, December, Treaty of Peace and Friendship with Dowlut Rao Scindia.

1804, January 9th, Additional Article to the Treaty with the Nizam, of 12th October, 1800.

1804, January 17th, Treaty of Amity and Alliance with the Rana of Gohud.

1804, February 6th, Treaty with the Sobahdar of Jhansi.

1804, February 27th, Treaty of Alliance and mutual Defence with Dowlut Rao Scindia.

1804, March 15th, Treaty concluded with Rao Raja Pareechect of Dutteea.

1804, April 28th, Partition Treaty of Hydrabad with his Highness the Sobahdar of the Deccan.

1804, May 14th Partition Treaty of Poona with his Highness the Peshwa.

1804, July 17th, Political Treaty with Raja of Colapore.

1804, July 17th, Maritime Treaty with ditto.

1804, September 2nd, Ikrar-namah, or obligation of allegiance and fidelity executed on the part of Maha Raja Beekrumajeet, Bajee Bahader, Raja of Chukary.

1804, September 2nd, Sunnud granted to ditto.

1804, November 25th, Treaty with the Raja of Pertaubgurh declaratory of his allegimee to be Company.

1805, January 12th, Treaty of Friendship and Alliance with the Raja of Travancore.

1805, April 17th, Treaty of Amity and Alliance with the Raja of Bhurtpore.

1805, April 21st, Definitive Treaty with Anund Rao Gwicowar, in confirmation of former Treaties, and for augmentation of the Subsidiary Force.

1805, August 21st, Engagement on the part of Zeiboo Nissa Begum of Sirdanah.

1805, November 22nd, Definitive Treaty of Amity and Alliance with Dowlut Rao Scindia.

1805, December 24th, Treaty of Peace and Amity with Jeswant Rao Holkar.

1805, Treaty of Friendship and Amity with Sirdars Runjeet Sing of Lahore, and Futteh Sing, Allowallah.

1806, January 10th, Treaty with the Rana of Gohud, for the relinquishment to the Company of the Country and Fort of Gohud and others, and for the investiture of the Rana in the sovereingty of the districts of Dholepore, Baree, and Bajkera.

1806, February 6th, Agreement made with Shaik Abdoolla Bin Croosh on the part of the Joasmee Chiefs.

1806, March 1st, Sunnud granted to Raja Nerender Gier.

1806, April 1st, Agreement entered into by the Agents of Bhunga Sing.

1806, April 4th, Ikrar-nameh, or obligation of allegiance presented by, and Sunnud granted to Kooar Soonee Sah.

1806, May 4th, Sunnud granted to Assud-oo-Dowlah Nujabut States Ali Khan Bahadur.

1806, May 4th, Sunnud granted to Abdool Mahomed Khan.

1806, May 13th, Perwannah granted to Ahmud Buksh Khan.

1806, May 13th, Perwannah granted to Ahmud Buksh Khan Bahadur.

1806, July 25th, Sunnuds granted to the Officers and Chiefs of Raja Bagojee Bhooslah, to whom pensions were assigned.

1806, August 24th, Engagement with the Raja of Berar for the Restitution of the Provinces of Sumbulpore and Patna by the British Government to the Raja.

1806, October 23rd, Treaty with the Rana of Calpee.

1806, November 22nd, Ikrar-nameh, or obligation of allegiance from Chobee Deriao Sing, Killadar of Calinger.

1806, December 9th, Ikrar-nameh, or obligation of allegiance from Duchmun Sing, Killandar of Adjyghur.

1807, January 10th, Political Treaty with the King of Persia.

1807, January 10th, Commercial Treaty with ditto.

1807, January 29th, Articles explanatory of the third article of the Treaty of Mysore, concluded in 1799.

1807, February 1st, Sunnud granted to Maharajah Kishore Sing.

1807, February 4th, Ikrar-namah, or obligation of Allegiance on the part of Maharajah Kishore Sing, Written 28th January.

1807, June 8th, Ikrar-nameh, or obligation of Allegiance, presented by, and Sunnud granted to Rajah Bukht Sing.

1807, June 21st, Ikrar-nameh, or obligation of Allegiance, presented by, and Sunnud granted to Rajah Mohun Sing.

1807, July 4th, Ikrar-nameh, or obligation of Allegiance, presented by, and Sunnud granted to Gopal Lall.

1807, September 19th, Ikrar-nameh, or obligation of Allegiance, presented by, and Sunnud granted to Keer Luchmon Sing.

1807, September 22nd, Ikrar-nameh, or obligation of Allegiance, presented by, and Sunnud granted at Dewan Aperbul sing and Dewan Chuthary.

1807, October 7th, Ikrar-nameh, or obligation of Allegiance, presented by, and Sunnud granted to Purseram.

1807, November 29th, Ikrar-nameh, or obligation of Allegiance, presented by, and Sunnud granted to Raja Ram.

1808, December 1807, January 1808, Agreements with the piratical Mahrattas.

1808, February 1st, Ikrar-nameh, or obligation of Allegiance, presented by, and Sunnud granted to Purtaub Sing.

1808, December 9th, Ikrar-nameh, or obligation of Allegiance, presented by, and Sunnud granted to , Dewan Deeraj Sing.

1809, March 11th, Ikrar-nameh, or obligation of Allegiance, presented by Laul Shew, Raja of Cucheerah and Nagode.

1809, March 12th, Treaty with the King of Persia.

1809, March 20th, Sunnud granted to Laul Shew, Raja of Cucheerah and Nagode.

1809, April 25th, Treaty of Alliance with the Raja of Lahore.

1809, May 3rd, Ittila-nameh, addressed to the Chiefs of the Country of Sirhind, on this side of the river Sutledge.

1809, May 6th Treaty of perpetual friendship and Subsidy with the Raja of Cochin.

1809, June 17th, Treaty of Alliance and Friendship with the King of Cabool.

1809, July 16th, Ikrar-nameh, or obligation of Allegiance, presented by Laul Amaun Sing, of Souhawal and Rygown.

1809, July 18th, Sunnud granted to Laul Amaun Sing.

1809, August 22nd, Promissory Agreement with the Ameers of Sinde.

1809, August 23rd, Ikrar-nameh or obligation of Allegiance, from Dewan Joogul Purshaud.

1809, August 25th, Sunnud granted to Dewan Joogul Purshaud.

1809, October 28th, Engagement with Dewan Hansraj of Mandavie.

1809, Agreement with Futteh Mahomed of cutch.

1810, August 16th, Ikrar-nameh, or obligation of Allegiance, from Laul Doonierputt.

1810, August 17th, Sunnud granted to Laul Doonierputt.

1811, January 7th, Sunnud granted to Dewan Jooggul Purshaud.

1811, March 22nd, Ikrar-nameh, or obligation of Allegiance, from Raja Kishore Sing, Bahadur Raja of Punna.

1811, March 22nd, sunnud granted to Raja Kishore Sing, Bahader Raja of Punna.

1811, March 25th, Sunnud granted to Raja Bajee, Bahader Raja of Churkary.

1811, March 26th, Ikrar-nameh, or obligation of Allegiance, from Raja Ruttun Sing, Raja of Bijawar.

1811, March 27th, Sunnud granted to Raja Ruttun Singh, Raja of Bijawar.

1811, July 16th, Engagement with the Raja of Macherry.

1811, August 22nd, Sunnud granted to Chiefs of the Country of Malwa and Sirhind, on this side of the river Sutlege.

1812, January 14th, Treaty with the Vizier of Oudh.

1812, February 24th, Sunnud granted to Dewan Gopaul Sing.

1812, March 14th, Treaty with the King of Persia.

1812, June 19th, Ikrar-nameh, or obligation of Allegiance, from Chobey Derrao Sing, late Killader of Calinger.

1812, July 4th, Sunnud granted to Chobey Derrao Sing, late Killadar of Calinger.

1812, June 19th, Ikrar-nameh, or obligation of allegiance, from Nawal Kishwur and the relic of Bherit Jew Chobey.

1812, Sunnud granted to Nawal Keshwur and the alie of Bherit Jew Chobey.

1812, June 19th, Ikrar-nameh, or obligation of Allegiance, from Chobey Chittersaul, and the mother of Chobey Chittersaul.

1812, July 4th, Sunnud granted to Chobey Chittersaul and the Mother of Chobey Chittersaul.

1812, June 19th, Ikrar-nameh, or obligation of Allegiance, from Gya Purshaud Chobey.

1812, July 4th, sunnud granted to Gya Purshaud Chobey.

1812, June 19th, Ikrar-nameh, or obligation of Alligriance, from Poker Purshaud Chobey.

1812, July 4th, Sunnud granted to Poker Purshaud Chobey.

1812, June 19th, Ikrar-nameh, or obligation of Allegiance, from Chobey Salagram.

1812, July 4th, Surmud granted to Chobey Salagram.

1812, July 4th, Ikrar-nameh, or obligation of Allegiance, from Gopaul Lall.

1812, July 4th, Sunnud granted to Gopaul Lall.

1812, July 4th, Sunnud granted to Thakoor Doorjun Sing.

1812, October 1st, Agreement with the Raja of Colapore.

1812, October 3rd, Agreement with Raja Pond Sawunt Boonshla Bahadur, Dessye or Sawant Warree.

1812, October 5th, Treaty of Friendship and defensive alliance with the Raja Rewah and Mookundpore.

1812, December 23rd, Treaty of Friendship and Defensive Alliance with the Raja of Oorcha or Tehree.

1813, June 2nd, second Treaty with the Raja of Rewah and Mookundpore with a supplemental Article.

1813, Engagement with the Raja of Rewah's son, binding himself to abide by the Treaties concluded with his father.

1814, March 11th, Third Treaty with the Rajá of Rewah and Mookundpore, under the seals and signatures of the Raja and his son.

1814, July 12th, Engagement with the Vizier of Oudh.

1814, August 3rd, Counterpart of engagement with the Vizier of Oudh by the British Government.

1814, November 25th, Treaty with the King of Persia.

1815, March 6th, Sunnud granted to Raja Maha Chund, of Belaspore.

1815, September 3rd, 4th, and 21st, Sunnuds granted to Rana Juggut Sing, of Baghal, to Rana Bhoop Sing, of Koobhar; same date, to Rooder Paul, of Boojye; September 4th, 1815, to Sunsaroo Thakoor, same date; to Mann Chund, of Boojye, same date; to Roy Mungree Deo, same date; to Thakoor Jugrah, September 21st, 1815.

1815, September 21st, Sunnud granted to Raja Futteh Sing of Nahan.

1815, October 20th, Sunnud granted to Raja Ram Sing (or Ram Surrun) for Hindore Hindoreea.

1815, October 20th, Sunnud granted to Raja Ram Sing, (or Ram Surrun), for Burrowlee.

1815, October 20th, Sunnud granted to Raja Kurrum Sing, of Putteala, for Pergunnah Mahalee, &c.

1815, October 20th, Sunnud granted to Raja Kurrum Sing, for Bugghaut and Juggutgurh.

1815, November 6th, Sunnud granted to Mehendra, Sing, of Bussahir.

1815, December 2nd, Treaty and Peace with the Raja of Nepal.

1816, January 16th, Treaty of Alliance with Rao Bharmuljee, of Cutch, with a supplemental article.

1816, March 4th, Ikrar-nameh, or obligation of Allegiance, executed on the part of the Rajah of Nepal.

1816, May 1st, Treaty with the Vizier of Oudh.

1816, May 27th, Treaty of defensive alliance with the Raja of Berar.

1816, June 18th, Treaty with the Rao of Cutch, supplemental to that of the 16th January 1816.

1817, January 11th, Sunnud granted to Purtaub Sing.

1817, January 11th, Sunnud granted to Nawab Kishore.

1817, January 11th, Sunnud granted to the widow of Bhurtjoo Chobey.

1817, February 10th, Treaty with the Raja of Siccim.

1817, April 7th, Sunnud granted to the Raja of Siccim.

1817, April 11th, Sunnud granted to Subadar Major Hoolas Pundit.

1817, June 13th, Treaty with the Peshwa.

1817, November 1st, Engagement with Nana Govind Rao, of Calpee.

1817, November 5th, Treaty with Dawlut Rao Scindia.

1817, November 6th, Supplement to the Definitive Treaty with the Gwicowar.

1817, November 9th, Treaty with the Raja of Kerowlee.

1817, November 9th, Engagement with Nawab Ameer Khan.

1817, November 12, Engagement with the Raja of Simpthur

1817, November 17th, Treaty with the Sobahdar of Jhansi.

1817, November 21st Sunnud granted to the widow of Gracoo Giyraj Misser.

1817, December 26th, Treaty with the Raja of Kotah.

1818, January 6th, Treaty with Mulhar Rao Holkar.

1818, January 6th, Treaty with the Raja of Joudhpore.

1818, January 6th, Provisional Treaty with the Rajah of Berar.

1818, January 13th, Treaty with the Rana of Oudeypore.

1818, February 10th, Treaty with the Raja of Boondee.

1818, February 20th, Supplementary Article to the Treaty with the Raja of Kotah dated December 26th, 1817.

1818, February 26th, Treaty with the Nawab of Bhopal.

1818, March 9th, Treaty with the Raja of Bickaneer.

1818, March 26th, Treaty with the Raja of Kishenghur.

1818, April 2nd, Treaty with the Raja of Jyepore.

1818, July 25th, Engagement with Dowlut Rao Scindia.

1818, July 31st, Treaty with the Raja of Dutteeah.

1818, September 16th, Treaty with the Raja of Banswarra.

1818 , September 16th, Supplementary Article to the Treaty with the Raja of Banswarra.

1818, October 5th, Treaty with the Raja of Dowleah and Purtaubghur.

1818, November 28th, Additional Article to the Supplementary Treaty with the Gwicowar.

1818, November 28th, Sunnud granted to Sujahut Khan.

1818, November 28th, Sunnud granted to Naumdhar Khan.

1818, December 11th, Treaty with the Raja of Doongerpore.

1818, December 12th, Treaty with the Raja of Jessulmere.

1818, December 12th, Treaty with the petty Chiefs of Dewass.

1818, December 25th, Treaty with the Raja of Banswarra.

1819, January 10th, Treaty with the Raja of Dhar.

1819, Ikrar-nameh, or obligation of Allegiance from Ram Chunder Buller.

1819, Sunnud granted to Ramchunder Buller, for villages in the district of Saugor.

1819, February 17th, Treaty with the Regency of Sawant Warree.

1819, April 22nd, Treaty with the King of Acheen.

1819, July 16th, Sunnud granted to Hurbullub Pundit.

1819, July 31st, Sunnud granted to Narain Pundit.

1819, July 31st, Sunnud granted to Nawab Saduk Ali Khan.

1819, August 13th, Sunnud granted to Kurreem Khan.

1819, August 13th, Sunnud granted to khandee Buksh.

1819, September 25th, Treaty with the Raja of Satara.

1819, September 25th, Sunnud granted to Maha Rao Omeed sing of Kotah.

1819, October 13th, Treaty with the Cutch Government.

1820, January 8th, Treaty with the Arab Tribes.

1820, January 8th, Preliminary Treaty with Hassan Bin Ramah.

1820, January 9th, Preliminary Treaty with Sultan Bin Sugger.

1820, January 9th, Preliminary Treaty with the Sheikh of Dubey.

1820, January 11th, Preliminary Treaty with Sheikh shakhbool Bin Dyab, of Abon Dyabee.

1820, January 15th, Preliminary Treaty with Hassan Bin Ali.

1820, February 6th, Engagement with Dowlut Rao Scindia.

1820, February 14th, Sunnud granted to Raja Ayoon Sing of Sah Gurh.

1820, February 14th, Sunnud granted to Raja Surmeet Sing of Ramnugger.

1820, February 17th, Treaty with the Regency of Sawunt Warree.

1820, March 4th, Sunnud granted to the Raja of Gurhwal.

1820, April 3rd, Sunnud granted to Takoor Zorawur Sing, of Hindoreea.

1820, April 15th, Sunnud granted to Sreedhur Pundit.

1820, May 20th, Sunnud granted to Raja Sunker Sah, of Ajnee.

1820, November 9th, Treaty with the Ameers of Sinde.

1821, January 15th, Treaty with the Imaum of Senns.

1821, January 15th, Sunnud granted to Bhugwant Sing Sobahdar.

1821, March 14th, Sunnud granted to Raja Maharag Sahy, Raja of Sumbulpore.

1821, June 16th, Sunnud granted to Rana Govind Rao Sobahdar Major.

1821, December 18th, Treaty with the Raja of Dhar.

1822, May 21st, Treaty with the Government of Cutch.

1822, July, Treaty with the Raghojee Angria of Colabs.

1822, August 29th, Treaty with the Imaum of Muscat.

1822, December 12th, Treaty with the Nizam.

1823, February 11th, Agreement from Maha Rawul Sree Bhunwannee Singh, Rawul, of Banswarra.

1823, April 11th, Sunnuds conferred on the Husht Bhayeh Jageerdars, viz. to Rao Bahadur Bukut Sing of Chirgaong, Dewan Soorjun Sing of Bijna, Dewan Boodh Sing of Dhoorwye, Rooard Hurpursand of Force, Dewan Bunka Esurree Sing of Puharee.

1823, Treaty with Rao Sheo Sing, Regent of Serohee, ratified 31st October, 1823.

1823, November 21st, Sunnud granted to Veetul Rao. Mulhar, Poorundary.

1823, November 21st, Sunnud granted to the widow of the late Madoo Rao Bhoskutta.

1823, December 9th, Agreement with Raja Pertaubghur.

1824, March 6th, Treaty with Raja Govind Chunder of Cachar.

1824, March 10th, Treaty with Raja Ram sing of Jyntheea.

1824, April 20th, Sunnud granted to Raja Ghunsham Sing.

1824, August 2nd, Treaty with the Sultan and Tumongong of Johore.

1825, July 31st, Provisional Treaty with the King of Siam.

1825, August 17th, Agreement with the King of Oudh.

1825, December 30th, agreement with the Raja of Colapore.

1826, February 24th, Treaty of Peace with the King of Ava, with additional article.

1826, June 20th, Political and Commercial Treaties with the King of Siam.

1826, November 23rd, Commercial Treaty with the King of Ava.

1826, November 30th, Agreement with Teerut Sing Acheembee, called the White Raja, Chief of Nungklow.

1826, December 1st, Treaty with the Raja of Nagpore.

1827, February 6th, Agreement with the Sheik of the Tribes of Hubberawal.

1827, October 23rd, Agreement with the Raja of Colapore.

1828, March 10th, Bond from His Royal Highness, the Prince Royal of Persia, annulling the 3rd and 4th articles of the Treaty dated 25th November, 1814.

1828, May 2nd, Sunnud granted to Teiz ool Khan Bungush. Sunnud granted to Nubbee Buksh Khan, and Hyder Buksh Khan.

1828, August 22nd, Sunnud granted to Wolly Mahomed Sobahdar Major.

1829, May 1st, Treaty with the King of Oudh.

1829, July 15th, Agreement with the Raja of Colapore.

1829, September 25th, Sunnud granted to Khadim Hossein Khan and Mahomed Hossein Khan.

1829, December 25th, Revised engagement with the Raja of Nagpore.

1831, September 20th, Engagement with the Nizam.

1832, April 4th, Treaty with the Government of Khyrpore.

1832, April 20th, treaty with the Government of Hyderabad in Sinde.

1832, April 22nd, Supplementary Article to ditto.

1832, September 20th, Treaty with the Government of Cutch.

1832, December 26th, Indus Toll Treaty with Maharaja Runjeet Sing of Lahore.

Supplementary Article to ditto.

1833, February 22nd, Indus Toll Treaty with the Nawab of Bahawulpore.

Supplementary Article to ditto.

1833, March 2nd, Treaty with Raja Poorunder Sing.

1833, March 12th, Treaty between Maharajah Runjeet Sing and Shah Shoojah-ool-Moolk.

1833, June 21st, Agreement with the King of Oudh, concerning the deposit of 3 lacs of rupees for the poor of Lucknow.

Modified Treaty with the Raja of Mysore.

1834, July 2nd, Treaty with the Government of Hyderabad.

1834, July 5th, Treaty with Government of Cutch.

1834, July 31st, Agreement with Deb Raja on the restoration of Dooar Booree Gooma.

1834, October 18th, Indus Toll Treaty with the Ameers of Sinde.

1834, November 3rd, Agreement with Toola Ram Seenapatty Articles proposed to be substituted for Articles 3rd, 4th, and 6th of the definitive Treaty with Persia.

1834, November 22nd, Proclamation by Government on Female Infanticide.

1835, January 24th, Supplementary Treaty with Maharajah Runjeet Sing, for abolishing a Toll on the Indus.

1835, March 5th, Supplementary Treaty with the Nawab of Buhawulpoor.

1835, December 7th, Engagement with the Raja of Joudhpore.

1836, January 18th, Bhownuggur, Engagements entered into by the Thakoor of Bhownuggur, exempting from Payment of Duty, Vessel putting into his Ports through stress of Weather.

1836, February 6th, Proclamation by the Ruo of Kutch, prohibiting Slave Trade.

1836, February 18th, Mahee and Rewa Kunta. Paper addressed to Acting Political Agent, by Maharaj Rithee Singjee Kururnsingjee.

1836, May 7th, King of Persia's Firman for British subjects trading with Persia.

1836, November 28th, Commercial Treaty with the Ameers of Sinde.

1837, September 11th, Treaty with the King of Oudh.

1838, January 3rd, Engagements by the Nawab of Joonaghur for thee Suppression of Suttee.

1838, January 7th, Engagement by the Seedee of Jafferabad for the Suppression of Suttee.

1838, January 23rd, Preliminary Engagement with Sultan McHassan of Lahij, for the Transfer of Aden to the British Government.

1838, April 8th, Treaty with the Raja Rana of Jhullawur, when that State was formed into a separate Principality out of the Koto Territory.

1838, April 8th, Treaty with the Raj Rana Mudun Sing of Kotah.

1838, April 10th, Treaty with Maha Rao Ram Sing of Kotah.

1838, April 17th, Agreement with thee Chief of Ras-ool-Khymah, for the Suppression of Slavery.

1838, June 26th, Tripartite Treaty between Shah Sooja ool Moolk of Cabool, Maha Raja Runjeet

Singh of Lahore, and the English East India Company.

1838, April 20th, Treaty with the Ameers of Sind.

1838, September 15th, Agreement with the Sudesaee.

1838, October 5th, Treaty with the Nawab of Bahawulpore.

1838, December 24th, Treaty with His Highness Meer Roostum Khan of Khyrpoor.

1839, July 3rd, Agreement for the Suppression of Slavery in the Persian Gulf.

1839, February 2nd, Engagement with the Sultan of Lahij, on behalf of himself and the Abdallees.

1839, February 4th, Further Engagement with the Sultan of Lahij.

1839, May 31st, Commercial Treaty with the Imam of Muscat.

1839, June 18th, Bond of Peace and Friendship, entered into by the Sultan of Lahij.

1839, January 31st, Engagement with the Huzzabee Tribe.

1839, February 2nd, Engagement with the Chief of Wakeel, and all under him.

1839, February 4th, Engagement of Peace and Friendship with the Chiefs of Hagrabees.

1839, February 18th, Engagement entered into between Shaikh Iwas Bin Sallaam el Abbadee and his Tribe.

1839, February 18th, Engagement with Shaikh Maidee.

1839, February 18th, Engagement with Shaikh of Zaidee.

1839, February 29th, Engagements with the Shaikhs of the Muswadie Territory of the Subees.

1839, February 20th, Engagement of Peace and Friendship with Shaikh Mahomet Bin Alee Busalee, of the Southern Division of the Subees.

1839, February 21st, Engagement of Friendship and Peace, with Shaikh Arsel Bin Hydee Bin Ahmed Musaidee, of a District of the Yaffaaes.

1839, March 10th, Treaty with Shah Kannan of Herat.

1839, March 10th, Egagement of Friendship and Peace, with Asun Bin Yorsoof Shirzebee.

1839, March 11th, Treaty with the Ameers of Scinde.

1839, September 4th, Treaty with the Raja of Satara.

1839, September 30th, Treaty with the King of Cabool.

1839, December 17th, Additional Articles to Treaty, with the Imaum of Muscat for the Suppression of Slavery.

1839, September 23rd, Proclamation by the Raja of Sattara, against Suttee.

1839, September 23rd, Proclamation by the Raja of Sattara abolishing Transit Duties.

1839, February 3rd, Agreement with Punt Sucheo.

1839, March 11th, Treaty with the Ameers of Hyderabad.

1840, April 13th, Proclamation by the Gwickwar, abolishing Suttee.

1840, June 23rd, Agreement subscribed by Meea Pretum Singh, of Koomharsain.

1840, September 8, Agreement with the Chief of Bhownuggur for relinquishing Land and Sea Customs.

1840, March 23rd, Renewed Engagement with Jhareja Chiefs for the suppression of Infanticide.

1840, April 16th, Egagement with the Chief of Soonawara.

1840, April 28th, Engagement with the Raja of Baria against Suttee.

1840, April 8th, Engagement by the Chief of Bhadurwa against Suttee.

1840, April 22nd, Engagement by the Chief of Chota Oodapoor against Suttee.

1840, May 9th, Engagement by the Raja of Rajpeepla against Suttee.

1840, May 12th, Engagement by Ranee Bhowanee Singjee of Soauth, against Suttee.

1840, May 8th, Engagement by Thakoor Sirdar Sing of Wankaneer, against Suttee.

1840, August 21st, Agreement entered into by Nawab Mohamed Syeed Khan.

1841, October 6th, Treaty with Meer Nusseer Khan, Chief of Kelat.

1841, March 11th, Proclamation by the Raja Kolhapoor, Prohibiting Suttee.

1841, June 18th, Treaty between the British Government and the Ameer of Meerpoor, Meer Cheer Cher Mahomed Khan.

1842, August 13th, Proclamation by the Raja of Rajpeepla, against Suttee.

1843, June 1st, Maritime Truce for Ten Years from 1st June 1843, by Arab Chiefs.

1843, February 11th, engagement with the Sultan of Lahij.

1843, September 11th, Agreement regarding the Levy of Duties of Merchandise in Transit through the Buhawulpoor Territory.

1844, February 20th, Further Bond entered into by the Sultan of Lahij.

1844, October 31st, Rulers by His Highness the Gwickwar exempting Vessels trading between Bombay and Sind, forced into his

Ports by stress of weather, from Payment of Duty at these Ports.

1844, November 8th, Treaty with the Sultan of Johanna for the Suppression of the Slave Trade.

1845, October 2nd, Further Agreement with the Imaum of Muscat for the Suppression of Slavery.

1846, March 19th, Engagement by His Highness the Nawab of Joonaghur, relative to the Customs on Vessels.

1846, March 22nd, Engagement by His Highness Jam Runmulgee of Nowanuggur, relative to the Customs on Vessels.

1846, March 9th, Treaty with the State of Lahore.

1846, March 11th, Agreement with the Lahore Durbar.

1846, March 16th, Treaty with Maharajah Golab Sing.

1846, December 16th, Agreement with the Lahore Durbar.

1846, April, Rules by the Imaum of Muscat regarding Duties to be charged on Cargoes of Vessels putting into his Highness's Ports.

1847, April 30th, with Shaik Sultan Bin Suggur, Chief of Ras-ool Kymah and Shurgah.

1847, April 30th, with Shaikh Muktoom, of Debaye.

1847, May 1st, with Shaikh Abdool Azeez, of Ejman.

1847, May 1st, with Shaikh Abdoollah Bin Rashid, of Amulgavine.

1847, May 3rd, with Shaikh Saud Bin Tohnoon, of Aboothabee.

1847, May 8th, Shaikh Mahomed Bin Khuleefa, of Bahrein.

1848, June 12th, Firmans by the Shah of Persia for the Suppression of the Slave Trade by Sea.

1849, May 22nd, Engagement with the Chief of Sohar for abolishing Slave Trade.

1849, May 7th, Final Treaty with the Sultan of Lahej.

1849, December 20th, Engagement by the Thakoor of Bhownuggur, relating to Customs on Vessels.

1849, March 29th, Terms granted to Maharajah Dulup Sing.

1850, June 3rd, Treaty of Friendship and Commerce with the Sultan of Johanna.

1851, October 8th, Rules by the Rao of Kutch, exempting, under certain circumstances, Vessels belonging to the Ports of Bombay from Payment of Duties on Goods.

1851, October, Agreement with the Persian Government for suppression of Slavery.

1853, February 22nd, Treaty of Friendship and Alliance with the Nawab of Buhawulpoor.

1853, May 4th, Perpetual Treaty of Peace, by Chiefs of the Arabian Coast.

1853, August 15th, Agreement with the Chiefs of Pahlunpoor for the Suppression of Infanticide.

1853, May 14th, Treaty with Meer Nusseer Khan, Chief of the Kelat.

1853, May 21st, Treaty with the Nizam.

1855, February 10th, Treaty with the Raja of Nepaul respecting the mutual surrender of Criminals.

1857, March 4th, Treaty of Peace between her Majesty the Queen, and the Shah of Persia.

REFERENCES

1. This stipulation arose probably from the circumstance that the Mahratta armies were at one time disciplined and commanded by French officers.
2. The representative of the British government in Mysore is called "Commissioner;" in Kolapore and Sawunt-Warree. "Political Agent."

11

Public Works in British India

Sect. I.— Educational, Institutions. Sect. II.—Public Works—Canals—Roads—Railways—Telegraphs. Sect. III— List of Government Measures Adopted to Promote the Culture of Cotton. Sect. IV—Measures Adopted to promote the Working of Iron Ores.

SECT. I. — EDUCATIONAL INSTITUTIONS

The existing system of Government education in India is as follows:—

There are Directors of Public Instruction in Bengal, the North - West Provinces, Madras, Bombay, and the Punjab respectively, and under them are Inspectors and Sub-Inspectors of different grades, in numbers proportioned to the territories to be super intended.

There are three Universities constituted under Acts of the Legislature of India at Calcutta,[1] Madras,[1] and Bombay. These Institutions were (by a dispatch of the Court of Directors, dated July 19, 1854), directed to be framed on the model of the University of London, and empowered to grant degrees to all who should produce certificates from certain affiliated Institutions, comprising all the principal Colleges and Schools in India, as to a previous course of study.

The functions of these Presidency Universities are thus defined in the dispatch above alluded to:––

> "The Universities in India will consist of a Chancellor, Vice-Chancellor, and Fellows, who will constitute a Senate. The Senates will have the management of the funds of the Universities and frame regulations, under which periodical examinations may be held in the different branches of art and science by examiners, selected from their own body, or nominated by them.
>
> The function of the Universities will be to confer degrees upon such persons as having been entered as candidates according to the rules which may be fixed in this respect, and having produced from any of the affiliated Institutions," which will be enumerated on the foundation of the Universities, or be from time to time added to them by Government, certificates of conduct, and of having pursued a regular course of study for a given time, shall have also passed at the Universities such an examination as may be required of them.
>
> The examination for degrees will not include any subjects connected with religious belief; and the affiliated Institutions will be under the management of persons of every variety of religious persuasion. As in England, various Institutions in immediate connection with the Church of England, the Presbyterian College at Caermarthen, the Roman Catholic college at Oscott, the Wesleyan College at Sheffield, the Baptist College at Bristol, are among the Institutions from which the University of London is empowered to receive certificates for degrees;— so in India, Institutions conducted by all denominations of Christians, Hindoos, Mahommedans, Parsees, Sikhs, Bhuddists, Janis, or any other religious persuasions, may be affiliated to the Universities, if they are found to afford the

requisite course of study, and can be depended upon for the certificates of conduct which will be required."

With respect to all existing vernacular and Anglo-vernacular Schools throughout India, whether established by individuals or societies, they are entitled, on certain prescribed conditions to grants in aid, on proof of attainment to a prescribed standard of secular instruction.

Among the schools entitled under existing Government regulations, to grants in aid, are those established at various periods by Christian Missionary Societies.

The total number of these schools scattered throughout the various districts of India, including vernacular and English elementary schools, both for boys and girls, was in 1853, 1657 schools, containing 64,806 scholars of both sexes, as will appear from the following statistical table:—

	Boys Schools.						Girls Schools.			
	Vernac		Boarding		Engligh		Day		Boarding	
Presidencies.	Schools	Boys	Schools	Boys	Schools	Boys	Schools	Girls	Schools	Girls
Bengal	140	6470	22	790	22	6005	24	689	29	830
North W. Provinces	61	3707	10	191	22	1754	10	242	10	175
Bombay	70	3480	2	21	7	1144	37	1222	6	101
Madras.	849	24,445	52	1165	41	4286	191	6619	52	1470
Total	1120	38,102	86	2167	92	13,189	262	8772	97	2576

These schools have been chiefly established by the twelve following Societies,[2] placed in the order of the commencement of their respective operations in India:—

1727. The society for the Propagation of the Gospel.

1793. The Baptist Missionary Society.

1805. The London Missionary Society.

1812. The American Board of Missions.

1814. The Wesleyan Missionary Society.

1815. The Church Missionary Society.

1822. The General Baptist Missions.

The Established Church of Scotland.

1830. The Free Church of Scotland.

The Basle Missionary Society.

1834. The American Presbyterian Mission.

1840. The American Baptist mission.

The chief existing higher Government Education Institutions in Bengal, which it is the object of the present system to affiliate to the University at Calcutta, are the following:—

1. The Madrissa, or Mahommedan College, at Calcutta, founded by Warren Hastings in 1782, for the study of Arabic and Persian (English having been since included). This institution contained in 1854, 314 pupils, all Mahommedans. The Hindoo College organized by a Native Committee for giving an English education to Hindoos in 1816, in which the pupils are taught Law, Medicine, and Civil Engineering; the Sanskrit College at Calcutta, and which has also an English department. This College was founded in 1823, and contained, in 1854, 386 pupils, all Hindoos. There is also a Medical College and Hospital with ten classes at Calcutta. There are also Government Anglo-Vernacular Colleges at Hoogly, Dacca, Kishaghur, and Berhampore.

There are other Collegiate Institutions in Bengal, some of which have been hitherto unconnected with and unaided by, the Government, which it is the object of the present system to affiliate with the University, or Presidency College. Among these are the Oriental Seminary, conducted by East Indians, the Bishop's college, the General Assembly's Institution, Dr. Duffs College, and the Baptist College of Serampore.

In the North-West Provinces, there are Government Colleges at Delhi and Agra, and at Benares a Sanskrit College, established in 1792. The Vernacular Schools in the North-West Provinces, first established by Mr. Thomason in 1843, and now brought within the scope of the grants in aid, amounted, in 1856, according to the statement of Lord Dalhousie, to 3669 in number. Hospitals and Dispensaries were also established in the North-West Provinces by Mr. Thomason. In the Civil Dispensaries, Medicines and Instruments are provided and Salaries paid by the Government. In Bengal there are now fourteen, and in the North-West Provinces thirty-six, Dispensaries.

In Bombay, the two chief Government Educational Institutions, which it is proposed to affiliate to the University to be established in that Presidency, are the Elphinstone College at Bombay, and the College at Poonah.

There are also about 235 Vernacular and Anglo-Vernacular Schools in that Presidency.

In the Presidency of Madras, there were said to be, in Sir Thomas Munro's time, 733 Schools and Colleges, containing 3750 Students, mostly Brahmins.

There are also in the Presidency of Madras thirty Government Civil Dispensaries, on the same footing with those above alluded to in Bengal.[3]

SECT. II—PUBLIC WORKS EXECUTED BY THE GOVERNMENT IN BRITISH INDIA

The portions of Canals and Irrigation Works actually completed, are as follows:—

Ganges Canal.— 449½ miles of the Ganges Canal were completed in April, 1856.

E. and W. Jumna Canals.— 445 miles of the W. Jumna Canal are completed.

Punjaub Canals.—425 miles of the Baree-Doab Canal in the Punjaub, were executed in May, 1856.

Madras Irrigation Works.—Tanks, reservoirs, and "annicuts," or dams, across the beds of the Cauvery, Godavery, and Kishna Rivers.[4]

The principal Trunk Roads in India now completed, are as follow:—

	Miles	Cost
From Calcutta to Peshawur	1,423	£1,423,000
" Calcutta to Bombay	1,002	500,000
" Madras to Bangalore	200	37,121
" Bombay to Agra	734	243,676
" Rangoon to Prome	200	160,000

The portions of Railroads in India now completed, under Government-guarantees are as follow:—

	Miles
From Calcutta to Burdwan	120
" Bombay[5] to Wassind	50
" Bombay to Campoolie	10
" Madras to Vellore	81

The electric Telegraphs now completed in India comprise about 4000 miles of telegraphic wire namely:—

From Calcutta to Peshawur.

" Agra to Bombay

" Bombay to Madras.

Other lines are in course of construction.

SECT. III— MEASURES ADOPTED AT DIFFERENT PERIODS BY THE GOVERNMENT TO PROMOTE THE CULTIVATION OF COTTON IN INDIA CHRONOLOGICALLY ARRANGED.[6]

1788 The Court of Directors called the attention of the Indian Government to the cultivation of cotton in India, "with a view to affording every encouragement to its growth and improvement." 500,000 lbs. weight of cotton are ordered to be sent. Reports are called for from the Collectors of districts.

1789 Screws for compressing cotton are at this time established, both by the Company and by individuals.

1790 Cotton (422,207 lbs.) received from India. Ahmood cotton-seed directed to be sent to Bengal. Reports of culture at Bombay, Benares, and Dacca received; also from Collectors of Bengal and Behar. Dr. Anderson employed in distributing cotton-seeds, from the Mauritius and from Malta, throughout the Peninsula of India.

1794 A machine sent out for cleaning cotton from seed, and other impurities.

1797 A plantation, under Mr. M. Brown, established at Randatarra in Malabar, chiefly for spices; but Mauritius and Nankeen cottons were grown in 1801, and the produce sent to this country.

1799 Nagpore cotton-send directed to be tried in the Circars, and a bounty offered to growers.

1802-3. Reports received on the cotton trade of Bombay and of the Gangetic Doab.

1809 Cotton ordered from India. 30,000,000 lbs. received in the following year.

1810 Samples of Georgian and Grenada cottons sent out, also seeds of West Indian and of American cottons. Directions sent out for the culture of cotton, prepared by Mr. R. Hunt and by the African Society.

1811 Bourbon seed procured, and distributed to Collectors of Surat and Broach, with directions for cultivation.

1813 Mr. B. Metcalfe, a cleaner of cotton from Georgia and New Orleans, sent to Tinnevelly, with saw-gins. Mr. Bruce directed to send cotton-seed from Persia to India. Seed from Bourbon and Seychelles Islands procured.

1814 Two or three hundred bales of the best and cleanest *Toomil* cotton directed to be sent annually.

1816 Collector at Caranga cultivates Bourbon cotton there. Drawback allowed "of the whole internal and see duties" on cotton exported to Great Britain. Two improved gins sent to Bombay, one for cleaning black-seed, the other for green-seed cotton.

1817 Mr. Assistant-Surgeon Gilder succeeds in cultivating Bourbon cotton at Kaira. Cotton culture attempted in Circars by commercial Residents. The Court suggest that, in addition to Caranja and Salsette, Malwan should be tried.

1818 Satisfactory report from Malwan, Pernambuco seed asked for Mr. Hughes successfully cultivates Bourbon cotton at Tinnevelly. Mr. Heath, having obtained instructions from Mr. Hughes, succeeds in Coimbatore. Memoir from Mr. Randall, Commercial Resident in Ceded Districts, proposing rewards for growing Brazil cotton in districts of Madras Presidency. Four cotton farms of 400 acres directed to be established at Tinnevelly, Coimbatore, Masulipatam, and Vizigapatam.

1819 Considerable success by Mr. Heath in Coimbatore. The cotton approved of in England and 500 bales of 300 lbs. each, sent to China, and sold there.

1823 Barbadoes and Brazil cotton grown at Tittyghur, near Barrackpore.

1828 Attention again called to the subject of cotton culture by Lord Ellenborough, President of the Board of Control, "in different and distant parts of India:" also in a Paper by one of the Directors, H. St. George Tucker, Esq.

1829 The court direct attention to the growth of new and better species; sent out machines for cleaning cotton; sent out seeds of Upland Georgia and of New Orleans Cotton; also sea Island, Pernambuco and

Demarara Cotton Seed with accounts of methods of cultivation;— five of Whitney's saw-gins sent out to India, with twelve more made up in England, and metallic work for twelve sets to be made up in India. —A quantity of Surant Cotton (500 bales) also ordered to be sent, of the best quality and well cleaned.— Rewards to be offered both to Ryots and to Wakarias for clean picking, and cleaning.—The Agricultural Society of India has an allowance of 1000/. a year, exclusive of rents, units 1833, to attempt the culture of cotton—20,000 rupees allowed for premiums for cotton and tobacco.

Dec. 31. Bombay Government report establishing a farm in Guzerat under Mr. Finney, another in Dharwar, &c., under Dr. Lush, another in Salsette. Land offered for cultivation of Cotton.

1830 Upland Georgia, Sea Island, Demarara, and other seed, also saw-gins received at Calcutta —300 bales of Toomil Cotton sent, and 25 bales from Broach Farm.

1831 Partial success at Cotton farm established at Akra, near Calcutta.

1832 The Court direct that land appropriated to the growth of Cotton should not (as theretofore) be subject to a higher assessment.—3000 to 4000 bales ordered to be sent, if procurable, at 115 rupees per candy.—Disposal of Cotton grown in the experimental farm of Guzerat for 152 to 156 rupees per candy.

1833 Reports from Collectors of Caddapah, Guntoor, Arcot, Salem and Coimbatore Farms, subsidiary to that at Danda in Guzerat, established, to be cultivated by Ryots. Farms established at Segee Hullee in Bedare District under Dr. Lush. White-seeded perennial, also the Pernambuco and

Egyptian succeeded. —Agency for the purchase of Cotton from Natives who had been instructed in picking it clean.—Screws and packing-sheds at Dharwar, Noulgond, and Gudduch Natives had the option of paying their rents in kind, or receiving a remunerating price. Foreign cotton-seeds also tried in Dhawar, Poona, and the Concan.

1838 Egyptian Cotton-seed and Egyptian cleaning machine applied for and supplied.

1836 Report of the proceedings of the East India Company in regard to the production of cotton wool, published.

1839 The Court of Directors first propose to procure planters from America, with a view to further experiments. Minute by Lord Auckland on this subject, with reports from Madras and Bombay, giving an account of the results of former experiments, as well as proposals for the present one.

1840 Mr. Elphinstone, Collector of Rutnagerry, succeeds in cultivating Sea-Island and Bourbon cotton.

Captain Bayles returns with ten planters from Cotton States of North America, bringing with him seeds and saw-gins, ploughs and hoes, with model of a gin-house. A hand saw-gin, prepared in Liverpool, where experiments are made, and three planters are sent to Broach, to Bombay.

1841 Three Planters sent to Madras, first stationed at Tinnevelly, then at Coimbatore. Four planters sent to Calcutta, and stationed in the Doab and Bundelcund. Dr. Burns appointed to the charge of the experiments in Broach.

1842 An Engineer sent to each of the three Presidencies, to repair and put up machinery. Mr. Shaw and Mr. Hadow, Collectors, cultivate New Orleans and

Bourbon cotton, in Dharwar. Mr. Mercer is stationed at Dharwar. Mr. Finnie explores the North-West for suitable sites.

1843 Unsuccessful experiments in Gorruckpore, and at Agra, by Mr. Blount and Mr. Finnie. Successful trial of New Orleans cotton by Mr. Wroughton, Collector of Coimbatore.

1845 Messrs. Simpson and Blount appointed to conduct experiments in Candeish. Cotton Committee appointed at Bombay.

1847 Mr. Landon appointed to carry on experiments in Broach.

(November.) Court of Directors order the following six queries to be sent out and circulated among the Collectors in the Presidencies, and the Political Agents in such Native States as are known to produce cotton.[7]

1. What is the pricc of cotton, freed from seed, at the principal mart or marts in your district?
2. At what prices does the Ryot sell his cotton, cleaned or uncleaned, and with or without advances?
3. What is the expense of cleaning cotton by the churka, or foot roller, or by any other method which may be in use?
4. What are the expenses of conveying cotton to the nearest port for shipment?
5. What is the average produce of cotton per beegah. or acre?
6. What is the quantity of land under cultivation with cotton, and to what extent is it probable that the cultivation could be carried in the event of an increased demand?

1848 Mr. Blount, having returned from America, is engaged to take charge of the culture in Dharwar.

1849 Mr. Simpson is engaged to procedure the experiments in Candeish,

200 cottage saw-gins prepared under the superintendence of the Manchester Commercial Association and of Mr. Petrie, sent by the Court of Directors to the three Presidencies. Seeds and saws sent at various times during these experiments.

1850 The Indian government offers, through the Agricultural Society of India, a reward of 5000 rupees for an improved cotton-cleaning machine.

SECT. IV— MEASURES ADOPTED BY THE GOVERNMENT TO PROMOTE THE WORKING OF IRON ORES IN INDIA

1850 In a Dispatch dated December 11, relating to the introduction of railways into India, the Court of Directors called the attention of the Government to the manufacture of iron in Bengal, pointing out several localities as most eligible for carrying on those works.

In the same year the Court addressed a Dispatch to the Government of Madras, calling attention to the subject of iron works within that Presidency.

The Madras government observed, in reply, that the various reports for seventeen years on the affairs of the Porto Novo Iron Company, would have put the Court in possession of the means and operations of that Company, which were then manufacturing superior ores at Beypoor. It was added, that additional capital alone was wanting to develop the resources of the Presidency as regards iron, the locations of which were stated to have been sufficiently shown in the correspondence which had taken place relating to the collection of specimens for the Great Exhibition.

Subsequently an arrangement was concluded with "The Indian Iron Company," the leading feature of which was the grant of fresh leases for thirty years to a new Company of the districts held on lease by the Old Iron Company, such leases to contain provisions for securing the due working of the iron ores on an enlarged scale.

In the same year the Court directed the institution of inquiries with regard to the capabilities of Western India, as regards the production of iron.

The reports received in reply show that iron ore exists in many parts of the Presidency of Bombay, and that in those districts iron is manufactured to a small extent by the natives for their own use. In consequence, however, of the general scarcity of fuel, and the wasteful manner in which the process of smelting is conducted, the iron imported from England seems to have the advantage both as regards quality and price. With reference to the iron of Belgaum, professor Oldham observes, "the absence of economical fuel and the scattered mode of occurrence of the ores appear to be abundantly sufficient to preclude the profitable extraction of the metal."

1853. Mr. Jacob, and afterwards Professor Oldham, were deputed to examine reports upon the mineral resources of the valley of the Nerbudda.

1854. (The existence of iron mines in the Province of Kumaon having been long known) Lieutenant-Colonel Drumnond of the Bengal Establishment was deputed to this Province to carry on the investigations necessary to satisfy the British public that sufficient inducement existed for the investment of capital in iron works in India. Colonel Drummond entered on his duties on the 18th October, 1854, and continued his researches for a period of about seven months. His inquiries appear to have been principally directed to the Bhabur district of Kumaon, and the results may be briefly summed up as follows:—

In order to obviate the necessity of carriage through a mountainous country, it became an object of importance to trace the existence of iron as near the plains as possible, and Colonel Drummond's first inquiries were consequently directed to the tract of country at the foot of the hills. At Dechouree the most western point of Colonel Drummond's route, a rich iron ore was discovered associated with clay. Here the deposits are stated to be readily discoverable not only by the large masses lying on the surface, but also by the beds being extensively exposed by deep ravines. In one part the solid bed of ore is exposed to a thickness of 30 ft.; in another it measured 24ft.; in a third it exceeded the depth of 50 ft. Where "a bed of such rich material," says Mr. Sowerby, one of the civil engineers connected with the East India Railway Company, "is ascertained to be at least 50ft. thick—a few feet more or less cannot be of much importance." The extent of ground examined at Dechouree was about a mile, and the quantity of ore at and near the surface was estimated to yield, if smelted, 100,000 tons of pig iron.

From Dechouree Colonel Drummond pursued his course in an easterly direction, passing by Loha Bhurbur, Kaleedoongee, Chowsilla, Beejapore, Jham, Burgote, and Burragur. The length of the route was about sixty miles, and rich deposits of iron ore were discovered at most of these places, varying in thickness from 25 ft. to 50 ft. At Loha Bhurbur the ore is associated with clay, not mere clay impregnated with iron, but solid iron stone. Huge blocks are here represented as lying exposed on the surface: several of these were measured, and found to be upwards of 10 ft. long, 6 ft. broad, and 4 ft. in thickness, each of which, it is said, if smelted into pig iron, would yield upwards of three tons of metal. These blocks were not occasional, but frequent, and common over the whole distance traversed, which was a mile in length, by a which of 175 yards. It was estimated, that upwards of 60,000 tons of metal could be obtained from the ore lying on the surface. The beds in the route, pursued by Colonel Drummond, fully show that an inexhaustible supply of workable iron ore yielding the quality of iron which is most useful for railway purposes can be obtained in an accessible tract, along the outer face of the lower Himalaya ranges, close to the plains.

1855. A Report on the Iron Ores of India, from Lieutenant– Colonel Goodwyn, Chief Engineer of the Lower Provinces of Bengal, in the Public Works Department, dated Fort William, June 27, contains the following passage:—

"That the Indian Iron can not only be successfully worked, but structurally applied, was proved many years ago, by Colonel Presgrave, formerly Mint-Master at Saugor, who smelted the iron in the neighbourhood, rolled it in the mint rollers, fashioned it into bars and rods, and then erected an excellent suspension bridge, near Saugor, entirely from the ore in the vicinity. Its manufacture in India is a subject of prominent importance, and scarcely less so than the establishment of railways and electric telegraphs.

"I will to here enter into details of the profits or percentage gained by native processes, or the nature of those processes: suffice it to notice here, that the result is most satisfactory, as a guarantee to enterprise, whilst the specimens that I have seen, and which are extant, show the metal to be of superior quality, where attention has been paid to locality, and if the postulates I have advanced are admitted, I deem that the Government would do well to expend a certain sum to place the matter beyond all possible doubt.

"As regards Central India, the Gwalior and Jubbulpore districts and the neighbourhood of hazareebaugh, place the question of the existence of good iron beyond doubt; but for the more ready consumption of the Presidency and its vicinity, it would probably, be worth while to enter on experiments in the Valley of the Damooda, near Raneegunge, on the Brohming in Cuttack, in Assam, and near Palamoas; and an outlay of from one lac to four lacs of rupees according to the extent of the operations, would, I am sure, end in the most advantageous results.

"Its *modus operandi* will be to call upon the authorities for an immediate brief return of the general character of the iron; information which has, at various times, been obtained on each district in which it is found; to select from these, under advice, two, three, or four districts, with especial reference to local facilities for the object in view, and, if possible, of after conveyance; to decide to spend not exceeding Rs. (400,000) four lacs upon the whole; to erect, at once, moderate-sized blast furnaces, at each place, the blast engines, &c, being constructed in Calcutta, while the furnaces are being built, the iron stone, or ore, fuel, and flux, being simultaneously collected in quantity, in readiness for the starting, and keeping up the supply, and placing each furnace in charge of some person who has been used to the work, and who may be found in the Calcutta foundries, giving to them certain latitude, to vary the proportions, and record the results, and give a large premium to the most successful, to send down the first pigs made to Calcutta; and, upon the result of this examination, and the reports of the blast furnace operations, and local supplies, there will be no difficulty in making over the whole to those who will complete the scheme by supplying all the rolling mills, puddling furnaces, and continuing the manufacture through all its stages, either returning the outlay to the Government, if made a condition or not, as may be considered most equitable at the time.

"I believe that no complete analysis by a regularly-trained ironviewer and smelter has yet been faithfully obtained, and it is very probable that greater value may, on the result of such analysis, be found in some localities, that will materially affect the prospect of working them; and I would fain hope that, under effective and scientific management, our public works may, at no distant period, receive that aid from native iron, without which their energies must be comparatively circumscribed."

1856. (March and April.) A blast furnace was erected at Deckouree, 50 miles from Moradabad in Kumaon; and, upon the works being completed, two experiments were made to test its efficacy for the smelting of iron ore, which were partially successful. The metal which was taken out of the furnace, when remelted, flowed out in a very liquid state into small pigs, which, when fractured, showed them to be iron of the best quality.— (*Vide* Mr. Sowerby's Report, April, 1856.)

REFERENCES

1. *Vide* Acts of the Indian Government, Nos. 2 and 27 of 1857.
2. It appears that the total number of Missionaries employed by these twelve Societies in 1853 was 383, and the total number of native Christians returned as belonging to their various communions was 94, 145.—Vide "Revised Statistics of Indian Missions," reprinted from the Calcutta *Christian Observer*, 1853.
3 It appears from Parliamentary returns that the total amount expended in aid of Native Education in India in 1853 was about 100,000/. sterling.
4. *Vide* Memorandum of Public Works, &c., completed by the Government of India during the last thirty years.
5. Of the Great Indian Peninsular Railway two branches have been commenced—the North-Eastern to Mirzapore, the South-Eastern to Madras. Thirty-Three miles of these two Railways, viz. from Bombay to Callianee, are on the same line.
6. Extracted from "The Culture and Commerce of Cotton in India," by Dr. Forbes Royle. 1850.—See also "Essay on the Productive Provinces of India," 1840; and "The Fibrous Plants of India," 1855, by the same Author.—See also a Paper read before the Society of Arts in London by J. B. Smith, Esq., M. P. May 13, 1857.
7. For replies to several of these queries, *vide* Report presented to the Board of Trade by Dr. Forbes Bovle. in 1857.

12

Lord Canning as Viceroy of India

Charles John Canning, the third son of George Canning, a great British Statesman (who became Foreign Secretary 1822-27 and then Prime Minister of England for a short time from April to August 1827)—was born on 14 December 1812. His mother was the daughter of General John Scott of Balcomie. He was educated at Eton and Christ Church, having Granville, Dalhousie, Gladstone and Elgin among his contemporaries at the latter place where he distinguished himself by winning a college prize for a Latin poem. His father, George Canning died on 8 August 1827 after which his mother became Viscountess Canning of Kilbrahan, co. Kilkenny. He took his degree in 1838 and was married in 1835 to Charlotte Stuart, a daughter of Lord Stuart de Rothesay, Ambassador at Paris (1815 to 1830). The Queen of George III was the godmother of his wife. In 1836 Charles became M.P. for Warwick, but the next year his mother died. He succeeded her and became a member of the House of Lords.

Lord Canning became Under-Secretary for Foreign Affairs in the Peel's Ministry in 1841, the following year his wife became Lady of the Bedchamber to the Queen which increased his influence further. In 1845 he became a Privy Councillor. Lord Aberdeen's Coalition Ministry made him Postmaster-General in 1852, but later when Palmerston came to power, he offered him the post of

Governor-General in India. Canning landed at Bombay on 26 January 1856, to assume charge of his new office from Lord Dalhousie.

EARLY CHANGES

Before Canning arrived in India, the Charter Act of 1853, as we have already seen, had renewed the Company's charter not for twenty years, as usual, but for any period the Crown pleased to grant it. It prepared the ground for the direct assumption of powers in India by the Crown at its will. Hardly two years passed after Canning's arrival, when this actually happened. But before the Crown directly took over, the Mutiny of 1857 took place. In the meanwhile assisted by the distinguished members of his Council, Peter Grant, Barnes Peacock, Sir John Low, J.A. Dorin and General Anson, Canning harnessed himself to the work.

War with Persia. The first important problem that Canning had to face in India, was the infiltration into Herat by the pro-Russian Persia. Herat which formed the western frontier of Afghanistan, was considered by some English statesmen as the 'key to India,' and Canning was afraid lest the extension of the Russian influence should "convert Persia, and perhaps her nearer neighbours into a perpetual blister upon us."[1] The British did not at the time enjoy good relations with Persia from where their envoy Charles Murray withdrew in protest for the insults he had suffered in the Persian Court. The English Cabinet was divided with regard to the Russian threat to India, which even if it existed, could be better operated upon "in Europe where we can do so with most effect,"[2] the Duke of Argyll held.

Canning, however, considered the Russian danger real, and he was sure that nothing short of a war could stop Persia from the course of action on which she had embarked. On 1 November 1856, therefore, the war on Persia was declared in the name of the East India Company. The British forces marched, Kharak in the Persian Gulf was occupied on 4 December, and on the 19th of the same month Bushire fell. There was not much of fighting, and on 4 March 1857 the peace treaty was signed by which the Shah of Persia undertook to evacuate Herat, to receive Murray at his Court, and to accept the Indian Government's mediation in disputes with Afghanistan. Some critics termed the treaty too lenient, for Kharak and Bushire already occupied, were returned and no indemnity as realised from the Shah. But peace with Persia came just in time, when mutiny broke out at Meerut and not a soldier could now be spared for an adventure abroad.

Afghanistan. In the meanwhile a friendly treaty was signed on 26 January, by Herbert Edwardes, with Dost Muhammad of Afghanistan, as a result of which Dost declared, "I have made an alliance with the British Government, and, come what may, I will keep it till death."[3] Dost kept his promise, and remained faithful to the British even during the Indian Mutiny when all temptations to the contrary existed.

Oudh. Of other developments before the mutiny, Oudh had been annexed, Canning appointed Coverly Jackson, a hot-headed man, as the Chief-Commissioner. Jackson, however, was later on succeeded on 1 January 1857 by Henry Lawrence under whom dislodgement of *Talukdars*, the quasi-feudal lords of villages who indulged in all types of extortion, was continued. This was to the benefit of the peasants; who however, thanks to their ignorant attachments to the old masters, could not appreciate it. Discontentment, therefore, spread among both the classes, and Oudh became a hot-bed of intrigues and agitation against the British.

Other Changes. Certain military reforms were also attempted. An order was thus issued making it incumbent on the new recruits to agree to be posted anywhere outside India. Among social reforms were the removal of some legal obstacles in the way of widow remarriage, followed by another Bill against polygamy among Kulin Brahmins who "permitted an almost illimitable number of wives, some of whom the husband never saw and with many of whom he never cohabited."[4] In 1856 the heir-apparent of the defunct Mughal Emperor Bahadur Shah died. Canning proposed that the new legal heir to the Emperor should be recognised only if he gave up the title of King and agreed to live outside Delhi. This aroused a lot of consternation among some people. Canning also gave his attention to the disorganised finance, deficit budgets and mounting debts which had become a more serious problem as a result of Dalhousie's expansionist policy. But before he could do much, the Persian war and the great mutiny of 1857 intervened, which reduced the whole thing to chaos. He had to postpone the consideration of these problems, and in the meanwhile to face what now befell the British.

THE MUTINY OF 1857

The most important event of the time of Lord Canning in India was the Mutiny of 1857 which rocked the whole land, and for once at least threw the mighty British power into a whirlwind of confusion. The character of this Mutiny has been variously commented upon. One view is thus held by persons such as V.D. Savarkar, according to whom it was an organised national movement. Its "great principles," writes Savarkar, "were Swadharma and Swaraj... (and) in these two, lies the root principle of the Revolutionary War."[5] Mr. Ashoka Mehta supports this view and forwards several arguments in this connection. He asserts that although the sepoys were the backbone of the Mutiny, yet it would be wrong to call it essentially a sepoy mutiny. The number of civilians killed was as large as that of the sepoys. At some places the sepoys themselves were rather egged on to action by the civil population. When General Havelock wanted to ferry his soldiers across the river, the refusal of the boatmen either to offer their boats or their services is a clear testimony to the part which the civil population played. Besides, the rapidity with which the mutiny spread clearly shows how in some areas at least it enjoyed a strong mass support. The Hindu-Muslim harmony which the Mutiny depicted also points towards the same direction. Bahadur Shah, the Mughal emperor, prohibited the slaughter of cows throughout the country, and wrote to the princes of Rajputana in clear words, as Mr. Ashoka Mehta quotes: "I have no desire left of ruling over India... I am willing to resign my imperial powers and authority in the hands of any confederacy of native princes who are chosen to exercise it." And all this clearly points towards the national character of the Mutiny.[6]

According to Outram, however, it was no national uprising. It was rather, in his view, a Muslim conspiracy which made capital of the Hindu grievances and was precipitated by the incident of cartridges.

The most widely supported view, however, is that of Sir John Lawrence who held that it was essentially a sepoy uprising. It broke out as a result of the cartridge incident, but was made use of by the other elements which being disgusted with the British in India, were in search of some such opportunity to re-assert their position. It was no national movement, as Rawlinson also supports: "It would be in accurate to describe the Mutiny as a national revolution, for nationalism was not as yet a factor in Indian politics."[7] According to Sir John Seeley too, it was "wholly unpatriotic and selfish sepoy mutiny with no native leadership and no popular support." P.E. Roberts also supports this view; and so does Dr. R.C. Majumdar in his recently published book. *The Sepoy Mutiny and Revolt of 1857*. Maulana Azad may also be quoted in this connection. He thus writes: "In the light of the available evidence, we are therefore forced to the conclusion that the uprising of 1857 was not the result of careful planning nor were there any master-minds behind it... This was due not to the conspiracy of a few individuals or groups but to the growing discontent of a large number of people...Patriotism had to be reinforced by an appeal to religious passion before the people rose."[8]

In fact several arguments can be forwarded to support the view that it was no organised national movement, but simply a sepoy outbreak advantage of which was taken by several interested elements. The widespread mutinous outbreaks occurred only at those places where the lead was given by the sepoys. For instance in Rajasthan there were no large-scale uprisings, became here "the ground was not prepared by a successful rising of the sepoys." Same among the Marathas. Although the Marathas just recently had suffered at the hands of the British, yet among them there were no large-scale uprisings, because there were no sepoy outbreaks in their midst. Moreover, rarely do we come across persons who should have been animated in their revolt by some enlightened principle of love for the nation. During the course of their action some might have developed this idea, but there are no proofs to show that an organised beginning towards this direction was made anywhere. Generally only local causes of love of booty, adventure, or superstitious belief, such as, one hundred years having passed after the Battle of Plassey of 1757, the time had come for the British departure, conditioned the uprising. In the Gaya district, for instance, the local *zamindars* thinking that the British had been destroyed, actually killed many persons and looted their property.

Nor did the so-called national heroes possess any well-knit plan of their campaigns or at least a regular contact with one another. There was no clear picture before them, of the sort of future they were going to build for the whole nation. They were all inspired by their selfish interests or conditioned only by local causes. Delhi was the backbone of the mutineers. Yet, when it was besieged by the British, Nana Saheb prevented the Kanpur troops from marching to relieve the capital perhaps because he feared that the mutineers' successes in Delhi would promote Bahadur Shah as the national ruler to whom he was not prepared to play the second fiddle.

Then, only one of the three provincial armies mutinied. Many chiefs and thousands of landlords remained loyal. Nor did every province rise in arms. The Punjab, one of the most important provinces of the British Indian empire, rather helped the British save their power in India. Clearly thus, it was no national movement based on any well-knit organisation, or on some enlightened principles of national independence.

Nor would it be correct to say that it was a Muslim conspiracy making capital of some Hindu grievances. Although Bahadur Shah did make use of it, there are reasons to believe that he was rather compelled to do so. "In fact the course of the trial made it clear," says Maulana Azad, "that the Mutiny was as much a surprise to Bahadur Shah as to the British."[9]

The facts are therefore clear. Right from the beginning of the British rule in India disaffection against them had been slowly piling up amongst the sepoys, the people and the princes of this country. Annexation of Oudh sent thousands of sepoys and civil servants of this state adrift. *Taluqdars* of the state suffered as a result of the new land policy. And then the way the states like Jhansi and Satara were extinguished, all these and many others were the political causes. Ruin of the Indian trade and industry, and the oppressive agrarian policy and other such factors constituted the economic causes. The Christian missionary activities, and some legal measures such as the Religious Disabilities Act of 1856, constituted the religious and social causes. Then there were the purely administrative causes. And all these created a combustible material in all parts of the country.

It may correctly therefore be repeated, though there was a disgruntled and disaffected mass of people all over the country, yet it was not so due to some single national cause, but due to different small and local issues. And further that, despite the fact that this disaffected mass of people existed, the Mutiny was primarily a sepoy Mutiny in which the interested hands later on joined. There was absolutely no national movement in the country. The fact will be clear from the following account.

The Causes

Of the various causes which brought about disaffection among the people and some princes and *zamindars* of this country, and which provided the combustible material for the Mutiny, the following may be mentioned.

Political Causes. The political causes of the Mutiny lay in the history of the development of the British power in India. The effort made in 1857 to overthrow the British rule in this country was not the first effort. Such efforts had in fact been made earlier as well, but they had all failed. The English got a chance to fish in the troubled waters of India when disintegration followed the death of Aurangzeb; Marathas establishing their supremacy in the Maharashtra proper and some parts of Southern India, and the Governors of Bengal, Oudh and the Deccan declaring themselves as virtually independent states. This disintegration was completed by Nadir Shah. When India was weak and divided, the English had their best chance. Their success was made easier by a triple factor: first that the Indian soldiers were less disciplined and less skilled than the English; secondly, that they could be easily made to fight against their own countrymen; and thirdly, that it was possible for the British to take sides in the local political quarrels and draw the best advantage out of them.

The British had their first great political gain in Bengal when they intrigued with the Mir Jaffar, a Commander of Nawab Siraj-ud-Daula. In the battle of Plassey in 1757 the Nawab's commanders standing aloof, the British were easily able to defeat the Nawab, who was beheaded and Mir Jaffar succeeded in his place and became a puppet in the British hands. The people of Bengal accepted the British control because they could not as yet realise the consequences of it, and moreover they had been accustomed to such changes.

As, however, the British developed their hold on this country, the political opposition grew. Shah Alam, the Emperor at Delhi led three expeditions against the British in Bengal between March 1759 and January 1761. But they all failed.

Mir Jaffar too, soon realised his folly. He and his successor Mir Kasim both chafed under the British yoke, and in the time of the latter the first real effort to overthrow the British rule was made when he joined hands with Shah Alam and Shuja-ud-Daula, the Nawab of Oudh, in a confederacy against the British. The confederacy however was defeated in the Battle of Buxar in 1764. Mir Kasim fled away, while Shah Alam and Shuja-ud-Daula signed humiliating treaties with the British; the former making a legal grant of the *Diwani* of Bengal, Bihar and Orissa to the English. This added a real strength to the British political power in India.

Slowly, but surely, the British went on developing their power, bringing under their yoke one principality after another. In the time of Warren Hastings another joint effort was made to overthrow the British power when Hyder Ali of Mysore tried to organise a confederacy with the Marathas and the Nizam of Hyderabad. Hastings' diplomacy however succeeded, and Hyder Ali failed in his designs. Towards the close of the 18th century, yet another effort was made between the Nawab of Oudh, Sindhia, Tipu Sultan, and Zaman Shah of Kabul, to organise a confederacy against the British; the details of which however are not known.

The British went on developing their power. Mysore was conquered in 1799. Gurkhas humbled in 1814-15 and the Marathas finally crushed in 1817-19. To disarm the criticism and suspicion, instead of conquering and annexing the Indian states, Wellesley had evolved the policy of "subsidiary alliance", under which those Indian princes who entered it, maintained British troops at their own expense, while the latter granted them internal autonomy and internal and external protection. Here was a master-stroke of the British political policy in India. The princes under the subsidiary alliance had neither to fear any external aggression nor an internal commotion. Nor was it the policy of the British to encourage an independent and original talent in them. Their policy, as the Tory Under-Secretary of State for India remarked in the

Commons, was rather to promote docile and unpretending mediocrity. Little wonder, these princes grew callous and irresponsible in their administrative duties.

As the administration of these states grew corrupt and oppressive under this system, the moral and material conditions of the people deteriorated fast, and the British, instead of realising their responsibility in it, began to put the entire blame on the shoulders of the princes; and declaring them unfit to rule, began to forward a new justification that their power should be ended, and the states be annexed for the benefit of the people.

A new turn therefore was given to the British policy towards these states when Lord Dalhousie arrived in India. The policy of Doctrine of Lapse was adopted, as we have already seen, and one state after another, one title and one pension after another began to be annexed and confiscated. The big state of Nagpur was declared lapsed. The Punjab was annexed, and Satara, Jhansi, Sambhalpur and others went the same way; the most tyrannical of such of his acts being the annexation of Oudh. The titles and pensions of Nana Saheb, the adopted son of Peshwa Baji Rao II, of the Nawab of Carnatic and of Tanjore, were swept away. And there was a proposal to abolish the title of the nominal Emperor of Delhi as well, though at the suggestion of the Court of Directors the action was deferred till the death of the beneficiary. Fuel was added to the fire of discontentment as a result of the utterances of some irresponsible officers like Sir Charles Napier, who declared: "Were I the Emperor of India for twelve years, no Indian prince should exist. The Nizam should be no more heard of—Nepal would be ours."

Dalhousie's ruthless policy of annexations and extermination brought about a commotion in the country, and every prince and *zamindar* of India began to fear his safety. Abolition of the pension of Nana Saheb, and annexation of Nagpur and Satara, extinguished the three historic and royal families towards whom the Marathas used to look with pride. Satara had been the seat of the descendants of the great hero Shivaji, and Nagpur had been held by the venerated family of Bhonsla. Nor was their extermination done in an honourable manner. In the case of Nagpur, for instance, as Kaye writes: "The livestock and dead stock of the Bhonsla were sent to the hammer...royal elephants, horses and bullocks were sold off at the price of carrion;...furniture was removed, and the jewels of the Bhonsla family, with a few propitiatory exceptions, were sent to Calcutta market. And I have heard it said that these seizures, these sales, created a worse impression not only in Berar, but in the surrounding provinces, than the seizure of the kingdom itself."[10]

After the annexation of these states, heavy rates of land revenue assessment were imposed on the peasants. The new settlement excluded the middle-man, sending his family adrift. The resumption of the rent-free tenures begun earlier was carried forward ruthlessly and relentlessly by Dalhousie. Inam Commission was set up under an Act of 1852, which enquired into the titles of the landowners and within five years preceding the Mutiny as many as 20,000 families were dispossessed of their estates. All this undoubtedly alienated every class of people against the British. Princes began to fear for their principalities, *zamindars* for their land, title-holders and pension-holders for their titles and pensions; while the peasants groaned under heavy assessment. Annexation of every principality made countless number of persons, such as the court girls, the musicians and other artists, and many others who lived on the bounty and money payments of the royal families, homeless.

John Sullivan, a member of the Madras Council remarked thus: "Upon the extermination of a native state...an Englishman takes place of the sovereign under the name of commissioner, three or four of his associates displace as many as a dozen of the native aristocracy, while some hundreds of our troops take the place of the many thousands that every native chief supports. The little court disappears, trade languishes, the capital decays, the people are impoverished, the Englishman flourishes and acts like a sponge, drawing up riches from the banks of the Ganges and squeezing them down upon the banks of the Thames."[11]

Economic Causes. Prior to the British many invaders had come to India, but they had all been absorbed and Indianised. The case with the British however was different. Although they remained for about two centuries and a half in this country, they kept their identity distinct, keeping contact with their own motheland and draining India of her wealth to enrich their coffers in England.

Besides realising large sums of money from those whom the British supported for political gains, as they did from Mir Jaffar and Mir Kasim, the servants of the Company developed their hold on the inland trade, creating monopolies in every article of trade and even the necessaries of life. Whenever they could, they made shameless discrimination against the Indians, subjecting their trade to heavy inland duties. Vansittart was charged by Scrafton of vast illegal acquisitions. Letters of Richard Barwell also show how he raised a colossal fortune by trade in every kind of article.

When the British came to power, they fashioned the whole Indian economy to meet the industrial requirements of England. Raw materials of India were exported to England at throw-away prices, and when the same raw materials were converted into manufactured goods, they were imported into this country at heavy prices. As the industrial revolution proceeded in England in the 19th century, the English industrial goods glutted the Indian markets. These goods being better finished and comparatively cheaper, pushed the Indian industry, which was as yet only a cottage and small-scale industry, to extinction. The masses of India were thrown back on agriculture the pressure on which increasing, divided the agricultural income into many parts, and thus increased the peoples poverty. Dr. Ishwari Prasad writes: "India became a milch cow to feed England while her own sons were gradually pushed to the starvation wage."[12]

Then, the agrarian policy that was followed in the territories held by the British, ruined the cultivators as well as the *zamindars*. The Permanent Settlement introduced by Cornwallis in Bengal, though ultimately beneficial, brought misery in the early stages. "The inexorable sale laws against the defaulting *zamindars*, in its ruthless course, unsettled many hereditary *zamindars* from their social and economic moorings. Great landholders and semi-royal families were more or less completely ruined, and that too, in some cases, for a temporary difficulty."[13] In Madras and Northern Circars where periodical settlements were made, the rates of assessment were raised at every new settlement, sometimes by as much as fifty per cent, thereby reducing the proprietors to mere farmers of revenue who could be ejected at any time for a default of revenue payment. The permanent settlement introduced later, rather ruined the *zamindars* for its sale-laws and over-assessment. In some parts of Madras the village system was tried, under which contracts were given for total assessment of a village. But assessments were generally heavy, the surplus going to the contractors who also realised unauthorised exactions. The peasants suffered heavily and they fled, thus putting the flourishing villages to a ruin.

The results of revenue settlements in Bombay and elsewhere were no better. Everywhere there were complaints of injustice and oppressive assessments. The peasants, as S.N. Sen writes, fell into "chronic debt and the bania, who was the village money-lender, was not an honest creditor."[14]

And then there was the damocles' sword—the resumption of rent-free holdings—hanging on their head, the awe of which robbed many of a peaceful night's sleep. The regulation in this connection was passed in 1793 which authorised collectors to recover such holdings as had no valid tenure, by a regular law-suit. The regulation of 1811 and those which followed made the practice of resumption harsh and offensive. In 1845 the tenure of these grants was restricted to the life-time of the then holders. And within the five years that preceded the mutiny as many as 20,000 estates were resumed in the Deccan, and their holders sent to the streets to spread the venom of disaffection and mutiny. Such thus were the economic causes which contributed to the gathering clouds of mutiny.

The Social and Religious Causes. Nor were the social and religious causes lacking, Ghulam Hussain remarked in 1780: "The English seldom visit or see any of us."[15] And Warren Hastings admitted in 1784 that "a few years ago most of the Englishmen regarded the Indians almost as barbarians, and though the feeling has decreased it has not entirely disappeared." If such were the arrogant beliefs the English held towards the Indians, the Indian sense of self-respect was not going to stand if for long, nor were even the good administrative intentions of the British going to be appreciated by the Indian masses. The Indian were dishonest to a man, not to be compared even to the most backward persons of the most backward of the European nations, thus wrote Charles Grant, a responsible English officer, in a book published in 1792. And the most vile and loathsome language which the *Calcutta Review* used regarding the Bengalis before the Mutiny, was bound to sting its Bengali readers some day to the bitterest action.

The overgrowing number of the Christian missionaries were granted unrestricted entry into India by the Charter Act of 1813, their growing numbers of schools in which Indian religions were ridiculed, and the so called Black Act which rendered some benefits to the Indians was criticised. All these were factors which slowly but surely prepared ground for the mutiny. The Indians were converted to Christianity by these missionaries by force or fraud. When there was a general famine in 1837, for instance, the missionaries discovered the best opportunity to exploit the situation and "numerous orphans were converted to Christianity," thus wrote Syed Ahmed.[16] The Religious Disabilities Act of 1856 gave protection to the rights of the Hindus converted to Christianity. Mangles, the Chairman of the Court of Directors of the East India Company, openly declared: "Providence has entrusted the extensive empire of Hindustan to England in order that the banner of Christ should wave triumphant from one end of India to the other. Everyone must exert all his strength that there may be no dilatoriness on any account in continuing in the country the grand work of making all Indians Christians."

Nor were under these circumstances, the good intentions of the British likely to be interpreted in the right spirit. The social legislation abolishing *sati* and legalising widow remarriage were supposed to be a naked British interference into the religious beliefs of the people. In the railways which the Englishman "began to construct, the telegraph wires by which he connected Calcutta with Peshawar and Bombay with Madras, the canal which he linked to the sacred stream of the Ganges, Brahmans fancied that sorcery was at work."[17]

There was a growing belief that the Indian religions were going to be destroyed and Christianity substituted in their stead. The people believed that the Government mixed dust of cow-bones in salt and other eatables. They adulterated ghee and threw the flesh of swine and cow into the wells to pollute the water. When, for instance, the prices of flour at Kanpur rose very high, a dealer from Meerut despatched large supplies of flour in Government steamers. But the people believed that dust of cow-bones had been mixed in it by the Government, and "although the flour was offered for sale at a greatly reduced price," thus wrote Sir Hope Grant in his private journal, "not a native would touch it preferring the pangs of hunger to the risk of contamination."[18] Under these circumstances, therefore, the time was fast approaching when the people's toleration reached the limit.

The Purely Administrative Causes. The there were grievances due purely to administrative causes. *Seir Mutakherin* explained in 1780 as to how in the early stages of the British occupation of Bengal, the people preferred their disciplined rule to the loose and corrupt administration of the Muslims. The real character of the British however, soon became manifest, and hatred against them began to grow. This happened particularly after the British got the grant of *Diwani*. The Indian grievances against the British, as listed by Ghulam Hussein in the above-named work, show that the worst features of their administration were that (1) the English officers were not easily accessible to those whom they ruled. (2) There being vast differences of language and customs between the English and the Indians, the administration given to the latter suited their character the least. (3) The English having no familiarity with the Indians, their administration was impersonal, and hence, slow, it frequently involved changes of policy, etc. (4) The discriminative policy of the British deprived the Indians of benefits from commerce; and they being not enlisted into the army to the same extent as before, had few careers open to them. There were many other grievances listed by the learned author to which a detailed reference may not be made.[19]

These grievances were dilated upon by Sir Syed Ahmed in 1860, who declared that the most important cause of the mutiny had been the non-admittance of the Indians into the legislative and the administrative branches of the Government because of which it failed to understand the Indian grievances in time.[20] The Muslims were perhaps the most dissatisfied lot in this respect. They had till recently occupied almost all the important civil and military posts in the Government, and had been the most privileged community of this country. Their old position having vanished, they now started lagging behind the other communities.

Government officers interfered in the transfers of land, and the collectors refused to enforce the decrees which went against the British interests, as it happened in the case of a *Raja* who got 138 villages out of 216 of his *taluka* confiscated. Flogging was abolished as a punishment for civil offences, and system of imprisonments substituted. This was not liked by the people.

The Sepoy Disaffection. Despite all the causes referred to above, however, the general civil population may not perhaps have mutinied at the time if there had been no mutiny among the Indian soldiers. The sepoys at Meerut mutinied, and killing their officers they reached Delhi where they declared Bahadur Shah as the Emperor of India. Even then it was not before the passage of some time that the civil population got affected by the mutinous spirit.

And so far as the mutinous spirit of the sepoys was concerned, it too had causes to exist. It was the Bengal army which played the dominant role in the mutiny, and this mutiny of the Bengal army was not its first. The Bengal army in fact consisted of the high-caste Hindus—Brahmins, Rajputs and Jats, who not only belonged to Bengal, but the whole of upper India. Though it also included a good number of sturdy Pathans, it belonged mainly to what later was called U.P. and to Oudh.

This army had a brilliant record of service to the British, yet as time passed their chances of promotion got limited. Holmes wrote regarding a sepoy in this army: "Though he might give signs of the military genius of a Hyder, he knew that he could never attain the pay of an English subaltern, and that the rank to which he might attain, after some thirty years of faithful service, would not protect him from the insolent dictation of an ensign fresh from England."[21]

Nor did the Government repose trust in the Indian officers. In every company there were two or three Indian officers who were discharged from service with full pay on retirement, on the pretext of rewarding them. And this was done as soon as they attained a good position of respect: "as soon as Sepoys become attached to them as soon as they encroach upon the admiration and respect which must be the exclusive property of the European officers..."[22]

As early as 1806, the Madras army mutinied as a result of the new regulations enforced on it, under which the sepoys were forbidden to wear caste-marks on their foreheads, and were ordered to shave off their heads and wear new turbans with leather cockades in place of the old.

There were mutinies at Barrackpur in 1824, and in Assam in 1825 in the Bengal army in the time of Amherst during the Burmese War when the sepoys were compelled to go across the sea to Burma against their caste prejudices, arrange their own carriage for their personal baggages and go to Arakan, a region of plague. These soldiers later hesitated from going to Afghanistan, but when completed to do so and eat the impure food in that country during the First Afghan War, they objected, though they did not mutiny. On return they had to perform many expiatory ceremonies.

Betweer 1764 and 1844 these sepoys mutinied for as many as a dozen times, for purely material grievances such as the low rates of pay and allowances. For instance, Bengal regiments refused to march to Sind in 1844, and demanded the restoration of their extra allowances as a condition for doing so. When the Army of occupation was sent to the Punjab in 1849, the mutinous spirit was discernible among these soldiers. In the time of Dalhousie too, mutinies occurred in Sind as well as in Burma. Dalhousie showed his weakness and refused to go to either of the places. And according to the Red Pamphlet: "from that moment a revolt became a mere question of time and opportunity."[23]

The general causes of discontentment which led the sepoys to mutiny earlier and stage a grand mutiny in 1857, were listed by Sheikh Hidayat Ali in a memorandum, the more important of them being: (1) The indignation of the sepoys at the annexation of Oudh to which many of them in the Bengal army belonged. (2) Recruitment of the Punjabi Sikhs and Muslims after the annexation of the Punjab, and the dismissal of many of them later when they refused to abide by the orders which, violating the earlier promises made to them, asked them to remove their beard and hair. (3) The General Service Enlistment Act and the general order in September 1856 asking the new recruits to take an oath to be prepared to go wherever required. Holmes commenting on this remarked that Canning had hoped that the recruitment would not be affected by it, but "being a new-comer, he did not realise that the Bengal army was a brotherhood, in which military service was hereditary."[24]

There were other causes besides the above. The activities of the Christian missionaries were becoming too offensive for the sepoys to bear. Proceedings of one of their schools read: "Some others now engaged in the degrading and polluting worship of idols shall be brought to the knowledge of the true God and Jesus Christ."

Then Sir Syed Ahmed Khan refers to a series of letters circulated by Edmond, and written for the public, but particularly for the responsible Indian officers in the army. These letters argued that since India now had one railway system, one telegraph system and one law for whole of the country, she must have one religion, which would best be Christianity. Sir. Syed remarked: "These letters so terrified the natives that they were as people struck blind, or from under whose feet the ground had suddenly slipped away."[25]

Some responsible officers like Major Mackenzie and Colonel Wheeler openly preached Christianity among the sepoys, to which the Government paid no heed. The active Christian propaganda coupled with the passage of the

Religious Disabilities Act, confirmed the religious apprehensions in the minds of the sepoys.

Then, the ordinary sepoys enjoyed no respect in the army. The most slanderous language and the most naked abuses were hurled on them, and the "English officer, instead of identifying himself with those under him, sought for interests, pleasures, and society in importation from home."[26] The only bond between the sepoys "and the Government was his pay and pension, and his pay and prospects were far from attractive."[27]

In the Bengal army, unlike in Madras and Bombay, promotions were given on seniority basis alone, and here was no retiring age. "The result," according to Rawlinson, "was that Subedars (highest rank of Indian infantry officer) of 50 years' service were no uncommon, and many of them were so old and decrepit that they could not keep up with the men on the march."[28] And the same was true of the British officers as well. Dalhousie himself remarked: "Commanding officers are inefficient, brigadiers are no better; divisional officers are worse than either, because older and more alone; and at the top of all they send a commmander-in-chief 70 years old." General Wheeler was actually 75 at the time of the Kanpur disaster.

There was a fear among the Bengal soldiers that a new war-like Sikh regiment would command superior respect and chances. There was a great disparity in number between the Indian and the English soldiers which encouraged them. At the time of the outbreak of mutiny, the whole effective English force all over India numbered only 36,000; while the Indian soldiers numbered as many as 257,000—armed police and lascars attached to artillery which constituted a large number being, excluded.[29] Then, "Lord William Bentinck's economy measures," writes Sen, "had caused great discontentment among the European officers and they openly talked of mutiny and his was no secret to the ordinary troops, Indian and European."[30]

The distribution of troops in the country too was faulty, there was no European soldier worth the name either in Bengal or Bihar, except there being a small number of them at Calcutta and Danapur near Patna. The major European force was concentrated far away in the Punjab and elsewhere. The Bengal army alone numbering 151,361 soldiers, they had a confidence in their future.

Not few amongst the Indian soldiers still possessed a deep veneration for the old royal family a Delhi, and that also animated their spirit for action. There was also the hope of plundering the private European property. The centenary of the Battle of Plassey was also to fall in June 1857, and the people had a superstitious belief that the end of the British rule in India had arrived. And last but not least, was the incident of a mysterious circulation of *chapaties*, and a similar circulation of the lotus flowers among the general public and the soldiers respectively. The origin and cause of these has not been known, yet occurring at the opportune moment as they did, they served to increase the general unrest.

And once the mutiny did break out, there were other causes which made their contribution to its sustainment and spread. There were the rumours of the Russian victory against England in the Crimean War. There was an ignorance of the resources and the real power of the English. And the courtiers of the ex-King of Oudh, if not he, did not spare their energy in spreading the disaffection. The King of Delhi also made promises of pay and grants of land. The soldiers disbanded from the army as a result of suspicion roamed about unemployed and added fuel to the mutinous fire.

The Immediate Cause. The immediate cause of the mutiny was the one connected with the greased cartridges. New Enfield rifle had been introduced for the use of the sepoys, for the loading of which the greased cartridges were used, the end of which as to be bitten off by the teeth of the user. There was a rumour that the fat of cows and pigs had been used to grease these cartridges, the object being to defile the Hindus as well as the Muslims. The British Government denied the charge and forced the sepoys to use these cartridges. The sepoys got infuriated and broke out into a mutiny at Barrackpore and later at Berhampore. The decisive mutiny of the sepoys, however, occurred at Meerut on 10 May 1857 when the British authorities acted foolishly by imprisoning the 85 sepoys for their refusal to use the cartridges. Later on it was actually proved that the fat of cows and pigs had been used, of which the British Government were ignorant.

The first shot of the mutiny had however been fired, and the situation could not now be brought back to normal. The regiments which broke out into mutiny at Meerut, murdered many Europeans and marched off to Delhi. The regiments at Delhi also mutinied. The mutineers murdering many Europeans in the capital, occupied the city and put Bahadur Shah the old Mughal Emperor on the throne. Soon the mutiny spread to Lucknow, Bareilly, Kanpur, Agra, Jhansi, Central India, Bundelkhand and many other places the mutineers killing the Europeans and throwing open the jails.

At Kanpur, the direction of the mutineers was in the hands of Nana Saheb. The British garrison here surrendered, and all but four of them were killed in cold blood. At Jhansi, Rani Laxmibai led the mutineers, and here too many Europeans were put to death. The other Indian leaders were Tantia Tope, Kunwar Singh, Azimulla Khan, Ahmed Shah and Maulvi Ahmed Shah of Fyzabad.

The greatest service to the British during the days of their trouble as rendered by the Punjab almost whole of which remained loyal, with a few exceptions here and there. And the major credit for this goes to its Commissioner Sir John Lawrence who disarmed the disaffected sepoys in time, raised new regiments of the Sikhs and sent them to Delhi to recapture it. Delhi being the heart of India, its capture was essential for the purpose of breaking the backbone of the mutiny. Bahadur Shah was arrested, his two sons were shot dead, and he himself was transported to Rangoon.

At Kanpur, Nana Saheb was defeated by General Havelock who took the city, and then marched off to Lucknow. After his departure, however, Kanpur was recaptured by the mutineers. Havelock entered Lucknow together with Outram, but here they themselves were besieged to be relieved only later by Campbell on 6 December 1857. Nana Saheb with his Gwalior sepoys was also defeated by Campbell. Tantia Tope, the minister of Nana and a veritable talisman for the mutineers, gave the best account, keeping the British troops running after him for nine months on a distance of three thousand miles. Finally, however, he too fell and with him ended the mutiny.

Such thus were the causes of the mutiny, and such its events in brief. The above account clearly shows that there was no organised movement for independence when the mutiny broke out, and that there was no spirit of nationalism that animated it. Different persons, different princes, the *zamindars* and the sepoys fought for different reasons. Some fought for their lost principalities, others for the lost titles and pensions, while yet others fought for their caste and religion which were in danger. Some fought just for the sake of adventure, while others fought for the love of plunder and booty. There were some common grievances, but none too common to inspire the whole mass of mutineers, the Hindus, the Muslims and the Sikhs, the princes, *zamindars* the rich and the poor together. The combustible material lay scattered, and the spark was provided by the sepoy mutiny.

Lord Canning himself wrote to Lord Elphinstone in a letter dated 6 May 1857: "It is not possible to say with confidence what the causes are, but with the common herd there is a sincere fear for their caste, and a conviction that this has been in danger from the cartridge and other causes…But upon the whole, political animosity does not go for much in the present movement, and certainly does not actuate sepoys in the mass."[31] Mr. Edwards, who was the magistrate and Collector of Budaon, the hot centre of mutiny, also commented: "I must solemnly declare my belief that with the mass of our soldiers the dread of these cartridges was the immediate and the most powerful cause of the revolt." The sepoys broke out into mutiny due to their own causes, and the others followed them, but they due to *their* own causes.

We may finally conclude with the words of Thompson and Garratt: "The Mutiny may be considered either as a military revolt, or as a bid for recovery of their property and privileges by dispossessed princes and landlords, or as an attempt to restore the Mughal Empire, or as peasants' war. From every aspect it was localised, restricted and unorganised."[32]

The Failure

Whatever be the character of the mutiny, it undoubtedly was a great event in the history of the Indian War of Independence. A good part of the nation up in arms; meagre resources of the British and their as yet difficult means of communication made yet more difficult by the openly hostile people. In fact the circumstances were very favourable for the people, and the British had been taken by surprise. Yet it was a wonder that the mutiny ultimately failed. It would be instructive to make a brief study of the causes of the failure.

The first and the foremost cause of the failure of the mutiny, it must be said, was the fact that the whole of India did not participate in the mutiny and those who did participate, had no solidarity among themselves. Those affected by the mutiny were only a part of the Punjab, U.P., Rohilkhand, Oudh, the territories between the Narbada and the Chambal rivers, and western part of Bihar and Bengal, while the territories of Rajputana, Central and Eastern Bengal and those south of the Narbada, all remained undisturbed. Sind was loyal, Dost Muhammad of Afghanistan rendered a loyal assistance, and Nepal in this respect did not remain behind. Not a single ruling chief of some importance joined the mutineers. Large civil population which included the intellectuals as a *class*, remained quiet, firstly, because they as yet completely lacked a national feeling, and secondly, because they had no reason to trust the ruling chiefs for any help. By diplomacy, rewards and threats, the Sikhs were not only kept aloof from the mutineers, they were made to render an important help against them.

Sir W. Russell indeed made a correct appraisal of the situation when he wrote: "Our siege of Delhi would have been quite impossible if the Rajas of Patiala and Jind had not been our friends and if the Sikhs had not remained in our battalions and remained quiet in the Punjab. The Sikhs at Lucknow did good service and in all cases our garrisons were helped, fed and served by the natives, as our armies were attended and strengthened by them in the field."[33]

The Raja of Jind in fact was the first man, European or Native, who took field against the mutiners; marching to Karnal with 800 men and securing supplies to the British. Patiala supplied 5,000 men and 8 guns, Nabha supplied 800 strong, while Kapurthala furnished 2,000. It was the Sikhs under the command of General Nicholson who finally captured Delhi for the British. Gordon wrote: "though the Khalsa has ceased to be a political power, it has entwined its military force with a strong chord of loyalty and sympathy for the British Crown."[34] His Royal Highness Prince Albert Victor of Wales on his visit to Lahore in 1890, called the Punjab "the guard-room of the Eastern Empire"[35] due to the part it played in 1857, but for which the history of the mutiny should have been different.

Then, the mutineers had neither a general plan of action, nor any liaison between different groups. Some sort of organisational talent was shown by the leaders like Rani Laxmibai of Jhansi, Tantia Tope and Kunwar Sigh. But there campaigns were local, and they too failed in having a regular contact with one another. While each of their armies were individually whole, all armies failed any where to combine together.

Nor, did the mutineers have an understanding of war strategy. Delhi was the backbone of a power which wanted to rule supreme in India. But while the British understood the psychology and the strategy attached to it, the mutineers absolutely failed in doing so. The first thing the British did was to collect every available soldier and concentrate round Delhi to besiege the Emperor and his troops within. The best thing for the mutineers outside should have been to prevent them from doing so, and attack them from the outside when they did concentrate. But they did neither of these.

The British position in Delhi could be maintained only by a regular and continuous supply of soldiers and arms from the Punjab which was done through a narrow passage which lay along the border of U.P. towards the north-west of the city. The passage lay in the midst of one of the most disaffected parts of the country. Yet it occurred to none to try to block it. Nana Saheb at Kanpur instead of sending the sepoys to do this job, dissuaded the Kanpur troops from doing so. Savarkar tries to justify Nana's action by saying that "the best interests would not be served by shutting up all the available forces in Delhi."[36] But comments Dr. Majumdar: "He forgets that what was wanted was to stop the succour coming to the besiegers of Delhi from the Punjab side, and the number of mutinous troops was so large that under proper leadership it should have been possible to cut off the communication between Delhi on the one side and the Punjab and Calcutta on the other."[37] Nana's selfish interests in fact seem to have been confined to Kanpur, and to securing Peshwahood for himself; he being concerned neither with Allahabad, nor Lucknow or Delhi. Nor in the case of Delhi being successful in holding out to the British, was he prepared to play second fiddle to Bahadur Shah.

There was in fact, no towering personality among the leaders of the mutiny who could organise or lead the mutineers on the national perspectives. The so-called leaders and heroes of the mutiny like Nana Saheb were in fact only traitors to the national cause. About Nana Saheb particularly, the less said the better. Selfish and incapable Nana Saheb had neither intelligence to plan nor nerve to fight battles on a large-scale. Near Kanpur he yielded a victory to Havelock with the least intelligent and courageous effort to retain it. His effort to dissuade the sepoys from marching to Delhi was not only unwise, but traitorous. Of the most heinous crime of killing the European women and children at Kanpur in cold blood, he could never entirely be absolved. Yet the worst part that he could play was in his repeated letters of appeal which he sent to the British praying for forgiveness and the restoration of his titles and pensions. He wrote to high British officials in a letter: "It is surprising that I who have joined the rebels from haplessness have not been forgiven." The killing of the women and children was done by "your sepoys and *Badmashas* at the time that my soldiers fled from Kanpur."[38]

Tantia Tope, Rani Laxmibai and Kunwar Singh should have been honest after they threw their lot with the mutineers; but none of them had the calibre to conduct a war on a national basis. Bahadur Shah was only figurehead.

Opposed to these, however were Lawrence, Outram, Havelock, Edwards and Nicholson; not only great soldiers, but also great organisers and planners. Lawrence's success in keeping the Punjab loyal and pacified and making it save an empire for the British, could any day be given the credit of great statesmanship, presence of mind, intelligence and foresightedness.

Nor could the courage and gallantry of the Indians be matched with those of the English. In fact the close study of any action fought between the two shows nothing but half-heartendess and resourcelessness on the part of the Indians, and precisely opposite behaviour on the part of the English. At Hindon, and at Badli-kasarai near Delhi for instance, in the pitched battles fought between the two, neither a superior number of the Indian soldiers nor their superior artillery could give them the necessary courage and morale to win a victory.

Only a few more instances may be quoted to enforce the point. At Kanpur the English sheltered themselves only in an improvised camp, with a weak entrenchment. They had only 400 English fighting men of whom as many as 70 were invalids, and had besides only a small band of faithful sepoys. Opposed to these were the three thousand mutinous sepoys, well trained, well armed, and well fed, assisted by the retainers of Nana Saheb and supported by the sympathies of a large civil population.[39] They, under the leadership of Nana Saheb, besieged the town for twenty days, and yet failed to reduce it; the town ultimately being reduced by Nana only by treachery.

At Jhansi the garrison under the command of the Rani numbered 10,000 Bundelas and Velaitees, and 1,500 sepoys.[40] The town was besieged by Sir Hugh Rose on 22 March 1858 with only 2,000 soldiers. On 31 March Tantia Tope arrived with 20,000 soldiers to relieve the garrison. Sir Hugh, however, leaving only a part of his army behind to continue the siege, attacked and defeated Tantia on 1 April. The latter fled the field hotly pursued by the English. After this Sir Hugh carried a direct assault and entered the fort on 3 April, the Rani stealing away to her safety. Thus the city was captured. Such was the demoralised state of the Indians. Even when the relieving army was engaged with more than half of the small besieging force, it occurred to nobody in the garrison to sally out and destroy the besiegers. Nor could the 20,000 soldiers of Tantia defeat a thousand or little more of the English.

The walled city of Delhi having a large well-equipped army, with a free access to the outside territory and having a strong fortification within, was reduced by the British only in four months. Such are thus the striking instances of the Indian weakness and demoralisation.

And then on the one hand were the British imbued with the spirit of revenge for the murdered women and children. They carried in their breasts, a zeal to retain an empire, a determination to save their national honour and a discipline and fellow-feeling to unite, fight and win. They had no alternative but to win in which alone lay the possibility of their life. If they fled the field there was no place in India to hide their heads and save life.

While on the other hand the Indians, were fighting more blindly than wisely. The problem of defending their religion having receded into the background, their fight was now animated only by hopes of material gains and a hatred against the British. There was no national ideal to inspire them, and no national zeal to enliven their spirit and unite them all together. To fight in the battle-fled was for the majority of them only an expediency, while to flee it and go back to the villages was to go to peace and safety of life.

Nor was the personal character of the Bengal troops a possession to be envied. Pride and arrogance in place of love and fellow-feeling was their trait which could hardly a tract others to unified action.

Such being the state of affairs in the Mutiny of 1857, there was no general appeal to peasants, the tillers and the common man of the nation to join. The main inspiration came from the ruined princes, and ruined title and pension-holders.

And then, in some parts of the country, as for instance in the Punjab and in Rajputana, some people preferred the disciplined administration of the British, however derogatory to the national economy, to the indisciplined administration of the Indian princes. Sir John Strachey writes: "The duty was once imposed upon me of transferring a number of villages which had long been included in a British district to one of the best governed of the native states. I shall not forget the loud and universal protests of the people against the cruel injustice with which they considered they were being treated."[41]

"The new middle-class created under British rule saw no hope in the 1857 revolt... They found the representatives of these 'middle classes' in the British rulers and thought it more prudent in their own class-interest to follow them, than to back the wrong 'feudal' horse."[42]

The time-factor too was against the Indians. Luckily for the British the Crimean war was over. Russia was defeated and the Indian rebels were internationally isolated. The only Indian hope lay in their quick victories, lest reinforcements should arrive from England. But thanks to the causes referred to above, the mutineers did not merit even a reinforcement.

Yet, ultimately it must be added that luck favoured the British in more than one cause. And the most important one of them was that the Indian princes sitting on the fence, were bound to join the mutineers if the suppression of the mutiny took just a little time more. Already, attractive offers were being made by Bahadur Shah and other leaders of the mutiny to them. The situation in the Punjab too was not very safe. Fierce tribes here watched a chance to pounce upon the British, 13,000 disarmed sepoys roamed about creating disaffection, and the large population though faithful, speculated whether the British should go or remain.[43] "If, with the last aid, Delhi were not taken, and that too speedily there could then be a struggle for European existence, within the Punjab."

Lawrence wrote in a Minute dated 19 April 1858: "Many thoughtful and experienced men now in India believe that it was only been by a series of miracles, that we have been saved from utter ruin."[44]

Be that as it may, the mutiny was suppressed with a heavy and uncompromising hand. But once it was so, Canning was not prepared to witness rabid and rancorous vindictiveness towards the people. For he declared that he did not want to govern in anger. Besides, expediency also required leniency. For it was impossible for a small number of Englishmen to rule over India without the good will of the people and the Indian soldiers. Many princes, *zamindars* and even common people had exhibited friendship towards the British. It was no good to develop unreserved hatred against the brown skin. Canning, therefore, issued a resolution to this effect, forbidding his officers from shedding needless blood, and burning villages which would threaten famine and also deplete revenue resources. Canning was conscious of the danger of racial animosity, and was anxious therefore to speedily bring about settled conditions.

The resolution that was issued carried detailed strictures regarding those who had indulged in violence and murder, but everything was to be done under law and no excess was to be perpetrated. It was well-intentioned and calculated to meet out justice and serve the long term interests of the British in India. But he was miscalculated, and there arose a storm of invective in the press and elsewhere condemning Canning's 'misplaced generosity'. An Indian newspaper termed it "impolitic, and iniquitous... it allows the blood of English and Christian subjects...to flow in torrents, and their wives, sisters, and daughters to be outraged and dishonoured without adequate retribution." *The Times* in London, in a lengthy article, called it the "Clemency of Canning,"[45] and contemptuously demanded if the "humanity and consideration are for the sole benefit of the mutineers..." In another article, *The Times* termed it a "silly proclamation". Other papers like *Punch* and the *Daily* News also made virulent attacks, but Canning remained unmoved and wrote to Grenville, that as "long as I have breath in my body I will pursue no other policy than that which I have been following."[46] Grenville agreed with him, and the Queen also heartily supported this policy.

Canning showed a remarkable calm at a time when exasperation, malice and indiscriminate vindictiveness were in the air. He refused to change his Indian guards for Englishmen, rejected the petition of the Whit community of Calcutta to impose martial law on the whole of Bengal, and in the midst of rancorous protests appointed Munshi Ameer Ali, a Muslim layer, as Deputy Magistrate in the Patna division. Open abuses, violent protests, petitions to the Queen to recall him, none could defect him from the path that he thought was right. His services were appreciated in England and he was gazetted GCB and promoted to Earldom in 1859.

As the storm blew over, the time came now also to reward those who rendered a faithful service to the British. The Chief Commissioner of Punjab, John Lawrence, was promoted Lieutenant-Governor. The rulers of Patiala, Nabha, Jind, Kapurthala, etc. who had done everything to help the British during their days of trouble, were all suitably rewarded. The territories which Nepal had ceded and were bestowed on Oudh in 1815, were returned to Jung Bahadur, the ruler, who was also awarded GCB in the Military division. Soldiers of this independent kingdom had marched during mutiny to Lucknow. Canning himself moved with the Viceregal cortege through Upper India, holding durbars and receiving distinguished and faithful princes at Ambala, Lahore, Peshawar, Sialkot and Simla.

CHANGES AFTER MUTINY

"The Mutiny cannot be dismissed as an unhappy incident which ended with its suppression," thus write Thompson and Garratt.[47] There was a complete reorganisation of the internal administration and of the relations with the Indian states; and "the reorganisation after the disturbances of the mutiny furnished an opportunity for transferring control from the company to the Crown in appearance as well as reality," writes Powell-Price.[48]

ACT FOR THE BETTER GOVERNMENT OF INDIA

The most important result of the mutiny was the Act for the Better Government of India 1858. This Act, in fact, was the termination of a process commenced by the Pitt's India Act in 1784. From 1784, the Crown's hold had slowly developed on the Indian affairs, while the powers of the Court of Directors were progressively curtailed till the Charter Act of 1853 was passed. This act clearly laid down that the Company was to hold the territories and the revenues of India in trust for Her Majesty till it was otherwise provided. The Company's monopoly of trade had already been dissolved and India was thrown open for any Englishman to settle in. The complete transfer of powers from the Company to the Crown in this circumstance could not wait for long.

Nor was the existing dual system of control at Home very conductive to efficiency in the Indian government. There were constant clashes and bitterness between the Court of Directors and the Board of Control entailing unnecessary delay and slothfulness. The thinking minds in India as well as England had already criticised it several times and this anomaly had therefore to be removed.

There was a growing belief also that a commercial concern such as the Company was incapable of ruling without self-interest. The Government of a land with a teeming population of millions could hardly be run by an association of merchants whose eyes rested more on profits than on administrative efficiency. Nor could the effects of the industrial revolution and the consequent evolution of liberalism in England go without an impact on the Indian system and life. A generation of liberals was taking birth in that country who believed a system of government with ministerial responsibility was the best. And they could find no consolation until it was introduced in India as in England.

The opportunity for the change came when India was thrown into conflagration by the great Mutiny of 1857. England criticised the system of the Company which was responsible for the great catastrophe involving the lives of hundreds of Englishmen, and a large-scale destruction of life and property of the Indians. The advocates of the direct control of the Crown became more vocal, and when the reorganisation after the mutiny came, "it furnished an opportunity for transferring control from the Company to the Crown in appearance as well as reality."

In the general elections of 1857 Palmerston succeeded and became the Prime Minister. In July of the same year he brought to the notice of the Parliament the evils of the double government, and expressed his desire to take over the Indian administration. The East India Company was alarmed and presented a "Grand Petition," arguing against the proposed step. The petition was very skilfully drawn up by John Stuart Mill, a well-known scholar of the time in the service of the Company, and in it the Company pleaded that if there was anything wrong with the double government, it was introduced by Pitt's India Act of 1784, and therefore it was the Government of England which was to blame. The petition recounted the great services the Company had rendered both to India and to the crown and mentioned how a great empire had been secured without any cost to the latter. It was asserted that the taking over directly of the Government of India would be attended by many dangers; and that, to "believe that the administration of India would have been free from error, had it been conducted by a Minister of the Crown, without the aid of the Court of Directors, would be to believe that the Minister, with full power to govern India as he pleased has governed ill, because he had the assistance of experienced and responsible advisers." Ross Mangles the Chairman of the Company also expressed a surprise that the existence of the Company was threatened even without a Parliamentary enquiry. He asserted that "an intermediate, non-political and perfectly independent body like the Company was an indispensable necessity for good Government in India."

All this, however, failed to convince Palmerston who, introducing in February 1858 a bill for the better government of India, said: "The principle of our political system is that all administrative functions should be accompanied by ministerial responsibility to Parliament, but in this case the chief functions in the Government of India are committed to a body no responsible to Parliament not appoint by the Crown, but elected by persons who have no more connexion with India than consists in the simple possession of so much India stock." Lord Palmerson's arguments were, however, dressed in a sympathetic language, and he said that the Bill was not intended to condemn or undermine the achievements of the Company, the aim was simply to remove some of the glaring defects in the existing system. Nor did Palmersoton agree that he direct take-over would involve any serious dangers from India or elsewhere. The Indian people would rather welcome the change, he said. Some members rather ruthlessly criticised the Company's administration, and among them Sir George Cornwell Lewis was perhaps the most outspoken.

The Bill went through the second reading. But unfortunately before it could become law, Lord Palmerston was defeated on the 'Conspiracy to Murder Bill', and was thrown out of office. Lord Derby with Disraeli as the Chancellor of Exchequer succeeded. A new Bill known as Disraeli's India Bill was introduced. But it was ridiculed by Lord Palmerston and his followers. The matter continued thus, till Stanley introduced yet another Bill, and it was passed as the 'Act for the Better Government of India'.

Provisions. The Act which had 75 Sections, declared that India henceforward would be "governed by and in the name of the Queen." Concerning the Home Government, the Act introduced the following changes: (1) The Board of Control and the Court of Directors were replaced by the Secretary of State for India. (2) The Secretary of State was to be assisted by a 'Council of India' consisting of 15 members, 8 of whom would be appointed by the Crown, while the remaining 7 would be elected by the sitting Court of Directors. (3) At least half of these members must have served in India for not less than ten years, and they must not have been away from that country for more than ten-years at the time of their appointment. (4) The vacancies among the Crown nominees would be filled up by the Crown; while among those elected by the Directors, would be filled up by the person co-opted by the Council. (5) The members would continue in office during good behaviour, and would be removed only on petition by both the Houses of the Parliament. (6) Their annual salary would be £1,200 each. (7) The Secretary of State would be a member of the Cabinet, he would sit in the Parliament, and be assisted by a Parliamentary Under Secretary. (8) The Secretary of State would preside over the meetings of the Council; and while in some matters such as issuing of securities for money, mortgage or sale of property and appropriation of property and revenue, he would be bound by the majority decisions, in others he would have the powers to overrule the Council's decisions—in which case, however, he himself or any other member of the Council may require that his opinion and arguments be entered in the Minutes of the proceedings. The Council itself had no initiative; it was only to advise on matters referred to it by the Secretary. (10) The Secretary of State could make rules for the efficient transaction of business by the Council, and he could constitute committees and distribute among them different departments of work. (11) The Council had to meet at least once a week, and its quorum would be of five. Any decision taken in the absence of the Secretary of State, was required to have his written approval. (12) The revenues of India would be used for India alone; and the salaries of the Secretary of State, and of the Councillors, the cost of the India Office, the East India Company's debts and dividends on its stock, were all to be paid by India. But all the orders of the Secretary of State regarding expenditure and loans, were required to have a concurrence of the majority of the Councillors. (13) All the communications from the Secretary of State to the Governor-General, were to be brought before the

Council or were to lie in its room for seven days. If the majority of the Councillors differed with the communication, but the Secretary of State still adhered to it, he had to record reasons why he did so. Certain matters concerning the declaration of a war, making of peace, or negotiations with princes, may, however, be marked secret and not brought before the Council. The Governor-General's despatches concerning these matters could also be kept secret. (14) The patronage was divided between the Secretary of State and the Government of India, as the Act said: all the appointments and promotions, "which by law or under any regulations, usage or customs are not made by any authority in India, shall continue to be made in India by the like authority." The appointments to the covenanted Civil Services were to be made by open competition under the rules laid down by Secretary of State with the help of the Civil Service Commissioners. (15) The Secretary of State was to place every year before the Parliament a report of the Indian accounts, and on the moral and material progress of the country. (16) And finally, the Secretary of State was declared to be a corporate body which could sue and be sued in England and in India.

Relating to the Government of India, the Act declared that (1) the responsibility of the Government of India was to be assumed directly by the Crown, and this assumption was to be declared to the Indian princes by a proclamation of the Queen. (2) All the treaties, contracts and liabilities entered into by the Company were to be binding on the Crown. (3) The Crown would appoint the Governor-General of India and the Governors of the Presidencies. The Lieutenant Governors, however, would be appointed by the Governor-General subject to the approval of the Crown; while the members of the various Councils would be appointed by the Secretary of State in Council. (4) The Indian naval and military control was transferred to the Crown; (5) while it was laid down that the Indian finances were not to be expended on military operations outside

India without the consent of the Parliament, except for repelling invasion or "sudden and urgent necessity."

A Review. There is a considerable significance of the passage of this Act in the history of India. The rule of the Company ended, and now that of the Crown in a direct manner commenced. "The Company," writes Marshman, "transferred to the Crown on relinquishing its functions, an empire more magnificent than Rome."[49] The differences between the Court of Directors on the one hand and the board of Control on the other had made the things too difficult to proceed with. Now both these bodies were replaced by the Secretary of State who was given strong powers to control the affairs of India effectively. This also replaced completely the hold of a body of merchants with that of pure politicians and administrators, and the Colonial Office and the Foreign Office now came into being. The dual government having been abolished and the control having passed entirely into the hands of a member of the British Cabinet, greater possibilities were created for the percolation through this machinery to India of the magnanimity of the new political spirit which was taking its birth in England. The members of the Court of Directors were not essentially those who had visited India, or whose experience of the Indian affairs was unsurpassed. The members of the Board of Control left much to be desired in this respect. The latter body was indeed considered to be a collecting ground for mediocrities. All this was now amended. The Secretary of State was to be assisted by a Council the majority of the members of which were required to have a vast experience in the Indian problems. The announcement of the direct take-over by the Crown was to be made to the princes in a proclamation, and this proclamation was a turning point in the history of the Government of India's relations with the States. This take-over offered an opportunity to the Crown to hold out great promises both to the Indian princes and to the Indian people. While the promises of the non-annexation of their territories to the princes were kept, those to the people for their welfare and uplift were violated, thereby offering a lever for the political agitation of the Indian people. In short the Act closed one chapter of the Indian history and commenced another. New hopes were inspired and new aspirations developed. The Indians had from ages looked upon a living person as an embodiment of sovereign power. The assumption of the Government by the Crown therefore was welcome.

The changes introduced by the Act, however, seem on a closer examination to be more in form than substance. "The transfer of the Indian Empire to the Crown," writes Ramsay Muir, "involved far less change than might at first sight appear; for the Crown had been steadily increasing its control over the Company's affairs almost since the beginning of its territorial sovereignty." The main rules under which India was governed in 1858, were already those of the British Parliament. The British administrators including the Governor-General though nominally the servants of the Court of Directors, knew that in reality they were answerable to the British Cabinet with its Indian Minister—who was the President of the Board of Control, and through them to the Parliament. From the Regulating Act of 1773, a series of statutes, of 1784, 1793, 1813, 1833 and 1853 had progressively reduced the powers of the Court of Directors till they became just nominal. At first the Company lost its trading monopoly, and then its trading practices were prohibited altogether. The chief officers in India had already become government nominees, while the rank and file came through the gates of the Haileybury College, the admission to which again was controlled by the Government.

It was in fact a constitutional anachronism that a private corporation had been left in possession of as vast a dominion as India. The Queen had already disapproved of the Company's grant of medals for military service. The Company system ill-fitted in the English principle of ministerial responsibility. The sovereignty of the Crown was therefore increasingly emphasised by the successive Charter Acts till ultimately it was frankly declared in the Act of 1853 that the Company was to hold the territories and the revenues of India in trust for the Crown till it was determined otherwise. The number of the Directors was reduced from 24 to 18 out of which 6 were to be the nominees of the Crown. The choicest flower in the bunch was indeed taken away when the Directors were deprived of their power of patronage. The result was that the Company now played no real effective part in the machinery of government; "but was only a superfluous fifth wheel; and when...the British Government stood frankly forth as responsible for the welfare of India, it was as if a ventriloquist were to throw aside his absurd doll and speak in his natural voice."[50]

Certain writers have pointed out defects in the Act. Thus, it has been said that the newly formed Council in England was incapable of imposing any check on the Secretary of State's authority. Though on matters referred to it, it could give a valuable advice, it was at best only "a place of repose for the distinguished servants of the Crown after their return from India."[51] There is no doubt that the Council was given some powers on the Indian revenues and expenditure, but it had no authority on war and peace and the huge expenses involved in it. Certain matters could be kept secret from it, and the Council had no initiative—being empowered to advise only on matters referred to it. The cost of the India Office, the Company's debts and dividends on its stock, and the salaries of the Secretary of State and of the Councillors, were all foisted on India, while for long no Indian member was taken on the Council. It was in fact a business accountancy with a vengeance. The Secretary of State was given large powers. Again, instead "of continuing boldly with the process of sweeping aside moth-eaten pretensions and vicious abuse of power, and thus rallying to her side all the forces of renascent India which she (England herself called into being." Writes Zacharias, "the Government of the day (of Lord Derby) preferred to make terms with the 'dominative' element of old, rather than with the 'political' ones of young India."[52] The princes of the country were recognised, and they were to continue. After the mutiny "the broad tendency was for more and more of the administration to be conducted from London."[53] The India Office in London directly controlled permanent officials in India and hence instead of criticising them identified itself with them and protected them. "These officials, therefore, became the practical owners of India; irremovable, irresponsible; and amenable to no authority but that of their fellow members." Previously under the fear of the renewal of the Charter, the Company did have an inducement to work more efficiently to satisfy the masters in the English Parliament. The Parliament too evinced a keen interest in the Indian problems. But now when the actual charge of India passed into the hands of the Parliament in form as well as reality, its interest slackened, and as Ramsay Macdonald writes, being too much preoccupied in the Irish and other problems, now "held no great debates on Indian questions."[54] Indian Civil Service was the costliest in the world, while on the other hand India was poor. The new officers were arrogant and haughty, and the gulf between the English and the Indians widened. Nor was the provision regarding the use of the Indian revenues very useful to India. These revenues were not to be used on military operations outside India without the consent of the Parliament, except for repelling invasion or "sudden and urgent necessity"—and these last words were very ambiguous.

Yet, the Act occupies an important position in our history inasmuch as it commenced a new era, the significance of which could be realised only in the years to come. The criticism of the weakness of the Council against the Secretary of State seems rather unjustified. The former could not dominate the latter, because he represented the opinion of the Cabinet and its domination over him should have signified a domination over the Cabinet thereby subverting the whole constitutional theory of England. The rest of the points of criticism may be important, yet the merits of the Act in the circumstances were greater than its defects.

THE PROCLAMATION OF THE QUEEN

The next significant development after the mutiny was the proclamation of the Queen which was read out by Lord Canning at a Durbar held on 1 November 1858 at Allahabad. The intentions of the Queen in issuing this proclamation are clear from her criticism of the original draft prepared by Lord Derby. Asking him to redraft it, she instructed that it should be framed bearing "in mind that it is a female sovereign who speaks to more than a hundred million of Eastern people, on assuming the direct Government over them and after a bloody war, giving them pledges, which her future reign is to redeem, and explaining the principles of her Government. Such a document should breathe feelings of generosity, benevolence and religious toleration, and point out the privileges which the Indians will receive in being placed on an equality with the subjects of the British Crown, and the prosperity following in the train of civilization."

The proclamation of the Queen, which declared the assumption of the Government of India directly by the Crown, marks the beginning of a new era in the history of India. It was a Charter of Rights for the Indians which declared the principles on which this country was to be governed.

After declaring the assumption of the Indian Government, the Queen re-appointed Lord Canning our "well-beloved cousin and councillor Charles John Viscount Canning, do hereby constitute and appoint him, the said Viscount Canning to be our first Viceroy and Governor-General in and over our said territories and to administer the government thereof in our name..." Thus, writes H.V. Lovett: "The chief of the government in India, the man on the spot there, was first styled 'viceroy and governor-general' in the famous proclamation of

1858." "Where the Governor-General is regarded as the representative of the sovereign he is spoken of as Viceroy; where he is referred to as the statutory head of the Government of India he retains his original title."[55]

With the reappointment of Lord Canning, the proclamation also declared: "We confirm all the civil and military officers employed by the East India Company." And then it went on to declare the principles of the government policy, which may be broken up as effecting the princes and the people of the country as under.

The Princes of India. For the princes of India, the proclamation said: "We hereby announce to the Native Princes of India that all treaties and engagements made with them by or under the authority of the Honourable East India Company are by us accepted, and will be scrupulously maintained, and we look for the like observance on their part." Then: "We desire no extension of our present territorial possession: and while we will permit no aggression upon our dominions or our rights to be attempted with impunity we shall sanction no encroachment on those of others."

And more, it said: "We shall respect the rights, dignity and honour of our Native Princes as our own, and we desire that they as well as our own subjects, should enjoy that prosperity, and that social advancement which can be secured by internal peace and good government."

The People of India. For the people of India it declared: "We hold ourselves bound to the natives of our Indian territories by the same obligations of duty which bind us to all our other subjects..." The proclamation promised non-interference in the religious affairs of the people, and non-discrimination as "...that none be any wise favoured, none molested or disquieted by reason of their religious faith and observances..."

Everybody, young, old, rich or poor, was granted an equal protection of law. Recruitment into services was to be done strictly on merit, as the proclamation said: "...so far as may be our subjects of whatever race or creed be freely and impartially admitted to offices in our service, the duties of which they may be qualified by their education, ability and integrity only to discharge."

A due protection and respect was to be given to the ancient rights, usages and customs of the people while framing laws. Similarly a full protection would be given in matters of inheritance and the possession of land.

An unconditional pardon and amnesty for the offences committed during the mutiny was to be granted, except in cases where direct part in murdering the British subjects had been taken.

The Queen declared: "...it is our earnest desire to stimulate the peaceful industry, to promote works of public utility and improvement and to administer its government for the benefit of all our subjects resident therein. In their prosperity will be our strengths in their contentment our security, and in their gratitude best reward."

Commenting on this proclamation, writes Ramsay Muir. "These were no new doctrines: they represented the consistent policy of the Company during at least the preceding generation."[56] But this seems wrong, more so at least with regard to the promises made to the princes. During the preceding generation the policy followed towards them was consistently aggressive, violent and against all treaties and engagements entered into. It was for the first time that the princes were assured of perfect territorial safety. The Doctrine of Lapse which had given the worst shock to their loyalty and faith for the British Government was abolished. And the right of adoption was recognised. Rawlinson therefore writes: "the most fundamental change of attitude was that which the proclamation foreshadowed in the relationship between the British Government and the Indian princes...the princes, therefore, heard with the utmost relief the announcement that their rights, dignity and honour should be respected, and that all treaties made with the Company would be maintained."[57]

The promises to the people, of non-interference in religious beliefs, of equal opportunity for recruitment into services, and of equal protection of law, were also significant. In fact the proclamation was actually, as it was said, the 'Magna Carta of Indian liberties.' "Its only fault indeed," Wilfred Seawan Blunt remarked, "has been that it has never been carried out."[58]

OTHER DEVELOPMENTS

The White Mutiny. The White Mutiny consisted of the mutinous demonstrations of a portion of the European force in the Indian army. Their grievance was that their services could not be transferred to the Crown without their consent, and therefore they should either be granted a fresh bounty money or be discharged from service. The disturbance arose just when Lord Canning completed his tours and pacified the mutinous India. The demonstration of these white soldiers took a serious turn in some cantonments such as those at Meerut and Allahabad. Lord Canning therefore was obliged to grant a discharge from service to those who desired, as a consequence of which the number of the European soldiers in India was depleted by 10,000.

Army Reconstruction. The White Mutiny resulted into a serious attention being paid to certain other defects in the army organisation which were forthwith removed. It was decided that henceforward the proportion of the Indians to the European in the army, was not to exceed two to one. An infantry brigade was to consist of one British and two Indian battalions. The Field and other Artillery was to be manned entirely by the Europeans. As a result of all these changes the whole number of the European soldiers in the Indian army became 72,000, while that of the Indians became 135,000.

Another defect removed was the increasing number of the locally recruited European Army, independent of the Home Government. Pitt had been very much conscious of the danger accruing from this, yet he having failed to remove the defect the number of the local European Army increased to about 1/3rd of the European Army in India by 1857. After a lot of controversy in May 1860 the Cabinet decided to amalgamate the two, and in August the same year the legislative sanction of the Parliament was secured which also laid down that in future no European should be recruited for local purpose in India.

The Bengal army, with the exception of a few loyal regiments had literally been annihilated: 120,000 out of the 128,000 sepoys having been killed in the battle-field, executed or having disappeared. They were now replaced by a new force which consisted chiefly of the Sikhs, the Jats, the Punjabi Muslims, Gurkhas, Baluchis and the other martial races who had proved loyal during the mutiny.

Before the mutiny, the Indian regiments had been divided into two classes, regular and irregular. In the regular units there was a staff of 25 British officers, of whom however only 12 were actually present at a time; the rest being engaged in the civil and other departments, and brought back only when the regiments were ordered into action. The military officers thus engaged in the civil services lost years of flirtation elsewhere when they were brought back to the army they were as unfit for the service as any layman. The results were disastrous.

In 1861, therefore, the Indian army was reorganised on the "Irregular System" in which the previous number of 3 specially selected British officers was raised now to 6, and it was further decided in the same year that every British officer here was to be duly selected and well paid. He was not to be attached to the Indian troops against his will. And he had to pass a test in a *Hindustani* language before he could join the Indian army. The more important feature of the reorganised "Irregular System" of 1861, however, was that Indians, in place of the Europeans, were to be the captains of Troops and the Companies.

As before, there were to be three Presidency Armies, "each with a staff corps which supplied the needs of the Indian regiments as well as officers for staff, political and judicial duties; but with the reorganisation of the civil services, the custom of seconding the best men for civil employment was no longer necessary.[59] The military police were disbanded and replaced by a civil force."[60]

The Financial Reforms. "The mutiny marks the inauguration of a new era in Indian finance," writes Sir H.S. Cunningham.[61] Among the results of the Mutiny were the terrible financial scars which it left on the Indian soil. Villages along the line of march of the armies of Neil and Havelock had been burnt to ashes, and cultivators fled to save their lives. A severe famine broke out in the Agra province in 1861 which destroyed many, and left lakhs of the rest physically weak, less able to work and produce revenue. Kanpur and Lucknow had been gutted, and Delhi was a city of the dead. The revenues were thus depleted; and when the entire cost of the mutiny too was thrown on India, her financial structure was seriously strained. The debt increased by about 40 million sterling. But when a proposal was made to license trade and the professions, there was a storm of objections.

Under these conditions Lord Canning requested the Home authorities for expert advice. James Wilson who had been the Finance Secretary to the Treasury and Vice-President of the Board of Trade, was sent to India in November 1859 as the first Finance Member of the Governor-General's Council.

Wilson after his arrival in this country undertook extensive tours in order to gather first hand knowledge of the existing financial problems. In his budget speech of February 1860, he surveyed the existing financial situation and described it as distressing. He told that a deficit of more than £ 30 million had been added during the three years of mutiny, and that the current year threatened to enhance it yet further by about £ 6½ million. The national debt had increased from 59½ million to as much as 98 million, adding thereby to the annual interest charges by 2 million.

Wilson estimated the gross revenue for 1860-61 at £ 33 million. The main source of revenue, he said, was the land revenue which amounted to about 40 per cent of the total. Next came opium, customs, stamps and salt; and then other sources of revenue.

The custom duties had been enhanced in 1859, which while increasing the revenue had decreased the imports. Moreover they had been hated by the British merchants in India, and Wilson had instructions from the Home authorities to do as much as he could for their satisfaction.

Wilson died within a year of his arrival in this country. But before that he had already made his recommendations which were based on two-fold remedy of new taxes and retrenchment. The new taxes proposed by him were three. First was the income tax which was to be imposed at the rate of 5 per cent on an income of Rs. 500 a year or more for five years. Second was the Licence Tax on different trades and professions, amounting to one, four or ten rupees a year. And the third was the tax on the Indian grown tobacco which was to correspond with the existing customs duty on the article imported into this country. A uniform import duty of 10 per cent was also proposed.

Among the retrenchments were those in the civil as well as the military expenditures, which were introduced in a drastic manner. For the purpose of watching and controlling the retrenchment in the military expenditure an efficient machinery was proposed.

Much was also done for the satisfaction of the British merchants in India. The government abolished the export duties on the raw products of this country such as hemp, jute and tea. On the other hand the import duties on the manufactured goods were also reduced to the detriment of the Indian industries. And all this was done under the pretext of free trade.

Such thus was the financial plan of Wilson, which was, however, only partially put into effect. Yet his proposals were considered sound, and formed the basis of the future financial policy of India.

Wilson was succeeded by Laing who had the credit of being the first to discover that "the revenue of India is really buoyant and elastic in an extraordinary degree". Under him the policy of retrenchment in the civil and military expenditure was continued; the former of which saved the Government ½ million while the latter saved 3¼ million. A paper currency was started, and salt duties were raised.

The most important feature of his financial policy, however, was his inauguration of the system of financial decentralisation which was carried on by his successors more vigorously. It was Laing who first proposed that the local governments should be entrusted with some of the items of taxation, the proceeds from which should be expended by them for local purposes, and should replace the Central assignments. To start with, the taxation on tobacco was entrusted. The best merit of the system was that in place of a tendency towards extravagance, a spirit of economy was introduced in the local governments. And the Centre also saved as much as £½ million.

"The result of these heroic remedies was that Mr. Laing found himself in the enjoyment of surplus,"[62] which he recommended to be spent, firstly, on the public works and education, secondly, for the purpose of lowering of duties on the Manchester goods, and thirdly for releasing from income-tax the class of lower income up to £ 50 a year.

The Agricultural Reforms. Lord Canning also introduced some agricultural reforms, the purpose being to free the cultivators from tedious and trouble some settlements and excessive state demands, and to secure for them the maximum of their hard-earned profits. The most important step was the passage of the Bengal Rent Act in 1859 which gave to the cultivators a fixity of rent and security of tenure, besides obviating some other defects of the Permanent Settlement. Under this Act, a ryot who had held a land for 20 years at the same rent was treated as if holding it since 1793, and was given the rights and privileges accordingly. Occupancy rights were given to tenants who held land for 12 years, and their rent could be enhanced only after an enquiry by a court of law. After this the other provinces also passed rent acts, taking the Bengal Rent Act as a model.

There took place some disputes between the European indigo planters and the Bengal peasantry in 1859 and 1860. As the matter became serious, a commission was appointed to investigate into the matter, which submitted its report. The Secretary of State intervened, and it was ultimately settled that for the non-fulfilment of a civil contract for growing indigo, the tenants would not be subjected to criminal prosecution.

Education. The principles to be followed for the educational development in India had been laid down by the Wood's Despatch of 1854. The progress however was slow. The situation was surveyed in 1859, and after some time a plan was chalked out. Under this plan a further impetus was given to the programme of establishing a department of education in every province, with a Director, teaching staff, and inspecting officers. Both primary and the higher education were made to expand. The financial hardship, however, continued, and the rate of progress in the field of education remained slow.

The Public Works Department. This Department had been organised by Lord Dalhousie. When peace was restored in the country, and the principles of the Queen's proclamation had to be given effect this department came under the special attention of the Government. Many new works of public utility were taken in hand. Numerous barracks, court houses and bridges were constructed, and vast dams began to rise. The Indian Forest Department was established with a conservator of forests and a trained subordinate staff in each division.

Law and Order. The problem of law and order in the country was serious. Under the prevailing system the sense of justice and equity in the judges alone was the guiding force to administer justice. Canning thought it essential to regularise the system, which could be done by codifying law. In 1860 therefore, the Indian Penal Code which had been drafted by Macaulay and the first Law Commission in 1837, became law. The Muslim Criminal Code was nullified. And the new Civil and Criminal Procedure Codes were passed.

The judiciary was reorganised by the passage of the Indian High Courts Act of 1861. Under this Act, in place of the Supreme Courts and *adalats* of the English Company. Chartered High Courts were established at Calcutta, Bombay and Madras. The Government were also authorised to establish one more such court, which was established in 1866 at Allahabad, to administer the territories of the North Western Provinces. The Company Sadr-Courts, and Supreme Courts of Presidencies were abolished in 1861; and a due provision for the protection of the European subjects being made in the Criminal Procedure Code, the exclusive jurisdiction of the Supreme Court over them was abolished.

The judges of the High Courts were to be appointed by the Crown, and were to hold office till the pleasure of Her Majesty. The qualification and powers of the judges were also laid down, which remain to guide as even today.

Another great achievement of Lord Canning was reorganisation of the Police Department. An Act was passed in 1861, under which each government got a separate Police Department presided over by an Inspector-General who was to be under the respective local government, and was to be assisted by Deputy Inspector-Generals. A Superintendent of Police was appointed in each district, who was to work in subordination and collaboration with the District Magistrate, and was responsible for maintaining law and order in his area, and for the management and discipline of the police force under him. The division of the district was placed each under a Deputy Inspector, who was to be assisted by a body of constables. The Superintendent of Police and all other police officers above him were to be Europeans whose recruitment was to be done in England.

Other Changes. Besides the above, some other administrative tidying up consisted of the creation of the Central Provinces under a Chief Commissioner in 1861. With the territories annexed from Burma after the First Burmese War under Amherst and second Anglo-Burmese War under Dalhousie, British Burma was set up in 1852. Due to the Company's China trade, Singapore and the Straits Settlements had been under the care of the Indian Government. Since the China monopoly had long since ceased to exist, and the East India Company also was now abolished, Canning no more felt the need of keeping under the Indian control such strategic ports and territories. He initiated the matter to get rid of this responsibility, though the ultimate hand-over could take place only later in 1866.

Famine Relief. Canning also made an important contribution in the development of the Famine Relief Policy in India. A short history of the earlier developments, and those that took place under him may not be out of place.

Throughout the Company's rule famine remained the "king of terrors" in India. For this is a country which depended too much on the monsoons. The general masses of the country, poverty-stricken and living from had to mouth, waited only for a signal to fall into the wide-open mouth of starvation. But their misery did not end with this. When the monsoons failed, not only did the crops fail to grow; the grass got burnt by the blazing sun and hot winds of March, April and May; the milch cows began to starve; and the plough and the transport-cattle, the working capital of the cultivators, were decimated; water level fell leaving the meagre supply of it spoiled with noxious germs; and cholera and pestilence followed closely to prey upon the helplessness and physical weakness in the people. The misery was thus complete. Lakhs died and among those who remained, lakhs failed to recover their lost vitality.

Under such conditions, besides the development of the irrigation facilities in this country, if millions of lives were to be saved every year from a miserable death, certain relief policy had to be developed.

During the eighteenth century, not much could be done by the British to revive the country from the horrors of famine calamities. For that was the time when they were still busy in their game of conquests and annexations, and the political diplomacy occupied much of their time. Nor were the means of communication yet properly developed so as to facilitate the transmission of the large quantities of grain at large distances; nor were the agricultural, the vital and the economic statistics readily available and nor had the science yet made it possible to forecast the climatic disturbances. And above all, as the Famine Commission of 1880 remarked: "the position of the British in India was not such as either to create any sense of general obligation to give relief, or to supply sufficient means of affording it".

The famines thus came and ravaged the country. Millions starved and died, but the Government could do nothing more than advance loans for sinking wells, store grain to meet certain emergencies, impose restrictions on the hoarding of grains, and do other odd jobs as the valour of the local and the district officers prompted. There was no national policy worth the name.

Nor did the conditions change much during the first half of the 19th century. It was for the first time perhaps that at the face of a terrible famine of 1837 in the upper regions of Ganges and Jumna, the local government admitted that the state should find work for the able-bodied, while the infirm and the helpless must be looked after by the whole community as in normal times. Even in the field where the responsibility was admitted, however not much was done, and a heavy mortality of men, women, children and cattle rendered the whole atmosphere full of wails and woes. There were riots which were suppressed.

The state of the things had not much changed when the mutiny came, and the East India Company was replaced by the Crown. It was only now that a systematic attention began to be given to the problem. Apathetic in the beginning, the Government of the Crown grew mindful later. And as the famines came, famine commissions began to be appointed to suggest measures to enable the Government to meet the monster of the famine more effectively the next time it came. And slowly the famine code matured, till it became helpful and workable and lives began to be saved.

Under the Crown, there was a great expansion in the means of irrigation. The railway lines and the other means of communication began slowly to measure the length and the breadth of this land. Trade and commerce grew, and so did grow the agrarian legislation for the cultivators' protection. The gradual change in the economic factors modified the very character of the famines, and this was one of the problems which every famine commission, as it was appointed, was called upon to face, and make its recommendations to suit the circumstance.

It goes to the credit of Canning, that the first famine commission came during his time in 1860 when in that year the monsoons failed and an area of 48,000 square miles, including Alwar, the North-West Provinces around Agra, and several other territories suffered a terrible famine. Over half a million of the people in the affected area left their homes. Luckily, the south-eastern districts of the North-West Provinces had plenty of rains, the East India Railways had considerably spread to help in bringing succour, and within the affected area also about 900,000 acres more of the land had since 1837 been brought under protection. The old policy of 1837 was repeated, and the

Government made efforts to provide work to the able-bodied, leaving the infirm to be looked after by the society; though the latter source having failed, here also the Government had to take up the responsibility itself. About 80,000 people were given relief through 26 central and 75 district relief houses.

It was for the first time that the Government decided to institute an enquiry into the matter, and Colonel Baird Smith was appointed for the purpose. Colonel Smith submitted his report, but it was unfortunate that this time no efforts were made to formulate any general principles for later guidance. Yet a start towards the direction was made, and the next commission of enquiry appointed in 1866-67 was able to take steps towards the evolution of a famine code which ultimately emerged as the result of the labour of several such commission. In the meanwhile during three years ending in 1861, Canning added 8,316 miles of new railway lines which considerably helped in the distribution of relief.

THE INDIAN COUNCILS ACT 1861

This was another great achievement of the reign of Canning in India. Between 1833 and 1861 in England, writes John Coatman, the "Chartist Movement had brought the revolutionary spirit of the Continent into our politics and had made it clear that political power would have to be extended from the upper and middle classes to at any rate the town workers, and the whole movement had quickened and strengthened the natural British instinct for free and democratic Government. This in turn worked powerfully in support of the movement of autonomy in the British colonies".[63] In India there was a strong feeling that when very far-reaching changes had been introduced at Home by the Government of India Act 1858, certain changes according to the circumstances were necessary in the Government of India as well. And it was lucky that the great liberal reformers of England like Gladstone, while anxious to extend democratic elements in England, were no less anxious to satisfy the Indian aspirations as well, though to a limited extent. Nor was it now possible to bear, as Sir Bartle Frere wrote in his Minute of 1860, "the perilous experiment of continuing to legislate for millions with few means of knowing except by rebellion whether the laws suit them or not". The Mutiny of 1857 had clearly brought forth that if the public feeling in India ad been properly gauged, and if certain means had been adopted to take regular counsel with Indians, much of the trouble that the British faced in 1857 could have been avoided. After the Mutiny the racial bitterness between the Indians and the Europeans developed at a fast pace. The Indians had no representation in the Legislative Councils wherefrom to exhibit their aspirations, and Sir Charles Wood in his speech in the Commons on 6 June 1861 aptly remarked: "it would be folly to shut our eyes to the increasing difficulties of our position in India, and it is an additional reason why we should make the earliest endeavour to put all our institutions on the soundest possible foundations".

There was yet another reason which necessitated a reform. The Charter Act of 1833, as we have seen, had centralised legislation which made utterly difficult for things to proceed smoothly. India was a vast country, the legislative problems of which could not be understood by a few members of the Central Government quite far away from the people whose destiny they tried to control. Nor had these members the will or the time to seek out certain common legislative standards applicable to all the parts of the country.

The working of the existing Legislative Council set up by the Act of 1833 was also supposed to be unsatisfactory. "The Council," writes Sir H.V. Lovett, "was working as a board and deciding all questions by a majority vote, the Governor-General possessing an overruling power in mates of grave importance".[64] Lord Canning was dissatisfied with this collective business. Nor was the

Council ever intended to become an Anglo-Indian House of Commons. Yet this is what it actually became in its legislative capacity. It adopted Parliamentary formalities such as three readings and reference to committees, etc. which all caused delay. There were as many as 136 standing orders to regulate the proceedings of a dozen members of the Council. Trying to act as an independent legislature, it sometimes stopped supplied and did not work entirely according to the wishes of the Home Government. Sometimes the members of the Council insisted on getting information on secret matters and asked questions which could not be replied. All this the authorities desired to correct. Such thus were the circumstances under which the Councils Act of 1861 was passed.

Executive Provisions. In its provisions the Act introduced certain changes in the Viceroy's Executive Council. In 1853 a Legal Member had been added to the Council who became its fourth member. Disorganisation of finances after the mutiny, necessitated a change, and the Legal Member was replaced by a trained financier. A jurist, however, was no less urgently needed, "as the law was in process of codification, and even the Penal Code, which had originally been drafted by Macaulay, was still incomplete".[65] So the Act of 1861 added to the Council the fifth required member. The Act also empowered the Secretary of State to appoint the Commander-in-Chief as the extraordinary member of the Council; while of the five above referred to, three were required to have served the Crown or the Company in India for not less than ten years. One of the five was to be a Military Member who would be a distinguished soldier. The other two were to be civil servants, the fourth was to be a financial expert who might or might not have served the Crown or the Company previously, while the fifth was to be a Legal Member who would be a barrister of England or Ireland, or a member of the

Faculty of Advocates in Scotland of at least five years' standing". The Commander-in-Chief "might be, and in practice always was, an extraordinary member who divided with the military member the responsibility for the military administration of the country".

Every ordinary member was to be assisted by a secretary and under-secretaries, and he was to have a full office establishment at his disposal.

The powers of the Governor-General were increased, and he was now authorised to act alone in all matters except the making of law. The Governor-General was also empowered to appoint a President who would preside over the meetings of the Council in his absence. He could make rules for the convenient transaction of business by the Council, and all acts done or orders passed under these rules were to be known as the acts or orders of the Governor-General in Council. Almost the first thing Lord Canning did under these powers was to stop the clumsy system of the exchange between the members of the boxes containing papers. He rather, by making certain new rules, created certain portfolios or departments of work and distributed them among the members, empowering them to dispose of unimportant business of their respective departments themselves, while placing the important matters before the Viceroy with the views of the member in charge. If the Viceroy differed with these views, the matter was to be brought before the Council where the President would have a casting vote. "Thus the Government of India," as Lovett writes, "became a cabinet government presided over by a Governor-General, being carried on departmentally and the Governor-General taking a more active and particular share in it than is taken by a prime minister in a western country or than had been taken by any of his predecessors".[66]

Central Legislature. For purposes of legislation, the Viceroy's Executive Council was expanded by an addition of not less than 6 and not more than 12 members who would be nominated by the Governor-General and would hold office for two years. Not less than half of these members were to be non-official. The old provincial representatives as introduced by the Charter Act of 1853, were sent back. Sir A.H. Layard in the Commons desired that a specific mention should be made that all the additional members would be Indians. But the Secretary of State replied that no such being either princes or big *zamindars*. They had absolutely no attraction for membership of the Councils, and hence, as K.V. Punniah comments, the "offers of seats in the Council were often declined and the members who were nominated showed the utmost reluctance to come and utmost hurry to depart".[67] Nor could the Councils themselves be called true legislatures either in composition or in functions. The Central and the Provincial Councils could discuss legislation immediately at issue, they could not call for information, nor could they impugn the administrative acts. Their laws merely represented Government wishes, they themselves acting only as "durbars which Indian rulers had traditionally held in order to sound their subjects' opinion".[68]

But then, this alone was the purpose of the creation of these Councils—to ascertain the public opinion and to secure the means to defend and justify the Government legislation. Publicity, information and discussion was the aim, and this aim to a limited extent the Act secured; laying at the same time the foundations of that system which the future Indian generations were to secure.

Sikkim. A few words regarding a small expedition to the small independent Himalayan kingdom of Sikkim before we sum up Canning's achievements after the Mutiny. The British had not been keeping good relations with this tiny state the ruler of which was said to be too provocative. In November 1860 Dr. A. Campbell's march into the territory with only 160 men was smartly defeated. An expedition of 2,600 men was thereafter despatched, which achieved complete success. No territory was annexed, but the peace treaty secured an indemnity of Rs. 7,000, a road into the kingdom was to be built and the British secured some commercial facilities in the state.

Thus, as it is clear, the effects of the Mutiny were great and far-reaching. The Crown assumed the direct administration of India which however, was only formal,[69] the Indian Army was completely reorganised, there was a great change in the policy towards the Indian states, and there were changes in the financial administration, agriculture, education, Public Works Department and the machinery connected with law and order in the country. Great constitutional changes took place as a result of the Government of India Act, 1858 and the Indian Councils Act, 1861.

"One indirect effect of the Mutiny is clearly seen in the birth and rise of extremism in Indian politics".[70] Russel, the Times' Correspondent in India observed in his diary: "the mutinies have produced too much hatred and ill-feeling between the two races to render any mere change of the rulers a remedy for the evils which effect India, of which those angry sentiments are the most serious exposition". The British unlike any previous invaders," write Thompson and Garratt, "became more aloof the longer they stayed, more foreign, more efficient".[71]

Retirement. Lord Canning retired from India on 18 March 1862 broken-hearted, as his wife had died at Calcutta few moths before. Reaching England, he himself died on 17 June the same year, leaving behind none to succeed to his titles. "Seldom in the annals of the Indian Empire," writes Rawlinson, "has any man been called upon to shoulder a heavier burden; his biographer relates that he sometimes worked without a break from midnight to midday until his pen literally fell from hand".[72] "He plunged eagerly into business," Cunningham writes, "and commenced from the outset the neglect of all considerations for health which he continued to the end with such disastrous effect". And indeed, all our praise goes for the "serene and resolute mood, the unbroken nerve, the firm justice, the loftiness of soul, with which Canning, rising nobly to the duties of a foremost post in an eventful epoch, piloted his country's fortunes in that dark hour across that tempest-driven sea".[73]

Lord Canning won laurels alike in war and peace. The resolute manner in which he fought against the storms of mutiny, deserve a credit indeed. But a greater credit goes to him due to the fact that once the peace was restored after the mutiny, he applied himself to the reconstruction of the country with a calm and serene mind which is the possession only of highly evolved souls. When there was a criticism of this policy, he wrote to Lord Grenville: "I don't want you to...do more than defend me against unfair or mistaken attack. But do take up and assert boldly that whilst we are prepared, as the first duty of all, to strike down resistance without mercy, wherever it shows itself, we acknowledge that, resistance over, deliberate justice and calm patient reason are to resume their way; that we are not going, either in anger from indolence, to punish wholesale, whether by wholesale hanging or burnings, or by the less violent but not one jot less offensive course of refusing the trust and countenance and favour and honour to any man became he is of a class of creed".

There was a persistent demand after the Mutiny, that he shoul l be recalled. He reacted in a firm manner and wrote to the Home authorities: "I believe that a change in the head of the Government of India at this time...would seriously retard the pacification of the country". And regarding any change in his policy, he remarked: "No taunts or sarcasm, come from what quarter they may, will turn me from the path which I believe to be that of my public duty".[74]

Such was Canning, kind-hearted, yet firm, and considerate yet merciless where the safety of the empire was involved. Rawlinson wrote: "England has always freely given of her best to India, and in that...George Canning.....holds an honoured place".[74]

REFERENCES

1. Maclagan, Michael, *Clemency Canning*, p, 52
2. *Ibid.*, p. 51.
3. *Ibid.*, p. 54
4. *Ibid.* p. 66
5. Savarkar, V. D., *The Indian War of Independence*, p. 7.
6. Ashoka Mehta's booklet, 1857—*The Great Rebellion*.
7. Rawlinson, *The British Achievement in India* (1948), p. 103
8. In an introduction to *Eighteen Fifty-Seven*, by S. N. Sen, pp. xiii-xv: see also Majumdar, R.C., *History of Freedom Movement in India* (1963), 3 vols; Majumdar, R.C., *Sepoy Mutiny* (1963); Majumdar, R.C., *Three Phases of India's Struggle for Freedom.*
9. Maulana Azad in his address to the 31st Session of the Indian Historical Records Commission, 1955.
10. Kaye, *op. cit.*, vol. I, p. 327-29.
11. Hilton, Major-General Richard, *The Indian Mutiny*, p. 17.
12. Prasad, I., and Subedar, S. K., *A History of Modern India*, p. 238.
13. Majumdar, Dr. R. C., *The Sepoy Mutiny and Revolt* of 1857, p. 18.
14. Sen, S. N., *Eighteen Fifty-Seven*, p. 34.
15. Khan, Chulam Hussain, *Siyar-ul Mutakhrin*, Kanpur, 1897.
16. Ahmed, Sir Syed, *Causes of Indian Revolt* (translated by W. N. Lees), p. 10.
17. Holmes, T. Rice, *Cambridge History of India*, IV, p. 169; see also Majumdar. R. C., *The Sepoy Mutiny.*
18. Grant, Sir Hope, *Incidents in the Sepoy Mutiny*, (1857-58), p. 12.
19. See Khan Ghulam Hussain, *Siyar-ul-Mutakhrin.*
20. Ahmed, Sir Syed, *Causes of Indian Revolt.*

21. Holmes, *Indian Mutiny*, p. 49.
22. *Ibid.*
23. *The Mutiny of the Bengal Army* (known as the Red Pamphlet), London, 1857. p. 9.
24. Holmes, op. cit., p. 172.
25. Ahmed, Sir Syed, *Essay on Causes of Indian Revolt*, translated by W. N. Lees, p. 20, also see Misra, Anand Swarup, *Nana Saheb Peshwa*.
26. The *Sepoy Mutiny* of Henry Knollys compiled from private journals of Gen. Sir Hope Grant.
27. Sen, S. N., *op. cit.*, p. 21.
28. Rawlinson, *op. cit.*, p. 96.
29. Roberts, P. E., *Modern India*, p. 434.
30. Sen. S. N., op. *cit.*, *pp.* 24-25.
31. Quoted in Kaye *op. cit.*, I, p. 618, f. n.
32. Thompson and Garratt, *Rise and Fulfilment of British Rule in India*, p. 436.
33. Russell, Sir W., *My Diary in India.*
34. Gordon, *The sikhs*, p. 222.
35. *Punjab Administration Report*, 1890-91.
36. Savarkar, V. D., *The Indian War of Independence*, p. 220.
37. Majumdar, *Sepoy Mutiny*, p. 271.
38. Majumdar, R. C., *Sepoy Mutiny and Revolt* of 1857.
39. See Holmes, *op. cit.*, p. 226.
40. *Ibid.*, p. 494.
41. Holmes, *op. cit.*, pp. 169-70.
42. *Rebellion* 1857, A Symposium, p. 117.
43. Chhabra, *History of Punjab*, II, p. 353.
44. *Punjab Administration Report*, 1856-58.
45. This is how Canning's name got currency as 'Clemency Canning'.
46. Maclagan, Michael, *Clemency Cannng*, pp. 132-41.
47. Thompson and Garratt, op. cit., p. 390.
48. Powell-Price, J. C., *A. History of India*, p. 559.
49. Marshman, J. C., *The History of India*, 2 vols.

50. Muir, Ramsay, *The Making of British India*, p. 380.
51. Prasad, Subedar, *A History of Modern India*, p. 279.
52. Zacharias, H. C. E., *Renascent India*, p. 92.
53. Dodwell, *Cambridge History of India*, VI, p. 213.
54. Macdonald, J. R., *Government of India*, p. 263.
55. Lovett, H. V., *Combridge History of India*, VI, p. 226; see also Curzon, *British Government of india*, II, p. 49.
56. Muir, Ramsay, *The Making of British India*, p. 381.
57. Rawlinson, *The British Achievements in India*, p. 115.
58. Blunt, W. S., *Indian Under Ripon*, p. 312.
59. For further details see chapter on Lord Lawrence.
60. Rawlinson, *op. cit.*, p. 116.
61. Cunningham, Sir H. S., *Earl of Canning*, (Hunter Series), p. 198.
62. Cunningham, *op. cit.*, p. 206.
63. Coatman, John, India, *The Road to Self-Government*, pp. 20-22.
64. Lovett, Sir H. Verney. *Combridge History of India*, VI, p. 226.
65. *Ibid.*, pp. 226-240.
66. See Lovett, *op. cit.*, pp. 229-30.
67. Punniah, K. V., *Constitutional History of India*, p. 104.
68. See Coupland, R., *Indian Problem*, p. 56.
69. See above, discussion of the Act of 1858.
70. Majumdar and others, *Advanced History of India*, p. 782.
71. T. and G., *op. cit.*, p. 412.
72. Rawlinson, *op. cit.*, p. 123.
73. Cunningham, *op. cit.*, p. 39.
74. Rawlinson, *op. cit.*, p. 123.

Index

N

O

P

R